The Legal Regulation of Cyber Attacks

The Legal Regulation of Cyber Attacks

Second Edition

Edited by

Ioannis Iglezakis

Wolters Kluwer

Published by:
Kluwer Law International B.V.
PO Box 316
2400 AH Alphen aan den Rijn
The Netherlands
E-mail: international-sales@wolterskluwer.com
Website: lrus.wolterskluwer.com

Sold and distributed in North, Central and South America by:
Wolters Kluwer Legal & Regulatory U.S.
7201 McKinney Circle
Frederick, MD 21704
United States of America
Email: customer.service@wolterskluwer.com

Sold and distributed in all other countries by:
Air Business Subscriptions
Rockwood House
Haywards Heath
West Sussex
RH16 3DH
United Kingdom
Email: international-customerservice@wolterskluwer.com

ISBN 978-94-035-0933-4

e-Book: ISBN 978-94-035-1020-0
web-PDF: ISBN 978-94-035-1065-1

Editor

Ioannis Iglezakis is a Full Professor of Law & Informatics at the Faculty of Law in the Aristotle University in Thessaloniki (Greece) and Attorney-at-Law at the Thessaloniki Bar Association. He graduated from the Faculty of Law of Aristotle University (Thessaloniki) in 1987. After completing a master's degree in the Universities of Thessaloniki in History, Philosophy and Sociology of Law (1990), he completed a master's degree (MLE) in European Law at the University of Hannover (1993). He received his PhD from the University of Thessaloniki in 1999, and his thesis was published in 2000.

He was scientific assistant in the University of Thessaloniki (2002–2003) and subsequently, he assumed the position of Visiting Lecturer in the same University (2003–2009). In 2009, he was elected Assistant Professor, and since 2020 he is serving as full Professor. He has authored several publications in Greece and also in several international legal reviews. He has participated in various EU funded projects related to Information law and EU law. His research interest include IT law, legal informatics, public, economic and EU law.

Contributors

Philippe Jougleux is an Associate Professor of Private Law at the Faculty of Law in the European University of Cyprus and Attorney-at-law at the Thessaloniki Bar Association. He graduated from the Faculty of Law of Lille II (France) in 1998. After completing a master degree in the University of Aix-Marseille III in MME Law in 1999, he worked in the same university as an assistant from 1999 to 2002.

He received his PhD in 2002 on the topic of the protection of information in the information society from University of Aix-Marseille III. He wrote various textbooks on private law in Cyprus and has various publications related to Copyright law and Computer law. His research interest include IT law, European intellectual property law and Cypriot private law.

Dr. Lilian Mitrou is a Full Professor at the University of the Aegean-Greece (Department of Information and Communication Systems Engineering) and Visiting Assistant Professor at the Athens University of Economics and at the University of Piraeus (Postgraduate Studies Program). She teaches information law and data protection law. Mitrou holds a PhD in Data Protection (University of Frankfurt-Germany). Her thesis concerned the so-called institutional control of data processing and more specifically the Data Protection Models and Authorities in the Federal Republic of Germany and France.

She has served as a Member of the Hellenic Data Protection Authority (1999–2003). From 1998 to 2004, she was the national representative in the EC Committee on the Protection of Individuals with regard to the Processing of Personal Data. She served and still serves as member of many Committees working on law proposals in the fields of privacy and data protection, communications law, e-government, etc. Recently she drafted the Law 3861/10 on the online publication of regulatory and governmental acts and decisions (Diavgeia) and the Law 3970/11 on the Electronic Governance. Her professional experience includes senior consulting and researcher positions in a number of private and public institutions on national and international level. Her research interests include privacy and data protection, e-democracy and e-Government services and Internet law. Mitrou published books and chapters in books (in Greek, German and English) and many journal and conference papers.

Tatiana-Eleni Synodinou is an Associate Professor at the Law Department of University of Cyprus. She completed her postgraduate studies at the University Aix-Marseille III and her doctoral and postdoctoral studies at Aristotle University of Thessaloniki receiving fellowships from the Greek Scholarship Foundation and by the Committee of Research of Aristotle University of Thessaloniki. Prior to her appointment at the University of Cyprus, Tatiana Synodinou worked as scientific collaborator with teaching duties at the Faculty of Law of Aristotle University of Thessaloniki (2001–2004) and as a full time Visiting Lecturer the Interdisciplinary postgraduate program of "Informatics and Management" of the Aristotle University of Thessaloniki.

She also worked as a full time Visiting Lecturer at the Department of Mass Media of Aristotle University of Thessaloniki and the Department of Accounting and Finance of the University of Macedonia, as a short-time Visiting Lecturer at the postgraduate program "M2 Recherche Droit de Propriete Intellectuelle" of the University of Nantes and as a scientific collaborator to the Centre of International and European Economic Law. She has worked as a short-time expert to EU twinning projects and was a member of the e-business Advisory Board for the study "Intellectual Property for ICT producing SMEs" in the context of the "Sectoral e-Business Watch" 2007–2008.

She is a case law reporter for "Kluwer Law International" to the legal database "Kluwer EU IP Cases" and a contributor to Kluwer Copyright Blog. She has participated as a speaker to numerous conferences-study days-seminars. She is founding member and President of the Union of Copyright Law of Cyprus (EDPI) which is the Cypriot affiliate of International Literary and Artistic Association (ALAI). She has numerous publications in the field of copyright law, information law, media law and commercial and private law.

Summary of Contents

Table of Contents

Preface

This volume provides a systematic analysis of the legal regulation of cyber attacks, in other words, of attacks against information systems, from a European, international and comparative law point of view. It aims at answering doctrinal and practical issues related to the application of the cybercrime regulation to new cybercriminal behaviors, and provides a guide for applying the offences under international and EU legal texts, such as the Cybercrime Convention and the EU Directive 2013/40/EU, to cyber attacks. Moreover, many issues relating to this specific type of cybercrimes are dealt with, such as the data protection issues with regard to the investigation of personal data, the forensics rules for the identification of cyber attackers, as well as procedural and other issues.

Chapter 1 was written by Lilian Mitrou. Chapter 2 was written by Philippe Jougleux (§2.01, §2.02 and §2.03), Lilian Mitrou (§2.04 and §2.06) and Tatiana-Eleni Synodinou (§2.05), Chapter 3 was written by Philippe Jougleux (§3.01) and Tatiana-Eleni Synodinou (§3.02). Chapter 4 was written by Lilian Mitrou (§4.01) and Tatiana-Eleni Synodinou (§4.02), while the concluding remarks were drafted by all the authors.[1]

1. This project has been funded with support from the European Commission. This publication reflects the views only of the authors, and the European Commission cannot be held responsible for any use which may be made of the information contained therein.

Introduction to the Second Edition

Ioannis Iglezakis

The second edition of this book adds important updates to the legal framework on cybercrime particularly as cyber attacks are concerned. These are referring not only to EU legislation related to cybercrime, but also to other aspects of information law such as data protection.

New measures on cybersecurity were introduced with the NIS Directive, i.e., Directive 2016/1148 on security of network and information systems, which was proposed in the framework of the EU Cybersecurity strategy. The NIS Directive is seen as a substantial step forward in the domain of cybersecurity as it provides legal measures to boost the overall level of cybersecurity in the EU, to create a culture of prevention and of damage mitigation. The deadline for implementation of this directive which was May 9, 2018 has passed, and it is now part of EU Member States' legislation.

The General Data Protection Regulation (GDPR) which took effect in May 2018 is another milestone in the development of a consistent legal framework for the information society, and it also has implications for cybersecurity and cybercrime, as it imposes a duty to report data protection infringements to supervisory authorities, in addition to existing reporting requirements. Breach notification requirements are inserted also in the NIS Directive, providing in Article 14 that Member States must ensure that operators of essential services notify the national competent authority and the national computer security incident response team (CSIRT) in case of an incident that significantly impacts the continuity of an essential service.

The EU legal framework applying to cyber-fraud has been revised with the Directive (EU) 2019/713 of the European Parliament and of the Council of 17 April 2019 on combating fraud and counterfeiting of noncash means of payment and replacing Council Framework Decision 2001/413/JHA. The Directive harmonizes the criminal conduct of natural or legal persons in relation to noncash means of payment, and it is important because it represents the EU's response to new technologies involving payment instruments, including virtual currencies and digital wallets.

Finally, this book also informs on the EU Commission's legislative proposals to enhance cross-border gathering of electronic evidence, i.e., the draft Regulation on European Production and Preservation Orders for electronic evidence in criminal matters and the draft Directive on the appointment of legal representatives for the purpose of gathering evidence in criminal proceedings.

CHAPTER 1

Attacks Against Information Systems: Technical Definitions

Lilian Mitrou

In many countries, laws are to a great extent focused on physical objects, not taking into account the particularities of intangible objects, such as information, which are associated with cybercrime and electronic evidence.[1] While traditional laws can principally apply to technical developments, such developments and the changing nature of cybercrime force legislators to deal with new concepts and objects not traditionally addressed by the law, such as information systems or computer data and to redefine concepts such as the notion of "attack." Analyzing these definitions and the underlying concepts is a prerequisite for understanding the issues raised and for implementing the respective law.

The first—not only methodological but also mainly legal—issue refers to the relation between the scientific concepts and the regulatory approach. A challenge that legislators have to respond is related to the framing of these concepts in a way independent from the technological state of the art, focusing as much as possible on fundamental descriptions. Technology neutral rules, initially proposed as new regulatory principle,[2] should neither impose nor discriminate in favor of the use of a certain type of technology.

1. United Nations Office on Drugs and Crime (hereinafter "UNODC"), *Comprehensive Study on Cybercrime*, Draft 2013, online available at: https://www.unodc.org/documents/organized-crime/UNODC_CCPCJ_EG.4_2013/CYBERCRIME_STUDY_210213.pdf, 51 (2013).
2. The principle of "technological neutrality" was officially presented by the European Commission as a regulatory principle in the Communications Review *Towards a New Framework for Electronic Communications Infrastructure and Associated Services* (1999).

Technology neutral or technology-independent regulation[3] is supposed to address the problem of distinction between online and offline world. Technology-independent rules can better resist "technological turbulence" or at least ensure that Information and Communication Technology (ICT) related rules may be responsive to rapid and revolutionary changes in this sector. Technology independence seems to be required not only in relation to the description of conduct when defining cybercrimes but also with regard to the definition of tools, assets (to be protected) as well as targets of cybercrime.

§1.01 "INFORMATION SYSTEMS" AND SURROUNDING CONCEPTS

Information systems are recognized as a key element of political, social and economic interaction.[4] The notion of "information systems" is, without doubt, a parameter of crucial importance for the legislation in the field of cybercrime. Especially with regard to EU policy, information systems and their security represent as umbrella term a good that has to be ensured and protected in a manifold way.

A rather functional definition of information systems which has been adopted by the International Standardization Organization (ISO) and the International Electrotechnical Commission (IEC) combines the definition of information systems with the notion of information. According to Definition 2.39 of ISO 27000:2014, an information system is "applications, services, information technology assets, or other information handling components."[5] Other definitions originating from the information systems community refer to the physical process that supports an organization by collecting, processing, storing and analyzing data, and disseminating information to achieve organizational goals. An information system collects, processes, stores, analyzes and disseminates information for a specific purpose.[6]

While these definitions reflect the technological and organizational aspects of information systems, the core feature of legal descriptions of "computer," "computer system" or "information system" is that the device must be "capable of processing

3. Koops points out that there is a significant difference between "technology independence" and "technology neutrality": Technology-independent regulation ought to abstract completely away from technology, whereas technology-neutral regulation might be closely related to or intertwined with technology, as long as it does not favor one specific technology over another. *See* B.-J. Koops, *Should ICT Regulation Be Technology-Neutral?*, in *Starting Points for ICT Regulation. Deconstructing Prevalent Policy One-Liners*, 77–108 (B.-J. Koops et al. (eds), IT & Law Series, vol. 9, The Hague 2006), Available at SSRN: http://ssrn.com/abstract=918746.
4. Directive 2013/40/EU of the European Parliament and of the Council off Aug. 12, 2013 on attacks against information systems and replacing council framework decision 2005/222/JHA, Recital No. 2.
5. International Organization for Standardization (ISO) and the International Electrotechnical Commission (IEC), International Standard 27000 - Third Edition 2014-15-01 Information technology—Security techniques—Information security management systems—Overview and Vocabulary. Information systems constitute a field of study and at the same time an academic doctrine that encompasses a variety of topics including systems analysis and design, computer networking, information security, database management and decision support systems.
6. K. Rainer, E. Turban & R. Potter, *Introduction to Information Systems* 6 (Wiley 2007).

computer data or information."[7] Both approaches refer to the multiple processing of information; however the European regulatory approach puts the emphasis on "devices" and relates the purpose to the data itself and not to the organization that performs an information system.

"Information systems" were initially defined in the Council Framework Decision 2005/222/JHA as "any device or related devices performing automatic processing of computer data, as well as computer data stored, processed, retrieved or transmitted by them for the purpose of their operation, use, protection and maintenance." The Directive 2013/40/EU has brought no substantial changes to the definition of the replaced Framework Decision.[8] Differently from the definition of "computer system" in the Cybercrime Convention, the terminology used in EU regulation includes also "computer data" in the definition of information system.[9]

In this context, it is useful to examine the surrounding concepts of device, computer data and information, as their meaning is inherent to understanding the scope and the protected legal interests with regard to legislation that deals with criminal acts.

As far as it concerns the "devices," the respective legal instruments are predominantly "technology-neutral" in order to mitigate the risk of the continuous and permanently existing and growing gap between the steadily developing technology and the legal provisions. The broad definitions adopted allow for flexibility as the meaning of computer (systems) evolves over time. By focusing on the underlying conduct rather than the technical mechanisms for its commission, the terms used in the Cybercrime Convention and the Directive 2013/40/EU enable the law enforcement to keep pace with developments not foreseen or fully appreciated at the time of their adoption.[10]

The legislators of Cybercrime Convention seem to regard "computer system" and "device" as identical to each other when clarifying that computer system under the Convention is a device consisting of hardware and software developed for automatic processing of digital data. It may include input, output, and storage facilities. It may be standalone or be connected in a network with other similar devices.[11] In this meaning the law may apply to devices such as mainframe and computer servers, desktop personal computers, laptop computers, smartphones, tablet devices, multimedia devices such as printers, MP3 players, digital cameras, and gaming machines.[12]

---

7. *See, for example,* Article 1 of the Council of Europe Cybercrime Convention (CETS No. 185).
8. However there is a slight change as the legislator of the Directive while defining information system has been more precise indicating one device as sufficient (use both singular and plural forms in the definition of information system). *See* E. Gruodyte & M. Bilius, *Investigating Cybercrimes: Theoretical and Practical Issues,* in *Regulating e-Technologies in the European Union – Normative Realities and Trends,* 229 (T. Kerikmae (ed.) 2014).
9. According to E. Gruodyte & M. Bilius "the term 'information system' used in the EU instruments indicates that its content should be broader than the term 'computer system'; however, no such extension is provided in the definition itself," 230 et seq.
10. *See* J. Clough, *The Council of Europe Convention on Cybercrime: Defining "Crime" in a Digital World,* 23 Criminal Law Forum 375 (2012).
11. *See* Explanatory Report on Article 1a of the Cybercrime Convention, No. 23.
12. Council of Europe, T-CY Guidance Note 1 on the notion of "computer system." T-CY (2012) 21, Nov. 14, 2012.

With regard to computer data, they are commonly described as a "representation of facts, information or concepts that can be read, processed, or stored by a computer." Both the definition in the Cybercrime Convention (Article 1b) and the one in the Directive 2013/40/EU (Article 2b), which are quite identical with slight differences build upon the ISO/IEC definition of data[13] especially focusing on their suitability to be processed by a computer—or an information system respectively.[14] Computer data as conceived by the legislator seem to correspond at least partially both to the notion of information and of data.[15]

Computer data in the context of cybercrime and its investigation may exist both in static form (recorder/stored) and fluid (in movement/in process of communication). Distinguishing the different types of computer data is of importance for applying the respective evidence collection mechanism as it is dependent on nature and form of data to be searched, seized and collected.[16] The differences may be much nuanced: different legal standards and requirements apply to the lawful interception of communications by law enforcement authorities than to the recovery of sensor or user input data stored on a smartphone, which may be regarded as personal biometric data.[17]

§1.02 THE NOTIONS OF "ATTACKS" AND THREATS

The Preamble of the Budapest Convention states as its purpose the necessity to detect action directed against the confidentiality, integrity, and availability of computer systems, networks, and computer data as well as the misuse of such systems. The EU legislator aimed at approximating the criminal law in the area of attacks against information systems by establishing minimum rules concerning the definition of criminal offenses and relevant sanctions.[18]

The Directive 2013/40/EU, likewise the Convention on Cybercrime, intends at protecting information systems, while regulating the cybercriminality *stricto sensu* by the introduction of the offenses against computer and/or information systems to be penalized: illegal access, illegal interception, data interference, system interference, and misuse of devices. However, the Cybercrime Convention and the Directive 2013/40/EU deal with cyber attacks and security without framing these concepts in a

13. According to the definition of ISO/IEC 11179-4:2004, data is defined (3.3) as reinterpretable representation of information in a formalized manner suitable for communication, interpretation or processing.
14. *See* Explanatory Report on Article 1b of the Cybercrime Convention, No. 25.
15. Data are defined as an elementary description of things, events, activities, and transactions that are recorded, classified and stored but are not organized to convey any specific meaning while information means data that have been organized so that they have meaning and value for the recipient. *See* K. Rainer, E. Turban & R. Potter, *Introduction to Information Systems* 5 (2007).
16. A. Nieman, *Cyberforensics: Bridging the Law/Technology Divide*, 1 J. Info. L. & Tech. (JILT), 6 et seq. (2009). Nieman points out that in most jurisdictions the powers of interception and monitoring of communications have traditionally been seen as more intrusive than the powers of searching and seizing, 11.
17. A. Mylonas et al., *Smartphone Sensor Data as Digital Evidence*, 38 Computers & Security (Special Issue: Cybercrime in the Digital Economy) 66 (2013).
18. Directive 2013/40, Recital No. 1.

legally binding way.[19] Neither of the aforementioned regulatory texts includes a formal definition of the legally protected goods.

In theory, cyber attacks are described as "computer to computer attacks carried out to steal, erase, or alter information, or to destroy or impede the functionality of the target computer system,"[20] while the ISO defines attack as an "attempt to destroy, expose, alter, disable, steal or gain unauthorized access to or make unauthorized use of an asset" (2.3).[21] In security theory and policy, there are several classifications and taxonomies of attacks based on various criteria, such as the vulnerabilities of a system, the impacts and implications of an attack, attackers' motivation, tools and objectives, etc.[22]

The European legislator when proscribing the types of conduct that are to be punished focuses on the process that results to interference with data and/or system[23] and, in the final analysis, to the interference with fundamental rights or legal interests. The criteria of impact(s) and/or motivation of the attacker can be detected in the aggravating circumstances enumerated in Article 9 of the Directive 2013/40/EU namely: (a) committing the punishable criminal offense within a framework of criminal organization, (b) causing serious damages, (c) attacking critical infrastructures[24] and (d) identifying theft. The legal classification resulting from the criminalized types of conduct is related to some type/taxonomy of attacks against information systems but there is no direct matching between them.

The technical understanding and content of the term "attack" and its relation to the respective terms used by the legislator to describe the criminal acts, i.e., interception or interference[25] should, however, not be underestimated: unclear definitions and/or a possible discrepancy between the steadily evolving content of these terms and

19. The term "attacks" appears only in the Recitals of the Directive 2013/40/EC.
20. E. Georgiades et al., *Crisis on Impact: Responding to Cyber Attacks on Critical Information Infrastructures*, 30 J. Marshall J. Info. Tech. & Privacy L. 31, 34-35, (2013).
21. Although threat, defined as potential cause of an unwanted incident, which may result in harm to a system or organization (ISO 27000-2014 2.83), is a crucial concept for ensuring security it is clear that both the Cybercrime Convention and Directive 2013/40/EU regulate the penalization of acts and not just threats.
22. For an overview of classifications/taxonomies, *see* P.S. Dowland & S.M. Furnell, Security Concepts, Services, and Threats, IPICS-handbook. *See also* S. Hansman & R. Hunt, *A Taxonomy of Network and Computer Attacks*, 24(1) Computers & Security 31–43 (2005). Interesting is also the taxonomy presented by ENISA in the document Good Practice Guide on Incident Management (2010).
23. Interference is defined indirectly in Article 4 of Directive 2013/40/EU as hindering or interrupting the functioning of an information system by inputting computer data, by transmitting, damaging, deleting, deteriorating, altering or suppressing such data, or by rendering such data inaccessible.
24. Critical infrastructure means an asset, system, or part thereof located in Member States which is essential for the maintenance of vital societal functions, health, safety, security, economic or social well-being of people, and the disruption or destruction of which would have a significant impact in a Member State as a result of the failure to maintain those functions (Article 2a of Directive 2008/114/EC of Dec. 8, 2008 on the identification and designation of European critical infrastructures and the assessment of the need to improve their protection). *See below*, Chapter 2, §2.01[B][2].
25. *See* further below, Chapter 2, §2.01[B].

the related legal terminology may raise problems. While providing for the criminalization of attacks that constitute a crime, the legislator has not delimited adequately the notions,[26] which relate to attacks, thus creating some ambiguity.[27]

Taking into consideration that legislators aimed at introducing technology neutral rules to ensure their sustainability, we should also keep in mind that flexibility and adaptability of law[28] should not be achieved at the expense of clarity and legal certainty. Clear and precisely defined, objective substantiation of a crime constitutes one of the basic principles of criminal law. Moreover, as prevention, enforcement and prosecution of cybercrime are largely dependent on the common understanding between technical and non-technical stakeholders, such as the prosecutors, lawyers, and the judges, providing consistency in understanding, language and taxonomies is of crucial importance.

Furthermore, it is noteworthy that the relevant legal framework ignores the concept of threat, although threat[29] is one of the more crucial concepts for ensuring security.[30] Actually, this choice is consistent with the fact that both the Cybercrime Convention and the Directive 2013/40/EU regulate by their nature the criminalization of conduct and they do not address threats, which seem to be more a matter of cybersecurity policy. Moreover, threats may be accidental (e.g., fire, power failure, operator error), environmental (e.g., flood, lightning) or deliberate (e.g., hacking, malicious software, eavesdropping), while the term "attacks" indicates a deliberate malicious action; this corresponds to the choice of the EU legislator to impose criminal liability only if the offense has been committed with criminal intent, regardless whether the objective criteria of the offenses laid down in the Directive are met.

§1.03 SECURITY OF INFORMATION SYSTEMS

The concept of attacks against information systems has to be understood in connection with the notion of security. Security, in a nutshell, is the absence of danger.[31] "*Security*

26. For example, the Council of Europe Convention contains no definition of interception while the Directive 2013/40/EU contains a quite general and vague reference in Recital No. 9.
27. Kaiafa-Gbanti, *Criminalizing Attacks Against Information Systems in the EU—The Anticipated Impact of the European Legal Instruments on the Greek Legal Order*, 20 Eur. J. Crime Crim. L. & Crim. Just., 59 (2012).
28. We should also keep in mind that notwithstanding the intentions of legislators to create technology-neutral rules the provisions usually mirror the state of the art of the time that legislation is adopted or in any case the perceptions of legislators thereof. It is worthy to mention the focus of the Directive 2013/40/EU on "botnets."
29. Defined as potential cause of an unwanted incident, which may result in harm to a system or organization (ISO 27000-2014, 2.83). Threat is also defined as a circumstance that has the potential to cause loss or harm.
30. Indicative of the importance of threat as a concept is the fact that the European Union Agency for Network and Information Security (ENISA) is almost exclusively referring to "threats" in its documents. However, we must take into consideration that in some cases these terms are also used in an interchangeable way.
31. European Commission, Ethical and Regulatory Challenges to Science and Research Policy at the Global Level, Directorate-General for Research and Innovation, Brussels, 2012, 14.

is the condition (perceived or confirmed) of an individual, a community, an organization, a societal institution, a state, and their assets (such as goods, infrastructure), to be protected against danger or threats such as criminal activity, terrorism or other deliberate or hostile acts, [and] disasters (natural and man-made)."[32]

The need for information and communication systems security essentially arises exactly from the growing dependence on information technology to support an ever-increasing range of activities. Attacks against information systems are not a technical issue, as the damages caused correspond to interference with rights and interests, harms and damages to persons, private organizations and government. Even without explicit references, both the Budapest Convention and the Directive 2013/40/EU aim at protecting security of information, security of information (and communication) technology and, last but not least, fundamental rights and freedoms such as communications secrecy, privacy and personality.

Information security has to be distinguished from ICT security. ISO/IEC defines information security in a functional way: "Information security is the protection of information from a wide range of threats in order to ensure business continuity, minimize business risk, and maximize return on investments and business opportunities" (ISO/IEC 17799).[33] In a more specific context, ISO/IEC states that security consists in preservation of the so-called CIA triad or the classic C-I-A triplet: (a) *confidentiality*,[34] which is actually the aspect that people or at least lawyers most closely associate with the concept of security and refers to the prevention of unauthorized information disclosure, (b) *integrity*, which relates to the prevention of unauthorized modification of information,[35] and (c) *availability*,[36] which corresponds to the need for data and systems to be accessible and usable (by authorized parties) whenever and wherever they are required.

ICT security is defined by ISO/IEC as all aspects relating to defining, achieving and maintaining the confidentiality, integrity, availability, non-repudiation,[37] accountability, authenticity,[38] and reliability[39] of information resources (ISO/IEC 13335-1, 2004).[40] Each of these components is critical to overall security. As they interact with

32. A.J. Sieber, *Presentation on CEN BT/WG 161 – Standards for Security and Protection of the Citizens*, in Security Research Conference, (Ankara 2008).
33. ISO/IEC 17799 ISO/IEC 17799 on Code of Practice for Information Security Management, 2005.
34. According to ISO 27000-2014 (2.12) confidentiality means the property that information is not made available or disclosed to unauthorized individuals, entities, or *processes*.
35. According to ISO 27000-2014 (2.40) integrity means the property of accuracy and completeness (2.40). In a formal security mode, integrity refers to the protection against unauthorized modification or destruction of information. J. Graham, R. Howard, R. Olson, Cybersecurity Essentials, CRC 2011, 5.
36. According to ISO 27000-2014 (2.9) availability means the property of being accessible and usable upon demand by an authorized entity.
37. According to ISO 27000-2014 (2.54) non-repudiation means ability to prove the occurrence of a claimed event or action and its originating entities.
38. According to ISO 27000-2014 (2.8) authenticity means the property that an entity is what it is claims to be.
39. According to ISO 27000-2014 (2.62) reliability means the property of consistent intended behavior and results.
40. *See* R. von Solms & J. van Niekerk, *From Information Security to Cyber Security*, Computers and Security 3, 897 e102 (2013).

each other, the failure of any one component may result in potential system compromise.[41]

Another slightly different approach of security definition is adopted by the European legislators in the so-called NIS Directive.[42] In Article 4(2) the "security of network and information systems" is related to the "ability of network and information systems to *resist*, at a given level of confidence, any action that compromises the availability, authenticity, integrity or confidentiality of stored or transmitted or processed data or the related services offered by, or accessible via, those network and information systems."

§1.04 CYBERSECURITY

In the past years, policy emphasis and the respective terminology are shifted toward the notion of cybersecurity. In Europe, the increased number of cyber attacks and the sophistication of the methods used, as well as the growing scale of the damage, have shifted cybersecurity in the top of the agenda.[43]

The term cybersecurity has been used in theory often interchangeably with the term information security. However, cybersecurity is conceived in a broader way as a notion encompassing protection of information, information systems and infrastructure from those threats that are associated with using ICT systems in a globally connected environment.[44] In the European Union's documentation and legislative approach, cybersecurity is conceived in a more general and vague way which combines institutional and organizational aspects: the European Commission states that cybersecurity "... commonly refers to the safeguards and actions that can be used to protect the cyber domain, both in the civilian and military fields, from those threats that are associated with or that may harm its interdependent networks and information infrastructure."[45]

Cybersecurity and cyber attacks are strictly related not only to computer systems but also to computer networks. Cyber attacks include actions that may undermine the functions of a computer system or a computer network, i.e., they may alter, disrupt, deceive, degrade, or destroy computer systems or networks or the information and/or

41. J. Graham et al., *Cybersecurity Essentials*, 3–6.
42. Directive (EU) 2016/1148 of the European Parliament and of the Council of 6 July 2016 concerning measures for a high common level of security of network and information systems across the Union. Official Journal of the European Union L 194/1, 19.7.2016.
43. European Commission, *Cybersecurity Strategy of the European Union: An Open, Safe and Secure Cyberspace*, Joint Communication to the European Parliament, the Council, The European Economic and Social Committee and the Committee of the Regions (2013).
44. U. Helmbrecht, *ENISA at the Service of the EU's Cyber Security, SEDE speech*, European Parliament Brussels (Mar. 16, 2015).
45. *Cybersecurity Strategy of the European Union: An Open, Safe and Secure Cyberspace*, Joint Communication to the European Parliament, The Council, The European Economic and Social Committee and the Committee of the Regions, Join (2013), (Feb. 7, 2013).

programs resident in or transiting these systems or networks.[46] A cybersecurity incident may also lead to breaches in the confidentiality, integrity, or availability of information.

Directive 2013/40/EU is a decisive step toward creating a cyberspace and cybersecurity policy for Europe. Cybersecurity touches on multiple aspects of security: individual, national, international, or even global security and stresses across the fields of internal market, justice and home affairs, and foreign policy to the extent that it angles to cyberspace issues. Directive 2013/40/EU aims to harmonize the criminalization of specific types of conduct (such as illegal access to information systems or illegal system and data interference) and does not address the prevention of Network and Information Security (NIS) risks and incidents, the response to NIS incidents and the mitigation of their impact. The Directive's ultimate goal is to address large-scale events and to contribute to the creation of a safer information society and of an area of freedom, security, and justice.[47]

As already mentioned the NIS Directive refers to "network and information systems security," but it does not define "cybersecurity" the term appearing only once in the Recitals. However, cybersecurity constitutes the main policy objectives of the EU.[48] The goal of the EU cybersecurity strategy, the NIS Directive being a central element thereof, is to protect European citizens, administration, infrastructure and economies from cyber disruptions. A range of legislative, organizational, and security measures are to be taken by Member States to create a cohesive approach with regard to cybersecurity measures, and minimize discrepancies within and between Member States.

§1.05 CYBERCRIME AND CYBERWAR

Large-scale momentums and malicious cyber attacks may disable infrastructures and cause their malfunction in ways and to an extent they impose severe sufferings on citizens or even physically harm them. Such attacks may threaten security and safety of persons and organizations and produce economic damages through the interruption of information and/or communications systems or loss of confidence in markets. At the same time, the growing number of cyber events reported on a regular basis has

46. *See* the comprehensive definition adopted by U.S. National Research Council in the Report Nat'l Research Council, Technology, Policy, Law, and Ethics Regarding U.S. Acquisition and Use of Cyberattack Capabilities 1 (William A. Owens et al.), 2009.
47. K. Pipyros, L. Mitrou, D. Gritzalis and Th. Apostolopoulos, *Cyberoperations and International Humanitarian Law: Obstacles in Applying International Law Rules in Cyber Warfare*, Information and Computer Security, Information and Computer Security 24(1), March 2016, pp. 38–52.
48. The NIS Directive consists of three major tools: (1) the introduction of certain national cybersecurity capabilities at a national level, e.g., individual EU countries must have a national CSIRT, (2) establishment of cross-border collaboration mechanisms, (3) obligation to organize national supervision of critical sectors. On Thursday Jun. 27, 2019, the Regulation (EU) 2019/881 of the European Parliament and of the Council of 17 April 2019 on ENISA (the European Union Agency for Cybersecurity) and on information and communications technology cybersecurity certification and repealing Regulation (EU) No. 526/2013 (Cybersecurity Act) entered into force. For more about visit the respective website of the European Commission https://ec.europa.eu/digital-single-market/en/cyber-security.

transformed "cyberspace" into a battlefield, bringing to light "cyberwarfare" as "the fifth domain or warfare" after land, sea, air, and space.[49] Attacks causing far-reached damages on public infrastructures or having national-security implications test the categories and limits of existing legal framework and expand the boundaries of cybercrime *lato sensu* to include also cyberwar.[50]

However, there is no commonly accepted definition for cyberwarfare. It refers to acts of war in cyberspace with means which are predominantly associated with information technology. The terms of cyberwar and cyber warfare are lacking an international generally accepted definition. Cyberwar is typically conceptualized as state-on-state action equivalent to an armed attack or use of force in cyberspace that may trigger a military response with a proportional kinetic use of force (Theohary and Rollins, 2015). Most policy makers and academics would agree that the term "cyber-war" is a loaded term, since there has yet to occur an act of aggression that comfortably meets the understandings of a "war." Therefore, the term "cyber warfare" is preferable in the international literature than the term "cyberwar." Cyber warfare "is a more open-ended term, more useful in exploring an environment that is not only virtual but also largely unchartered."

Probably the most important problem relating to cyber attacks, cyber operations, and cyber warfare is the lack of clear-cut legal framework to define, assess, and face such attacks. Today, no international, legally binding instruments exist to regulate the interstate relations in cyberspace. As a result, states and organizations perceive the notion of cyber warfare differently, depending on their priorities and specific interests. Despite the fact that there has been considerable progress at the European and International level toward the development of European and National Cyber Security Strategies[51] and the adoption of an effective comprehensive legal framework of prevention measures for NIS and against cyber attacks, it is doubtful if such strategies and rules can deal adequately and effectively with cyber warfare. More specifically, it has not been clarified in which cases cyber attacks could be treated as an "armed attack," making it possible for a state to respond by exercising its legitimate right of self-defense under Article 51 of the UN Charter.

Actually, there is currently no institutional framework for the evaluation of the "use of force" concept in cyberspace. However, experts have proposed evaluation criteria that could escalate a security incident into cyberwar. Such criteria may be "severity" (severity of attacks), "immediacy" (i.e., the speed with which consequences manifest themselves), "directness" (i.e., the causal relation between a cyber attack and its consequences), "invasiveness," "measurability of the effects," "military character of the cyber operation," "extent of State involvement" and "presumptive legality" (i.e.,

49. W. Lynn, *Defending a New Domain: The Pentagon's Cyberstrategy*, Foreign Affairs, vol. 89, No. 5, available at: www.foreignaffairs.com/articles/66552/william-j-lynn-iii/defending-a-new-domain (2010).
50. NATO Cooperative Cyber Defence Centre of Excellence, *Ten Rules for Cyber Security* (Talinn 2011).
51. *See* the Reports of ENISA Study on CSIRT landscape and IR capabilities in Europe 2025 (2019) and NIS Directive and national CSIRTs (2016).

acts not expressly prohibited by international law).[52] The most typical problem arising from the form of cyber attacks and from the way they are conducted is the inability to positively identify the key actor of the attacks, resulting thus in an inability to handle the issue of "attribution" which means that we can never be absolutely certain who is behind a cyber attack.[53] In addition, in cyber warfare, the activities of key actors (states) can often not be easily distinguished from the activities of non-state actors (such as cybercriminals and terrorist groups), rendering the terrain of cyber conflict complicated. The combination of anonymity and parallel action from both state and non-state actors and the difficulty in distinguishing military from criminal actions makes the management of this type of conflicts complicated and the implementation of international humanitarian law rather problematic.[54]

52. This set of criteria proposed by M. Schmitt seems to be widely adopted. *See* M. Schmitt, *Computer Network Attack and the Use of Force in International Law: Thoughts on a Normative Framework*, 37 Columbia J. Transnational L., available at: http://papers.ssrn.com/sol3/papers.cfm?abstract_id = 1603800 (1999).
53. K. Pipyros, et al., *A Cyber Attack Evaluation Methodology*, in Proc. of the 13th European Conference on Cyber Warfare and Security, 264–270 (2014).
54. *See* K. Pipyros et al., A new strategy for improving cyber-attacks evaluation in the context of Tallinn Manual, Computers & Security 74, 371–383 (2018).

CHAPTER 2

Criminalization of Attacks Against Information Systems

Philippe Jougleux, Tatiana-Eleni Synodinou & Lilian Mitrou

Until recently, the regulation of attacks against information systems was not recognized as a separate field of study. This topic was incorporated in the vast and heterogenic notion of cybercriminality. Therefore, it has to be reminded that the definition of cybercriminality itself has provoked a great deal of confusion among academics, politicians and practitioners. Even if the notion is still in progress and no consensus still exists on its definition, we can distinguish three periods, three successive definitions, which correspond to an evolution of the concept. First, cybercriminality has been understood as a simple transposition of the general rules of criminal law on the Internet as a new medium of communication. In this sense, the notion of cybercriminality covers various and very different topics such as child pornography or intellectual property enforcement. We can then see various efforts of more precise definitions, such as the distinction proposed between one type of cybercrime, which is mostly technological in nature, and another kind of cybercrime, which has a more pronounced human element.[1] On the basis of a third approach, which will be adopted by this study, cybercriminality *stricto sensu* does not concern any offense committed through the use of an electronic device, but only the offenses related by nature to the protection of information systems. In order to avoid any confusion, we will in this study use the notion of "cyber attacks" instead of cybercrime when referring to these offenses. Alternatively, based on Wall's work,[2] cybercrime is also classified by distinguishing three various kinds of crimes: the cyber-assisted, cyber-enabled, and

1. Sarah Gordon & Richard Ford, *On the Definition and Classification of Cybercrime*, 2(1) J. Computer Virology, 13, 20 (August 2006).
2. David S. Wall, *Cybercrime: The Transformation of Crime in the Information Age* (Polity 2007); Wall, *Crime, Security and Information Communication Technologies: The Changing Cybersecurity Threat Landscape and Implications for Regulation and Policing*, pp. 1075–1096 (2017).

cyber-dependent crimes. Cyber-assisted crimes consist of crimes that could occur in the real world but received help from information on digital forms (e.g., Internet recipe to create a bomb). Cyber-enabled crimes category encompass crimes such as fraud, which are escalated by the globalized "cyber" element of networked and digital technologies, but which will still take place at a more limited (probably local) level if the Internet was removed from the equation. Finally, cyber-dependent crimes category refer to crimes that would not exist without digital and networked technologies. Cyber attacks fall within this last category.

"Cybercrimes *stricto sensu*" or "cyber attacks" then are those offenses where a computer is itself the target, i.e., three fundamental offenses: (1) illegal access to information systems, (2) illegal system interference, (3) illegal data interference, which protect the integrity of a computer system. A fourth offense may be added to this list, specifically, the offense of illegal interception, which does not refer to the integrity of a system, but is related to the protection of electronic communication privacy. These offenses are complemented with other provisions, which will be analyzed further below under "prevention,"[3] since they incriminate acts executed in order to prepare or facilitate the execution of one of these four offenses. To understand this *summa divisio* of cybercrime regulation, we first need to focus on the international and European history of this legal framework, in order to analyze each offense in its specific elements.

§2.01 THE MILESTONES OF THE EUROPEAN LEGAL FRAMEWORK

[A] The Long Road to the Harmonization of Cybercrime Law

[1] Before the Budapest Convention

Although the Budapest Convention on Cybercrime of 2001 is the most important point of reference concerning the subject matter of this book, it is noteworthy to remember that various individual initiatives aimed at creating a harmonized legal framework against cybercriminality had already appeared in the early 1970s.[4] Interpol has also historically played a major role in the repression of cybercrime; for example, it created the first "Interpol Training Seminar for Investigators of Computer Crime," in 1981.

Even if cybercriminality is often seen by the public as a notion interrelated with malevolent practices on the Internet, it has to be reminded that it is not accurate: cybercriminality, both as a concept and as a reality, existed before the democratization of the Internet in the 1990s. In fact, cybercriminality was present for as long as information systems existed; that is how the enigma machine code was broken in the World War II,[5] the various "phreaking boxes" used to interact with automated

3. *See* Chapter 3.
4. S. Schjolberg, *The History of Global Harmonization on Cybercrime Legislation—The Road to Geneva* (Cybercrime Law December 2008), available at: cybercrimelaw.net.
5. McGrayne & Sharon Bertsch, *The Theory That Would Not Die: How Bayes' Rule Cracked the Enigma Code, Hunted Down Russian Submarines, & Emerged Triumphant from Two Centuries of Controversy* (Yale University Press 2011).

telephone systems in the 1960s decade,[6] to the creation of the first associations of hackers in 1981.[7]

The Council of Europe (CoE) Recommendation on computer-related crimes of 1989[8] had already distinguished various forms of cybercriminality. Basically, the recommendation only asked the Member States to take into account, when reviewing their legislation or initiating new legislation, the report on computer-related crime elaborated by the "European Committee on Crime Problems" (CDPC),[9] and in particular the guidelines for the national legislatures.[10]

The report dealt with various computer-related offenses; in more particularly, it defined some offenses, which will serve as a basis for the discussions of the Budapest Convention. "Computer fraud" is defined as "the input, alteration, erasure or suppression of computer data or computer programs, or other interference with the course of data processing that influences the result of data processing thereby causing economic or possessory loss of property of another person with the intent of procuring an unlawful gain for himself or for another person."

"Computer forgery" is defined as "the input, alteration, erasure or suppression of computer data or computer programs, or other interference with the course of data processing, in a manner or under such conditions, as prescribed by national law, that it would constitute the offense of forgery if it had been committed with respect to a traditional object of such an offence." Third, the offense of "damage to computer data or computer programs" is defined as "the erasure, damaging, deterioration or suppression of computer data or computer programs without right," whereas "computer sabotage" as "the input, alteration, erasure or suppression of computer data or computer programs, or interference with computer systems, with the intent to hinder the functioning of a computer or a telecommunication system." The offense of "unauthorized access" criminalizes the act of "access without right to a computer system or network by infringing security measures." Last but not least, "unauthorized interception" is defined as "the interception, made without right and by technical means, of communications to, from and within a computer system or network."

[2] The Budapest Convention on Cybercrime (2001)

The Budapest Convention on Cybercrime of November 23, 2001,[11] often more simply called "the Budapest Convention," was drawn up by the CoE and constitutes the first contemporary international framework of harmonization against cybercrime. However, the scope of the Convention is very extended, adopting a broad definition of the cybercriminality and including in its dispositions child pornography, copyright law infringement, computer-related forgery and computer-related fraud. Concretely, the

6. Patrick S. Ryan, *War, Peace, or Stalemate: Wargames, Wardialing, Wardriving, and the Emerging Market for Hacker Ethics*, 9 Va. J.L. & Tech. 1 (2004).
7. The Chaos Computer Club (CCC) based in Germany. *See* http://www.ccc.de.
8. CoE, *Recommendation on Computer-Related Crimes*, No. R. (89)9 (Sep. 13, 1989).
9. Available at: http://www.coe.int/t/DGHL/STANDARDSETTING/CDPC/default_en.asp.
10. Recital R (89)9 on computer-related crime.
11. CoE, Budapest Convention on Cybercrime of Nov. 23, 2001, CET.185.

Convention distinguishes four different categories of cybercrimes: (1) offenses against the confidentiality, integrity and availability of computer data and systems; (2) computer-related offenses; (3) content-related offenses; (4) offenses related to infringements of copyright and related rights. Therefore, with the first and the second categories of offenses, the Convention regulates the cybercriminality *stricto sensu* and defines the notion of illegal access, illegal interception, data interference, system interference and misuse of devices.

The Budapest Convention can be seen as a huge success. Indeed, it introduces some common definitions at a world level, since important non-CoE States, such as the USA, Canada, South Africa, Australia and Japan, also adopted the Convention. On March 1, 2006, the Additional Protocol to the Convention on Cybercrime came into force, with regulations incriminating racist and xenophobic communications on the Internet.

The Convention of Budapest has been widely adopted. This success is proved not only by the huge number of ratifications of the Convention but also by the fact that the convention has also served as a model and an inspiration for non-subscripting countries worldwide. It has been thus estimated that more than a hundred countries have used the Budapest Convention as a model for their domestic legislation.[12]

The Convention also establishes general principles of criminal law applicable to cybercrime. First of all, it proclaims that cybercrime offenses are based on intentionality. Also, it excludes petty and insignificant situations from the scope of repression. In each offense, it is mentioned as an element the absence of right, in order to protect the behaviors normally protected under legal defenses.

[3] The Council Framework Decision of 2005

The Budapest Convention came into effect on July 1, 2004. One year later, the EU institutions adopted their own instrument on cybercrime repression and national authorities' coordination. The Council framework decision of 2005[13] constitutes the first legislative approach on cybercrime at the European Union's level. It follows closely the Convention of Budapest, not only chronologically but also in its philosophy. However, whereas the international Convention used a very broad approach of the notion of cybercriminality, the European institutions preferred to distinguish cybercriminality *stricto sensu* from other kinds of criminality, that only use computers as a means, such as child pornography or intellectual property violation. Also, it has to be noted that the Framework Decision does not merely constitute the adoption by EU law of the general principles of the Budapest Convention, but it has followed its own

12. Zahed Jamil, *Cybercrime Model Laws, Discussion Paper Prepared for the Cybercrime Convention Committee*, available at: https://rm.coe.int/1680303ee1 (Dec. 9, 2014).
13. Council Framework Decision 2005/222/JHA of Feb. 24, 2005 on attacks against information systems.

process of reflection, which can be traced back to a recommendation in 2000 on computer-related crime.[14]

The framework decision of 2005 proposed a strategy focused on enhancing the security of information infrastructures and giving law enforcement authorities the means to act. Emphasis is placed on the need for an effective police and judicial cooperation.[15]

Decision 2005/222 was apparently not designated to last long. The decision to reform it was made very early. Indeed, as described in a communication of the Commission in 2008, this reform was judged indispensable in order to "combat the use of botnets for criminal purposes and to promote the use of the same contact points used by the Council of Europe and the G8 to react rapidly to threats involving advanced technology."[16]

[4] Other Unilateral, Bilateral and Multilateral Approaches

It should be reminded that the European approach does not preclude other legislative frameworks. Both the international tool that constitutes the Budapest Convention and the EU legal framework propose a minimum level of protection. They do not pretend to monopolize competency on the topic of cybercrime.

Therefore, first of all, many countries decided to go further and to criminalize some acts related to the Internet's misuse that are not dealt by the EU regulation, or to put emphasis on a specific type of coordination. As mentioned in a recent report, some cultural blocs can be distinguished as regards the unilateral approach. The authors of the report explain that:

> Several distinct cyber-blocs have formed with their unique cyber security strategies and emphases. The Anglosphere, led by the US and the UK, emphasizes a leading private sector role, an educated workforce, outreach and diplomacy. The EU, led by Germany, focuses on a robust legal and regulatory framework, and on the promotion of the Council of Europe (Budapest) Convention of Cybercrime as a blueprint for international cooperation and enforcement. The Baltic States are in tight cooperation with NATO in the development of their national cyber-security strategies. The post-Soviet CIS bloc, led by Russia with some degree of Chinese cooperation, focuses on internal threats, abhors extra-territorial judicial action, and promotes a corresponding international framework under the auspices of the UN.[17]

In the same vein, a bilateral approach traditionally constitutes an advantaged solution for countries which wish to deepen their relationship on the topic of

14. Communication from the Commission to the Council, the European Parliament, the Economic and Social Committee and the Committee of the Regions: *Creating a safer information society by improving the security of information infrastructures and combating computer-related crime* (COM(2000) 890 final – not published in the Official Journal (OJ)).
15. Recitals 5, 7, 8 and 12 of the Framework Decisions.
16. Commission Report to the Council on Article 12 of the Council Framework Decision of Feb. 24, 2005 on attacks against information systems (COM(2008) 448 final).
17. Avner Levin, Paul Goodrick & Daria Ilkina, *Securing Cyberspace: A Comparative Review of Strategies Worldwide*, Privacy and Cyber Crime Institute (Ryerson University 2013).

cooperation. We can cite, for instance, the China-US Bilateral on Cybersecurity "Fighting Spam to Build Trust" of 2011.[18]

Other multilateral initiatives also exist. The General Assembly of the United Nations adopted a resolution[19] in 2000, stressing out the need of an efficient protection against cybercriminality, with the development of national legislations which would provide a relevant enforcement.[20] One year later, in another resolution,[21] the same assembly refers explicitly to the Budapest convention and invites the States "when developing national law, policy and practice to combat the criminal misuse of information technologies, to take into account, as appropriate, the work and achievements of the Commission on Crime Prevention and Criminal Justice and of other international and regional organizations." In 2010, in a third resolution,[22] the UN promotes better cooperation in this topic and they "recommend that the United Nations Office on Drugs and Crime, upon request, provide, in cooperation with Member States, relevant international organizations and the private sector, technical assistance and training to States to improve national legislation and build the capacity of national authorities in order to deal with cybercrime, including the prevention, detection, investigation and prosecution of such crime in all its forms, and to enhance the security of computer networks."[23]

The International Telecommunications Union (ITU), one of the oldest international organizations,[24] and now incorporated in the UN as a special agency, has extended its field of competence to cybersecurity, acknowledging in 2010 that one of its fundamental roles "is to build confidence and security in the use of Information and Communication Technologies."[25] The institution, therefore, develops various projects related to cybercrime, such as the assistance in the establishment of a National Computer Incident Response Team (CIRT), which serves as a national focus point for coordinating cybersecurity incident response to cyber attacks in the country, the promulgation of clear security principles for IMT (3G and 4G) networks, the development under ITU's Study Group 17 of confidence and security in the use of Information and Communication Technologies, and the creation of a Global Cybersecurity Index (GCI), which is a project to measure the cybersecurity capabilities of nation states and hence enable informed decisions to foster a global culture of cybersecurity.

In parallel, other international institutions have been found to give a lot of attention to legal issues of cybercrime. One of these is the Organization for Economic

18. https://www.m3aawg.org/system/files/china-us-fighting-spam-final.pdf.
19. UN General Assembly Resolution 55/63, on combating the criminal misuse of information technologies.
20. The resolution indicates that "Legal systems should protect the confidentiality, integrity, and availability of data and computer systems from unauthorized impairment and ensure that criminal abuse is penalized."
21. UN General Assembly Resolution 56/121, Combating the criminal misuse of information technologies, Dec. 19, 2001.
22. UN General Assembly Resolution 65/230, Twelfth United Nations Congress on Crime Prevention and Criminal Justice, Dec. 21, 2010.
23. Point 42.
24. ITU was founded in Paris in 1865 as the International Telegraph Union.
25. The position has been explicit following the World Summit on the Information Society (WSIS) and the 2010 ITU Plenipotentiary Conference.

Co-operation and Development (OECD). The OECD regularly publishes reports, guidelines and analysis concerning cybercrime: the notion of critical information system,[26] the identity theft,[27] the spam[28] and the virus and malware propagation.[29]

Finally, it has also been proposed to apprehend the issue of cybercrime not only as a criminal matter, but also as a threat to national and global economies. The lack of harmonization on cybercrime repression would lead to distortion of the free competition. Therefore, the WTO could be competent to interfere in these matters by negotiating a "Competitive Fairness and Cybercrime Agreement."[30]

[B] Directive 2013/40/EU

[1] The Adoption of the Directive

The Directive 2013/40/EU constitutes the last step of the regulation of cybercrime in Europe. Although it replaces the 2005 Framework Decision, it does not revolutionize the legal framework of cybercrime. Contrary to the Budapest convention and following the 2005 Framework Decision, it only concerns cybercrime *stricto sensu*. Therefore, it confirms the orientation adopted by the European legislator, which is to abandon the idea of a general and unified legal framework applicable to every offense on the Internet in profit of a pragmatic, sectorial approach, with separate regulations of cyber attacks, child pornography or criminal media law. Recital 15 of the Directive expresses the idea that the Directive should be viewed as complimentary to the Convention on Cybercrime, indicating that "this Directive builds on that Convention."[31]

The Directive does not aim to modify *de profundis* the legal framework. On the contrary, it aims to reinforce its efficiency, with a focus on the mechanisms of enforcement, which means better police cooperation, faster judicial cross-border procedures, and easier flux of information. Therefore, it should not be seen as a stand-alone legal framework, but has to be conjugated with other mechanisms of cooperation, such as Council Framework Decision 2009/948/JHA of November 30, 2009 on prevention and settlement of conflict of jurisdiction in criminal proceedings.[32]

---

26. OECD, *Guidelines for the Security of Information Systems and Networks: Towards a Culture of Security* (Paris, OECD Publishing 2002). This Recommendation has been replaced by the Recommendation of the Council on Digital Security Risk Management for Economic and Social Prosperity (Oct. 1, 2015).
27. OECD, *Policy Guidance on Online Identity Theft* (Paris, OECD Publishing 2008).
28. OECD Task Force on Spam was established in 2004 and delivered a report in 2006.
29. OECD, *Computer Viruses and Other Malicious Software: A Threat to the Internet Economy* (Paris, OECD Publishing 2009).
30. Patrick Stewart, *Trading Cybercrime for Jobs and Commerce or Paying Up: Using the WTO to Combat Cybercrime*, 48 Geo. Wash. Int'l L. Rev. 475 (2016).
31. "(15) The Council Conclusions of 27–28 November 2008 indicated that a new strategy should be developed with the Member States and the Commission, taking into account the content of the 2001 Council of Europe Convention on Cybercrime. That Convention is the legal framework of reference for combating cybercrime, including attacks against information systems. This Directive builds on that Convention. Completing the process of ratification of that Convention by all Member States as soon as possible should be considered to be a priority."
32. As mentioned explicitly in Recital 27 of the Directive.

Recital 33 of the Directive better explains its purpose and justification: "Since the objectives of this Directive, namely to subject attacks against information systems in all Member States to effective, proportionate and dissuasive criminal penalties and to improve and encourage cooperation between judicial and other competent authorities, cannot be sufficiently achieved by the Member States, and can therefore, by reason of their scale or effects, be better achieved at Union level, the Union may adopt measures in accordance with the principle of subsidiarity as set out in Article 5 of the Treaty on European Union. In accordance with the principle of proportionality, as set out in that Article, this Directive does not go beyond what is necessary in order to achieve those objectives."

[2] Main Principles of the Directive 2013/40/EU

The Directive introduces a regime of criminal liability for legal persons. A wider recognition of the liability of legal persons corresponds to the evolution of the sociology of hacking, in the sense that more and more organizations are involved in practice in illegal activities on Internet. Nowadays, the hacker's profile has shifted from the antisocial computer genius to complex groups of mercenaries, associated with the mafia or just working as mercenaries for the account of non-scrupulous companies that wish to neutralize the access to a competitor's website or to steal some sensitive information from another company. In other words, their action can be one of economic intelligence or more directly of nuisance to the online infrastructure of the competitor (through a Distributed Denial-of-Service (DDoS) attack for instance) and either way in this case they should be held liable. Article 10 of the Directive states that a legal person could be held liable for the cyber attacks "committed for their benefit," at the condition that the author of the attack possesses either a power of representation of the legal person, an authority to take decisions on behalf of the legal person or an authority to exercise control within the legal person.

Another approach of the Directive is to graduate the legal response according to the criminal behavior, using the classic mechanism of aggravating circumstances. While the main offenses are punishable "by a maximum term of imprisonment of at least two years" according to Article 9(2), the sanction can increase in case of aggravating circumstances, listed by the European legislator at Article 9.

The first aggravating circumstance requires four cumulative conditions in order to take effect: the specific offenses referred to in Articles 4 and 5, an intention, a significant number of information systems have been affected and, finally, this has been realized through the use of a tool, referred to in Article 7, designed or adapted primarily for that purpose. In this case, the act can be punished with an imprisonment of at least three years. This situation aims to cover the event where hackers provoke massive damages to a network. Indeed, this circumstance does not apply in case of illegal access or of illegal interception, but just in case of data or system interference. Moreover, the criterion of "a significant number of information systems" implies in this context massive damages and as a result we can say that the mass of the damages constitutes a requirement for the fulfillment of this provision.

On the contrary, the references to the intention, on the one hand, and to the specific hacking tool, on the other, should be criticized. Indeed, the reference to the intention of the author could lead to the conclusion that the offenses of illegal interference to the system or to the data could be committed unintentionally. Moreover, reference to the tools used to commit the cybercrime merely complicate without obvious reasons the application of this situation.

Article 9(4) introduces a second step of aggravating circumstances, deemed to be even more serious than the first one, since the penalties have increased to at least five years of imprisonment. The legislator distinguishes between three various situations that constitute the second step of aggravating circumstances. All these three situations refer only to the offenses of data interference or system interference. Therefore, an aggravating circumstance is to considered where: (a) the offenses of data interference or system interference "are committed within the framework of a criminal organization, as defined in Framework Decision 2008/841/JHA, irrespective of the penalty provided for therein; (b) they cause serious damage; or (c) they are committed against a critical infrastructure information system."

The first situation is clear enough and well defined. According to Article 1(1) of the Framework Decision 2008/841/JHA "on the fight against organized crime," "'criminal organization' means a structured association, established over a period of time, of more than two persons acting in concert with a view to committing offences which are punishable by deprivation of liberty or a detention order of a maximum of at least four years or a more serious penalty, to obtain, directly or indirectly, a financial or other material benefit."

The question of the eventual application of this disposition could arise and pose some difficulties as regards the movement of "Anonymous." Indeed, a lot of cyber attacks have been organized by individuals claiming that they are acting under the ideology of this informal group. The application of this aggravating circumstance to "Anonymous" members is deemed in most cases invalid, since two conditions are missed: the association cannot be seen as "structured" and also, because of the ideological aim of the attacks, no "financial or other material benefit" occurs.

The second situation of aggravating circumstances expressed by Article 9(4) of the Directive refers to attacks which cause serious damage. However, this reference could be described as quite unclear. What does "serious damage" mean? And how does this situation differ from the first step of aggravating circumstances analyzed above? We can distinguish two cases: either the system or data interference inflicts serious damage cumulatively, in which case the first situation of aggravating circumstance applies (attack against a significant number of information systems), or the attack inflicts serious damage to the society, and by definition, this means that the attack was aimed at very sensitive information systems. In this case, the third category should apply. In conclusion, this specific aggravating circumstance seems too general to apply within the frame of a criminal procedure.

Finally, a last situation is left to the discretion of the national legislator, who may choose whether to regard it as an aggravating circumstance or not. Article 9(5) of the Directive states that the legislator is free to institute an aggravating circumstance when instances of data or system interference "are committed by misusing the personal data of another person, with the aim of gaining the trust of a third party, thereby causing prejudice to the rightful identity owner," "unless those circumstances are already covered by another offense, punishable under national law." This provision certainly aims to counter the growing phenomena of identity theft on the Internet. Even if identity theft is a well-known issue of criminal law,[33] it is traditionally essentially a means for an illegal activity (such as, most of the time, bank fraud or deceit). The Directive, by consequence, reflects this traditional logic and considers identity theft as an aggravating circumstance. However, in the era of social networking, identity theft has ceased being a means and has become the purpose, since the identity itself constitutes the value. For instance, the creation of fake accounts of famous persons on social networks relies on the naivety of the people in order to exploit their personal data, to disseminate false information or even just as a kind of joke. It could have been interesting, however, to enhance protection by creating a specific offense on this issue, and some countries have already taken some initiative in this field.[34]

Also, the question remains to comprehend the nature of cyber identity and therefore of cyber identity theft;[35] it is a matter of interpretation to determine whether identity theft, defined in the European Directive as the misuse of personal data of another person, could also cover cyber identity data, but the famous broad definition of personal data, enacted by Directive 95/46/EC[36] as any information relating to an identifiable person, directly or indirectly, should authorize an interpretation in favor of the incorporation of cyber identity theft to the application of Article 9(4).

[3] Cyberwar and the Directive

As mentioned above, legal persons are liable on the basis of the Directive 2013/40. However, Article 2(c) excludes the State from the definition of legal person. This exclusion corresponds to a certain pragmatic view of cybercrime enforcement. Indeed, on the one hand, it seems difficult to imagine a situation of inter-state espionage in the post-Cold War background to end up in court. On the other hand, this exclusion can be seen as a very unfortunate development because of the modern evolution of cybercrime. Based upon Edward Snowden's revelations about the American mass surveillance programs,[37] it can be held as certain that at least two cases of cyber attack have been organized directly by States. Indeed, the virus which was aimed to destroy the

33. Sean B. Hoar, *Identity Theft: The Crime of the New Millennium*, 80 Or. L. Rev. 1423 (2001).
34. For a comparative analysis of the national legal approaches, *see* N. Robinson et al., *Comparative Study on Legislative and Non Legislative Measures to Combat Identity Theft and Identity Related Crime: Final Report*, TR-982-EC, available at: https://ec.europa.eu/home-affairs/sites/homeaffairs/files/e-library/documents/policies/organized-crime-and-human-trafficking/cybercrime/docs/rand_study_tr-982-ec_en.pdf (June 2011).
35. L.D. Roberts, *Cyber Identity Theft*, in *Cyber Crime: Concepts, Methodologies, Tools and Applications*, 21–36 (Hershey 2012).
36. European Parliament and Council Directive 95/46/EC of Oct. 24, 1995 on the protection of individuals with regard to the processing of personal data and on the free movement of such data.
37. Andrew Hammond & Richard J. Aldrich, *Afterword: Securing Freedom. Obama and the World: New Directions*, US Foreign Policy 303 (2014).

infrastructure of Iranian's nuclear power plant was – according to these revelations, even if a lot of suspicions already had existed on the hackers' identity – the creation of Israeli and American special services. Also, the mass surveillance of European communications operated by the United States National Security Agency (NSA), quite certainly constitutes the crime of data interference. One could also mention the hacking of Hilary Clinton's emails during the USA elections in March 2016. Information acquired by this hacking—and the divulgation of the vulnerability of the email itself—destabilized the population and it might have played a role in the results of the election. Even if it has not really been proven, investigations tend to demonstrate that a foreign power might have been behind this hacking. [38]

It is arguable under public international law that this kind of intervention constitutes a violation of the principle of territoriality.[39] Criminalization of this kind of attacks would be in this context counter effective, unless new Treaties and extraterritorial jurisdiction are agreed at a global level. However, so far, international law has failed to recognize the use of cyber attacks as a weapon of national strategy in any legally binding text.[40]

[4] The Protection of Critical Infrastructure Against Cyber Attacks and Cyber Terrorism

As mentioned above, attack against Critical Infrastructure is referred in the Directive as an aggravating circumstance on Article 9(4). The European institutions have clearly given a lot of importance to thoughts about cyber terrorism in the Communication from the Commission to the European Parliament, the Council, the European Economic and Social Committee and the Committee of the Regions of March 30, 2009 on Critical Information Infrastructure Protection.[41] This significance was affirmed two years later in another Communication on the same topic.[42] The idea is that in the information society, i.e., a society is where computers rule every aspect of the management and logistics of the cohabitation of millions of people in "meta-cities," cyber attacks can be directed not only against private persons or companies but also against vital resources of the society. We can think of water/electricity plants, light management, gas distribution, mass broadcasting tools, communication servers, traffic management for trains, airplanes, subways, etc. The list of critical infrastructures which, if destroyed, could paralyze an entire society, is here nonexhaustive. Also, this provision has to be

---

38. Lam C., *A Slap on the Wrist: Combatting Russia's Cyber Attack on the 2016 US Presidential Election*, 59 BCL Rev.2167c (2018).
39. Terry PC, *Don't Do as I Do-The US Response to Russian and Chinese Cyber Espionage and Public International Law*, 19 German LJ 613 (2018).
40. Eimear Bourke, *A War Without Bullets: Protecting Civilians in the Technology*, 28 Alb. L.J. Sci. & Tech. 1 (2018).
41. Protecting Europe from large-scale cyber attacks and disruptions: enhancing preparedness, security and resilience (COM(2009) 149 final).
42. Communication of Mar. 31, 2011 from the Commission to the European Parliament, the Council, the European Economic and Social Committee and the Committee of the Regions on Critical Information Infrastructure Protection "Achievements and next steps: towards global cybersecurity" (COM(2011) 163 final).

read in conjunction with the legal framework created by the Directive 2008/114/EC of December 8, 2008 on the identification and designation of European critical infrastructures (ECIs).[43]

The attack against a critical information infrastructure is then treated as an aggravating circumstance. It could have been pertinent to create a specific offense, as the psychology of the perpetrator, the modus operandi, and the results of the incriminated act, diverge a lot from a casual cyber attack on the Internet. This reflection rejoins the general discussion surrounding terrorism. While terrorism is apprehended in criminal law in a specific way and often goes with derogative procedures, cyber terrorism should also be considered as an ontologically different act from a mere cyber attack. Cyber terrorism possesses two characteristics that differentiates it from both cyber attacks and terrorism. Contrary to cyber attacks, cyber terrorism aims at terror. However, contrary to terrorism, cyber terrorism is in position to really affect and paralyze a society by targeting its critical infrastructures. The European legislator finally adopted this line of reasoning by amending its existing legislation on terrorism with a new Directive in 2017.[44] Indeed, Article 3 of the Directive 2017/541 specifically states as a terrorist offense the "(i) illegal system interference, as referred to in Article 4 of Directive 2013/40/EU of the European Parliament and of the Council in cases where Article 9(3) or point (b) or (c) of Article 9(4) of that Directive applies, and illegal data interference, as referred to in Article 5 of that Directive in cases where point (c) of Article 9(4) of that Directive applies;" or the threat to do it, when it may causes serious damage given their nature or context.

The Directive defines a critical infrastructure as an asset, system, or part thereof, located in Member States, that is essential for the maintenance of vital societal functions, health, safety, security, economic or social well-being of people, and the disruption or destruction of which would have a significant impact on a Member State as a result of the failure to maintain those functions, and distinguishes this general notion from the European Critical Infrastructures ("ECIs"), defined as the critical infrastructure in Member States, the disruption or destruction of which would have a significant impact on at least two Member States. Even if the energy sector[45] is logically the first answer that appears when one thinks about critical infrastructure, the large definition adopted does not stop there. Therefore, for instance, a submarine cable access for the European continent, which is vital for the Internet access of the population, should be seen as an ECI.

In conclusion, cyber terrorism has been discussed for two decades now,[46] and effective measures of both prevention and repression have been taken. If it is true that

43. Council Directive 2008/114/EC of Dec. 8, 2008 on the identification and designation of European critical infrastructures and the assessment of the need to improve their protection.
44. Directive (EU) 2017/541 of the European Parliament and of the Council of Mar. 15, 2017 on combating terrorism and replacing Council Framework Decision 2002/475/JHA and amending Council Decision 2005/671/JHA.
45. Kumar VS, Prasad J & Samikannu R, *A Critical Review of Cyber Security and Cyber Terrorism–Threats to Critical Infrastructure in the Energy Sector,* 14(2) Intl J Critical Infrastructures 101–119 (2018).
46. Furnell SM & Warren MJ, *Computer Hacking and Cyber Terrorism: The Real Threats in the New Millennium?,* 18(1) Computers & Security 28–34 (Jan. 1, 1999).

terrorist organizations adopted the digital tools and make a lot of use of it, it seems that for now this is for propaganda purposes only. In other words, cyberterrorism can be seen (thus far) as a "narrated catastrophe", a type of disaster that does not really exist beyond popular stories and narratives, since terrorist groups have not yet managed to orchestrate cyber attacks with lethal consequences or significant economic damage.[47]

[5] Next Steps after the Directive

In 2017, the Commission published a report on the States' status of compliance with the Directive.[48] It concludes that "the Directive has led to substantive progress in criminalising cyberattacks on a comparable level across the Member States, which facilitates the cross-border cooperation of law enforcement authorities investigating this type of offenses. Member States have amended criminal codes and other relevant legislation, streamlined procedures, and set up or improved cooperation schemes. The Commission acknowledges the major efforts by the Member States to transpose the Directive." Therefore, no step will be taken in the near future to amend the existing European legislation.

However, the EU activities did not stop here. On 2016, the European legislator adopted one more regulation on cybersecurity, the so-called NIS Directive.[49] The new Directive does neither amend the 2013/40 Directive nor change substantive criminal law. Still, the NIS Directive is seen as a substantial step forward in the domain of cybersecurity as it provides legal measures to boost the overall level of cybersecurity in the EU, to create a culture of prevention and of damage mitigation. Mainly, the NIS Directive focuses on the creation of a legal framework related to the operator of "essential service" and to the provider of digital service. It provides measures aimed to promote information and collaboration between national cybersecurity centers.

§2.02 CRIMINAL OFFENSES

[A] Illegal Access to Information Systems

[1] The Offense and Its Application

According to Article 3 of Directive 2013/40/EU, "Member States shall take the necessary measures to ensure that, when committed intentionally, the access without right, to the whole or to any part of an information system, is punishable as a criminal

47. Myriam Dunn Cavelty, *Is cyberterrorism a real threat?* in Richard Jackson, Daniela Pisoiu (eds) *Contemporary Debates on Terrorism*, London: Routledge, 2d ed (2018).
48. Report from the Commission to the European Parliament and the Council assessing the extent to which the Member States have taken the necessary measures in order to comply with Directive 2013/40/EU on attacks against information systems and replacing Council Framework Decision 2005/222/JHA, COM/2017/0474 final.
49. Directive (EU) 2016/1148 of the European Parliament and of the Council of Jul. 6, 2016 concerning measures for a high common level of security of network and information systems across the Union.

offence where committed by infringing a security measure, at least for cases which are not minor." This offense could be seen as a first approach to the legal understanding of hackers' activity.

Obviously, the notion of illegal access seems to be related, upon initial examination, with the consent or absence of consent by the person who owns the data.[50] For instance, a person mandated to test the "defenses" of an informational system cannot be pursued for illegal access. On the contrary, the so-called white hats, who take the initiative by themselves to test the protection of famous online systems and to alert the population in case vulnerability is found, have typically acted without the consent of the system owner. Independent of their very legitimate motive, their intention is criminal.[51] The intent to penetrate a nonauthorized computer system constitutes, therefore, the mental element of the offense. However, it has been mentioned that "due to the potential broad reach of some cybercrime offenses, such as illegal access to computer data, it is important that the mental element of cybercrime acts is clearly defined in law."[52] The various criminal traditions of the Member States as regards the estimation of the mental element could potentially create some gaps in the harmonization of the sector: does the intent refer to the will, the knowledge, the purpose, whereas some legal systems incorporate reckless behavior in the range of intentional acts? The only answer to these questions could come from the Court of Justice of the European Union (CJEU), through the mechanism of the autonomous notions of the European Union.

The intent constitutes only one requirement, and it has to be proved that access has been realized without right. The absence of right to access is directly related to the authorization by the administrator of the system. Any access without express authorization constitutes an access without right.[53] The reference of the "without right" element pre-existed in the Cybercrime Convention of 2001 and thus, the analysis provided in the Explanatory Report of the Convention could be extremely useful for its understanding. The authors of the Explanatory Report thus wrote that this:

> reflects the insight that the conduct described is not always punishable per se, but may be legal or justified not only in cases where classical legal defenses are applicable, like consent, self-defense or necessity but also in cases where other principles or interests lead to the exclusion of criminal liability. The expression "without right" derives its meaning from the context in which it is used. Thus, without restricting how Contracting Parties may implement the concept in their domestic law, it may refer to conduct undertaken without authority (whether

50. In fact, this contract-based theory of authorization has to be rejected since the European legislator adds a second criteria to the application of the offense of illegal access: the circumvention of a technical measure of protection, as we will see below.
51. C. Le Stanc, *Du "Hacking" considéré comme un des beaux arts et de l'opportun renforcement de sa répression*, Communication Commerce électronique n° 4, chron. 10 (April 2002).
52. United Nations Office on Drugs and Crime (UNODC), *Comprehensive Study on Cybercrime* 79 (New York: United Nations, February 2013).
53. For instance, *see* in France the case law *CA Toulouse*, 3e ch. corr., 21 janv. 1999, n° 98/00307: JurisData n° 1999-040054.

legislative, executive, administrative, judicial, contractual or consensual) or conduct that is otherwise not covered by established legal defenses, excuses, justifications or relevant principles under domestic law. The Convention, therefore, leaves unaffected conduct undertaken pursuant to lawful government authority (e.g., where the Party's government acts to maintain public order, protect national security or investigate criminal offences). Furthermore, legitimate and common activities inherent in the design of networks, or legitimate and common operating or commercial practices should not be criminalized."[54]

Various purposes motivate the hacker when he decides to illegally access a system. The data contained can be of value, by themselves as personal data, sensitive commercial information, trade secrets, political secrets or as tools such as passwords and credit card numbers, and therefore justify the intrusion. Also, at other times, the intrusion targets the system itself, as when a professional of copyright law infringement or of child pornography searches for some virtual space in order to host his illegal files, creating, in other words, a kind of illegal cloud storage.

It has to be noted that the offense does not distinguish whether access is related to another computer or concerns situations where a person physically accesses a stand-alone computer. This theory has been formulated, for instance, in the UK, where it has been advocated that the offense should only concern the first situation, since the legislator's intention is to incriminate hacking behavior. However, this restrictive view has been rejected on appeal.[55]

The offense distinguishes between access to the all information system and the access to only a part of it. The Commission's report highlights the fact that most countries did not give attention to this in transposing this offense in national law. This omission, however, should not be seen as substantial, since the elastic notion of information system itself should provide a solution to it.

[2] The Issue of Illegal Access with or Without Use of Technological Measures

Article 3 of Directive 2013/40/EU, in contrast to the 2005 Framework decision, specifically refers to the infringement of security measures as a condition of the offense.[56] Also, the reference to the use of technological measures adds some clarity to the definition of illegal access, while it has been criticized that the mere notion of illegal access as a legal standard is "remarkably naïve"[57] because its broad interpretation could lead to very divergent jurisprudences.

This condition makes sense at first glance: how to determine the illegality of the access without proof of the criminal intent, as in proof of the knowledge that the access was unauthorized? For instance, does a person authorized to access parts of a

54. Convention on Cybercrime ETS 185, Explanatory Report, paragraph 38.
55. Attorney-General's Reference (No. 1 of 1991) (1992) 3 WLR 432.
56. Pedro Miguel, F. Freitasa & Nuno Gonçalvesa, *Illegal Access to Information Systems and the Directive 2013/40/EU*, 29(1) Intl. Rev. of L. Computers & Tech. 50–62 (2015).
57. Orin S. Kerr, *Cybercrime's Scope: Interpreting "Access" and "Authorization" in Computer Misuse Statutes*, 78 New York U. L. Rev. 1596 (2003).

computer system, which accessed other parts without permission, commit the offense of illegal access? In the past, this issue had created most of the discussions in national courts. For instance, in the UK, in *DPP v. Bignell*[58] in 1997, two police officers who used an official database for a private purpose were found innocent of this offense. In Greece, the Supreme Court[59] has also refused to apply the criminal framework to the case where an employee used some sensitive information in the framework of a judicial disagreement with his formal company. Even though the employer protested that the employee could not have accessed this information without entering the company's system while his authorizations were removed, the judges found that there was no real proof of the material act of accessing the system.

On the contrary, the act of circumventing a technological measure of protection by itself is deemed to be characteristic of an act of system interference. However, this causes an overlap with the other offenses created by the directive, either the illegal system interference (with the assumption that infringing the protection of a system is deemed to seriously hinder or interrupt the functioning of the system) or the illegal data interference (assuming that a technological measure of protection is also data, the act of circumventing it automatically constitutes an act of altering data).

A solution should be to give a broader definition to the notion of security measure. Indeed, a strict application of this condition would have as a consequence to exclude a lot of the classic hacking activities from the regulation. For instance, a computer specialist in a company installs a backdoor, which is a special routine that offers him access to the system without need of authentication, with the idea that in case of a problem with his contract he would have the means to blackmail the company. In a strict and technical approach, he does not have illegal access to the data, since he has just used a hidden function of the system. In a broad legal approach, the use of the backdoor by itself should be ruled as a way to circumvent a technological measure of protection.

Even if firewalls should be regarded as the first destination of this condition, the notion of technical measure of protection extends, for instance, to online paywalls. The specific issue of Wi-Fi networks is characteristic. To access a nonprotected Wi-Fi network is not illegal. However, to crack the password by brute force or by exploiting a flaw of the cryptographic method of protection of the password conduces to the offense of illegal access. But what about the use of a protection measure which is largely known as inefficient? For instance, the WEP method of encryption of a Wi-Fi network is known to possess some serious flaws and hackers have, in the past, created some software to automatically crack the password in less than five minutes. In this case, if some personal data are enclosed due to the illegal access, the Wi-Fi owner could be held civilly liable. Nevertheless, the hacker is still liable for illegally accessing the system, since the law does not distinguish according to the efficiency of the protective measure. It should be reminded that this condition is mainly present in order to establish without doubt the presence of the criminal intent.

58. *DPP v. Bignell* [1998] 1 Cr App R8.
59. Decision No. 1294/2007.

Also, the illegal acquisition of a password is incriminated as a separate offense related to the illegal distribution of hacking tools, which criminalizes the intentional "procurement for use" of sensitive information. Nonetheless, it has to be noted that password misuse is in practice the more frequent mean to unauthorized access, "either for obtaining erotic materials, uncovering information about a previous or current partner, or simply reading messages."[60] In this context, it is important to interpret the offense of illegal access to the system in conjunction with the offense stated in Article 7 of the Directive, entitled "tools used for committing offenses."[61] The offense criminalizes the acts of distribution of software or codes which would be used to facilitate cyber attacks. Indeed, since for the EU legislator the intentional production, sale, procurement for use, import, distribution or otherwise making available of a password has constituted a preliminary phase for the offense of illegal access, it means that the legislator intended that the mere use of a password without authorization is interpreted as illegal access.

Another practical issue is the use of the same password to access multiple services. Even though experts strongly disapprove of this practice, the common user would have difficulties by definition to remember his unique credentials to his numerous services (photography sharing, texting, social networks, clouding services, fora, dating applications, etc.). A classic approach from hackers when they find a list of passwords (either by hacking, phishing or the use of a keyboard noting) is to test it on other very popular online services. Recently, for instance, Dropbox has been accused of a major breach of security, whereas most probably the passwords had been stolen from elsewhere.[62] From a strict legal point of view, without the use of a technical measure to circumvent the protection, there is no illegal access. We can see that this reference to the violation of security measure apparently marks the end of the "contract-based theory of authorization,"[63] which is accused to endanger constitutional liberties. However, a jurisprudential synthesis could be found between the contract-based theory of authorization and the very restrictive notion of technical digital trespass, by using a comprehensive and technological neutral interpretation of

---

60. Gřivna T & Drápal J, *Attacks on the Confidentiality, Integrity and Availability of Data and Computer Systems in the Criminal Case Law of the Czech Republic*, 28 Digital Investigation 1-3 (Mar. 1, 2019).
61. Article 7 of the Directive states:

> Member States shall take the necessary measures to ensure that the intentional production, sale, procurement for use, import, distribution or otherwise making available, of one of the following tools, without right and with the intention that it be used to commit any of the offences referred to in Articles 3 to 6, is punishable as a criminal offence, at least for cases which are not minor:
>
> (a) a computer programme, designed or adapted primarily for the purpose of committing any of the offences referred to in Articles 3 to 6;
> (b) a computer password, access code, or similar data by which the whole or any part of an information system is capable of being accessed.

62. Reuters, *Dropbox Passwords Leaked* (Oct. 14, 2014).
63. Orin S. Kerr, *Cybercrime's Scope: Interpreting "Access" and "Authorization" in Computer Misuse Statutes*, *supra* n. 57.

the notion of security measure and, as explained above, by interpreting the offense in conjunction with the offense of Article 7 of the Directive. In conclusion, it has to be admitted that a security measure is mandatory for the illegal access offense to apply, while the notion of breach of security has to be interpreted extensively.

The relative weak degree of protection offered by a password led the EU legislator to impose a two step verification procedure for all digital services of payment, with the "PSD2 Directive of 2015."[64] The Directive defines the "strong customer authentication" as "an authentication based on the use of two or more elements categorised as knowledge (something only the user knows), possession (something only the user possesses) and inherence (something the user is) that are independent, in that the breach of one does not compromise the reliability of the others, and is designed in such a way as to protect the confidentiality of the authentication data."[65] The Directive applies this procedure for access from the user to his payment account online, when the user initiates an electronic payment transaction or when he carries out any action through a remote channel which may imply a risk of payment fraud or other abuses.[66]

In practice, this obligation has led to an increasing significance of smartphone devices, as often two-step verification procedures are based on call, SMS or use of a specific app. In the context of cybersecurity, this means that mobile devices become more and more the targets of hacking. Through SIM swapping or zero-day vulnerability's exploitation, the personal code of verification sent to the mobile device is intercepted by the pirate in order to validate his illegal access to the information system. The requirement of a breach of the protection, in order to access the protection offered by the offense of illegal access, can also be analyzed as an incentive to better protect a computer system. From a criminologist's point of view, the role of the victim in the perpetration of the crime is substantial. In other words, "security plays a crucial, pervasive role in the fight against computer misuse."[67]

Finally, in the same way, a simple file sent, for instance, by email, does not constitute an illegal access. If it occurs that the file is a Trojan or a virus, the other infractions of the Directive will apply according to the case.

In conclusion, the requirement of technical protection circumvention could potentially create legal uncertainty in court, as it is not clarified whether identity's usurpation constitutes or not a kind of technical protection circumvention. Characteristically, according to the Commission's Report, almost half of EU Member States have not transposed this requirement in their national law. Even if this approach could be seen as more effective, it leads to greatly minimize the harmonization effect of the European regulation.

64. Directive (EU) 2015/2366 of the European Parliament and of the Council of 25 November 2015 on payment services in the internal market, amending Directives 2002/65/EC, 2009/110/EC and 2013/36/EU and Regulation (EU) No. 1093/2010, and repealing Directive 2007/64/EC (Text with EEA relevance), OJ L 337, 23.12.2015, pp. 35–127, ELI: http://data.europa.eu/eli/dir/2015/2366/oj.
65. Article 4(30) of the Directive.
66. Article 97(1) of the Directive.
67. N. MacEwan, *The Computer Misuse Act 1990: Lessons from Its Past and Predictions for Its Future*, 12 Crim. L.R. 955–967 (2008).

[3] *Illegal Access and Theory of Information Goods*

The notion of illegal access to data implies a kind of monopoly that is an exclusionary right on data, similar to a property right. Nevertheless, it does not aim to cover every case of "information theft." Illegal access to information by violation of a contract or of a work policy is clearly outside the scope of the Directive, as explained in Recital 17:

> in the context of this Directive, contractual obligations or agreements to restrict access to information systems by way of a user policy or terms of service, as well as labor disputes as regards the access to and use of information systems of an employer for private purposes, should not incur criminal liability where the access under such circumstances would be deemed unauthorized and, thus, would constitute the sole basis for criminal proceedings.

Recital 17 also adds that: "this Directive is without prejudice to the right of access to information as laid down in national and Union law, while at the same time it may not serve as a justification for unlawful or arbitrary access to information."

The offense does not intend to protect the information itself contained in the system, but the system itself. However, the incrimination of illegal access has an indirect consequence: data indirectly acquire the status of confidential data. In other words, a legal monopoly is created, regulating the access to the information contained on a system.

This indirect protection of information as an asset could shed some light on a very uncertain issue at the European level, the nature of information itself. To restrict the discussion to the framework of criminal law, can information be assimilated to a good, in the sense that it would be possible to "steal" it? For instance, a recent decision of the French Supreme Court applied the concept of "good" to the information stocked in a server of the company and condemned for breach of trust the employee who, by violation of the general charter of utilization of the information system, downloaded and stored for private use some sensitive data of the server.[68] For the offense of breach of trust to apply, in French law, a transfer of possession on the goods has to occur, but in this case the judges were satisfied with the idea that the owner of the information could no longer enjoy it in the monopolistic way it was intended to be. In the digital era, one could easily remark that the digital copy does not prevent the exercise of a possession. However, as the judges tend to answer, the copy itself corresponds to a violation of the property rights on information, since the information good escapes from the owner's sphere of control.

[B] Illegal System Interference

[1] *Overview of the Offense*

Article 4 of Directive 2013/40/EU states that:

68. Cour de cassation, chambre criminelle, Oct. 22, 2014, Thierry x., Available at: legifrance.gouv.fr.

> Member States shall take the necessary measures to ensure that seriously hindering or interrupting the functioning of an information system by inputting computer data, by transmitting, damaging, deleting, deteriorating, altering or suppressing such data, or by rendering such data inaccessible, intentionally and without right, is punishable as a criminal offence, at least for cases which are not minor.

It should be noted that, in general, the Directive 2013/40/EU (as previously the Budapest Convention) offers to the national legislator the discretionary possibility not to apply the legal framework of cyber attacks in case of minor incidents. However, there is no indication of a minimum level of interference needed in order for the offense to apply. The interference, according to Article 4, has to be enough to provoke an obstruction and even an interruption of the system: the illegal system interference offense aims to condemn disruptive attacks, whereas the illegal data interference offense applies to destructive attack.[69] Even if no duration is indicated, the text refers to "serious" interferences. By consequence, the systematic exploitation of the freely accessible online resources of a system by itself should not be seen as illegal, even if it increases the upkeep cost of the system.

For instance, it has been ruled out by a French court that a person who used a robot to repeatedly connect to the website of a competitor in order to check for new information was not guilty, since no proof of a disruption of the service was brought.[70] On the contrary, it has been ruled that a person who provoked serious perturbation of the email service of a company, by systematically sending emails with large, empty attached files, committed the offense of illegal system interference.[71]

However, this statement should be combined with other relevant legal frameworks, such as the sui generis protection of databases.[72] Indeed, it has been recently ruled by the CJEU[73] that the repeated extraction of insubstantial parts of the content of a database of a website may constitute an infringement of the database sui generis right. In this case, a meta-search engine, specialized in car searches, systematically exploited data stocked in a website specialized in classified ads about cars' sells. The judges considered that an operator who makes available on the Internet a dedicated meta-search engine infringes a database, where that dedicated meta engine provides the end user with a search form which essentially offers the same range of functionality as the search form on the database site, "translates" queries from end users into the search engine for the database site "in real time," so that all the information on that

69. C. Lotrionte, *State Sovereignty and Self-Defence in Cyberspace: A Normative Framework for Balancing Legal Rights (Symposium: International Law and the Internet: Adapting Legal Frameworks in Response to Online Warfare and Revolutions Fuelled by Social Media)*, 26 Emory Int'l L. Rev. 825, 1 (2012).
70. TGI Bordeaux, 4e ch., 6 janv. 2011, Min. publ. c/ Cédric M. Available at: www.legalis.net. Note A. Capriolli, *Absence d'intention de nuire et requête automatisée et répétitive*, Communication Commerce électronique n° 11, comm. 109 (November 2011).
71. *See* the French Decision: CA Toulouse, 3e ch. corr., 21 janv. 1999, n° 98/00307: JurisData n° 1999-040054, note Le Stanc, C. Communication Commerce électronique n° 1, Janvier 2002, comm. 5.
72. Directive 96/9/EC of the European Parliament and of the Council of Mar. 11, 1996 on the legal protection of databases.
73. CJEU, Case C-202/12, *Innoweb BV v. Wegener ICT Media BV*, Wegener Mediaventions BV, Dec. 19, 2013.

database is searched through and presents the results to the end user using the format of its website, grouping duplications together into a single block item, but in an order that reflects criteria comparable to those used by the search engine of the database site concerned for presenting results. In other words, the systematic misappropriation of an online database, such as a search engine, operated by a meta-search engine, even if it does not enter into the definition of system interference, may still lead to some legal consequences (database maker's sui generis right infringement).

Interference to the computer system becomes a criminal offense where it occurs "intentionally and without right." It is often needed to test, in computer science, the solidity and the lack of vulnerability of a system, and the right to interfere with the system is obviously gained by asking for the consent of the system administrator. As the acts described as *actus reus* of the offense are very specific and do not leave a wide margin of interpretation about the presumed intent of the author, the intention does not seem to raise particular issues regarding the framework of illegal system interference. The intention to create the interference is deemed to suffice and national courts do not seem to require an intention to provoke damage.[74] However, the situation changes when someone is pursued on the basis of attempt of illegal system interference, for instance because the interference was not serious enough to cause a real dysfunction of the system. In fact, the attempt could be pursued only if there is very solid proof of an intention to provoke serious damages.

Illegal system interference is defined not only as material acts modifying the system but also alternatively as acts rendering such data inaccessible. It means that the offense of illegal system interference is autonomous from the offense of illegal access, since no access to the system is needed for the legal framework to activate.

Could the Internet as a whole be considered as an information system? It is now established that a common strategy in war is to cut the enemy lines of communication and for instance Russia, both in the Georgian war (2008) and the Ukrainian war (2014), used cyber attacks against the communications infrastructure.[75] However, the story of the retired 75-year-old woman without any technological knowledge, who has single-handedly managed to cut off the Internet connection of two countries, is famous.[76] In this case, while scavenging for copper to sell as scrap, she accidently sliced through an underground cable that apparently was a vital Internet infrastructure. It is noteworthy that the text of the offense does not limit only to "digital" acts (transmitting, damaging, deleting, deteriorating, altering or suppressing such data) but also to any other acts, virtual or in real life, rendering the data of an information system inaccessible.

74. For instance, in France, TGI Paris, 12e ch., 19 mai 2006, Min. public c/ Clément P., Elypsal, Thomas P.: Jus Luminum J31327; Gaz. Paljanvp. 35.
75. H. Shane, *Hack Attack, Russia's First Targets in Ukraine: Its Cell Phones and Internet Lines*, available at: http://www.foreignpolicy.com/articles/2014/03/03/hack_attack (Mar. 3, 2014).
76. T. Parfitt, *Georgian Woman Cuts Off Web Access to Whole of Armenia*, The Guardian (Apr. 6, 2011).

[2] DDoS Attacks

The independency of the offense of illegal system interference from the offense of illegal access to data is clearly described by the case of DDoS attacks. The criminalization without ambiguity of DDoS attacks has been one of the main objectives of the new European Directive as it explicitly states that one case of illegal interference is the mere act of "rendering inaccessible" the system. The initials DDoS stand for denial-of-service (DoS) or DDoS attack. It describes the use by someone of an illegal botnet, that is to say, of a park of connected computer systems that have been corrupted by a malware (typically, a Trojan horse) and answer to the orders of a specific controller. This botnet is asked to connect to a server, saturating the target machine with external communications requests. It has to be noted that, even if it is considered one of their main activities, botnets are not only used for DDoS Attacks. Cybercriminals may also utilize the brute computing capacity of their botnet, for instance, in order to crack by brute force some passwords that would instead need months to crack on a single computer or, as a new trend, in order to mine for cryptocurrency.[77]

Depending on the defenses of the target and the resources committed to expand the bandwidth of his servers, the result of such an attack may vary from the point of view of the user, from the integral blocking of access for hours, and sometimes even days, to the disruption of some services or a simple feeling of slowness. The structure of the attack is related to the structure of the Internet itself, which is the liberty to ask for a connection with every single online device.

This kind of attack is used for various motives. A new phenomenon of DDoS attack renting services appeared which demonstrates once more the growing mercantilism of illegal activities online.[78] It has been observed that the attacks sometimes also serve some political purpose and the attacks have even been compared to a kind of street manifestation.[79] On the contrary, DDoS attacks serve very well as weapons of choice in the framework of cyber wars, as it has been demonstrated when a foreign botnet cut all Estonian connection to the Internet in April 2007.[80]

The capacity of nuisance that a DDoS attack can cause is strictly related to the size of the botnet. But, for the most important parts, the attacks are able to menace even the major sites online, with huge economic consequences. It is estimated that the economic loss for one hour offline are, for instance, USD 102,898 million for Amazon, USD 743,834 million for Google and USD 254,392 million for Paypal, to name three companies who have been notorious victims of DDoS attacks.[81] This means that influent online companies may very likely be targeted with various attempts of

77. Lillian Ablon et al., *Markets for Cybercrime, Tools and Stolen Data, Hackers' Bazaar*, 22 (Santa Monica, California; Washington, District of Columbia: RAND Corporation, 2014).
78. P. Leeson & C. Coyne, *The Economics of Computer Hacking*, 1 J.L. Econ. & Pol'y 511 (2005).
79. R. Stallman, *The Anonymous WikiLeaks Protests are a Mass Demo against Control*, The Guardian, www.guardian.co.uk/commentisfree/2010/dec/17/anonymous-wikileaks-protest-amazon-mastercard (Dec. 17, 2010).
80. Joshua Davis, *Hackers Take Down the Most Wired Country in Europe*, Wired Magazine (September 2015).
81. R. Ottis, *Proceedings of the 10th European Conference on Information Warfare and Security* 233 (Academic Publishing Limited 2011).

extortion and commercial blackmail based on DDoS attack potentials. Commercial blackmail has nowadays become a real phenomenon.[82] The victim will also search for a way to minimize the fact of its vulnerability, by keeping it in confidentiality. Furthermore, the attack is based on the mediation of a botnet, which makes even more difficult the possibility of tracing the attack back to the identity of the botnet controller. Consequently, an efficient repression at an international level of DDoS attacks should probably not be based on the offense of illegal system interference, but would have to use autonomous police investigation on the illegal botnets. At the same time, an efficient police investigation would have to negotiate with a third party involved in this field: the researchers. Indeed, IT researchers find themselves in a position sometimes where they could easily have taken possession of a criminal botnet, claiming a right of "self-defense."[83] From a legal point of view, however, there is a real danger of these practices being characterized as an obstruction to the investigations.

The national transposition of this offense has lacked attention. As the Commission's report noted[84], in nine cases the State purely omitted to add the term "rendering inaccessible" in its legislation. This should be seen as a negligent transposition of the EU legislation with the potential effect to create uncertainty as to the repression of DDoS attacks.

[3] Other Fields of Application

Even if DDoS attacks clearly constitute the main objective of repression, other fields of application can be found on the offense of illegal system interference. For instance, the growing issues of Sybil attacks should be analyzed with attention, since it also possesses some applications in the field of cryptocurrencies, with the practice of selfish-mining.[85] Wikipedia states that "In a Sybil attack the attacker subverts the reputation system of a peer-to-peer network by creating a large number of pseudonymous identities, using them to gain a disproportionately large influence."[86] Indeed, a peer-to-peer network draws its strength from the additional value brought by each member. The massive use of false users can therefore easily destabilize a network.

It has to be mentioned that, from an economical point of view, developing and increasing the "noise" of an illegal cybercrime market constitute one of the most effective ways to fight its development, following the nowadays classic theory of "lemon markets," that is a market where the seller is in a better position as regards to

82. L. Edwards, *Dawn of the Death of Distributed Denial of Service: How to Kill Zombies*, 24 Cardozo Arts & Ent LJ 23 (2006).
83. D. Dittrich, F. Leder & T. Werner, *A Case Study in Ethical Decision Making Regarding Remote Mitigation of Botnets, Financial Cryptography and Data Security*, 216 (IFCA/Springer-Verlarg Berlin Heidelberg 2010).
84. Report from the Commission to the European Parliament and the Council assessing the extent to which the Member States have taken the necessary measures in order to comply with Directive 2013/40/EU on attacks against information systems and replacing Council Framework Decision 2005/222/JHA, *supra*.
85. Ittay Eyal & Emin Gün Sirer, *Bitcoin Is Broken*, Hacking, Distributed, available at: http://hackingdistributed.com/2013/11/04/bitcoin-is-broken/#sthash.7cVk9Fvc.dpuf (Nov. 4, 2013).
86. http://en.wikipedia.org/wiki/Sybil_attack.

information possessed, the market naturally tends to collapse.[87] For instance, a massive creation of false users could easily paralyze an illegal peer-to-peer network of exchange of copyrighted materials. However, it can easily be argued, from a legal point of view, that such practices are deemed to be considered as illegal interference, independent of the nature of the information system targeted that might be using illegal practices.

[C] Illegal Data Interference

[1] Overview of the Offense

According to Article 5 of Directive 2013/40/EU, the "Member States shall take the necessary measures to ensure that deleting, damaging, deteriorating, altering or suppressing computer data on an information system, or rendering such data inaccessible, intentionally and without right, is punishable as a criminal offence, at least for cases which are not minor."

The offense should be seen as an attempt to give a legal dimension to the phenomenon of computer malware. In other situations, the data interference only constitutes the mandatory means to the execution of another criminal offense. Indeed, most of the time an illegal access to the system would also mean an alteration of the data, since a technical measure of protection has to be violated, or just for the perpetrator of the offense to ensure that he wipes his personal traces from the system. However, it is possible to conclude on the existence of illegal data interference without any illegal system access. For instance, in the case of a malware, most of the times it is inserted in the system by the user himself, either by opening an attached file in his/her emails, or by executing a script while surfing on the Internet, or more traditionally through storage devices.

The computer virus is a specific malware which has the ability to auto-multiply and to infect by itself other systems, either through automatic storage devices infection or through the contact list of the user. As regards the *mens rea* of the offense, it has been very recently established by case law (for instance in USA, in 1986[88]) that the requisite is not proof of the real intention to infect a particular system, but the intention to spread the virus.

[2] New Forms of Malware and Repression

According to the Article 1 of Directive 2013/40/EU, an information system "means a device or group of interconnected or related devices, one or more of which, pursuant to a programme, automatically processes computer data, as well as computer data stored, processed, retrieved or transmitted by that device or group of devices for the

87. C. Hoe, M. Kantarcioglu & A. Bensoussan, *A Game Theoretical Analysis of Lemonizing Cybercriminal Black Markets*, 7638 Computer Science, 60–77 (2012).
88. *United States v. Morris*, 928 F.2d 504 (2d Cir. 1991) cert. Denied, 502 US 817 (1991).

purposes of its or their operation, use, protection and maintenance." There is no doubt, following this definition, that a cell phone is a device capable of processing computer data, however, until recently the limited capacities of the phone comprised the main technical obstacle to the proliferation of cyber attacks. Obviously, the situation has radically changed now and cell phones have become a main target of cyber attacks.

The logical concern of most people, about overcharged calls through a malware application, should not be seen as the most important and new threat. On the one hand, the hacker quickly ensures a large benefit from the overcharged calls. But, on the other hand, in this domain the enforcement of the law is deemed to be easier for the special police units in charge.

However, the cell phone is particularly vulnerable to a wide range of attacks, from the interception of communication and privacy issues (remote access to the camera or the microphone of the phone), to more original malware. For instance, the virus BadLepricon is an application that can be downloaded through the playstore interface of an Android, and it is the exact characteristic of the new threats posed by the virus.[89] This app exploits the calculation resources of the cell phone while it is apparently sleeping in order to create some electronic money. Basically, it does not constitute an illegal access, since it has been installed with the consent of an innocent user. The app also does not interfere with the data and personal data of the cell phone. But, the use without consent of the calculation resources of the cell phone, with consequences such as a diminution of battery capacities, should be ruled as a form of illegal system interference. On the contrary, Google will be protected by the intermediaries' safe harbor, on the condition that it promptly removes the malware from its database of applications once it has been alerted.

Also, the reference in Article 5 of "rendering such data inaccessible" has cleverly been added, in order to give an answer to the growing threat of cryptoware. Crypto ware could be defined as a specific kind of ransomware, which is a computer program used in order to commit illegal data interference with the intention of blackmailing the target. In the case of cryptoware, however, the data are not in threat of imminent destruction, but already altered, encrypted in fact. Then a message appears and announces to the victim that he/she has a certain amount of time to proceed to the payment of a sum (through a cryptocurrency mechanism of course) in order to have access to the decryption key. The novelty stays in the psychological part: contrary to the situation of a classic virus, the victim there knows that somehow it is possible to retrieve the data.

From a legal point of view, to encrypt the data is already a form of alteration. However, the mention of "inaccessibility" of the data should cover a large range of options and offer an efficient protection. The main issue is at the enforcement level: the so-called dark figure of criminality, in other words, the difference between the real

89. Mikhail Kazdagli et al., *Morpheus: Benchmarking Computational Diversity in Mobile Malware*, Proceedings of the Third Workshop on Hardware and Architectural Support for Security and Privacy (ACM, 2014).

numbers of cybercriminality and the declared cases, is already huge.[90] The main causes of the dark figure are typically the innocence, the unawareness of the shame of the victim.[91] Now, in the case of ransomware, enforcement will become ten times more difficult, since the criminal plays with the victim's hope to retrieve some precious data that is only kept in the hard disk.

Similarly, scareware is based on the appearance of ransomware. Unlike the ransomware, there is no real threat to the system or the data, but a message appears which aims to convince the user of the contrary. The aim is to force the user to pay scammers for a bogus service which allegedly would protect them from the treat. In the same way, the criminal also uses—one could say quite cleverly—the guilt and fear related to the massive use of pirated cultural products. A message appears and explains that "the special Internet force" of the police has found him guilty of IP infringement and, in order to avoid judicial consequences, a fine has to be paid to a specific account.

[3] The States as Perpetrators of the Offense

Nowadays, the extensive and increasing amount of time and money needed in order to develop activities of cyber warfare means concretely that this kind of activities has become the privilege of a small number of States, as only the most major players of the international scene have the financial capacity to invest on these fields. However, the nature of cyber warfare eventually makes it very attractive to less well-heeled combatants, forced to engage in an asymmetric conflict.[92] Both the Budapest Convention and the EU legal framework leave in the dark a matter which has lately become very sensitive. Even if nowadays legal persons can be found guilty of cyber attacks, by application of the Article 10 of Directive 2013/40/EU, nobody has foreseen or wanted to prepare for the multiple offenses committed by States themselves.

For instance, a state involvement in virus creation has been discovered in the creation of the Stuxnet virus, which was a dormant virus, until it touched the Iranian nuclear complex. Strong suspicion exists that the Israel service named "Unit 8200" is involved in its creation, in collaboration with the USA, and Edward Snowden confirmed it in an interview in 2013. The difference between this and a classic operation of sabotage is that the virus Stuxnet, in order to be operational, had to infect a wide range of computers and by definition infect a lot of innocent users.

International law recognizes the significance of the principle of State sovereignty as an essential foundation of international relations. It is nowadays established that cyber operations against another state's territorial infrastructure can violate a state's

90. M. Tcherni, A. Davies, G. Lopes and A. Lizotte, *The Dark Figure of Online Property Crime: Is Cyberspace Hiding a Crime Wave?*, 33(5) Justice Quarterly, 890-911 (2016), DOI: 10.1080/07418825.2014.994658.
91. Julie L. Marble et al., *The Human Factor in Cybersecurity: Robust & Intelligent Defense, Cyber Warfare*, Springer Intl. Pub., 173–206 (2015).
92. J. Jurich, *Cyberwar and Customary International Law: The Potential of a "Bottom-up" Approach to an International Law of Information Operations*, 9 Chi. J. Int'l L. 275 (2008).

sovereignty.[93] On this very sensitive issue, it has even been proposed that whereas "passive defenses are not available or would be ineffective in stopping or preventing the attacks, the victim state could use forcible measures – cyber 'active defenses,' such as the sending of destructive viruses to the attacker's computer – as long as the use of the active defenses were proportionate to the threat from the adversary."[94]

On the contrary, it can also be argued that the use of viruses as cyber weapons is de facto illegal, because it violates international law's principle of neutrality.[95] Since it is traditionally forbidden for a belligerent actor to launch an attack from a neutral territory and because it is by definition impossible to control the online dissemination of a network virus, the broad use of this cyber weapon could indeed be analyzed as a violation of neutrality's law, on the condition, however, that the virus is active (otherwise, the information is just transmitted in neutral territory and no violation of sovereignty exists).

[D] Illegal Interception

[1] Overview of the Offense

The offense of illegal interception of private communication differs from other kinds of cyber attacks in the sense that it is by essence closely related to the protection of privacy. It would be, nonetheless, an error to assimilate this offense to a simple criminalization of illegal personal data processing, as the offense does not rely on the nature of the data. Similarly, for an illegal interception to occur, it is irrelevant whether the data processed is put into an archive or not.

Article 6 of the Directive states that "Member States shall take the necessary measures to ensure that intercepting, by technical means, non-public transmissions of computer data to, from or within an information system, including electromagnetic emissions from an information system carrying such computer data, intentionally and without right, is punishable as a criminal offence, at least for cases which are not minor."

The criminalization of illegal interception cannot really be described as a novelty and, on the contrary, in most cases, national legislators in Member States will have to resolve the issue of the need for a legislative change, as, generally, the criminalization of illegal interception has been raised as an offense since the emergence of modern communications. However, the illegal interception of electronic transmissions differs in some points from the traditional "tapping" of a telephone or the recording of an oral conversation.

93. C. Joyner & C. Lotrionte, *Information Warfare as International Coercion: Elements of a Legal Framework*, 12 Eur. J. Int'l L. 825, 842 (2001).
94. C. Lotrionte, *supra* n. 69, 26 Emory Int'l L. Rev. 825 (2012).
95. E. Jensen, *Sovereignty and Neutrality in Cyber Conflict* (Symposium: Cyber Attacks: International Cybersecurity in the Twenty-First Century), 35(3) Fordham Int'l L.J. 815 (2012).

The act is illegal only where technical means have been used in order to intercept the transmission. According to the explanatory report of the Cybercrime Convention of 2001:

> Interception by "technical means" relates to listening to, monitoring or surveillance of the content of communications, to the procuring of the content of data either directly, through access and use of the computer system, or indirectly, through the use of electronic eavesdropping or tapping devices. Interception may also involve recording. Technical means includes technical devices fixed to transmission lines as well as devices to collect and record wireless communications. They may include the use of software, passwords and codes. The requirement of using technical means is a restrictive qualification to avoid over-criminalization.[96]

A grey zone subsists as regards the notion of interception. Should it be interpreted in a way where a third person acknowledges the content of the communication or, on the contrary, does interception occur when the communication's content is automatically analyzed by an automatic system, for instance, for the purpose of individual marketing? From a legal point of view, it seems safer to adopt the policy that an automatic analysis does not constitute an interception per se, leaving the issue of the legality of this practice to be ruled under the field of personal data protection.

[2] The Distinction Between Private and Public Communication

The offense's field of application is limited to private communication. What do nonpublic transmissions mean? As it has been highlighted in decisions of the European Court of Human Rights (ECtHR) about surveillance effectuated by an employer on the activity of an employee, the use of a public terminal does not preclude the nature of the communication.[97] In other words, even an employee at work has a right to private communication, which includes the act of consulting the Internet.[98] In the same way, the nature of the information is indifferent to the characterization of the communication's medium as public or private. For instance, the use of a public Wi-Fi service does not preclude the right to the secrecy of the communication. Also, and even if the offense refers to a surveillance "without right," the existence or not of consent does not help in this case, since the employee is placed in a position of subordination that annihilates the free character of the consent.

Therefore, only the purpose between the parties to communicate confidentially can serve as a characteristic of the nature of the communication. This purpose should be ascertained by objective criteria. For instance, the adjustment of the level of clarity of a message posted on a social network from "friend only" to "public" would define the will to keep the communication private or not. The mere intention, however, without objective measures limiting the access, should not be considered as sufficient.

96. Explanatory report, No. 53.
97. ECHR, *Halford v. UK*, 1997.
98. ECHR, *Copland v. UK*, 2007.

For instance, in the USA, in the case *Snow v. DirecTV Inc*,[99] it has been ruled that a newsletter on a website which required users to create an account and exhorted that certain parties should not join was not a private communication, in absence of a specific configuration designated to limit the access to the general public.

This reasoning possesses the quality that it frees the notion of private communication from mere technological concerns. However, it also contains a substantial flaw. In order to analyze the purpose of the communication, it is necessary to have some knowledge of its content, whereas the offense serves as an absolute interdiction to do it. In other words, the offense requires a priori qualification of private communication, whereas the purpose works as an a posteriori condition. By consequence, it is necessary to relativize the purpose's criterion by adopting a series of presumptions related to the technological medium. Emails and Voice over Internet Protocol ('VoIP') communication in this sense would be presumably considered as private communication, whereas posts in social media, regardless of their status or of the number of actual members, should be deemed to be assimilated to forms of public communication.

[3] The Principles Guiding Lawful Interceptions

The privacy of private communication is raised in most European countries to the rank of constitutional value. Therefore, the offense of interception of electronic private communication merely constitutes one criminal application of a constitutional principle, also protected by the European Convention on Human Rights (ECHR) through Article 8 of the Convention, which mentions the protection of correspondence. In this framework, an interception would be ruled as lawful under specific circumstances related particularly to the existence of a judicial warrant, as a general rule.

At the European Union level, the details and principles of application of the lawful interception are explained by the Resolution of 1995,[100] which was inspired by the USA's legal framework "CALEA." It is noteworthy to mention that the Resolution indicates about cryptography that: "If network operators/service providers initiate encoding, compression or encryption of telecommunications traffic, law enforcement agencies require the network operators/service providers to provide intercepted communications *en clair*."

The conditions of intention and lawfulness play a substantive role for the determination of the criminal liability of the network administrator. For instance, a specific technique, called "sniffing" could be defined as the use of a computer program called packet analyzer, in order to intercept traffic passing over a digital network or part of a network. This technique could be employed legally as a method of evidence

99. *Snow v. DirecTV, Inc*, 450 F.3d 1314 (11th Cir. 2006).
100. The European Council Resolution of Jan. 17, 1995 on the Lawful Interception of Telecommunications (OJ C 329).

collection in the framework of the repression of a cybercriminal activity, after which an interception warrant has been issued.[101]

However, this technique is also often used by the network administrator outside of the framework of a judicial activity, for controlling the existence of anomaly in the network. The administrators therefore have, with good reasons, some concerns about the legality of their methods.[102] Do they really have the intention to intercept private communications? The network administrator uses sniffing for network troubleshooting. If technically it cannot be denied that the administrator truly intends to intercept all the communications transferring in the network, the judges would be sensible to the fact that the sniffing tools are a very common mechanism for detecting network issues and it could be acceptable to conclude that the administrator does not have the intention to intercept the private communication itself.

It is noteworthy to mention that in the USA exists a relevant ruling. In the 2013 case *Joffe v. Google, Inc.*,[103] the plaintiff criticized Google and more particularly, its Google Street view service, on the fact that, when the vehicle (the "Google cars") approached an open Wi-Fi network, it connected and started to automatically sniff information transferred on the network. The judges decided that the protection of the privacy of private communication also covers the interception of unencrypted Wi-Fi communications, and therefore this automatic sniffing could not be assimilated to a lawful interception.[104]

Also, a service which would systematically analyze the content of private information for the scope of personal data collection is deemed to be characterized as an illegal interception, even if the users have been alerted. This issue had been raised when a lawsuit was filed against Google for its service "Gmail," because of its practice of electronically scanning the contents of people's Gmail accounts to help sell ads.[105] The interception is "without right," since no consent is given from the other users, the ones who send emails to Gmail users.

[4] The Snowden Revelations and Their Lessons

The recent NSA scandal has profoundly shocked the public opinion of the European Union and provoked some legal reflections about the need for better protection against

101. J. Broadway, B. Turnbull & J. Slay, *Improving the Analysis of Lawfully Intercepted Network Packet Data Captured for Forensic Analysis*, in *The Third International Conference on Availability, Reliability and Security* 1361 (2008).
102. D. Sicke, P. Ohm & D. Grunwald, *Legal Issues Surrounding Monitoring During Network Research*, Proceedings of the 7th ACM SIGCOMM conference on Internet measurement, ACM, 141 (2007).
103. *Joffe v. Google, Inc.*, 729 F.3d 1262 (9th Cir. 2013), amended by No. 11-17483, 2013 WL 6905957 (9th Cir. Dec. 27, 2013).
104. S.L. Garfinkel & M. McCarrin, *Can We Sniff Wi-Fi?: Implications of Joffe v. Google, Security & Privacy*, IEEE (2014).
105. Dominic Rushe, *Google: Gmail Users Shouldn't Expect Email Privacy*, The Guardian. (Aug. 15, 2013).

massive State intrusion in the privacy of individuals. For instance, a complaint has been filed against the UK to the ECHR by the organism "Big Brother Watch."[106]

The exhaustive description of the scandal in the framework of the case should constitute a good start for the discussion:

> The applicants concern was triggered by media coverage following the leak of information by Edward Snowden, a former systems administrator with the United States National Security Agency (NSA). According to media reports, the NSA has in place a programme, known as PRISM, which allows it to access a wide range of Internet communication content (such as emails, chat, video, images, documents, links and other files) and metadata (information permitting the identification and location of Internet users), from United States corporations, including some of the largest Internet Service Providers (ISPs) such as Microsoft, Google, Yahoo, Apple, Facebook, YouTube and Skype. Since global Internet data take the cheapest, rather than the most direct route, a substantial amount of global data passes through the servers of these American companies, including possibly emails sent by the applicants in London and Berlin to their international contacts. The applicants submit that the NSA also operates a second interception programme known as UPSTREAM, which provides access to nearly all the traffic passing through fiber optic cables owned by United States communication service providers such as AT&T and Verizon. Together, these programmes provide very broad access to the communications content and metadata of non-United States persons, to whom the provisions of the Fourth Amendment (the United States Constitutional privacy guarantee) apply, and allow for this material to be collected, stored and searched using keywords. According to the documents leaked by Edward Snowden, the United Kingdom Government Communications Head Quarters (GCHQ) has had access to PRISM material since at least June 2010 and has used it to generate intelligence reports (197 reports in 2012).
>
> In addition, the revelations based on Edward Snowden's leaked documentation have included details about a United Kingdom surveillance programme called TEMPORA. According to the applicants, TEMPORA is a means by which GCHQ can access electronic traffic passing along fiber optic cables running between the United Kingdom and North America. The data collected include both Internet and telephone communications. GCHQ is able to access not only metadata but also the content of emails, Facebook entries and website histories. The TEMPORA programme is authorized by certificates issued under section 8(4) of the Regulation of Investigatory Powers Act 2000 (RIPA). The applicants allege that United States agencies have been given extensive access to TEMPORA information.

It is not considered in this case whether this huge scandal related with the illegal interception of European communication by American authorities belongs to the offense of illegal interception of data because UK law seems to give such powers to UK information services and, therefore, interception occurs "with right." However, the same finding cannot stand in every European country concerned by mass surveillance. The challenges raised by a potential judicial action are related with the absence of real proof of a specific monitoring. On the one hand, the existence of mass surveillance is now well known, but, on the other hand, it is impossible for a specific individual to

106. *Big Brother Watch and others against the United Kingdom*, lodged on Sep. 4, 2013, Application No. 58170/13.

prove that one of his private communications has been subject to this mass surveillance mechanism. It has been argued that on this point a modification of the ECHR's jurisprudence would be profitable.[107] It could take the form of an acceptance of an *in abstracto* personal prejudice or of an *actio populis* claim.

The UK case is based on a claim of breach of Articles 8 and 10 of the ECHR. While the implication of Article 8 (protection of privacy) is obvious enough, the reference to Article 10 is justified by the alleged chilling effect on freedom of speech of the knowledge or even suspicion that all electronic communications are followed by information agencies. The UK court, in a secret judicial process, then had two issues to address: whether there are publicly known rules for the interception of communications, whose content is sufficiently indicated, and whether these rules are subject to proper oversight. The Court answered positively to both questions in February 2015.[108]

Since the fundamental principle of secrecy of correspondence has encountered a lot of difficulties in its efficient enforcement, the main lesson from the NSA scandal seems to be that a technological answer could be the best solution. The generalization of cryptography or even the recognition at a legal level of a right to encrypt private messages as a new subdomain of the right to data self-determination would, indeed, slow down the activities of information agencies. Of course, this also means that the various national antiterrorist regulations will not be as effective. In any case, a public debate is already raging about the need to continue on the road of strict antiterrorism measures, or whether it is time to finally leave behind the trauma of the 9/11 attacks.

[E] Relationship of Cyber-Attack Offenses with Other Offenses

[1] Consecutive and Concurrent Sentences

As it has already been noticed, the very precise definition of the offenses of cyber attacks may create an overlap between the offenses. Not only these offenses are interrelated but also it is necessary to ascertain also their relationship with other offenses which are applicable, depending on the circumstances. It is, therefore, important to determine where cyber attacks could be punished—alternatively or cumulatively—under the legal framework of generally applicable crimes.

In some cases, the illegal acts of access or interference to information systems can only be a means for the perpetration of a more serious offense. For instance, the hacking of an "intelligent" car can lead to a lethal accident. Illegal acts of interference to data can be seen also as a form of illegal misappropriation of an intangible good. Illegal access to online client databases means most of the time that the legal framework of personal data protection is also violated.

In case where the general interest protected by the offenses is exactly the same, the general legal principle *specialia generalibus derogant* shall be applied. This means

107. Sloot, Bart van der, *Privacy in the Post-NSA Era: Time for a Fundamental Revision?*, 5(1) JIPITEC 1 (May 2, 2014).

108. *Liberty (The National Council of Civil Liberties) & Others v. The Secretary of State for Foreign and Commonwealth Affairs & Others*, [2015] UKIPTrib 13_77-H.

that the more specific offense, as *lex specialis*, should prevail upon the most general one. However, in case whereas the various applicable offenses refer to a different philosophy, the question of the cumulative application of those offenses is legitimately posed according to the ECHR case law.[109] In criminal law theory, this issue is resolved by the application of the theories of accumulation of offenses. First, it should be noted that the plurality of offense does not raise by itself any difficulty: in case of culpability, the defendant is liable separately for each one of the offenses. The issue is to ascertain the sanction. Is it possible for the sentences to run concurrently? Should the privations of freedom cumulate? With or without limit? Unfortunately, the *corpus juris*, namely the EU *acquis* related to criminal law, does not solve the issue, which is left to national legal systems. In practice, very different systems apply, even if informally most European systems tend to adopt a "totality principle" which requires the court to consider the overall sentence in relation to the totality of the offending.[110]

Furthermore, it has to be highlighted that the principle *non bis in idem* is well established in EU criminal law.[111] The EU Charter of Fundamental Rights enshrines this principle in Article 50 ("Right not to be tried or punished twice in criminal proceedings for the same criminal offence") and the same principle is mentioned on Article 4 of Protocol No. 7 to the ECHR. The rule forbids the accumulation of two penalties of the same kind. This means practically that independently of the chosen offense, the same cyber attacks cannot be prosecuted twice. The rule prohibiting concurrent application of sentences refers to the accumulation of two penalties of the same kind, that is to say, to criminal law penalties. But also, it is clear that, in accordance with Article 50, the *non bis in idem* rule applies not only within the jurisdiction of one State but also between the jurisdictions of several Member States.[112] In other words, in case of a European-scale cyber attack, even if rules exist in order to avoid jurisdictional conflicts (*see* section 2.05), a possibility of accumulation of prosecution cannot totally be avoided. In this case, the principle *non bis in idem* will have the effect to prevent a second prosecution in another country for the same attack.

[2] The Concurrent Application of "Computer-Related" Offenses with Cyber Attacks Offenses

It should be added that the Budapest Convention inserts under the title "computer-related offenses" two very specific offenses, the offenses of "computer-related forgery"[113] and of "computer-related fraud,"[114] which are very closely interrelated with the

109. ECHR, *Oliveira c/ Suisse*, Jul. 30, 1998, §22.
110. Andrew Ashworth, *Sentencing and Criminal Justice* 170 (Cambridge University Press 2010).
111. For instance, *see* decision of the Court of First Instance of Apr. 20, 1999, Joined Cases T-305/94 *Limburgse Vinyl Maatschappij NV and others v. Commission* [1999] ECR II-931.
112. Explanations relating to the charter of fundamental rights, 2007/C 303/02.
113. Article 7 of the Budapest Convention:

> Each Party shall adopt such legislative and other measures as may be necessary to establish as criminal offences under its domestic law, when committed intentionally and without right, the input, alteration, deletion, or suppression of computer data, resulting in inauthentic data with the intent that it be considered or acted upon for legal

cyber attacks offenses.[115] Indeed, the Budapest Convention's Explanatory Report characterizes them as "two specific kinds of manipulation of computer systems or computer data."[116] The Convention stipulates that those offenses should be punished as criminal offenses. Both offenses are inspired by the Convention's general cybercrime principles: only intentional acts without right are criminalized.

The computer-related forgery has a narrow field of application, since it applies to forgery of computer data for legal purposes only. It is a matter of interpretation whether this offense applies to the specific kind of cyber attack which is related with certificate falsification. Most platforms of online application distribution nowadays impose a system of software certification in order to create a form of developer's liability and therefore prevent the dissemination of malware. Similarly, the mechanism of certificates is used for HTTPS-based web sites, usually for e-commerce purposes. The certificate here authenticates the website and ensures the user that it has not been hacked. Even in the case where the data have not a legal purpose, the eventual alteration of these certificates would qualify as a data alteration in the scope of the related offense.

It is worth mentioning that a new European cybersecurity certification scheme has been implemented by the Regulation (EU) 2019/881 of the European Parliament and of the Council of 17 April 2019.[117] This policy covers ICT products, services and processes, under the supervision of the European organism European Network Information Security Agency (ENISA). The purpose of the certification is to inform upon the security of the ICT product or service, with three indicators: "basic," "substantial" or "high" level of protection, given that the assurance level shall be commensurate with the level of the risk associated with the intended use of the ICT product, ICT service or ICT process, in terms of the probability and impact of an incident.[118] Article 65 of the

---

> purposes as if it were authentic, regardless whether or not the data is directly readable and intelligible. A Party may require an intent to defraud, or similar dishonest intent, before criminal liability attaches.

114. Article 8 of the Budapest Convention:

> Each Party shall adopt such legislative and other measures as may be necessary to establish as criminal offences under its domestic law, when committed intentionally and without right, the causing of a loss of property to another person by:
>
> (a) any input, alteration, deletion or suppression of computer data,
> (b) any interference with the functioning of a computer system, with fraudulent or dishonest intent of procuring, without right, an economic benefit for oneself or for another person."

115. Venancio, Pedro Dias, *Similarity and Competition Between Cybercrimes Related to Computer Data in the Council of Europe's Convention on Cybercrime*, 7 Masaryk UJL & Tech. 97 (2013).
116. Explanatory Report – ETS 185 – Cybercrime (Convention), 80.
117. Regulation (EU) 2019/881 of the European Parliament and of the Council of Apr. 17, 2019 on ENISA (the European Union Agency for Cybersecurity) and on information and communications technology cybersecurity certification and repealing Regulation (EU) No. 526/2013 (Cybersecurity Act) (Text with EEA relevance), OJ L 151, 7.6.2019, pp. 15–69, ELI: http://data.europa.eu/eli/reg/2019/881/oj.
118. Article 52 of the Regulation 2019/881.

Regulation 2019/881 ensures that this certificate is protected and penalties are applicable to infringements of European cybersecurity certification schemes. In any case, the offense of computer-related forgery still possesses a wide importance when applied in respect of digital signatures. This field of law has just been completely revised by the European legislator. The Regulation 910/2014[119] on electronic identification and trust services for electronic transactions in the internal market creates a new general legal framework related to digital identification, distinguishing between the legal regime of electronic signatures,[120] electronic seals,[121] electronic time stamps,[122] electronic registered delivery services[123] and website authentication[124] (section 8). Each time these electronic identifications are used for legal purposes (public, such as relationship with public services, or private, such as contractual purpose), the intentional alteration of their authenticity leads to the application of the computer-related offense. The Regulation adds that in case of security breach which questions "the reliability of the cross-border authentication of that scheme, the notifying Member State shall, without delay, suspend or revoke that cross-border authentication or the compromised parts concerned, and shall inform other Member States and the Commission."[125] Furthermore, in parallel of the question of criminal liability, the Regulation imposes civil liability "for damage caused intentionally or negligently to any natural or legal person"[126] of the various implicated actors of the identifying process (the State, the party issuing the electronic identification means and the party operating the authentication procedure) according to the obligation's failure.

The offense of "computer-related fraud" has also to be interpreted very narrowly. It would not apply to the general activities of phishing which are alarmingly developing on the Internet. Indeed, whereas the hacker uses a fraudulent means, such as a false email (for instance the famous "Nigerian scam"), or even a fake website mirroring the appearance of a genuine website (which raises also issues of copyright law infringement), Internet is used only as a means of communication and the legal response can be found accordingly to the rules applying to the general offense of fraud or even to extortion (in case of romance scam). The condition of "economic benefit for oneself or for another person" is certainly met in these cases. However, the cumulative condition of alteration of computer data or interference with the functioning of a computer system is not met.

By consequence, the offense of "computer-related fraud" should be seen as a specific application of the offenses of cyber attack, when the fraudulent intent of economic benefit is established. This could apply to direct attacks against systems of electronic money distribution or even of cryptocurrencies' systems.

---

119. The Regulation 910/2014 of the European Parliament and of the Council of Jul. 23, 2014 on electronic identification and trust services for electronic transactions in the internal market and repealing Directive 1999/93/EC.
120. Chapter III, section 4.
121. Chapter III, section 5.
122. Chapter III, section 6.
123. Chapter III, section 7.
124. Chapter III, section 8.
125. Article 10 of the Regulation 910/2014.
126. Article 11 of the Regulation 910/2014.

[3] *The Legal Evolution of Cyber Fraud with the Directive 2019/713/EU*

The EU legal framework applying to cyber fraud has been revised with the Directive (EU) 2019/713 of the European Parliament and of the Council of 17 April 2019 on combating fraud and counterfeiting of noncash means of payment and replacing Council Framework Decision 2001/413/JHA.[127] One of the most significant updates of this mechanism is the importance given to new payment technologies. As stated by the Recital 6 of the Directive, "Recent years have brought not only an exponential increase in the digital economy, but also a proliferation of innovation in many areas, including payment technologies. New payment technologies involve the use of new types of payment instruments, which, while creating new opportunities for consumers and businesses, also increase opportunities for fraud. Consequently, the legal framework must remain relevant and up-to-date against the background of those technological developments, on the basis of a technology-neutral approach."

Therefore, the Directive defines as "digital means of exchange" not only electronic money (as in the previous EU legislations) but also, for the first time, "virtual currency." The term obviously refers to crypto currencies. As it is defined at Article 2 of the Directive, "'virtual currency' means a digital representation of value that is not issued or guaranteed by a central bank or a public authority, is not necessarily attached to a legally established currency and does not possess a legal status of a currency or money, but is accepted by natural or legal persons as a means of exchange, and which can be transferred, stored and traded electronically."

The Directive is based on the model of the Cyber-Attack Directive 2013/40. It proposes a list of specific offenses (Title 2), it regulates the jurisdiction and investigation legal issues (Title 3) and creates a legal framework related to exchange of information and reporting of crime (Title 4). As for the Cyber-Attack Directive, production or distribution of tools used for committing offenses (Article 7), incitement, aiding and abetting and attempt are punishable as criminal offenses. In the same way, criminal liability of legal persons is also provided.

Article 3 criminalizes the fraudulent use of a stolen or otherwise unlawfully appropriated or obtained noncash payment instrument or the fraudulent use of a counterfeit or falsified noncash payment instrument. For instance, the use of a stolen credit card is criminalized, which will certainly not change a lot the national laws of the vast majority of EU Member States.[128]

The directive distinguishes between corporeal and noncorporeal forms of payment. A corporeal form of payment has a physical existence. For instance, a credit card is a corporeal form of payment while the credit card number is a noncorporeal form of payment. In the same way, hardware cryptocurrency wallet (installed on USB disk for instance) would constitute a corporeal form of noncash payment.

---

127. Directive (EU) 2019/713 of the European Parliament and of the Council of 17 April 2019 on combating fraud and counterfeiting of noncash means of payment and replacing Council Framework Decision 2001/413/JHA, OJ L 123, 10.5.2019, pp. 18–29, ELI: http://data.europa.eu/eli/dir/2019/713/oj.

128. A.A. Gillespie & S. Magor, *Tackling Online Fraud*, ERA forum 1–16 (2019), https://doi.org/10.1007/s12027-019-00580-y.

Both the fraudulent use of corporeal and noncorporeal forms is criminalized by Articles 4 and 5 of the Directive. However, while, as regards corporeal forms of payment, are criminalized the intentional acts of theft or other unlawful appropriation, the fraudulent counterfeiting or falsification, the possession and the procurement of a stolen, counterfeit or falsified corporeal noncash payment instrument for fraudulent use, the non-corporeal noncash payment instruments' protection focuses also on their unlawful obtainment, "at least when this obtainment has involved the commission of one of the offenses referred to in Articles 3 to 6 of Directive 2013/40/EU" (Article 5). This expression opens a window to national legislators, who are free to implement Article 5 in two different ways: either the unlawful obtainment of a noncorporeal instrument is criminalized per se or it is criminalized only when obtained through illegal access, illegal interference to the system or to the data.

The most important and innovative part of the Cyber Fraud Directive concerns Article 6, related to "Fraud related to information systems." The article states that: "Member States shall take the necessary measures to ensure that performing or causing a transfer of money, monetary value or virtual currency and thereby causing an unlawful loss of property for another person in order to make an unlawful gain for the perpetrator or a third party is punishable as a criminal offence, when committed intentionally: (a) without right, hindering or interfering with the functioning of an information system; (b) without right, introducing, altering, deleting, transmitting or suppressing computer data." This criminal protection of monetary value and virtual currency is certainly a big step toward the recognition of a form of legal property, while, at the same time, the question remains uncertain under the light of a civil law approach.

However, the offense is subject to significant restrictions: the performing or causing of the transfer has to be the cause of an unlawful loss of property, which should exclude the case of malicious cryptomining (where the hacker uses the computing power of the victim's device to mine cyber currencies). The act has to create an unlawful gain, which also could be problematic in the context of cyber currencies. Lastly, only the combination of the fraud with either an illegal interference with an information system or an illegal interference with the data is criminalized. The online fraud which is purely based on human deception (the victim willingly transfers the monetary value) is therefore left aside. It creates a dangerous and potential confusion, as some online frauds are regulated thought the specific offense of cyber fraud, while others still belong to the general and nonharmonized criminal offense of fraud.

Generally speaking, the Directive offers a wider protection against cyber fraud than the previous EU legislation. In this context, it could be advanced that the EU legislator's understanding has evolved in order to better encompass the cyber fraud's reality. However, practice has evolved too and the legislation still does not apply to specific forms of fraud, such as auction fraud (misrepresentation of a product advertised for sale through an Internet auction site or the non-delivery of products purchased through an Internet auction site), confidence trick (attempt to defraud a person or group after first gaining their trust) or even Nigerian Prince's fraud.[129]

§2.03 PRIVATE LAW ASPECTS OF THE REGULATION OF CYBER ATTACKS

[A] Civil Liability for Cyber Attacks

Neither the Budapest Convention nor the European legislation touch upon civil law issues related to cyber attacks. Civil liability poses issues both in respect of the liability of the perpetrator of the cyber attack and in respect of the intermediaries' liability. The specific issue of the intermediaries' liability plays a substantial role in general in Internet regulation and, therefore, it is discussed in detail in the Chapter 3 of this book.[130] However, the direct civil liability of the perpetrator of a cyber attack has not been clearly defined yet by the legislator. In general, the legal framework of civil liability has not been harmonized in the European Union yet. However, a common Roman law heritage, centuries of discussions and the concerted efforts of scholars in the past twenty-five years (such as the European Principles of Tort law PETL,[131] which were published in 2005[132]) led to some practical results. The civil law arsenal in this matter includes on the one hand, injunctive relief and disclosure orders to ISPs against perpetrators. On the other hand, the person who has been harmed by the cyber attack is also entitled to civil claims in order to recover the loss caused by the cyber attack. Therefore, the private aspect of cyber attacks can be dealt mostly by applying the standard reasoning of civil law, "though to novel factual settings."[133]

As it has already been mentioned above, cyber attack offenses require intention. From a private law perspective, this means the application of a fault-based liability regime. Indeed, as stated in the PETL, "a person is liable on the basis of fault for intentional or negligent violation of the required standard of conduct."[134] From a continental law approach, this should be enough to ensure that the liability of the person behind a cyber attack is established. From a common law approach, an additional difficulty appears. The intention should exclude the application of the tort of negligence. However, the criminal aspect of a cyber attack could be used as a direct legal basis for an action for compensation under the "breach of statutory duty" tort. The criteria for the application of this tort are certainly related to the intention of the legislator. In other words, the judge has to ask himself if, by promulgating a general interdiction, the legislator also presumes that the perpetrator should be civilly liable. Even if, in general, the existence of criminal sanctions works as a presumption that the

129. *Ibid.*
130. *See* Chapter 3, section 3.02.
131. European Principles of Tort law PETL, http://www.egtl.org/.
132. European Group on Tort Law, *Principles of European Tort Law, Text and Commentary*, XII, 282 (Springer 2005).
133. A. Koch, Bernhard, *Cyber Torts: Something Virtually New?*, 5.2 J. Eur. Tort Law 133–164 (2014).
134. Article 4:101.

legislator did not wish to impose a civil sanction, in the case of cybercrime, a reasonable approach would be to recognize that the intention of the law is to cover also the loss inflicted by a cyber attack. Therefore, even if in principle, the existence of criminal sanctions works as a presumption of the legislator's intention not to accept civil sanctions, civil law actions shall not be excluded.

Both in common law and civil law jurisdictions, causation has to be established. In other words, a casual relationship between the cyber attack and the loss has to be proven. As stated in the PETL, "An activity or conduct (hereafter: activity) is a cause of the victim's damage if, in the absence of the activity, the damage would not have occurred,"[135] while the liability is limited to the extent of the foreseeability of the damage.[136] The application of these general principles depends on the specific type of the cyber attack. For example, in case of computer-related fraud, the causation between the fraud and the loss is evident. Similarly, in case of a direct intrusion to a system, the intentional intrusion is the cause of the data breach.

However, in case of a virus or of a DDoS attack, the perpetrator could be tempted to use the rules of causality in his benefit in order to avoid liability. Viruses, malware and DDoS attacks most of the time imply the act of a third person, which is often the innocent "medium" for the transmission and the perpetration of the attack. In this context, could the perpetrator use the defense of *nova actus interveniens* ("breaking the chain")? Furthermore, in case of a virus or a malware, the perpetrator has often no control on the dissemination of the tool and no idea of the real extent of the damage that it will be caused. Could this signify that the total damage is not foreseeable? Also, the DDoS attack exploits the vulnerability of connected devices in order to create a zombie network. The force of the DDoS attack depends on the size of the network. Could, therefore, the tortfeasor validly claim that his liability has to be limited by application of the rules of third party's liability for negligence? For all those complex questions, the reckless attitude of the tortfeasor should serve as a justification for a flexible application of the rules of causation by the judge.

Finally, in certain circumstances, the issue of civil liability as regards cyber attacks would be resolved differently. The offense of illegal access to information system, mainly, has to be seen in relation with the new European Directive on the protection of trade secrets.[137] Indeed, according to Article 4 of the Directive, unlawful acquisition, use and disclosure of confidential information is prohibited. The text explicitly refers to access to electronic files as a mean of unlawful acquisition. It is worth noting that a "trade secret" is broadly defined as any confidential information that possesses commercial value and "has been subject to reasonable steps under the circumstances, by the person lawfully in control of the information, to keep it secret."[138]

135. Article 3:101.
136. Article 3:201.
137. Directive (EU) 2016/943 of the European Parliament and of the Council of 8 June 2016 on the protection of undisclosed know-how and business information (trade secrets) against their unlawful acquisition, use and disclosure (Text with EEA relevance).
138. Article 2(1)(c) of the Directive 2016/943.

Therefore, the perpetrator of an act of an unlawful acquisition which is defined mainly as unauthorized access, theft, bribery, deception, breach or inducement to breach confidentiality, is primary liable for this action. The trade secrets create a regime of secondary liability which is currently absent in most countries. More precisely, the third party who obtains access to the protected information with knowledge of their unlawful acquisition is also civilly liable. In conclusion, the legal framework of trade secrets institutes a quasi-intellectual property right[139] on trade secret, which is deemed to play a substantial role in the framework of civil law conflicts related to cyber attacks.

[B] The Calculation of Damages

One particularity of the civil aspect of cyber attacks is that in most cases the court has to deal with issues of solidary and several liability. In this context, underground networks which are responsible for DDoS attacks, malware programming and other cyber attacks should be seen as multiple tortfeasors. In the same time, viruses, malware, massive Internet frauds and general online communication surveillance mean that a plethora of victims exists. The general rules governing the calculation of damages set out that, in case of solidary liability, each tortfeasor is liable for the entire damage.[140] This could lead to some extreme situations. For instance, in a case of child pornography in USA, a perpetrator who was convicted for illegal detention of pictures of child pornography, was sued by the family of the child which appeared in the photos. Most probably he was one of the thousands of people who shared this photo. However, according to the general rules of civil law, the holder of the photo was held liable for the entire sum of the prejudice, which means millions of dollars of damages.[141]

---

139. J. Heitto, *The Trade Secret Directive Proposal and the Narrow Path to Improving Trade Secret Protection in Europe*, 16(5) Computer L. Rev. Intl. 140–144 (2015).
140. *See* PETL, Article 9:101:

> (1) Liability is solidary where the whole or a distinct part of the damage suffered by the victim is attributable to two or more persons. Liability is solidary where:
> (a) a person knowingly participates in or instigates or encourages wrongdoing by others which causes damage to the victim; or
> (b) one person's independent behaviour or activity causes damage to the victim and the same damage is also attributable to another person.
> (c) a person is responsible for damage caused by an auxiliary in circumstances where the auxiliary is also liable.
>
> (2) Where persons are subject to solidary liability, the victim may claim full compensation from any one or more of them, provided that the victim may not recover more than the full amount of the damage suffered by him.
>
> (3) Damage is the same damage for the purposes of paragraph (1)(b) above when there is no reasonable basis for attributing only part of it to each of a number of persons liable to the victim. For this purpose it is for the person asserting that the damage is not the same to show that it is not. Where there is such a basis, liability is several, that is to say, each person is liable to the victim only for the part of the damage attributable to him.

141. Supreme Court, *Paroline v. USA*, No. 12-8561, Apr. 23, 2014, 701 F. 3d 749.

Class actions are a well-known mechanism in US civil law.[142] Class actions offer to a large portion of the population a way to obtain reparation even if the loss that occurred individually does not justify the expenses of a trial. For various reasons, this mechanism has not really been adopted at a European level, even if at a national level and mostly for the protection of the consumer, some States have enacted various forms of class actions.[143] In case of cyber attacks, in our opinion it could be very profitable for the general interest if a similar mechanism of class action is instituted.

The calculation of damages, by definition, encompasses material and moral damages. First of all, as regards material damages, it has to be noted that in some cases a mechanism of automatic protection protects the victim. For instance, in case of an online fraud which affects the bank account of the victim, by application of consumer protection rules, the Bank has to cover all the material loss which was inflicted to the victim. According to the Payment Service Directive, the payer's liability for unauthorized payment transactions is of EUR 150 maximum.[144] However, a new legislation in 2015 limited this liability to EUR 50 maximum.[145]

The type of loss covered by a civil action depends strictly of the kind of cyber attack which occurred. In case of an illegal access to a system, the access by itself causes damage to the victim, since it compromises the confidentiality of the information. In case of an illegal interference with a system, the loss of data or the loss of profit should be fairly estimated. A DDoS attack which blocks a popular commercial website could provoke millions of euros of damages by hour of inactivity. In continental law, this situation enters into the definition of the loss of profit, which is covered by the reparation.[146] Nonetheless, in common law jurisdictions the theory of pure economic loss[147] could apply if the attack did not provoke any material damages. According to this rule, a distinction shall be made between the loss of certain profit and potential future profit (which is not covered by the reparation). A DDoS attack not only disrupts actual transaction, but also and, more importantly, blocks potential transactions. In order to avoid this difficulty related to the tort of negligence, certain common law courts seem ready to adopt an extensive definition of another tort, the tort of trespass to the chattels which becomes a tort of "trespass to chattels online." These case law

142. Coffee, John C., *Class Wars: The Dilemma of the Mass Tort Class Action*, 95(6) Columbia L. Rev. 1343–1465 (1995).
143. In Italy, Law No. 99/2009 (from Jul. 1, 2009) has introduced Article 140-*bis* in the Consumers Code, allowing consumers to group together in order to file a single suit bringing collective court claims; in France, Law No. 2014-344 (from Mar. 17, 2014) introduced collective actions in consumer and competition disputes.
144. Directive 2007/64/EC of the European Parliament and of the Council of Nov. 13, 2007 on payment services in the internal market.
145. Directive (EU) 2015/2366 of the European Parliament and of the Council of Nov. 25, 2015 on payment services in the internal market, amending Directives 2002/65/EC, 2009/110/EC and 2013/36/EU and Regulation (EU) No. 1093/2010, and repealing Directive 2007/64/EC (Text with EEA relevance).
146. Y. Gotanda John, *Recovering Lost Profits in International Disputes*, Georgetown J. Intl. L. 61–112 (Fall 2004).
147. Jennifer A. Chandler, *Security in Cyberspace: Combatting Distributed Denial of Service Attack*, 1 Uni. Ottawa Law & Tech. J. 231 et seq. (2003).

responses show that "the loss of use, without permanent physical damage, ought to be recoverable."[148]

Furthermore, moral damages should not be underestimated. This is obvious in case of attacks with high level of prejudice for the personality, such as a romance scam. Mass surveillance systems, data breach and malware are deemed also to inflict moral damages.

[C] The Negligent Protection of an Information System

It should be reminded that in practice most often the intrusion to an information system is successful due to human errors.[149] Should the company, which has the duty to supervise and train its employees, be liable for the damage caused to a person as a consequence of a data breach? Generally speaking, does the digital service provider have a positive duty to protect the interests of the users who are using its service? In the banking sector, the courts have already examined this question and answered in the affirmative. For instance, in Portugal in 2016 a bank has been found liable after a phishing attack against its clients, because it had been demonstrated that the company did not take the relevant measures of protection against this kind of attack.[150] In common law, this specific duty of banks to protect their clients' interest—through technical measures of security, but not only—is coined as "Quincecare duty" (the name comes from the *Barclays Bank plc v. Quincecare Ltd* case law,[151] where the duty has first been formulated) and as recently been confirmed by new case law.[152]

Furthermore, if the cyber attack was facilitated by zero-day vulnerability, the question of the liability of the Software manufacturer emerges.[153] For instance, if a firewall does not work correctly, an operating system contains a backdoor and a browser automatically installs malware programs. An obvious vulnerability (even if it is invisible to the consumer) means that the software manufacturer or distributor is strictly liable, while at the same time the various clauses of liability exemption would be normally set aside as being abusive. The situation of open source software is more delicate, since it is most often distributed free of charge and this fact could play a substantive role both in the application of the defective products and of abusive clauses regulations. However, the proposal of a directive on certain aspects concerning contracts for the supply of digital content aims to impose a two-year guarantee on this

148. *Ibid.*
149. Hatchimonji Grant, *"Report Indicates Insider Threats Leading Cause of Data Breaches in Last 12 Months"*, available at: csoonline.com (Oct. 8, 2013).
150. Supreme Court of Portugal, Ruling 1063/12.1TVLSB.L1.S1 as cited in ICLG (eds), Cybersecurity Laws and Regulations 2019, iclg.com (2018).
151. *Barclays Bank plc v. Quincecare Ltd* [1992] 4 All ER 363.
152. *Singularis Holdings Limited (in liquidation) v. Daiwa Capital Markets Europe Limited* [2018] EWCA Civ 84.
153. Emily Kuwahara, *Torts v. Contracts: Can Microsoft Be Held Liable to Home Consumers for Its Security Flaws*, 80 S. Cal. L. Rev. 997 (2006).

issue.[154] In consequence, the lack of correction of known vulnerabilities of a software would raise automatically the contractual liability of the software retailer.

The recent NIS Directive[155] created a statutory duty of care of the operator of an essential service ("a service which is essential for the maintenance of critical societal and/or economic activities"). Specifically, in Article 14(1), it is stated that such operators have to "take appropriate and proportionate technical and organisational measures to manage the risks posed to the security of network and information systems which they use in their operations. Having regard to the state of the art, those measures shall ensure a level of security of network and information systems appropriate to the risk posed." In the same way, Article 14(2) completes this provision by stating that they also have the duty to "take appropriate measures to prevent and minimise the impact of incidents affecting the security of the network and information systems used for the provision of such essential services, with a view to ensuring the continuity of those services." A similar framework applies to digital service providers (Article 16). This provision should be interpreted as creating a presumption of liability for negligence against the digital service provider in case a user suffers damage from a cyber attack organized through the digital service provider's information system.

In parallel, if as a result of the attack personal data are leaked, on the basis of the General Data Protection Regulation (GDPR)[156] civil liability of the digital service provider is also activated through the provider's duty to protect the integrity of the treatment.[157] In this matter, Article 32 of GDPR does not systematically impose encryption of the data as a solution to protect the user's privacy against attacks. However, this solution must be seriously taken in consideration according to "the state of the art, the costs of implementation and the nature, scope, context and purposes of processing as well as the risk of varying likelihood and severity for the rights and freedoms of natural persons."

In both the cases of an essential service and a digital service, the operator/provider has to notify the relevant national point of contact which is competent in matters of cybersecurity. Alternatively to civil or administrative sanctions and based on the model of the data breach notification which has been adopted for personal data protection[158], the operator/provider may be "condemned" to reveal to

154. Proposal for a Directive of the European Parliament and the Council on certain aspects concerning contracts for the supply of digital content, COM/2015/0634 final - 2015/0287 (COD).
155. Directive (EU) 2016/1148 of the European Parliament and of the Council of Jul. 6, 2016 concerning measures for a high common level of security of network and information systems across the Union, OJ L 194, 19.7.2016, pp. 1–30, ELI: http://data.europa.eu/eli/dir/2016/1148/oj.
156. Regulation (EU) 2016/679 of the European Parliament and of the Council of Apr. 27, 2016 on the protection of natural persons with regard to the processing of personal data and on the free movement of such data, and repealing Directive 95/46/EC (General Data Protection Regulation) (Text with EEA relevance).
157. Article 5 of GDPR states that "Personal data shall be: (...) (f) processed in a manner that ensures appropriate security of the personal data, including protection against unauthorised or unlawful processing and against accidental loss, destruction or damage, using appropriate technical or organisational measures ('integrity and confidentiality')."
158. *See* Articles 33 and 34 of GDPR.

the public the extent of the attack. This can be interpreted as a form of reputational sanction. Data breach notification laws and reputational sanctions are regarded as positive measures since they encourage businesses to adopt stricter policies as regards cybersecurity.[159]

Furthermore, if a specific protection cannot apply, the general law of negligence will apply in order to cover the loss endured by the client whose data were held by a vulnerable informational system. For instance, in France, the court accepted the civil liability of a company that had installed a telephonic center in another company without warning it that the protection system was left in their default setting. More particularly, the root password was "0000." The liability was based on the breach of duty to inform the client of the danger related with the use of default password. Indeed, unknown persons used the center for their own purposes for months.[160] In a very similar case, the Supreme Court of Cyprus had arrived to the same conclusion and condemned the IT company to pay general damages,[161] since it was not possible to distinguish how many connections were used for the personal benefit of the intruder.

§2.04 FORENSIC ISSUES

[A] The Enforcement of Cybercrime Legislation and the Problem of Evidence

Cybercrime and conventional crime differ significantly both in commission and in prosecution. Cybercrimes are difficult to investigate, prosecute and punish. In any case evidence has to be gathered, considered and evaluated, but in the digital world, where the number of crimes involving digital devices and network is growing rapidly, there are neither fingerprints nor even physical presence. Considerable technological changes occur, and the extent and the way in which technological devices are used evolve constantly. These changes refer to the exponentially increasing amount of data that is produced, processed and transferred globally, the use of multiple devices, encryption and anonymization tools, the increasing use of cloud computing services as well as the possible involvement of innocent users, whose devices may be easily compromised and used for criminal purposes such as the so-called botnet attacks.[162]

This, also, results in new law enforcement challenges. However, law enforcement is an information-intensive process, its effectiveness relying on the information

159. ML McMichael, *Cybersecurity on My Mind: Protecting Georgia Consumers from Data Breaches*, 51 Ga. L. Rev. 265 (2016).
160. Tribunal de commerce de Nanterre, 3ème chambre, Feb. 5, 2015, AFJ Nerim venant aux droits de la sas Normaction / Fast Lease, available at: http://www.legalis.net/spip.php?page=jurisprudence-decision&id_article=4506.
161. Supreme Court, *Galatariotis Telecommunications Ltd* v. *1. Dimitri Sioukiouroglou 2. Premier Chemical Co Ltd* (2008) 1 C.L.R. 29.
162. Cybercrime Convention Committee (T-CY), Ad-hoc-group on Jurisdiction and Transborder Access to Data, *Transborder Access and Jurisdiction: What Are the Options?*, Report adopted by T-CY, 9 (Dec. 6, 2012).

gathered and reported.[163] Evidence in judicial proceedings is increasingly being stored, transmitted or processed in electronic form. A fundamental question that needs steadily to be considered is whether, how and to what extent, digital traces and computer data can be treated as documentary evidence. Data, which can eventually be classed as evidence, can be easily deleted or disappear. The digital evidence is fragile, as it can be also easily destroyed by inexperienced access and handling. Cyber evidence is undoubtedly easier to destroy or to alter by the perpetrator without obvious traces.[164]

Furthermore, the transnational element is common for cybercrime in general and for cyber attacks: Physical location of victims and/or damaged information systems, offenders and evidence may be different as the digital environment enables cybercriminal to operate across national borders and consequently, transjurisdictionally. It has been stressed out that "today, armed with a computer and a network connection, anyone can commit a crime halfway around the world without ever physically entering the jurisdiction of the crime scene."[165]

To address the challenges of new forms of cybercrime, policing and law enforcement has been also revolutionized through digital forensics and the development of specialized tools to aid investigative processes into cybercrime offending.[166] In order to assist investigation for acquiring, preserving and analyzing evidence specific tools, procedures and techniques have been created and introduced.[167] Forensic science uses technology to assist in the establishment of facts.

[B] Digital Forensics and E-Evidence

Originally used as a synonym for computer forensics,[168] the term digital forensics has expanded to include the investigation of any device capable of storing information in digital form.[169] Potential sources of digital evidence are computers, storage devices, mobile devices or network devices.[170] Digital forensics indicates the scientific discipline, branch of both computer science and forensics, which is concerned with recovering information that may have evidential value.

163. M. Karyda & L. Mitrou, *Internet Forensics: Legal and Technical Issues, WDFIA*, International, Workshop on Digital Forensics and Incident Analysis, International 2007, 3 (2007).
164. O. Leroux, *Legal Admissibility of Electronic Evidence,* 18(2) Intl. Rev. of L. Computers & Tech. 193 (2004).
165. J. Herrera-Flanigan & S. Ghosh, *Criminal Regulations,* in *Cybercrimes: A Multidisciplinary Analysis,* 286 (Ghosh S. & E. Turrini eds, Springer 2011).
166. A. Pichan et al., *Cloud Forensics: Technical Challenges, Solutions and Comparative Analysis,* 13 Digital Investigation 38 (2015).
167. S. Simou et al., *Cloud Forensics: Identifying the Major Issues and Challenges,* in *Advanced Information Systems Engineering* 271 (Springer International Publishing 2014).
168. Computer forensics focuses on analyzing traditional desktop computers and laptops as found in both homes and businesses. *See* UNODC, *Cybercrime Study, supra* n. 52, 160.
169. S. Simou et al., *supra* n. 167, 141.
170. ENISA refers to an indicative list of devices that includes computers (PC's, laptops, servers or even game consoles), storage devices (CDs, DVDs, USBs and memory cards), hand-held devices than include not only mobile phones but also digital cameras, satellite navigation systems and last but not least Network devices (like hubs, switches, routers and wireless access points). ENISA, *Electronic Evidence – A Guide for First Responders*, 4.

More specifically, digital forensics refers to the use of scientifically derived and proven methods toward the preservation, collection, validation, identification, analysis, interpretation, documentation and presentation of evidence derived from digital sources.[171] Digital forensics focuses on developing evidence pertained in the digital world for use in criminal or/and also civil court proceedings and for the purpose of facilitating or improving the reconstruction of events relevant for the case to be judged.

[1] Electronic Evidence

Facts relevant for a trial and for the judgment of the court are established and reconstructed by the means of evidences. Evidence may consist of facts, testimony, documents as well as physical exhibits, and it was traditionally collected in physical form. New technologies and their impacts on almost all aspects of life, including the way crimes may be committed, have posed new challenges with regard to extracting evidences from electronic devices and they gave rise to a new form of evidence called in general "electronic evidence."[172]

There are various definitions of electronic evidence and in some cases the term is used interchangeably with the term "digital evidence."[173] Electronic evidence as concept encompasses any material in electronic or digital form that may be used and admitted to prove the facts in question.[174] Electronic evidence is conceived as "any information obtained from an electronic device or digital medium which serves to convince the truth of a deed."[175] In the Electronic Evidence Guide developed by the CoE, electronic evidence is defined in a more generic way.[176] Bonnici et al. suggest as

171. These elements have been emphasized in a quite comprehensive definition given by Palmer (G. Palmer, *A Road Map for Digital Forensic Research*, DFRWS Technical Report, Air Force Research Laboratory, Rome, New York (2001) while K. Kent, S. Chevalier, T. Grance & H. Dang, defined digital forensics as "the application of science to the identification, collection, examination, and analysis of data while preserving the integrity of the information and maintaining a strict chain of custody for the data" in *Guide to Integrating Forensic Techniques into Incident Response*, NIST Special Publication, 800 (2006).
172. ENISA, *Digital Forensics – Handbook*, 3 (2013).
173. *See* J.P.M. Bonnici, M. Tudorica, & J.A. Cannataci, *The European Legal Framework on Electronic Evidence: Complex and in Need of Reform*, in M.A. Biasiotti, J.P. Mifsud Bonnici, J. Cannataci & F. Turchi (eds.), *Handling and Exchanging Electronic Evidence Across Europe*, 189-235, at 190 (Law, Governance and Technology Series; Vol. 39), Cham: Springer (2018) https://www.rug.nl/research/portal/publications/the-european-legal-framework-on-electronic-evidence(135ebdcb-2d62-4c1e-8820-2f8889eda63b).html.
174. Cameron S.D. Brown, *Investigating and Prosecuting Cyber Crime: Forensic Dependencies and Barriers to Justice*, 9(1) Intl. J. Cyber Criminology 83 (January–June 2015).
175. CYBEX, *The Admissibility of Electronic Evidence in Court – Fighting against High-Tech Crime – Study*, available at: www.cybex.es (2006). The simplest definition is this adopted by the CoE which defines electronic evidence as evidence that can be collected in electronic form of a criminal offense (CoE, Cybercrime Convention—Explanatory Memorandum) while the US Department of Justice defines electronic evidence as "information stored or transmitted in binary form that may be relied on in court." US Department of Justice, Office of Justice Programs, National Institute of Justice, *Forensic Examination of Digital Evidence: A Guide for Law Enforcement*, 46 (2004), https://www.ncjrs.gov/pdffiles1/nij/199408.pdf.
176. Digital evidence is defined as the electronic evidence which is generated or converted to a numerical format. Maria Angela Biasiotti & Mattia Epifani, *Bridging the Gap in the Collection,*

definition of electronic evidence "any information (comprising the output of analogue devices or data in digital format) of potential probative value that is manipulated, generated through, stored on or communicated by any electronic device."[177] In this perspective, electronic evidence and a (suitable) legal framework are of vital importance not only with regard to cybercrime but increasingly to crime and effective crime response in general.[178] In the Draft Regulation of the European Parliament and of the Council on European production and preservation orders for electronic evidence in criminal matters, the "electronic evidence"[179] it is defined as "evidence stored in electronic form by or on behalf of a service provider at the time of receipt of a production or preservation order certificate, consisting in stored subscriber data, access data, transactional data and content data" (Article 2(6)).

The collection of electronic evidence involves the assessment of a given situation and the identification and recovery of relevant sources of information that could be of evidential value to a criminal investigation.[180] Digital evidence can be found in nearly any computerized system processing data. Digital data can be stored or transient. They can exist in the form of digital documents, emails, logs digital photographs, software programs, or other digital records, and network data or metadata.

In the literature a taxonomy of evidence is proposed that responds to a set of questions, i.e., *who, where, when, what, why, how.* [181] This taxonomy includes: (a) *identity Evidence,* identifying subjects that are part of an event that constitutes an attack to an information system, (b) *location Evidence,* defining the approximate or exact location, where an event takes place, (c) *time evidence,* for inferring the time that an event takes place, (d) *context evidence,* providing adequate context, such as user actions and activities for an event description, or the event nature, (e) *motivation evidence,* including data that are used to determine event motivation and (f) *means evidence,* describing the way that an event took place, or the mean that were used for the attack.

Digital Forensics investigators have a variety of tools at their disposal, proprietary and open source to conduct their analysis. Their investigation is organized based on one of the many digital forensic methodologies that exist[182] although obtaining digital

---

Use and Exchange of Electronic Evidence in Europe – Presentation in context of European Informatics Data Exchange Framework for Court and Evidence (EVIDENCE) Project. *See also* CyberCrime@IPA, EU/COE Joint Project on Regional Cooperation against Cybercrime, N. Jones, E. George & F. Insa Mérida, *Electronic evidence guide – A basic guide for police officers, prosecutors and judges*, Version 1.0.

177. M. Bonnici et al., *supra* n. 173, 190.
178. UNODC, *Cybercrime Study, supra* n. 52, 5, 147.
179. Council of the European Union, Regulation of the European Parliament and of the Council on European production and preservation orders for electronic evidence in criminal matters – general approach, Brussels, Jun. 11, 2019 (OR. en), 10206/19 (Interinstitutional File: 2018/0108(COD)).
180. ENISA, *Electronic Evidence – A Basic Guide for First Responders*, 4 (2014).
181. *See* C. Blackwell, *An Investigative Framework for Incident Analysis* In *Advances in Digital Forensics*, Part VII, 22 (G. Peterson & S. Shenoi eds, Springer 2011). Also W. Jansen & R. Ayers, *Guidelines on Cell Phone Forensics,* NIST Special Publication 800: 101 (2007).
182. More in Karyda and Mitrou, *supra* n. 163, 137.

evidence often requires a combination of digital forensics and traditional methods and techniques.[183]

Taking into consideration the function of evidence there are no intrinsic differences between digital and more traditional types of evidence. The admissibility of evidence from computer records and digital devices in courts depends to a great extent on the underlying fundamental principles of evidence in the respective country. In Europe, continental legal systems operate according to the principle of free introduction and free evaluation of evidence and provide that all means of evidence, irrespectively of the form they assume, can be admitted in legal proceedings.[184] Legal systems based on these principles in general do not hesitate to introduce computer records as evidence.[185]

However, digital evidence has some special characteristics that separate it to some degree from its real-world counterparts; rather the problems are raised from the fragility and vulnerability and the transience of many forms of computer evidence.[186] Therefore, digital forensics puts special emphasis on the correct treatment of potential evidence to prevent it from being altered or tampered with.

[2] Principles

Digital evidence must have all the attributes of conventional evidence, any tool, method or procedure used during an investigation has also to meet strict standards. Investigating agencies as well as their agents have to ensure that the possession of and access to electronic evidence is compliant with the law as well as the general procedural and forensic principles.[187] They have to demonstrate that *they abide by applicable laws;*[188] *otherwise they risk having their digital or physical* exhibits *declared*

183. A. Mylonas et al., *Smartphone Forensics: A Proactive Investigation Scheme for Evidence Acquisition*, in *Information Security and Privacy Research* 249 (Springer Berlin Heidelberg 2012), available at: http://www.aueb.gr/users/amylonas/docs/SEC-12Smartphone%20ForensicsTechRe.pdf.
184. In the past, the use of computer-generated evidence in court has posed legal difficulties only in common law countries, and especially in Australia, Canada, the United Kingdom and the United States of America: these countries are, to a greater extent, characterized by an oral and adversarial procedure. Knowledge from secondary sources, such as other persons, books, or records, is regarded as "hearsay evidence," and is, in principle, inadmissible but there are several exceptions to the hearsay evidence rule.
185. CYBEX, *The Admissibility of Electronic Evidence in Court – Fighting against High-Tech Crime – Study*, available at: www.cybex.es (2006).
186. P. Sommer, *Digital Footprints: Assessing Computer Evidence*, Criminal Law Review – Special Edition, 61–78 (1998).
187. Legality is one of the five main principles adopted as a part of EU and CoE project to develop a seizure of e-evidence guide.
188. As collection of e-evidence is understood the process of gathering items that contain potential electronic evidence in the widest sense, meaning search, seizure,interception and any other forms of gathering evidence by law enforcement agencies (LEAs), but also capture of evidence by the private sector and any other forms of gathering potential electronic evidence. *See* Bonnici et al., *supra* n. 173.

inadmissible at court.[189] In order to be *admissible*, digital evidence has to comply with the legal principles and requirements in a criminal procedure.

E-evidence must also be "irrefutable authentic," i.e., it must be possible to positively tie evidentiary material to the security incident.[190] Furthermore, authenticity implies that it has to be certifiable to tie the evidence to the case under investigation.[191] Digital evidence is regarded authentic if the information obtained is a true and accurate representation of the original data contained on the device.[192] In this context, authenticity relates strictly with the principle/requirement of integrity.

Perhaps the most important element in the digital forensics is to maintain the integrity of the digital evidence, i.e., both device and data that are presented as evidence have to be the same as that which was originally discovered. The evidences have to be considered and evaluated, but in most attacks against information systems there is no physical evidence at place. Electronic devices and data must remain unchanged in relation to either hardware or software.[193]

Data, which can eventually be classed as evidence, are volatile: they can be easily modified, deleted or disappear either purposely or even through normal use.[194] Digital information is by its nature vulnerable to manipulation. Computer artifacts can be easily or imperceptibly modified, overwritten or deleted, thus posing challenges with regard to authentication and verification of digital information.[195] Digital evidence, as traditional evidence, has to be free from tampering and/or alteration.

Electronic evidence and especially online content is by its nature ephemeral raising specific issues with regard to its proper collection and authenticity: for example it is possible that the content in question to be removed, so investigators have to acquire and provide evidence of what a web page looked like at a certain point of time. In order to validate authenticity several validation procedures have been proposed and employed around the world. However, procedures such as witness cause too many controversies and concerns which often result in nonadmissibility of the electronic evidence.[196]

The accuracy of the computer or any other device in the retention and retrieval of the information at issue has to also to be ensured. Evidence integrity, authenticity and

---

189. Cameron S.D. Brown, *supra* n. 174, 87, with further references.
190. CoE, *Explanatory Report to the Convention on Cybercrime (ETS 185)* (2001), available at: http://www.coe.int.
191. ENISA, *Digital Forensics – Handbook*, 3 (2013).
192. UNODC, *Cybercrime Study*, *supra* n. 52, 158.
193. ENISA, *Digital Forensics – Handbook*, 4 (2013).
194. As noted in ENISA *Handbook on Digital Forensics*, Devices constantly change the state of memory. *See* ENISA *Digital Forensics – Handbook*, 6. Also RAND Europe, *Handbook of Legislative Procedures of Computer and Network Misuse in EU Countries – Study for the European Commission*, Directorate-General Information Society (2002).
195. UNODC, *supra* n. 52, 158.
196. E. Lalas, L. Mitrou & C. Lambrinoudakis, *ProCAVE: Privacy-Preserving Collection and Authenticity Validation of Online Evidence*, in Proceedings of the 10th International Conference on Trust, Privacy & Security in Digital Business (TRUSTBUS-2013), 137–148 (Springer (LNCS 8058) Czech Republic, August 2013).

continuity are to be maintained for both the physical device[197] storing the information and the information stored on the device.[198] The integrity, and thus the reliability and trustworthiness, of a digital evidence has to be guaranteed and demonstrated the entire time period between its seizure *to the point that it is introduced in court*. Preservation of continuity—as element of integrity—of evidence (and investigation process) requires the detailed recording and documentation of seizure steps to track any digital exhibit and establish the chain of evidence.

The investigation process itself should not result in any action that could change data which may subsequently be relied upon in a judicial proceeding.[199] The collection and handling must guarantee the authenticity,[200] integrity and continuity of evidence. However, it has to be taken into consideration that sometimes the collection of evidence may not take place without altering it.[201]

As indicated, digital evidence has to be collected in accordance with formal requirements to establish its reliability. The reliability and consequently the admissibility of digital information as evidence may be challenged when the system generating the information does not have robust security and respective security controls. Information security practices can be used to safeguard the quality and reliability of collected information.[202] Establishing the integrity and authenticity of material in court, requires standard techniques and methods for the collection, preservation and presentation of stored evidence material.

As the use and handling of data and information collected by detection tools are closely related to standardization, the European Commission has emphasized the need to create procedural and technical standards to ensure that the data collected complies with the requirements of law for the use of such data in court proceedings.[203] In order

197. It is also required that the physical device sought to be introduced as evidence is identical to that which was initially discovered and subsequently taken under inquiry; Cameron S.D. Brown, *supra* n. 174, 58, with further references.
198. These requirements refer to what is understood as "evidence continuity" or "chain-of custody." Evidence continuity is typically a question of fact and the chain-of-custody process is the mechanism applied for maintaining and documenting the chronological history of the evidence as it moves from one place to another. *See* E. Casey, *Digital Evidence and Computer Crime: Forensic Science, Computers and the Internet*, 21 et seq., 60 et seq. (Elsevier 2011).
199. ACPO, *ACPO Good Practice Guide for Digital Evidence*, https://www.digital-detective.net/digital-forensics-documents/ACPO_Good_Practice_Guide_for_Digital_Evidence_v5.pdf.
200. The authenticity is often contested either with regard to the source of computer-stored records or the subsequent corruption, manipulation or alteration of evidence gathered; *see* C. Brown, *supra* n. 174, 87.
201. A major problem that investigators have to face is how to ensure the integrity of evidence when investigations are taking place on live systems, as any live procedure performed on a running device creates changes to the system state itself. Once power or device is removed it may change data on the system under investigation making impossible to replicate the live state to verify and validate findings. *See* B.D. Carrier, *Risks of Live Digital Forensic Analysis, Communications of the ACM*, 49(2), 56 et seq. (2006). *See also* ENISA, *Electronic Evidence – A Basic Guide for First Responders* that recommends that documentation and explanation of gathering steps and actions taken gains in importance (p. 7).
202. A. Mitrakas & D. Zaitch, *Law, Cybercrime and Digital Forensics: Trailing Digital Suspects*, in *Digital Crime and Forensic Science in Cyberspace* 267 et seq. (P. Kanelis et al. eds, London 2006).
203. Commission of the European Communities, *Green Paper on Detection Technologies in the Work of Law Enforcement*, Customs and other Security Authorities, COM(2006) 474 final. In this

to ensure the integrity of the procedure it has to be considered if and to what extent "the technical means and methods should be subjected to independent testing and certification."[204]

In this context there has been a shift to the development of "practical principles" that could be accepted internationally regardless the differences between national legislations with regard to admissibility of reference. ISO/IEC has developed a group of standards[205] that serve to promote good practice methods and processes for forensic capture and investigation of digital evidence.[206] Another interesting set of non-legally binding guidelines is included in the *Electronic evidence guide – A basic guide for police officers, prosecutors and judges,* which has been developed within the framework of the European Union and the CoE joint project (CyberCrime@IPA project). This Guide is addressed to "countries that are developing their response to cybercrime and establishing rules and protocols to deal with electronic evidence and aims at providing support and guidance in the identification, handling and examination of electronic evidence."[207]

[3] Problems and Shortcomings of Digital Evidences

Despite the increasing elaboration of forensic tools, the capacity of investigators to forensically acquire and use digital evidences remains restricted. Investigators face steadily new challenges that relate not only to the need to comply with integrity, authenticity and continuity requirements but also to inherent characteristics of the digital environment. First, electronic evidence is invisible to the human eye or at least it is invisible to the untrained eye and in any case, it becomes visible often only indirectly and after appropriate procedures have been followed.[208]

---

context, a set of Guidelines that could be considered is the OLAF Guidelines on Digital Forensic Procedures aiming at establishing "rules for conducting digital forensic operations in a manner that ensures the integrity and the chain of custody of potential evidence to be admissible in administrative, disciplinary and judicial procedures." These internal rules are to be followed by OLAF staff with respect to the identification, acquisition, imaging, collection, analysis and preservation of digital evidence.

204. RAND Europe, *Handbook of Legislative Procedures of Computer and Network Misuse in EU Countries – Study for the European Commission,* Directorate-General Information Society (2002).
205. ISO/IEC 27037 *Guidelines for Identification, Collection, Acquisition, and Preservation of Digital Evidence* (2012), 27041 *Guidance on Assuring Suitability and Adequacy of Incident Investigative Methods* (2015), 27042 *Guidelines for the Analysis and Interpretation of Digital Evidence* (2015), 27043 *Incident Investigation Principles and Processes (2015).*
206. It is expected that standardization will (eventually) lead to the adoption of similar if not identical approaches internationally, making it easier to compare, combine and contrast the results of such investigations even when performed by different people or organizations and potentially across different jurisdictions, http://www.iso27001security.com/html/27037.html.
207. CyberCrime@IPA, *Electronic Evidence Guide – A Basic Guide for Police Officers, Prosecutors and Judges.*
208. ENISA, *Digital – Forensics Handbook,* 4. Also A. Nieman, *Cyberforensics: Bridging the Law/Technology Divide,* (1) J. Info. Law & Tech. (JILT) 19 (2009).

The vast and steadily augmenting storage capacities in combination the wide range of devices and the scope of evidence increases the complexity of digital forensics and burdens law enforcement authorities.[209] The process of identifying and capturing relevant forensics data becomes more complicate due to the variety of file formats, operating systems, application software and hardware particulars.[210] Each device may eventually necessitate a different process as well as different forensic tools and methods for collecting evidences.[211]

Taking into account the volatile nature of electronic evidences investigators have to face additional problems caused by delays on accessing the "crime scene" and/or on results, stemming from time-consuming processes in the forensics lab. In this context the notion of onsite forensics and mobile live memory forensic techniques is proposed to enable or facilitate the acquisition of volatile data, which reside in device's memory are gaining importance.[212]

The second major barrier to investigation and successful prosecution of cybercrime lies in the difficulty to attribute an act to an individual. The establishment of an uncontested link between captured electronic evidence and a person is especially difficult if there are multiple users of the device in seizure. Additional difficulties may also arise with regard to attribution of authorship of computer-stored information or the identification of communicating parties and/or involved offenders/attackers. Such problems may lead to uncertainties that could undermine the accuracy and reliability of electronic evidence[213] or—worse—they may implicate or exonerate mistakenly a person with serious impacts on her freedom and life. For this reason electronic evidence is usually supplemented by evidence obtained through traditional police investigations to demonstrate that evidence can be attributed to the offender and/or the device was under his/her control.[214]

209. Several countries by responding to UNODC Study Cybercrime questionnaire identified evidentiary issues as major obstacles to successful prosecution of cybercrime. Such issues include "the large volume of evidence," "the short period of time during which service providers store information needed for investigation purposes" and "maintaining integrity of electronic evidence from the time of seizure to the point of completion of the case," "failure to establish chain of custody of evidence," and lack of proper storage facilities to maintain evidence. UNODC, *Cybercrime Study, supra* n. 52, 169.
210. UNODC, *Cybercrime Study, supra* n. 52, 158.
211. For this reason, one of the principles recommended by the Evidence Guide is the so-called specialist support. Such a support needs to be requested as there are so many different systems and technical situations that it is almost impossible for a digital forensics expert to have the specific know-how on how to deal with all these sorts of electronic evidence.
212. A. Mylonas et al., *Dynamic Evidence Acquisition for Smartphone Forensics*, in *Proceedings of the 27th IFIP International Information Security and Privacy Conference*, Springer (IFIP AICT376), Greece (June 2012).
213. Uncertainties are regarded by some authors as a quite inherent characteristic of digital forensics. E. Casey states that when criminal activities on a computer network are being reconstructed using digital records, every aspect has some degree of error. The origin and time of the events, as well as who was responsible for the events, can be uncertain. Lost data can give an incomplete picture of the crime. It is even possible that an event never occurred but that a digital record was fabricated to misdirect investigators or implicate an innocent person. *See* E. Casey, *Error, Uncertainty, and Loss in Digital Evidence*, 1(2) Intl. J. Digital Evidence 2 (2002).
214. *See* Cameron S.D. Brown, *supra* n. 174, 86.

Presentation of collected evidence to the court is also of grave importance for its reliability and admissibility.[215] Legal systems are mostly tailored to traditional types of crime and evidentiary processes. The probative value of electronic evidence depends also upon the perceptions, attitudes and the (lack of) expertise of nontechnical stakeholders, such as the police, prosecutors, lawyers and the judges.

[C] Specific Forensics Categories

As noted in the comprehensive ENISA report, over time, the technical aspects of forensic investigations have evolved into subfields relating to the special conditions of the evidence involved, like toxicology, fingerprint analysis, etc. with digital forensics being the branch of forensic science encompassing the recovery and investigation of material found in digital devices.[216] Investigators, law enforcement authorities and judges are facing specific problems concerning the acquisition and use of electronic evidence that is to be gained either though smartphones devices or in cloud environments. These additional difficulties are due to the hybrid nature and functionality of new communication devices such as smartphones or the challenges posed by the inherent characteristics of cloud computing such as multiplicity of location sites.

[1] Network Forensics

Recently, the ENISA has presented a detailed study concerning a subbranch of digital forensics that seems to gain in importance: Network forensics is the subcategory that relates to the monitoring and analysis of computer network traffic for the purposes of information gathering, legal evidence or intrusion detection. Network forensics come to the epicenter of interest as it is no longer adequate to think about computers in isolation since computing has become network-centered as more people rely on e-mail, e-commerce and other network resources.[217] Forensics investigation are increasingly following the "cybertrails" to find related digital evidence on the public Internet, private networks, and other commercial systems.

The Report of ENISA categorizes the different types of network based evidence as following: (a) Full content data that it is every single piece of information that passes across a network (or networks); in this evidence collection process nothing is being filtered, exact copies of all the traffic (often called "packet captures") are being stored; (b) Session data, which usually consists of aggregated traffic metadata and usually refers to the conversation between two network entities, grouped together into "flows" and/or groups of network packets related to one another. (c) Alert data that are generated whenever network traffic triggers a predefined item of interest (such as a particular pattern of bytes, or counts of activity, or other characteristics); (d) Statistical data that provide the forensics analysts with network-related aspects such as the

215. P. Pichan et al., *supra* n. 166, 39.
216. ENISA, *Introduction to Network Forensics, Final*, January 2019, 10.
217. *Ibid.*

number of bytes contained in a packet trace, start and end times of network conversations, number of services and protocols being used, most and least active network nodes, average packet size, etc. that could be proved as a useful source for the so-called anomaly detection.

As in other cases of forensics, the general forensic and procedural principles have to be respected both to the access to electronic evidence and the possession thereof. According to ENISA, network forensics will inevitably collect privacy-related data, foremost IP addresses. Moreover, packet captures as well as log files may contain all kinds of data, including passwords, usernames, credit-card numbers, etc. The application of GDPR as well as of national laws implementing the Police (and Justice) Directive 2016/680/EU affect the conditions under which such data may be collected and stored, already due to the fact that an IP address is now explicitly considered as personal data.

[2] Smartphone Forensics

Since smartphones host a plethora of heterogeneous data generated from hardware or software sources, they offer law enforcement authorities "a treasure trove of evidence,"[218] creating a new branch/sector of digital forensics, the so-called smartphone forensics. "A smartphone[219] combines the features of a cell phone along with PC-like functionalities. It permits access to saved and sent messages and files and provides tools for accessing data not presently stored on the device."[220]

A smartphone offers law enforcement authorities "a window into their suspect,"[221] first via a rich set of evidences including: (a) *messaging data*, i.e., the content and metadata (e.g., sender, delivery time, etc.) from messaging services, (b) *device data*, i.e., data that are stored in the device storage media and are not related to any application (multimedia files, software and hardware identifiers, etc.), (c) *(U)SIM Card Data*, (d) *usage history data*, i.e., user logs (e.g., call logs, browsing history, etc.) and system logs kept for monitoring and debugging, (e) *application data*, i.e., permanent or temporal data that are used during application execution (e.g., flat files, databases, etc.), (f) *sensor data*, which are created by sensors that are found in most devices (e.g.,

218. S. Morrissey, *IOS Forensic Analysis: for IPhone, IPad and IPod Touch* 71 (Apress 2010).
219. The majority of smartphones, as well as feature phones, include multimedia hardware such as a microphone and camera (often a pair of front and back cameras), location sensors (i.e., Global Positioning System (GPS), motion sensors (i.e., accelerometer, gyroscope) and environmental sensors (e.g. magnetometer, proximity, light, temperature, pressure). Spyware authors have already used smartphone sensors in order to acquire context awareness either for research reasons, or for commercial ones, for instance spyware software used for family affairs (e.g., FlexiSPY2).
220. A. Mylonas et al., *supra* n. 183.
221. S. Morrissey, *supra* n. 218.

camera, microphone, Global Positioning System (GPS)), motion sensors (accelerometer, gyroscope), or environment sensors (magnetometer, proximity, light, temperature, etc.) and (g) *user input data*, i.e., data from keystrokes, gestures, etc., which are processed on the fly, or stored in a keyboard cache for performance reasons.[222]

Furthermore law enforcement authorities may gain information and insight into valuable information, concerning the character, the habits and the context of a—eventually law infringing and punishable—behavior. With the increasing use of such devices for every kind of communications, including social networking, the importance of digital evidence gathering is increasing as well. A smartphone itself, alone or in its technical networking, can contain personal data to such a degree and in such diversity that it may provide a revealing picture of her personality, and/or facilitate insight even into the core area of private life of a person.[223]

Even if in some jurisdictions[224] there are no conceptual differences between searching a person's body and searching electronic equipment that this person possesses or carries with, a smartphone stores and reveals apparently and tremendously more information, thereby providing law enforcement with access to information that a person would never carry in her pocket.[225] In this perspective, the acquisition of evidence through a smartphone is comparable to a search of premises.[226]

[3] Cloud Forensics

When carrying out forensic investigation in cloud environments,[227] basic legal principles and processes have to be respected. Cloud-derived evidence must have all the

222. A. Mylonas et al., *supra* n. 183.
223. Alexios Mylonas, Vasilis Meletiadis, Lilian Mitrou, and Dimitris Gritzalis, *Smartphone Sensor Data as Digital Evidence*, available at: http://www2.aueb.gr/users/amylonas/docs/cosef.pdf.
224. As in the case of the attachment of a GPS device to the defendant's vehicle the acquiring of information through smartphones sensors and applications is much more intrusive. In USA the Supreme Court upheld in the case *United States v. Jones* (2012) the D.C. Circuit finding that an attachment of a GPS device to the defendant's vehicle to monitor the vehicle's movements constituted a search under the Fourth Amendment and should be subject to a warrant. *See* M. Reid, *United States v. Jones: Big Brother and the "Common Good" Versus the Fourth Amendment and Your Right to Privacy*, available at: https://papers.ssrn.com/sol3/papers.cfm?abstract_id =2291997 (2012).
225. A. Gershowitz, *The iPhone Meets the Fourth Amendment*, available at: http://works.bepress.com/adam_gershowitz/3 (2008).
226. A. Wiebke, Agents, *Trojans and Tags: The Next Generation of Investigators*, 23(1-2) Intl. Rev. L., Computers & Tech. 99 (2009). The German Constitutional Court has (2008) placed strict limits upon the ability law enforcement authorities to remotely access computers, PDAs and mobile phones. The Court has specified the rights to "informational self-determination" and "absolute protection of the core area of the private conduct of life" and has lifted "security and integrity of information systems" as a fundamental right of the user, expressing a right to the unhampered development of her personality in the information era. A. Wiebe, *The New Fundamental Right to IT Security—First Evaluation and Comparative View at the U.S.*, Datenschutz und Datensicherheit, 713 et seq. (2008).
227. The commonly referred definition of Cloud computing is this given by the US National Institute of Standards and Technology (NIST) as "a model for enabling convenient, on-demand network access to a shared pool of configurable computing resources (e.g., networks, servers, storage, applications, and services) that can be rapidly provisioned and released with minimal management effort or service provider interaction." *See* P. Mell & T. Grance, *The NIST*

attributes of conventional evidence. However, it seems that forensics experts face specific legal challenges, when identifying, labeling, recording and acquiring forensic data in the cloud. Where cloud-derived material is obtained, its admissibility as evidence and evidential weight may be challenged not only on the basis of the conduct of investigators in the course of gathering such material but also the quality of the forensic process itself, which will depend in large part on peculiarities/specificities of cloud computing systems.

In the early stages of cloud computing, investigations on cloud environments were based on methodologies and tools from the digital forensic field. Rapid advances in cloud computing have required new methodologies, frameworks and tools for performing digital forensics in cloud environments. *Cloud computing forensic science* is the application of scientific principles, technological practices and derived and proven methods to reconstruct past cloud computing events through identification, collection, preservation, examination, interpretation and reporting of digital evidence.[228]

Forensics experts face specific legal challenges, when identifying, labeling, recording and acquiring forensic data in the cloud, as they have to differentiate their tools and procedures in accordance to the cloud service model.[229] The identification of evidence in cloud environments itself is a difficult process due to the different deployment and service models.[230] Difficulties may arise due to uncertainty as to the characterization of the evidence being "at rest" or "in transmission," or the entities against which such powers may be exercised as cloud computing involves usually also a lot of subcontractors.

Additional difficulties are related to the centralization of storage as well as to shared tenancy of physical hardware, two inherent characteristics of cloud computing.[231] Another challenge for investigation and evidence gathering concerns the ephemeral and ethereal nature of the cloud: infrastructure and services can be utilized on demand and often repurposed for other cloud customers.[232]

Perhaps the most important issue is that the evidence can reside everywhere in the world in a virtualization environment. While cloud is borderless the investigation and prosecution of crime and lawsuits are strictly related to territorial sovereignty and

---

Definition of Cloud Computing, NIST, accessible at https://nvlpubs.nist.gov/nistpubs/Legacy/SP/nistspecialpublication800-145.pdf (2009).

228. A working definition for cloud forensics proposed by Ruan et al. defines cloud forensics as the application of digital forensic science in cloud environments. *See* K. Ruan et al., *Cloud Forensics: An Overview*, in *Advances in Digital Forensics* 7, 36 (2011).

229. The identification of evidence is apparently more difficult in public cloud provisioned for use by the general public than in a private cloud environment where cloud infrastructure is used explicitly by a single organization.

230. Simou et al., *supra* n. 167.

231. Cloud resources are shared to serve multiple cloud clients by the use of a multitenant model. These physical and virtual resources are dynamically assigned and reassigned according to demand. P. Balboni, *Data Protection and Data Security Issues Related to Cloud Computing in the EU*, TILBURG University legal Studies Working Paper series, accessible at http://ssrn.com/abstract=1661437 (2010).

232. N. Marangos et al., *Digital Forensics in the Cloud Computing Era*, First International Workshop on Management and Security Technologies for Cloud Computing, IEEE 779 (2012).

territorially defined jurisdiction: search and seizure warrants refer to the geographical scope of the warrant issued by a judge or a court authorizing access to digital data.

Location is of outmost importance, as it determines not only the applicable law and the competent law enforcement authorities but also the rights of suspects. The "loss of location" leads to significant incertitude with regard to the place where sought computer data—evidence are stored. It may become impossible for a national agency to confiscate "a cloud" for seizure given pending advances around long distance hypervisor migration[233] and the fact that physical servers are spread across different countries.[234]

[4] Internet of Things Forensics

The emergence and the increasing intrusion of Internet of Things[235] (IoT) in everyday life give rise to a new category of forensics, the so-called IoT forensics. On the one side, smart devices and sensors may help in providing a lot of evidence, as motion detection, location, etc. IoT poses new challenges for digital investigators when they encounter IoT devices in criminal scenes. On the other side the explosive growth of smart objects and their dependency on wireless technologies for communication increases the vulnerability of IoT to cyber attacks:[236] the IoT technology can create more opportunities for cybercrimes to attack areas, such as smart city, medical care, social domains, smart home and smart vehicle, resulting in a direct impact on users.

IoT devices are directly associated with objects in our daily lives. Like smartphones, digital evidence pertaining to IoT devices is a rich and relatively unexplored domain. From the forensic perspective, each IoT device will provide important artifacts that could help in the investigation process.[237] The sources of evidence in IoT forensics include home appliances, cars, medical implants, sensor nodes and tag readers, etc. Unlike in traditional forensics wherein data is mostly available in an electronic document or standard file formats, regarding types of evidence data, IoT data can be available in any vendor-specific format.[238]

233. ENISA, *Cloud Computing Benefits, Risks and Recommendations for Information Security*, 45 (2009).
234. K. Ruan et al., *supra* n. 228, 7, 40 (2011).
235. The concept of the Internet of Things (IoT) refers to an infrastructure in which billions of sensors embedded in common, everyday devices—"things" as such, or things linked to other objects or individuals—are designed to record, process, store and transfer data and, as they are associated with unique identifiers, interact with other devices or systems using networking capabilities.
236. *See* I. Yaqooba, I.A.T. Hashemb, A. Ahmed, S.A. Kazmia & C. Seon Honga, *Internet of Things Forensics: Recent Advances, Taxonomy, Requirements and Open Challenges*, 92 Future Generation Computer Systems, 265–275, at 265 (March 2019).
237. Saad Alabdulsalam, Kevin Schaefer, Tahar Kechadi and Nhien-An Le- Khac, Alabdulsalam S., Schaefer K., Kechadi T. & Le-Khac NA., *Internet of Things Forensics – Challenges and a Case Study*, in: Peterson G. & Shenoi S. (eds), *Advances in Digital Forensics XIV*. Digital Forensics, IFIP Advances in Information and Communication Technology, vol 532. Springer, Cham, 35–48, at 36 (2018).
238. *Ibid.*, 38 (2018).

As underlined by many authors,[239] IoT forensics investigation involves many challenges due to the nonsuitability of currently available digital forensics tools and standard forensics methodologies in the IoT environment.[240] Furthermore, as most of IoT data are stored in the cloud, forensics will face some of the problems of collecting evidence from the cloud. If technical challenges refer to the diversity of data formats, limited visibility, short "survival" period of evidences and lack of real-time log analysis solutions, IoT forensics pose also serious informational privacy concerns.

As emphasized by the Article 29 Data Protection Working Party, the IoT relies on the principle of the extensive processing of data through these sensors that are designed to communicate unobtrusively and exchange data in a seamless way, it is closely linked to the notions of "pervasive" and "ubiquitous" computing.[241] According to Article 29 DPWP IoT could go as far as develop a form of surveillance of individuals that might be considered as unlawful under EU law. Specific IoT forensics procedures should be adopted to ensure that during investigation, special attention is paid to principles related to data quality and limitation of use, retention and disclosure and in general the data privacy compliance of the system.[242]

§2.05 PERSONAL DATA PROTECTION AND THE LEGAL STATUS OF THE IP ADDRESS

The enforcement of the legislation on cybercrime and, more precisely, the issue of collection and use of evidence in criminal proceedings related to cybercrime, are of high importance in the fight against cybercriminality. The identification of cyber criminals is based on digital evidence. The IP address constitutes, therefore, a crucial source of identification of cybercriminals. Of course, other enforcement methods can be used with parsimony, such as the example of the infiltration of the Tor network by the FBI in order to shut down the Silkroad 2.0 website.[243]

---

239. *See* among others Áine MacDermott, Thar Baker & Qi Shi, *IoT Forensics: Challenges For The IoA Era*, 9th IFIP International Conference on New Technologies, Mobility and Security (NTMS), 2018, 1-5.

240. Due to these challenges, other authors regard IoT forensics as a "Myth" or not mature enough. However, they do recognize also that IoT forensics is an essential topic, and its importance will increase with every passing day. *See* B. Karabacak, K. Aydin & A. Igonor, *IOT Forensics Curriculum: Is It a Myth or Reality?*, Annual ADFSL Conference on Digital Forensics, Security and Law (2019).

241. *See* Article 29 Data Protection Working Party, Opinion 8/2014on the on Recent Developments on the Internet of Things, 4.

242. *See* A. Nieto, R. Rios & J. Lopez, *IoT-Forensics Meets Privacy: Towards Cooperative Digital Investigations*, Sensors 2018, 18, 492; https://doi.org/10.3390/s18020492.

243. *See* Alistair Charlton, *Silk Road 2.0 Agent Within: How the FBI Infiltrated Illegal Drug Website and Shut it Down*, at: http://www.ibtimes.co.uk/silk-road-2-0-agent-within-how-fbi-infiltrated-illegal-drug-website-shut-it-down-1473705 (Nov. 7, 2014); Donna Leinwand Leger, *How FBI Brought Down Cyber-Underworld Site Silk Road*, at: http://www.usatoday.com/story/news/nation/2013/10/21/fbi-cracks-silk-road/2984921/ (May 15, 2014).

But in the majority of cases, a significant trace of a cyber attack takes the form of the IP address.[244] As it is stated in the U.S. Department of Justice Special Report on "Investigations Involving the Internet and Computer Networks": "All communications on the Internet and across networks rely on an IP address to reach their destination. The key to investigating crimes relating to the Internet and networks is to identify the originating IP address and trace it to a source. These skills enable an investigator to locate additional sources of evidence, corroborate victim and witness statements, and potentially locate a suspect."[245]

ICANN allocates IP addresses to ISPs, who decide to attribute it either dynamically or statically (most of the times a static IP address costs more, but permits the user to create a personal server). ISPs have the obligation to keep the log of the IP addresses allocated to their subscribers at any given time. The real identity of a person connected to the Internet can be ascertained, consequently, by analyzing the ISP log which had a specific IP address at a specific moment.[246] The use of the IP address as digital evidence raises the question of Internet surveillance, thus the interception of communications associated with a suspect, and of the disclosure by the ISPs of information about their customers.

The issue of the legal nature of the IP address does not concern only cyber attacks, but also cybercrimes, such as child pornography, intellectual property enforcement, libel, etc., and more broadly the application of legal rules to the Internet. Indeed, without the identification of the perpetrator of a criminal activity, no repression can occur and, in the end, no law exists.

As shown in the following, a lot of uncertainty exists whether and under which circumstances the IP address shall be considered as personal data. Indeed, the IP address cannot always lead with certainty to the identity of the natural person who committed a cybercrime. Problems arise in general when the same computer device is shared by many natural persons without registration and identification prior to any use. This can occur under many circumstances, such as the use of the same computer device by the employees of a company or in Internet cafes, public libraries, universities or in an open wireless network, VPN or Tor exit relay[247] used by any number of people.

244. Computers on the Internet recognize each other through IP addresses. Each computer connected to the Internet has its own IP address that is allocated to it permanently or temporarily. The IP address has the form of a series of numbers. *See* G. Smith, *Internet Law and Regulation*, 148 (4th edn, Thomson, Sweet & Maxwell 2007).

245. Alberto R. Gonzales, Regina B. Schofield, David W. Hagy, US Department of Justice, Special Report on Investigations Involving the Internet and Computer Networks, January 2007, 15, available at: https://www.ncjrs.gov/pdffiles1/nij/210798.pdf.

246. For tracing a suspect, it is sometimes necessary for an investigator to connect his computer to that of a suspect in order to derive its IP address. The ISP typically holds a log of which customer had ISP address at what time in what is called a RADIUS log. An investigator who has obtained an IP address of a suspect will first have to identify the ISP who owns it—which can be done via a general Internet resource—and then ask the ISP to identify their customer. *See* Peter Sommer, *Evidence in Internet Paedophilia Cases*, Computer & Telecommunications L. Rev. 183 (2002).

247. An exit relay is the last computer that Tor traffic goes through before it reaches its destination. Since Tor traffic exits through these computers, their IP addresses may be misinterpreted as being the origin of the traffic, although the exit node operator is neither the true origin of that

In some cases, these obstacles to the identification of the natural person behind the computer device can be lifted by the overlap with other information,[248] while in other cases identification on the grounds of the IP address might not be possible. This will normally be the case of IP address spoofing, which permits either the falsification of the IP address from where the packets come from or its replacement with another IP address in order to commit a cyber attack.

The discussion on the legal status of the IP address becomes complex, given the concurrent application of the regime of protection of the secrecy of communication to IP addresses. Indeed, as it will be shown in the following paragraphs, the IP address appears to have a double identity, since it could be cumulatively applied to it the legal qualification of personal data and of an exterior element of a communication, which is protected by the rule of confidentiality of communications.

[A] The Double Nature of the IP Address in EU Privacy Law

The double identity that seems to be allocated by EU privacy law to IP addresses results in the concurrent application of different legal sources and norms, which complicates even more the question of the determination of the legal nature of the IP address and, therefore, interferes with law enforcement.

[1] The IP Address and Personal Data Protection

The legal qualification of the nature of the IP address, and more precisely, the question whether IP addresses are personal data, to which the protective regime of the EU data protection legislation applies, has been debated in doctrine and case law since the adoption of the Data Protection Directive in 1995.[249]

Indeed, the flexible definition of personal data in Directive 95/46/EC leaves the door open for an interpretation in favor of the qualification of IP addresses as personal data. In practice, this approach has also been followed by national courts. Nonetheless, there has also been a significant stream of case law resisting the application of the legal regime of personal data to IP addresses.[250] The main argument favoring such an approach has been that an IP address is a series of numbers, which is by no means a

---

traffic nor able to identify the user who is. *See* M. Hoffman, *Why IP Addresses Alone Don't Identify Criminals*, Electronic Frontier Foundation, available at: https://www.eff.org/ (Aug. 24, 2011).

248. M. Cahen, *L'adresse IP est-elle une donnée personnelle?*, available at: https://www.murielle-cahen.com/publications/p_donnees3.asp (2015).

249. Directive 95/46/EC of the European Parliament and of the Council of Oct. 24, 1995 on the protection of individuals with regard to the processing of personal data and on the free movement of such data, OJ L 281, 23/11/1995, pp. 0031-0050.

250. For a general overview, *see* Timelex, *Study of Case Law on the Circumstances in Which IP Addresses are Considered Personal Data*, Final Report (May 2, 2011).

personal data related to a person, in so far as it relates to a machine and not to the individual who uses the computer.[251]

According to Article 2(a) of Directive 95/46/EC, personal data is defined as:

> any information relating to an identified or identifiable natural person ("data subject"); an identifiable person is one who can be identified, directly or indirectly, in particular by reference to an identification number or to one or more factors specific to his physical, physiological, mental, economic, cultural or social identity.

Moreover, according to Recital 26 of the Directive, "account should be taken of all the means likely reasonably to be used either by the controller or by any other person to identify the said person."

So, a central element of this definition is the ability of information to reveal the identity of the person to whom the information is relating, regardless of whether this identification is done directly or indirectly.

Although the IP address is allocated to a specific device, it is able to disclose the identity of the user of the device at a later stage when combined with other elements, such as the traffic data (the user login and the log files). Thus, it could be argued that the IP address falls within the category of information that can lead indirectly to the identity of an Internet user.[252] On the other hand, it shall not be forgotten that the IP address, strictly speaking, does not identify a natural person, but a specific network device, and is generally issued only temporarily. Thus, a very narrow reading of Recital 26 might lead to the opposite finding, namely that the IP address typically cannot be used to identify a natural person, but only to establish and log electronic communication between two network devices.[253]

The Article 29 Working Party 4/2007[254] calls for a broad, flexible and nonliteral interpretation of Recital 26 of Directive 95/46. In order to determine "all the means likely reasonably to be used" to identify the persons, the purpose pursued by the data controller in the data processing is of great importance. As the Opinion states, "in fact, to argue that individuals are not identifiable, where the purpose of the processing is precisely to identify them, would be a sheer contradiction in terms. Therefore, the

251. *See, for example,* Cour d'appel de paris, 13ème chambre, section A, 15 mai 2007, *Monsieur H. S. c/ ministère Public, Société civile des producteurs phonographiques,* n° RG 06/01954, available at: http://www.forumInternet.org. For similar argumentation in the US, *see* the order of the US District Court Southern District of Florida, Mar. 19, 2014 in respect of the processing of IP addresses from alleged BitTorrent pirates in conjunction with the use of geo-location software in order to pinpoint the right location (residential address, and not a public hotspot): "There is nothing that links the IP address location to the identity of the person actually downloading and viewing Plaintiff's videos, and establishing whether that person lives in this district."

252. J. Frayssinet, in: Lucas, Frayssinet, Deveze, *Droit de l'informatique et de l'Internet* 78 (PUF 2001).

253. Timelex, *Study of Case Law on the Circumstances in which IP Addresses are Considered Personal Data,* Final Report (May 2, 2011).

254. Article 29 Working Party, *Opinion 4/2007 on the concept of personal data,* WP 136, Jun. 20, 2007, available online at: http://ec.europa.eu/justice/policies/privacy/docs/wpdocs/2007/wp136_en.pdf.

information should be considered as relating to identifiable individuals and the processing should be subject to data protection rule."

Having established this principle of teleological interpretation, the Working Party focuses on the specific case study of dynamic IP addresses. First, it briefly explains the identification of uncertainties, which might arise from some sorts of IP addresses, such as in the case of IP addresses attributed to a computer in an Internet café, where no identification of the customers is requested. In this case, it could be argued that the data collected on the use of a computer during a certain timeframe does not allow for the identification of the user with reasonable means, and therefore it is not personal data. Nonetheless, as the Working Party states, "the Internet Service Providers will most probably not know either whether the IP address in question is one allowing identification or not, and that they will process the data associated with that IP in the same way as they treat information associated with IP addresses of users that are duly registered and are identifiable."

Subsequently, the Working Party refers to its earlier finding to the Opinion of 2000, on the issue of the legal qualification of IP addresses:

> Internet access providers and managers of local area networks can, using reasonable means, identify Internet users to whom they have attributed IP addresses as they normally systematically "log" in a file the date, time, duration and dynamic IP address given to the Internet user. The same can be said about Internet Service Providers that keep a logbook on the HTTP server. In these cases there is no doubt about the fact that one can talk about personal data in the sense of Article 2a of the Directive ... .

Finally, it comes to a clear conclusion that favors the qualification of IP address as personal data in case of doubt: "unless the Internet Service Provider is in a position to distinguish with absolute certainty that the data correspond to users that cannot be identified, it will have to treat all IP information as personal data, to be on the safe side."

The question of the legal qualification of the IP address has also been discussed in 2008, in the Article 29 Working Party's Opinion on data protection issues related to search engines.[255] The Working Party first affirmed that an IP address is a kind of data, which is processed by search engines. Then, it confirmed that IP addresses may lead to the identification of individuals. As it was explained:

> an individual's search history is personal data if the individual to which it relates, is identifiable. Though IP addresses in most cases are not directly identifiable by search engines, identification can be achieved by a third party. Internet access providers hold IP address data. Law enforcement and national security authorities can gain access to these data and in some Member States private parties have gained access also through civil litigation. Thus, in most cases - including cases with dynamic IP address allocation - the necessary data will be available to identify the user(s) of the IP address.

255. Article 29 Working Party, *Opinion 1/2008 on data protection issues related to search engines*, WP 148, available at: http://ec.europa.eu/justice/policies/privacy/docs/wpdocs/2008/wp148_en.pdf (Apr. 4, 2008).

Finally, the finding of Opinion WP 136 on the definition of personal data also applies to search engines, stating that:

> unless the Internet Service Provider is in a position to distinguish with absolute certainty that the data correspond to users that cannot be identified, it will have to treat all IP information as personal data, to be on the safe side.

This view has also been affirmed in Opinion 1/2009 on the proposals amending Directive 2002/58/EC on privacy and electronic communications, where it is further explained that:

> IP addresses relate to identifiable persons in most cases. Identifiability means identifiable by the access provider or by other means, with the help of additional identifiers such as cookies or in interactions with internet services with which the data subject is identified explicitly or implicitly.[256]

The impact of the authoritative view of the Article 29 Working party on the determination of the legal nature of the IP address in the national law of EU Member States is undeniable. Two main tendencies appear.

On the one hand, a more absolute approach classifying all IP addresses as personal data is a matter of standard practice. This maximalist approach is illustrated in France, where for some time in the past the debate was focused on the possibility to consider the IP address not simply as personal data, but as sensitive personal data related to offenses, criminal convictions or security measures, which require more rigorous processing rules. The issue was finally decided by the French Supreme Court (*Cour de Cassation*), which stated that IP addresses are not sensitive data, but indirect personal data.[257]

On the other hand, a more vigilant approach, favoring the application of the personal data regime on a case-by-case basis depending on the circumstances of each case and particularly on the availability of additional information that would allow the dynamic or static IP address to be associated to an individual should be favored.[258] In this view, IP addresses are technical data which are inherently incapable to provide identification.

Nonetheless, their processing combined with other information render IP addresses indirect personal data. This approach appears to be more consistent with the technical complexity of the IP address. Although the IP address is often paralleled to the telephone number or the registration number of a car, the capability of the IP address to provide identification is much more limited than in the aforementioned cases. While the combination of the telephone number with other information can be easily

256. Article 29 Working Party, *Opinion 1/2009 on the Proposals Amending Directive 2002/58/EC on Privacy and Electronic Communications*, available at: https://ec.europa.eu/justice/article-29/documentation/opinion-recommendation/files/2009/wp159_en.pdf.
257. Cour de Cassation (crim.), Jan. 13, 2009, n 08-84088. *See* C. Castets-Renard, *Droit de l'Internet: Droit français et européen*, 88–89 (Montchrestien, Lextenso editions 2012).
258. Timelex, *Study of Case Law on the Circumstances in Which IP Addresses are Considered Personal Data*, Final Report (May 2, 2011).

obtained through easily accessible sources, such as a telephone directory, in the case of IP addresses there is not any general directory of IP addresses available.

Furthermore, it is not possible to directly access an individual via the IP address as in the case of telephone number, where with a simple phone call privacy intrusion occurs. The IP address does not allow setting a similar relationship, since the machine-to-machine communication only allows in principle to verify the connection from the computer to the network.[259] Nonetheless, the matching of the IP address with other information renders it personal data, since it enables the identification. In this context, a simple IP address associated with relevant traffic data is sufficient to also be covered by the data breach notification obligation.[260] Similarly, when a static IP address is used in a private network the data controller could identify at least the computer associated with that IP address and, as a result, that IP address could be considered as personal data relating to the regular user of that computer.[261]

Although the two main tendencies follow a different line of thinking, they permit the rather easy qualification of IP addresses as personal data. The possibility of the combination of IP addresses with other information, and the fact that they can potentially be accessed by law enforcement and national security agencies, favors the qualification of IP addresses as personal data.

For some commentators, this argumentation creates an intriguing "data protection limbo."[262] Indeed, the application of the regime of personal data to IP addresses has significant consequences in the field of digital evidence. If IP addresses are considered personal data indistinctively in any case, then their simple collection prior to any combination and conjunction with other information is subject to personal data processing rules and cannot be conducted without a judicial order. Nonetheless, this absolute approach might seriously impede the collection of digital evidence.

An interesting illustration is the Cypriot case *General Attorney v. Isaia and others*. The case was about a Facebook profile in which injurious statements against the holder of the profile were made via hacking. The victim found the IP address of the computer from which the account was hacked and delivered this evidence to the police, who matched this information with data provided by ISPs for filing an accusation. When the question of the legal status of the IP address was raised by the defense, the Court considered that the collection of the IP address privately by the victim without a judicial order was illegal personal data processing and dismissed the accusation. On appeal, this decision was reversed. The main argument was that the IP address is public data and its collection from the victim did not require a judicial order permitting this processing. An IP address becomes personal data only when the ISP has to reveal

259. de Frédéric Lecomte, Marie-Hélène Lemaitre, *Inconnue juridique à cette adresse (IP), Ou les affres du débat autour de la qualification de donnée à caractère personnel de l'adresse IP*, Expertises (May 2008).
260. Kristof Van Quathem, *Security Breach Notification in the European Union: First Step taken, More to Come*, 01/10 World Data Protection Report, 19 (2010).
261. Graham J.H. Smith, *Internet Law and Regulation* 696 (4th edn, Sweet & Maxwell 2007).
262. Eneken Tikk, *IP Addresses Subject to Data Protection Regulation*, in *International Cyber Security Legal and Policy Proceedings* (E. Tikk & A.M. Taliharm, NATO Cooperative Cyber Defense Center of Excellence 2010).

the identity of the individual behind a specific IP address. Since the ISP revealed the identity of the person to whom the specific IP address was allocated on the grounds of a judicial order, the processing of the IP address was legal.[263]

Similarly, the French Court of Appeal of Rennes has recently confirmed that IP addresses are not necessarily personal data even indirectly, since they refer to a computer and not to an individual. In this context, it was held that the collection and preservation of IP addresses referring to computers connected to the internal network of a company, in order to later discover the persons who accessed the company's internal network, does not constitute processing of personal data, provided that there is no link between the IP addresses and any natural persons.[264] This decision, however, contradicts another recent decision of a French Court, in which a bank was condemned for having communicated to a client the log files related to her account, since the files comprised also of IP addresses.[265]

Clarifying the legal status of the IP address is essential for the legitimate processing of IP addresses and their use as evidence in cybercrime investigation. National courts have been struggling for years to provide adequate answers but, as it seems, no homogenous answers have been given. The uncertainties surrounding the legal status of IP addresses as personal data shall be dealt with by the European Court of Justice (CJEU), in order to arrive to harmonized and consistent findings.

Thus, the preliminary reference filed in October 28, 2014, by the German Federal Court of Justice (GFCJ) in respect to the question of whether an IP address constitutes personal data under the EU Data Protection Directive 95/46/EC is more than welcome.[266] The German court referred the question to the CJEU for a preliminary ruling, in connection with a case that arose in 2008, when a German citizen challenged the German federal government's storage of the dynamic IP addresses of users on government websites.[267]

In the case pending at the GFCJ, the plaintiff, a German politician and data protection activist, seeks an order against the Federal Republic of Germany to desist from storing his assigned dynamic IP addresses beyond the end of use of government websites. On most German government websites, the users' IP addresses are stored together with the name of the website and the time of the request. The government stores this data in log files beyond the termination of the actual use of the website, in order to repulse hacker attacks, and to enable the prosecution of attackers. The plaintiff argues that the assigned IP addresses can be linked to him, and therefore qualify as personal data, therefore the recording and storage of the IP addresses required his

263. Supreme Court, *General Attorney v. Isaia and others*, Jul. 7, 2014, available online at: www.cylaw.org.
264. CA Rennes, ch. com., Apr. 28, 2015, n°14/05708, *SARL Cabinet Peterson c/SARL Groupe Logisneuf, SARL C-Invest, SARL European Soft*. For a commentary, *see* Éric Caprioli, *Données à caractère personnel et sécurité de l'information*, Communication Commerce électronique, 46–47 (July 2015). *See also* CA Paris, 13e ch. Corr., 15 mai 2007, n°06/01954 Juris Data n°2007-336454.
265. TGI Paris, réf., Jul. 7, 2014, Communication Commerce électronique, comm., 81 (2014).
266. CJEU Case C-582/14.
267. *See* http://juris.bundesgerichtshof.de/cgi-bin/rechtsprechung/document.py?Gericht=bgh&Art=pm&Datum=2014&Sort=3&nr=69184&pos=0&anz=152.

explicit consent.[268] The central argument of the German state was that the logs to its websites were justified by the purposes of preventing and blocking network attacks, since the logs could be used in the context of criminal prosecution of cyber attackers.

The citizen's claim was initially rejected by the court of first instance. The claim was granted, however, by the court of second instance to the extent that it referred to the storage of IP addresses after the users left the relevant government websites. Subsequently, both parties appealed the decision to the GFCJ.

The GFCJ has suspended the proceedings and referred two questions to the CJEU. The first is whether, under Article 2A of the EU Data Protection Directive, an IP address is personal data (i.e., any information relating to an identified or identifiable natural person), when the IP address is stored by an ISP and a third party (e.g., the ISP) possesses sufficient additional data to identify the user. Indeed, it is questionable whether a dynamic IP address is personal data in cases where the plaintiff did not provide further personal information to the recipient that would enable his identification based on the assigned IP address. This happened to the pending case, since the government authorities had no access to such information. Furthermore, the plaintiff's Internet access provider was not permitted to transfer any such information on the plaintiff's identity to the defendant.[269]

The second question is whether the EU Data Protection Directive is contrary to a provision of the German Telemedia Act, which provides that a website provider may collect and process the personal data of users without their consent, only to the extent that is necessary to enable the general functionality of the website or to arrange payment.[270] In this context, it could be argued that storing the logs for the prevention and repression of cyber attacks falls within the general purpose of the functionality of the website, since a Denial of Service attack could paralyze the website and, consequently, prevent any access of the users to the networked system.[271]

According to section 12 of the German Telemedia Act, a service provider may only collect and use IP addresses (assuming they qualify as personal data) without the users' prior approval to the extent that the Telemedia Act, or another statutory provision referring expressly to the Telemedia Act, permits it. In that case, IP addresses were stored in order to ensure and maintain the security and functionality of the government websites. However, the German Federal Court has doubts whether this is sufficient for permission under section 15 of the Telemedia Act.[272] Specifically, assuming that IP addresses qualify as personal data even though the information which is necessary for the identification is held by ISPs and not by the websites' administrators, their processing continued even after the data subject left the website. So, it has

268. Martin Munz & Markus Mette, *Are Dynamic IP Addresses "Personal Data"? German Federal Court of Justice seeks advice from the European Court of Justice*, at: http://www.whitecase.com/articles/122014/are-dynamic-ip-addresses-personal-data/#.VJBgzsnLJpk (December 2014).
269. Martin Munz & Markus Mette, *ibid.*
270. Hunton & Williams LLP, *German Court Asks European Court of Justice if IP Addresses are Personal Data*, Privacy and Information Security Law Blog, at: https://www.huntonprivacyblog.com/2014/11/articles/german-court-asks-european-court-justice-ip-addresses-personal-data/ (Nov. 6, 2014).
271. *Case C-582/14, Breyer – Seeing the logs from the trees in privacy law*, EU Law Radar.
272. Martin Munz & Markus Mette, *supra* n. 268.

been essential to check further whether the processing taking place after the use of the website could still be justified by the exception of Article 7(f) of the Data Directive (Directive 95/46/EC)[273] which in this context should be interpreted as also covering general web security purposes.[274] The extension of the exception's scope in order to recognize as a data controller's legitimate interest the security of the website or the network does not comply with the principle of restrictive interpretation of the Data Directive's exceptions in Case C-468/10 *ASNEF*.[275]

In the meantime, the current version of the Proposal for a Regulation on the protection of individuals with regard to the processing of personal data adopts in this respect, the concept of "online identifiers."[276] Indeed, Article 4 of the EU Regulation states that "personal data means any information related to an identified or identifiable natural person 'data subject'; an identifiable person is a one who can be identified, directly or indirectly, in particular by reference to an identifier such as name, an identification number, location data, online identifier, or to one or more factors specific to the physical, physiological, genetic, mental, economic, cultural or social identity of the person."

Furthermore, according to Recital 24 of the EU Regulation:

> individuals may be associated with online identifiers provided by their devices, applications, tools and protocols, such as Internet Protocol addresses, cookie identifiers or other identifiers such as Radio Frequency Identification tags. This may leave traces which, in particular when combined with unique identifiers and other information received by the servers, may be used to create profiles of the individuals and identify them." [277] The current provision of the recital 24 differs significantly from a previous version of the Proposal [278] which seemed to embrace a case by case evaluation of the legal status of IP addresses as persona data. [279]

In this context, the coupling of the IP address with other data in the possession of third parties, namely ISPs, for the identification of data subjects, will still be considered as personal data processing. In the meanwhile, despite the clear classification of the IP address as an "online identifier," significant questions still pose interpretative and

273. According to this provision, "Member States shall provide that personal data may be processed only if: ...(f) processing is necessary for the purposes of the legitimate interests pursued by the controller or by the third party or parties to whom the data are disclosed, except where such interests are overridden by the interests for fundamental rights and freedoms of the data subject which require protection under Article 1(1)."
274. *Supra* n. 271.
275. *Asociación Nacional de Establecimientos Financieros de Crédito (ASNEF)* (C-468/10) and *Federación de Comercio Electrónico y Marketing Directo (FECEMD) v. Administración del Estado,* (C-469/10) Judgment of the Court (Third Chamber), paragraphs 29–32 (Nov. 24, 2011).
276. Éric Caprioli, *Données à caractère personnel et sécurité de l'information,* Communication Commerce électronique, 47 (July 2015).
277. For the draft text of the Regulation on Dec. 15, 2015, *see* https://www.lawspot.gr/sites/default/files/images/nea/misc/proposal-eudatap-regulation-final-compromise.pdf.
278. Proposal for a Regulation of the European Parliament and of the Council on the protection of individuals with regard to the processing of personal data and on the free movement of such data (General Data Protection Regulation) (COM/2012/011 final - 2012/0011 (COD)).
279. Indeed, Recital 24 stated that, "It follows that identification numbers, location data, online identifiers or other specific factors as such need not necessarily be considered as personal data in all circumstances."

judicial conundrums. For example, shall website or network traffic monitoring in order to detect anomalies and prevent possible attacks be subject to the personal data processing rules?[280] Shall a distinction be made between real-time monitoring and monitoring which is combined with IP addresses storage? In this respect, the IP legal status saga will not cease.

[2] The IP Address and the Secrecy of Communications

The legal status of the IP address is complemented by the qualification of IP address as an external component of private electronic communications under the light of the protection of confidentiality of communications. In this context, the main legal challenges do not concern the legal qualification of the IP address, but the proper calibration of the confidentiality of the IP address with other conflicting interests, such as national security and crime repression.

Directive 2002/58/EC provides the definition of "traffic data." "Traffic data" means any data processed for the purpose of the conveyance of a communication on an electronic communications network, or for the billing thereof. Recital 15 of the Directive further explains the concept of traffic data as following:

> A communication may include any naming, numbering or addressing information provided by the sender of a communication or the user of a connection to carry out the communication. Traffic data may include any translation of this information by the network over which the communication is transmitted for the purpose of carrying out the transmission. Traffic data may, inter alia, consist of data referring to the routing, duration, time or volume of a communication, to the protocol used, to the location of the terminal equipment of the sender or recipient, to the network on which the communication originates or terminates, to the beginning, end or duration of a connection. They may also consist of the format in which the communication is conveyed by the network.

IP addresses fall within this broad definition of traffic data. Traffic data are covered by the protective veil of the confidentiality of communication established in Article 5 of the Directive, which states as following:

> Member States shall ensure the confidentiality of communications and the related traffic data by means of a public communications network and publicly available electronic communications services, through national legislation. In particular, they shall prohibit listening, tapping, storage or other kinds of interception or surveillance of communications and the related traffic data by persons other than users, without the consent of the users concerned.

Nonetheless, exceptions to this rule can be introduced on the grounds of Article 15(1) of the Directive, which enables Member States to restrict the scope of the rights and obligations provided for in Article 5 when such restriction constitutes a necessary, appropriate and proportionate measure within a democratic society to safeguard

---

280. *See*, on this issue, Eneken Tikk, *IP Addresses Subject to Data Protection Regulation*, at: https://www.sbs.ox.ac.uk/cybersecurity-capacity/system/files/IP%20addresses%20subject%20to%20Personal%20Data%20Regulation.pdf.

national security (i.e., State security), defense, public security and the prevention, investigation, detection and prosecution of criminal offenses or of unauthorized use of the electronic communication system, as referred to in Article 13(1) of Directive 95/46/EC. To this end, Member States may, *inter alia*, adopt legislative measures providing for the retention of data for a limited period, justified on the grounds laid down in this paragraph. All the measures referred to in this paragraph shall be in accordance with the general principles of Community law, including those referred to in Article 6(1) and (2) of the Treaty on European Union.

Article 15(1) of Directive 2002/58/EC is the equivalent of Article 13 of the Data Protection Directive. As it is stated in Recital 11 of the Directive 2002/58/EC:

> like Directive 95/46/EC, this Directive does not address issues of protection of fundamental rights and freedoms related to activities which are not governed by Community law. Therefore it does not alter the existing balance between the individual's right to privacy and the possibility for Member States to take the measures referred to in Article 15(1) of this Directive, necessary for the protection of public security, defense, State security (including the economic well-being of the State when the activities relate to State security matters) and the enforcement of criminal law. Consequently, this Directive does not affect the ability of Member States to carry out lawful interception of electronic communications, or take other measures, if necessary for any of these purposes and in accordance with the European Convention for the Protection of Human Rights and Fundamental Freedoms, as interpreted by the rulings of the European Court of Human Rights. Such measures must be appropriate, strictly proportionate to the intended purpose and necessary within a democratic society and should be subject to adequate safeguards in accordance with the European Convention for the Protection of Human Rights and Fundamental Freedoms.

The CJEU gave a broad interpretation of Article 15(1), so as to include the protection of the rights and freedoms of others as an additional exception.[281]

Member States have introduced exceptions on the grounds of Article 15(1) in a balanced way. For example, the German Telecommunications Act permits the processing of traffic data where an unauthorized use of a service is taking place.[282] In a landmark case involving a major Internet access provider, the courts have held that

281. A. Dix, *Directive 2002/58/EC, Article 15*, in: Bullesbach, Gijrath, Poullet, Prins, *Concise European IT Law* (2d edn, 2010), Article 15 of Directive 2002/58/EC, 235. *See* Judgment of the Court (Grand Chamber), *Productores de Música de España (Promusicae) v. Telefónica de España SAU*, Case C-275/06 (Jan. 29, 2008): ("It is clear, however, that Article 15(1) of Directive 2002/58 ends the list of the above exceptions with an express reference to Article 13(1) of Directive 95/46. That provision also authorises the Member States to adopt legislative measures to restrict the obligation of confidentiality of personal data where that restriction is necessary inter alia for the protection of the rights and freedoms of others. As they do not specify the rights and freedoms concerned, those provisions of Article 15(1) of Directive 2002/58 must be interpreted as expressing the Community legislature's intention not to exclude from their scope the protection of the right to property or situations in which authors seek to obtain that protection in civil proceedings") and Order of the Court (Eighth Chamber), *LSG-Gesellschaft zur Wahrnehmung von Leistungsschutzrechten GmbH v. Tele2 Telecommunication GmbH*, Case C-557/07 (Feb. 19, 2009).

282. Section 100 TKG.

traffic data could only be collected on a case-by-case basis, whereas a blanket collection of all customers' communications data for "security purposes" was illegal.[283]

Rules on the processing of traffic data are established in Article 6 of the E-Privacy Directive. According to Article 6, traffic data relating to subscribers and users processed and stored by the provider of a public communications network or publicly available electronic communications service must be erased or made anonymous when it is no longer needed for the purpose of the transmission of a communication, without prejudice of Article 15(1). Recital 28 states that the obligation to erase traffic data, or to make such data anonymous when it is no longer needed for the purpose of the transmission of a communication, does not conflict with such procedures on the Internet as the caching in the domain name system of IP addresses, or the caching of IP addresses to physical address bindings, or the use of log-in information to control the right of access to networks or services. It is not clear what the exact scope of this recital is. It appears to allow the retention of traffic data for the purpose of caching or log-in procedures, despite the erasure rule.[284] According to Article 6(2), traffic data necessary for the purposes of subscriber billing and interconnection payments may be processed. Such processing is permissible only up to the end of the period during which the bill may lawfully be challenged or payment pursued. The service provider must inform the subscriber or user of the types of traffic data, which are processed and of the duration of such processing. Article 6(5) appears to permit the processing of traffic data for other purposes too, since it considers that persons handling customer enquiries or fraud detection are also entitled to process traffic data.[285]

On the basis of the above, it is clear that traffic data, such as IP addresses, may only be collected and stored for reasons directly related to the communication itself, including billing, traffic management and fraud prevention purposes. Afterwards, the data must be deleted.[286] It is also clear that Article 6 applies to the relation between the providers of electronic communication services and the subscribers or users of such services, while the possibility of processing of IP addresses in criminal cases shall be regulated by the national law of the Member States on the legal grounds of Article 15 of the E-Privacy Directive.

Although the processing of traffic data for the purposes defined in Article 15(1) ("to safeguard national security (i.e. State security), defense, public security, and the

283. LG Darmstadt, 25 S 118/2005 (Dec. 7, 2005).

284. Rosier, in: Bullesbach, Gijrath, Poullet, Prins, *Concise European IT Law* (2d edn, 2010), Art. 6 of Directive 2002/58/EC, 201.

285. Article 6(5): "Processing of traffic data, in accordance with paragraphs 1, 2, 3 and 4, must be restricted to persons acting under the authority of providers of the public communications networks and publicly available electronic communications services handling billing or traffic management, customer enquiries, fraud detection, marketing electronic communications services or providing a value added service, and must be restricted to what is necessary for the purposes of such activities."

286. Opinion of the European Data Protection Supervisor on the current negotiations by the European Union of an Anti-Counterfeiting Trade Agreement (ACTA), 2010/C 147/01, available at: http://www.edps.europa.eu/EDPSWEB/webdav/site/mySite/shared/Documents/Consultation/Opinions/2010/10-02-22_ACTA_EN.pdf (2010).

prevention, investigation, detection and prosecution of criminal offences or of unauthorized use of the electronic communication system") is a matter of national law, constitutional values and the principles of the European Convention of Human Rights impose a cautious and proportionate processing of traffic data for these purposes. As the Article 29 Working Party stressed out in its Opinion 04/2014 on surveillance of electronic communications for intelligence and national security purposes:

> under no circumstance surveillance programmes based on the indiscriminate, blanket collection of personal data can meet the requirements of necessity and proportionality set out in these data protection principles. Limitations to fundamental rights have to be interpreted restrictively, following case law from the European Court of Human Rights and the Court of Justice of the European Union.[287]

In the meantime, a Proposal for a Regulation on the respect for private life and the protection of personal data in electronic communications was published on 10 January 2017. The text was subject to scrutiny and several amendments. The legislative process is formally still ongoing,[288] but its future is highly uncertain given the rejection of the latest version of the Council's position on November 22, 2019 by the Permanent Representatives Committee of the Council of the European Union (COREPER). Now it is up to the Commission to either withdraw the entire proposal, and leave citizens unprotected, or to the Council to prepare a new text.[289]

The aim of the proposed Regulation is to replace Directive 2002/58/EC (E-Privacy) and be a *lex specialis* to the GDPR.[290] The proposed Regulation establishes rules for the processing of electronic communications content, electronic communications metadata and for electronic communications data, which comprise both electronic communications content and electronic communications metadata. Specifically, while a general prohibition to the processing of electronic communications data is established, processing can be based on various legal bases, which vary for electronic communications content and electronic communications metadata.

Processing of IP address falls within the scope of processing of "electronic communications metadata," which are defined in the proposed Regulation as "data processed by means of electronic communications network services for the purposes of

287. Article 29 Working Group, Opinion 04/2014 on surveillance of electronic communications for intelligence and national security purposes, WP 215 (Apr. 10, 2014).
288. *See* version of October 2019: Proposal for a Regulation of the European Parliament and of the Council concerning the respect for private life and the protection of personal data in electronic communications and repealing Directive 2002/58/EC (Regulation on Privacy and Electronic Communications, Brussels, Oct. 30, 2019, Interinstitutional File: 2017/0003(COD), available at: https://eur-lex.europa.eu/legal-content/EN/TXT/PDF/?uri=CONSIL:ST_13632_2019_INIT&from=EN.
289. *See* e-Privacy: EU Member States push crucial reform on privacy norms close to a dead end, available at: https://edri.org/eprivacy-eu-member-states-push-crucial-reform-on-privacy-norms-close-to-a-dead-end/.
290. The Finish Presidency presented its last compromise proposal on the e-Privacy regulation in November 2019. No agreement on the text of the proposed Regulation was reached until 22 Nov. 22, 2019. *See* Legislative Train Schedule, Proposal for a regulation on privacy and electronic communications, available at: http://www.europarl.europa.eu/legislative-train/theme-connected-digital-single-market/file-jd-e-privacy-reform.

transmitting, distributing or exchanging electronic communications content; including data used to trace and identify the source and destination of a communication, data on the location of the device generated in the context of providing electronic communications services, and the date, time, duration and the type of communication; ... ."[291] The Proposal affirms the principle of secrecy/confidentiality of communications for electronic communications data (content and metadata). Specifically, Article 5 states that: "Electronic communications data shall be confidential. Any interference with electronic communications data, including listening, tapping, storing, monitoring, scanning or other kinds of interception, surveillance and processing of electronic communications data, by anyone other than the end-users concerned, shall be prohibited, except when permitted by this Regulation."

According to Article 6 of the proposed Regulation, providers of electronic communications networks and services shall be permitted to process electronic communications data only if: it is necessary to achieve the transmission of the communication; it is necessary to maintain or restore the security of electronic communications networks and services or detect technical faults and/or errors and/or security risks and/or attacks in the transmission of electronic communications; it is necessary to detect or prevent security risks and/or attacks on end users' terminal equipment; or it is necessary for compliance with a legal obligation to which the provider is subject laid down by Union or Member State law. Therefore, provided that there are no significant changes to this provision, processing of both content and metadata would be possible in order to detect also attacks in the transmission of electronic communications.

Furthermore, the IP address and other metadata may also be processed on the grounds of Article 6b of the proposed Regulation, if it is necessary for the purposes of: network management or network optimization or to meet technical quality of service requirements; for calculating and billing interconnection payments; or for the performance of an electronic communications service contract to which the end user is party; in particular, if necessary for billing; or if it is necessary for detecting or stopping fraudulent, or abusive use of, or subscription to, electronic communications services to protect the vital interest of a natural person; in the case of emergency, in general upon request of a public authority, in accordance with Union or Member State law, is necessary for statistical purposes or for scientific research purposes. Metadata processing is also possible when the end-user concerned has given his or her consent to the processing of his or her communications metadata for one or more specified purposes. The proposed text establishes also separate rules and conditions for the compatible processing of metadata and for detection of child sexual abuse material.[292]

As it stated in the Recital 7a, the Regulation should not apply to the protection of fundamental rights and freedoms related to activities which fall outside the scope of Union law, and in any event activities concerning national security and defense. It is further stated in Recital 26 that the proposed Regulation should not affect the ability of Member States to carry out lawful interception of electronic communications or take

291. Article 4 of the proposed Regulation.
292. *See* Articles 6c and 6d.

other measures, such as legislative measures providing for the retention of data for a limited period of time, if necessary and proportionate to safeguard the public interests mentioned above, in accordance with the Charter of Fundamental Rights of the European Union and the European Convention for the Protection of Human Rights and Fundamental Freedoms, as interpreted by the CJEU and of the ECtHR.

Interceptions are not generally inconsistent with the European Convention of Human Rights and EU law, but they are subject to serious scrutiny. The CJEU, in the seminal judgment of April 8, 2014 that annulled the Data Retention Directive, affirmed that the processing of personal data related to electronic communications, and more precisely data retention, constitutes a particularly serious interference with the right of privacy, but it is not such as to adversely affect the essence of this right, given that the directive does not permit the acquisition of knowledge of the content of the electronic communications as such.[293] In *Tele2 Sverige* and *Watson*, the CJEU stressed in relation to metadata retained by providers of publicly available electronic communications that "taken as a whole, [they] may allow very precise conclusions to be drawn concerning the private lives of the persons whose data has been retained, such as the habits of everyday life, permanent or temporary places of residence, daily or other movements, the activities carried out, the social relationships of those persons and the social environments frequented by them" and "[provide] the means [...] of establishing a profile of the individuals concerned, information that is no less sensitive, having regard to the right to privacy, than the actual content of communications."[294] More recently, it was held in the *Ministerio fiscal* case that "[i]n accordance with the principle of proportionality, serious interference can be justified, in areas of prevention, investigation, detection and prosecution of criminal offences, only by the objective of fighting crime which must also be defined as 'serious'" and "in [those areas], only the objective of fighting serious crime is capable of justifying public authorities' access to personal data retained by providers of electronic communications services which, taken as a whole, allow precise conclusions to be drawn concerning the private lives of the persons whose data is concerned."[295]

Some international treaties even impose a duty on Contracting States to employ special investigative measures, such as phone interceptions, in order to combat certain forms of crime. The CoE Criminal Law Convention on Corruption[296] obliges Signatory States to adopt "such legislative measures as may be necessary (...) including those permitting the use of special investigative techniques' to facilitate the gathering of

293. Joined Cases C-293/12 and C-594/12, *Digital Rights Ireland Ltd (C-293/12) v. Minister for Communications, Marine and Natural Resources, Minister for Justice, Equality and Law Reform, Commissioner of the Garda Síochána, Ireland, The Attorney General, intervener: Irish Human Rights Commission, and Kärntner Landesregierung* (C-594/12), Michael Seitlinger, Christof Tschohl and others, paragraph 39 (Apr. 8, 2014).
294. CJEU, Joined Cases C-203/15 and C-698/15, *Tele2 Sverige and Watson*, ECLI:EU:C:2016:970, paragraph 99.
295. CJEU, Case C-207/16, *Ministerio fiscal*, ECLI:EU:C:2018:788, paragraphs 54 and 56.
296. Criminal Law Convention on Corruption Strasbourg, 27.01.1999, available at: http://conventions.coe.int/Treaty/en/Treaties/Html/173.htm.

evidence and confiscation of proceeds" (paragraph 23) in corruption cases. The explanatory report[297] to this Convention clarifies that:

> this provision includes an obligation for the parties to introduce special investigative techniques' such as 'wiretapping, bugging, interception of telecommunications (paragraph 114).[298]

The protection of the confidentiality of communications on the legal grounds of Article 8 of the European Convention of Human Rights also covers the external communication elements, thus not only the content of the letter but also the "envelope."[299] This has been clearly affirmed in the leading case *Malone v. UK*,[300] where it was held that it also amounts to an interference with Article 8 paragraph 1, when authorities do not take note of the content of phone conversations, but only record which phone numbers are called from a certain phone and how long the conversations last (so-called *metering*).

The ECtHR has scrutinized the conditions of legitimate interceptions. In the *Huvig* and *Kruslin* cases,[301] the Court has pronounced the criteria which could afford adequate safeguards:

> independent judicial authorization, avenues for judicial review, exclusion of subterfuge or ruse, classifications of persons liable to have their communications intercepted, classes of offences in respect of which interception can be sought, reporting requirements, preservation of the integrity of the recordings, as well as rules governing their destruction.[302]

One of the conditions set by the Court is that the law providing the legal basis for interceptions has to specify the categories of crimes which may give rise to an interception. In respect to phone interceptions, in *Kennedy v. UK*, it was held that the condition of the foreseeability of the law enabling interceptions did not require the setting of an exhaustive list of offenses which are apt to justify phone interceptions, and held that the interpretation of the term "serious crimes" contained in the relevant British law provided citizens with sufficient information as to the circumstances in which phone interceptions could be authorized.[303] In *Iordachi v. Moldava*,[304] the Court examined the Moldovan "Operational Investigative Activities Act" of 1994, which provided that phone interceptions could be undertaken for the investigation of serious,

297. Criminal Law Convention on Corruption (ETS No. 173), Explanatory Report, available at: http://conventions.coe.int/Treaty/EN/Reports/Html/173.htm.
298. Phone interceptions in light of Article 8 ECHR, available at: https://human-rights-law.eu/echr/article-8-echr-right-to-private-life-family-life-correspondence-and-home/phone-interceptions-and-surveillance-of-communication-in-light-of-article-8-echr/.
299. For the relevant discussion in the US, *see* Matthew J. Tokson, *The Content/Envelope Distinction in Internet Law*, 50 William & Mary Law Review, 2105 (2009), http://scholarship.law.wm.edu/wmlr/vol50/iss6/5.
300. ECtHR, *Malove v. UK* (Application No. 8691/79) (Oct. 2, 1984).
301. ECtHR, *Kruslin v. France* (Application No. 11801/85) and *Huvig v. France* (Series A No. 176-B; Application No. 11105/84 (Apr. 24, 1990).
302. CoE, *Problems of Criminal Procedural Law Connected with Information Technology*, Recommendation No. R(95)13 and Explanatory Memorandum, Legal Issues (1998).
303. ECtHR, *Kennedy v. UK* (Application No. 26839/05) (Aug. 18, 2010).
304. ECtHR, *Iordachi v. Moldava* (Application No. 25198/02) (Sep. 14, 2009).

very serious and exceptionally serious offenses and the Criminal Code contained a definition of these terms. While the category of crimes liable to give rise to an interception was thus clearly defined, the Court criticized that "more than half of the offences provided for in the Criminal Code fall within the category of offences eligible for interception warrants."[305]

The latest addition to this rich case law on the topic of mass surveillance has been made by the Grand Chamber of the Court on December 6, 2015 in the case *Roman Zakharov v. Russia*. In this case, the Court examined the compatibility of a Russian legislation that authorizes mass surveillance of communication through cell phones for purposes of national security and without any intervention of judicial authorities with the Article 8 of the convention. A nongovernmental organization of human rights defense had tried without success to challenge the legality of the law on a national level and then asked for the Court to condemn Russia.

The Court noted, first, that the request's admissibility is an issue by itself, since there is no real and specific facts to the case, but just a general estimation of the potential danger for the human rights of the new legislation. Applying and confirming its previous jurisprudence, the court decides on this point that this danger, associated with the lack of available therapies, justifies in this case the admissibility of the request.

The Court then resumed and applied the conditions of legitimacy of a mass surveillance mechanism. To be justified, a data interception must be in accordance with the law (which does not only mean that a legal basis should be provided but also that this legal basis states a transparent and foreseeable legal framework), pursue a legitimate aim listed in Article 8(2) and be necessary in a democratic society. The main idea of these conditions is that the legal framework should provide strict mechanisms of control and/or of limitations which would protect the citizen against the danger of abuse of any discretion left to the authorities. One such fundamental mechanism is for the court the direct implication of the judicial powers in the process. By consequence, the court ruled that the Russian legislation, which both permitted general surveillance and lacked any judicial involvement, was not compatible with Article 8.

Article 8 of the European Convention of Human Rights can also act at the opposite direction, imposing the disclosure (thus the processing) of personal data, in order to efficiently protect the private life of an individual. In this context, the ECtHR held that the denial of an ISP to provide the necessary information in order to identify the author of defamation violates Article 8. More precisely, in *KU v. Finland*,[306] the ECtHR held that there was a violation of Articles 8 and 13 of the Human Rights Convention, when an ISP refused to provide the identity of an individual who published a sexually explicit advertisement involving a minor.

305. Paragraph 44. *See Phone Interceptions in Light of Article 8 ECHR*, available at: http://echr-online.com/art-8-echr/phone-interceptions-in-light-of-article-8-echr.
306. ECtHR, 2872/02 [2008].

[3] IP Address and Presumption of Liability in the CJEU's Case Law: An Alternative Approach?

While the IP address is a crucial means for identifying the person who committed a cybercrime, finding a specific user's IP can be difficult and is complicated by factors such as whether the IP address is static or dynamic, whether the user was on an unsecured or secured network and whether the same address is shared by people in the private circle of the alleged perpetrator. These factors play an important role in the reliability and specificity of information that the IP address reveals to law enforcement authorities.[307]

Similar to a crime scene where a single fingerprint is not sufficient evidence to prove without reasonable doubt that the person whose fingerprint matches the one found at the crime scene committed the crime, IP addresses pose hurdles for investigators.[308] Since the IP address might be shared by many people,[309] the identification of the specific person who committed the infringement is not evident. Indeed, in criminal cases IP addresses are often seen as a starting point to trace criminal activity, but they cannot alone lead to the suspect. This has often been confirmed by courts worldwide. For example, in France in the case *Rentabiliweb Europe v. Hi-Media*, the Court of appeal of Paris affirmed that the IP address is not sufficient evidence for the identification of a person who have maliciously deleted information about its competitor in Wikipedia.[310] Similarly, in the US case *United States v. Broadhurst*,[311] it was held that due to unsecured wireless networks, it was impossible to conclude the source of child pornography file-sharing solely by using an IP address.

---

307. Erin Larson, Tracking Criminals with Internet Protocol Addresses: Is Law Enforcement Correctly Identifying Perpetrators?, 18 N.C. J.L. & Tech. 316 (2017), at p. 319, available at: https://scholarship.law.unc.edu/ncjolt/vol18/iss5/10.
308. Identifying Cybercriminals: Is An IP Address Sufficient? Feb. 11, 2016. Available at: https://www.securityskeptic.com/2016/02/identifying-cybercriminals-is-an-ip-address-sufficient.html.
309. Indeed, CGN technologies are used by ISPs to share one single IP address among multiple subscribers at the same time. This has been highlighted by Europol as a significant hurdle for law enforcement. In the Press Release of Oct. 17, 2017 entitled *Are you sharing the same IP address as a criminal? Law enforcement call for the end of Carrier Grade NAT (CGN) to increase accountability online*, Europol and the Estonian Presidency of the EU Council at this moment had addressed the serious online capability gap in law enforcement efforts to investigate and attribute crime created by CGN technologies. As it is stated "it has become technically impossible for ISPs to comply with legal orders to identify individual subscribers. This is relevant as in criminal investigations an IP address is often the only information that can link a crime to an individual. It might mean that individuals cannot be distinguished by their IP addresses anymore, which may lead to innocent individuals being wrongly investigated by law enforcement because they share their IP address with several thousand others – potentially including criminals." *See Are you sharing the same IP address as a criminal? Law enforcement call for the end of Carrier Grade NAT (CGN) to increase accountability online*, Press Release of Oct. 17, 2017, available at: https://www.europol.europa.eu/newsroom/news/are-you-sharing-same-ip-address-criminal-law-enforcement-call-for-end-of-carrier-grade-nat-cgn-to-increase-accountability-online.
310. Cour d'appel de Paris Pôle 5, chambre 5 Arrêt du 3 octobre 2013, Available at: https://www.legalis.net/jurisprudences/cour-dappel-de-paris-pole-5-chambre-5-arret-du-3-octobre-2013/ (accessed on Nov. 19, 2019).
311. No. 3:11–cr–00121–MO–1, 2012 WL 5985615, at *1 (D. Or. Nov.28, 2012).

The strength of the IP address as evidence for the identification of the infringer of an online illegal activity has been expressly addressed at the EU level only in relation to cases of online copyright law infringement. In this context, the CJEU was called to clarify the legal consequences of the use of an IP address for copyright infringement for the owner of an IP address.

Specifically, certain EU Member States, such as Germany and Denmark, have adopted the presumption that the owner of the IP address is responsible for infringements committed from the owner's IP address.[312] Specifically, in Germany in the case *Sommer unseres Lebens*,[313] the Bundesgerichtshof (BGH) held that a private owner of an unprotected Wi-Fi network was liable for copyright infringement committed by an unidentified third party, because the owner of the network should have protected it with safety measures to prevent its misuse. As a result, Wi-Fi operators should password-protect their connections in order to avoid any third-party copyright infringements.

This legal framework has been examined by the CJEU in the *Lübbe* case.[314] Lübbe, the owner of copyright in an audio book, accused a German citizen, Strotzer, for copyright infringement of an audio book. Strotzer is the owner of an Internet connection, and therefore of the IP address, through which the audio book had been illegally shared in a peer-to-peer network. Mr. Strotzer denied that he had committed the copyright infringement, but also maintained that his Internet connection was sufficiently secure. He, furthermore, asserted that his parents had access to the Internet connection but that he did not know whether they had committed the infringement. Under German law, if it is shown that an Internet connection was used to infringe copyright, the owner of that Internet connection is presumed to have committed the infringement. However, this presumption can be rebutted by the owner, if he or she can show that other persons had independent access to the Internet connection and were therefore capable of committing the infringement. Further, if a family member of that owner had access to the Internet connection, the owner can, on the basis of the right to the protection of family life, escape liability merely by naming a family member without being required to provide further details as to how and when the Internet connection was used by that family member.[315]

The main question that has been brought in front of the CJEU is whether this legal regime is compatible with the need to safeguard effective copyright enforcement. In order to answer, the Court carries out a balancing act between, on the one hand, the protection of intellectual property rights as guaranteed by the German Copyright Act and Article 17 of the EU Charter of Fundamental Rights in relation to the protection of the right of property and, on the other hand, the proper discovery process for

312. J. Brogaard Clausen & E. Svensson, *Copyright infringement: The burden of proof is on the owner of the IP address*, available at: https://www.njordlaw.com/copyright-infringement-the-burden-of-proof-is-put-on-the-owner-of-the-ip-address/ (accessed on Jul. 5, 2019).
313. Bundesgerichsthof, Judgment of May 12, 2010, *Sommer unseres Lebens*.
314. *Bastei Lübbe GmbH & Co. KG v. Michael Strotzer*, Case C-149/17, Judgment of the Court (Third Chamber) of Oct. 18, 2018.
315. Paragraph 36 of the judgment.

evidence[316] and the respect of other fundamental rights. For the CJEU, it is not compatible with the rights holders' fundamental rights to an effective remedy and to intellectual property if the owner of the IP address can avoid a presumption of liability merely by stating that a family member also has had access to the Internet connection. As regards the protection of family life, the Court affirms that the members of a family enjoy special protection in that they need not incriminate each other. However, if a national law would always make the right to private life prevail over the right to intellectual property in infringement proceedings, then this national legislation would fail to correctly ensure the effective enforcement of intellectual property rights. Such a national law would make it practically impossible to obtain evidence on an alleged infringement of copyright.[317]

Furthermore, the liability and the possible obligations of the owner of an IP address which is used by others has been examined by the CJEU in the past in an another landmark ruling in the *McFadden* case,[318] although in a different context, since this was a case of an injunction against an Internet access provider as regards copyright infringements committed by third parties. In *McFadden*, the CJEU was called to answer whether an injunction which requires an owner of a shop who offers access to a Wi-Fi network to the general public free of charge to prevent third parties from making copyright-protected work available in a peer-to-peer exchange platform is compatible

316. Article 6(1) of the Enforcement Directive (Directive (EU) 2019/633 of the European Parliament and of the Council of 17 April 2019 on unfair trading practices in business-to-business relationships in the agricultural and food supply chain OJ L 111, 25.4.2019, p. 59–72). According to this provision:

> 1. Member States shall ensure that each of their enforcement authorities has the necessary resources and expertise to perform its duties, and shall confer on it the following powers: (a) the power to initiate and conduct investigations on its own initiative or on the basis of a complaint;(b) the power to require buyers and suppliers to provide all necessary information in order to conduct investigations of prohibited trading practices; (c) the power to carry out unannounced on-site inspections within the framework of its investigations, in accordance with national rules and procedures; (d) the power to take decisions finding an infringement of the prohibitions laid down in Article 3 and requiring the buyer to bring the prohibited trading practice to an end; the authority may abstain from taking any such decision, if that decision would risk revealing the identity of a complainant or would risk disclosing any other information in respect of which the complainant considers that such disclosure would be harmful to its interests, and provided that the complainant has identified that information in accordance with Article 5(3); (e) the power to impose, or initiate proceedings for the imposition of, fines and other equally effective penalties and interim measures on the author of the infringement, in accordance with national rules and procedures; (f) the power to publish its decisions taken under points (d) and (e) on a regular basis.

317. Paragraphs 51–52 of the judgment. For a different outcome where the protection of family life and of the presumption of innocence prevailed in a case of an online copyright infringement in cases judged by the IP court in Taiwan, *see Prosecutors of the Taichung District Prosecutors Office v. Jian*, 107 Xing-Zhi-Shang-Yi 59, IP Court (November 2018); *Prosecutors of the New Taipei District Prosecutors Office v. Chen*, 108 Xing-Zhi-Shang-Yi 24, IP Court (June 2019). Available at: Tony Tung-Yang Chang, Taiwan: IP Address as Digital Footprint Evidence Questioned in Copyright Cases, 30 July 2019, http://www.mondaq.com/x/831352/Copyright/IP+Address+As+Digital+Footprint+Evidence+Questioned+In+Copyright+Cases.
318. CJEU, *Tobias Mc Fadden v. Sony Music Entertainment Germany GmbH*, Case C-484/14, Judgment of Sept. 15, 2016.

with the protection of fundamental rights. The referring court stated that it is inclined to apply, by analogy, the Bundesgerichtshof's ruling in the *Sommer unseres Lebens* case holding the view that this judgment, which concerned private persons, should also apply in the case of a professional who operates a Wi-Fi network that is accessible to the public.

The CJEU has made a strict scrutiny of the measures that can be taken by the access provider in order to prevent the making available of particular copyright-protected content. In the view of the CJEU, measures consisting in terminating the Internet connection completely or in monitoring all communications transmitted via a given network shall be rejected because they cannot strike a fair balance between the conflicting fundamental rights.

The only measure which could be adopted is a single measure consisting in password-protecting the Internet connection, provided that the users are required to reveal their identity in order to obtain the required password and may not therefore act anonymously. Although such a measure interferes with freedom to conduct business and freedom of expression, it does not damage in their essence of those fundamental rights. [319] As regards the issue whether such a measure is an effective means to prevent copyright infringements, the Court answers in the positive, since, for the CJEU, this measure can make it difficult for users to gain unauthorized access to protected material and can seriously discourage Internet users from accessing protected material. The reasoning of the court gives rise to some doubts, since simply a password and an obligation of the user of the connection to identify herself/himself cannot really establish a link to the infringer, since the latter can be registered with false details. Lastly, it should be emphasized that this judgment does not create a legal obligation on free Wi-Fi providers to password-protect their network and/or register users' details, unless they are required to do so in order to comply with an injunction.

Given the importance given in both cases to the use of the IP address as evidence for attributing liability to the IP address holder or for assuming preventive obligations for the IP address holder, a question that could be posed is whether a similar line of reasoning could also apply to cybercrime, including cyber attacks', cases either at a national or even at an EU level. In other words, could a legal mechanism of presumption of criminal responsibility against the holder of the IP address be established in relation to other online illegal activities, including cybercrimes? In this context, the mechanism of a presumption of liability against the holder of the IP address could be seen as a precursor for similar presumptions in other legal fields, beyond intellectual property law. However, the severity of the criminal conviction and the fundamental axiom of the presumption of innocence would not enable such an extension. Moreover, in cases of cyber attacks the attacks are usually committed through use of the IP address of an innocent third party. It is extremely difficult to establish a direct link between the IP address of the machine that originated the attack and the person that set the attack in motion. Indeed, the cyber attacker can forge or hijack an IP address and thus "leave some other person's fingerprints." Hackers

319. Paragraphs 90–92 of the judgment.

regularly attempt to hide their tracks by destroying or modifying system logs or other data, and seeding misinformation. The ability to link an IP address to a particular person has also been undermined by the proliferation of "pay as you go" ISPs and the growth of prepaid Internet access cards, which require no or little identification.[320] Therefore, a careful and detailed scrutiny of hardware and of other multiple supportive evidences is necessary and the basic finding that the IP address is crucial, but only a starting point still remains.

[B] The Processing of the IP Address as Evidence in Criminal Litigation

[1] The IP Address in the Cybercrime Convention

Apart from establishing specific, substantial cybercrime law rules, the Cybercrime Convention also addressed the tricky question of evidence in cybercrime investigation. Indeed, a significant problem for law enforcement is that cybercrimes are extremely difficult to investigate, prosecute and punish. The acquisition and preservation of evidence that will prove an offender's identity and possible crimes is difficult to collect, while there have been great national divergences in the ability to investigate and punish cybercrimes.[321] As it is explained in the Explanatory Report of the Cybercrime Convention, the procedural law of the Convention aims at giving a response to the major criminal procedure challenges related to cybercrime.

Indeed:

> the technological revolution, which encompasses the "electronic highway" where numerous forms of communication and services are interrelated and interconnected through the sharing of common transmission media and carriers, has altered the sphere of criminal law and criminal procedure. The ever-expanding network of communications opens new doors for criminal activity in respect of both traditional offences and new technological crimes. Not only must substantive criminal law keep abreast of these new abuses, but so must criminal procedural law and investigative techniques. Equally, safeguards should also be adapted or developed to keep abreast of the new technological environment and new procedural powers.[322]

As it is further stated:

> one of the major challenges in combating crime in the networked environment is the difficulty in identifying the perpetrator and assessing the extent and impact of the criminal act. A further problem is caused by the volatility of electronic data, which may be altered, moved or deleted in seconds. For example, a user who is in control of the data may use the computer system to erase the data that is the

320. Howard F. Lipson, Tracking and Tracing Cyber-Attacks: Technical Challenges and Global Policy Issues, November 2002, Special Report CMU/SEI-2002-SR-009, available at: https://resources.sei.cmu.edu/asset_files/SpecialReport/2002_003_001_13928.pdf.
321. N. Marion, *The Council of Europe's Cyber Crime Treaty: An exercise in Symbolic Legislation*, 4(1&2) Intl. J. Cyber Criminology 700 (January–July 2010/July–December 2010).
322. Explanatory Report, paragraph 132.

> subject of a criminal investigation, thereby destroying the evidence. Speed and, sometimes, secrecy are often vital for the success of an investigation.[323]

One way in which the Convention overcomes these problems is by adapting traditional procedures, like search and seizure, to an ever-changing technological landscape. Moreover, in order to make these traditional crime investigation methods effective, new measures have been created, such as the expedited preservation of data, real-time collection of traffic data and the interception of content data.[324]

The definition of traffic data is also established in the Convention; "traffic data" means any computer data relating to a communication by means of a computer system, generated by a computer system that formed a part in the chain of communication, indicating the communication's origin, destination, route, time, date, size, duration or type of underlying service. The Explanatory Report stresses out the importance of the processing of traffic data in cybercrime investigation. Indeed:

> in case of an investigation of a criminal offence committed in relation to a computer system, traffic data is needed to trace the source of a communication as a starting point for collecting further evidence or as part of the evidence of the offence. Traffic data might last only ephemerally, which makes it necessary to order its expeditious preservation. Consequently, its rapid disclosure may be necessary to discern the communication's route in order to collect further evidence before it is deleted or to identify a suspect. The ordinary procedure for the collection and disclosure of computer data might therefore be insufficient. Moreover, the collection of this data is regarded in principle to be less intrusive since as such it doesn't reveal the content of the communication which is regarded to be more sensitive.[325]

The Explanatory Report also provides insightful clarifications in respect of the definition of "traffic data" which shall be processed under the procedural rules of the Convention. As it is explained:

> the definition lists exhaustively the categories of traffic data that are treated by a specific regime in this Convention: the origin of a communication, its destination, route, time (GMT), date, size, duration and type of underlying service. Not all of these categories will always be technically available, capable of being produced by a service provider, or necessary for a particular criminal investigation. The "origin" refers to a telephone number, Internet Protocol (IP) address, or similar identification of a communications facility to which a service provider renders services. The "destination" refers to a comparable indication of a communications facility to which communications are transmitted. The term "type of underlying service" refers to the type of service that is being used within the network, e.g., file transfer, electronic mail, or instant messaging.[326]

It is clear from the Explanatory report that the IP address is "traffic data" related to the origin of the communication and it is, therefore, covered by the Convention's

---

323. Explanatory Report, paragraph133.
324. M. Keyser, *The Council of Europe Convention on Cybercrime*, (12) J. Transnational L. & Policy 311 (2003).
325. Paragraph 29.
326. Paragraph 30.

procedural rules. The processing of traffic data, including IP addresses, is subject to the general conditions and safeguards of Article 15 of the Convention, while the specific processing procedural rules of Articles 16 (Expedited preservation of stored computer data[327]), 17 (Expedited preservation and partial disclosure of traffic data[328]) and 20 (Real-time collection of traffic data[329]) apply to traffic data. Articles 16, 17, 29 and 30 establish provisional measures, which have been put in place in order to gain time in

327. Article 16 states:

> 1. Each Party shall adopt such legislative and other measures as may be necessary to enable its competent authorities to order or similarly obtain the expeditious preservation of specified computer data, including traffic data, that has been stored by means of a computer system, in particular where there are grounds to believe that the computer data is particularly vulnerable to loss or modification. 2 Where a Party gives effect to paragraph 1 above by means of an order to a person to preserve specified stored computer data in the person's possession or control, the Party shall adopt such legislative and other measures as may be necessary to oblige that person to preserve and maintain the integrity of that computer data for a period of time as long as necessary, up to a maximum of ninety days, to enable the competent authorities to seek its disclosure. A Party may provide for such an order to be subsequently renewed. 3. Each Party shall adopt such legislative and other measures as may be necessary to oblige the custodian or other person who is to preserve the computer data to keep confidential the undertaking of such procedures for the period of time provided for by its domestic law. 4. The powers and procedures referred to in this article shall be subject to Articles 14 and 15.

328. Article 17 states:

> 1. Each Party shall adopt, in respect of traffic data that is to be preserved under Article 16, such legislative and other measures as may be necessary to: a) ensure that such expeditious preservation of traffic data is available regardless of whether one or more service providers were involved in the transmission of that communication; and b) ensure the expeditious disclosure to the Party's competent authority, or a person designated by that authority, of a sufficient amount of traffic data to enable the Party to identify the service providers and the path through which the communication was transmitted. 2. The powers and procedures referred to in this article shall be subject to Articles 14 and 15.

329. Article 20 states:

> 1. Each Party shall adopt such legislative and other measures as may be necessary to empower its competent authorities to: a) collect or record through the application of technical means on the territory of that Party, and b) compel a service provider, within its existing technical capability: i) to collect or record through the application of technical means on the territory of that Party; or ii) to co-operate and assist the competent authorities in the collection or recording of, traffic data, in real-time, associated with specified communications in its territory transmitted by means of a computer system. 2. Where a Party, due to the established principles of its domestic legal system, cannot adopt the measures referred to in paragraph 1.a, it may instead adopt legislative and other measures as may be necessary to ensure the real-time collection or recording of traffic data associated with specified communications transmitted in its territory, through the application of technical means on that territory. 3. Each Party shall adopt such legislative and other measures as may be necessary to oblige a service provider to keep confidential the fact of the execution of any power provided for in this article and any information relating to it. 4. The powers and procedures referred to in this article shall be subject to Articles 14 and 15.

situations where it is time wasting to make a request in line with existing formal procedures.[330]

Data preservation procedures of Articles 16 and 17 of the Cybercrime Convention must be distinguished from the data retention obligation that has been introduced under the EU Data Retention Directive of 2006,[331] which has been annulled in 2014 by the CJEU.[332] Indeed, data preservation, also known as expedited preservation of stored data or "quick freeze," refers to situations where a person or organization is required by a state authority to preserve specified data from loss or modification for a specific period of time.[333] This may include traffic but also content data. This could include preservation of what IP addresses connect to and from another IP address, or what phone numbers connect to a VoIP number. This may also include information about what types of protocols a customer makes use of, size and use of packets, and so forth.[334]

Data preservation may include data not only held by a service provider but also by any other physical or legal person. That person or organization, which may be a communications service provider or any physical or legal person who has the possession or control of the specified computer data, may then be required, often by means of a court order, to disclose this data, usually on the ground that the data relates to specific individuals who are suspected to be connected to a particular criminal investigation or prosecution. On the contrary, data retention measures generally aim at requiring (some or all) operators, such as ISPs, to retain traffic data processed as a result of activities of all users of operators' communications or network services, so

330. European Commission, Evidence of Potential Impacts of Options for Revising the Data Retention Directive: Current approaches to data preservation in the EU and in third countries, Center for Strategy & Evaluation Services, Final Report – Task 2, available at: http://ec.europa.eu/dgs/home-affairs/what-we-do/policies/police-cooperation/data-retention/docs/drd_task_2_report_final_en.pdf (November 2012).
331. Directive 2006/24/EC of the European Parliament and of the Council of Mar. 15, 2006 on the retention of data generated or processed in connection with the provision of publicly available electronic communications services or of public communications networks and amending Directive 2002/58/EC, L 105/54, 13.4.2006. IP addresses were expressly mentioned as data that had to be retained by Internet service providers. *See* Article 5(2) (Categories of data to be retained): "concerning Internet access, Internet e-mail and Internet telephony:(i) the date and time of the log-in and log-off of the Internet access service, based on a certain time zone, together with the IP address, whether dynamic or static, allocated by the Internet access service provider to a communication, and the user ID of the subscriber or registered user;(ii)the date and time of the log-in and log-off of the Internet e-mail service or Internet telephony service, based on a certain time zone."
332. Judgment of the Court, Apr. 8, 2014, Joined Cases C-293/12 and C-594/12, *Digital Rights Ireland Ltd (C-293/12) v. Minister for Communications, Marine and Natural Resources, Minister for Justice, Equality and Law Reform, Commissioner of the Garda Síochána, Ireland, The Attorney General, intervener: Irish Human Rights Commission, and Kärntner Landesregierung, Michael Seitlinger, Christof Tschohl and others.*
333. A maximum of ninety days under the Cybercrime Convention.
334. Alana Maurushat, *Australia's Accession to the "Cybercrime Convention": Is the "Convention" Still Relevant in Combating Cybercrime in the Era of Botnets and Obfuscation Crime Tools?* 33(2) Uni. New South Wales Law J. 431–473 (2010); UNSW Law Research Paper No. 2011-20, available at SSRN: http://ssrn.com/abstract=1800503.

that they can be accessed by state authorities and used for "public order" purposes when necessary and lawful.[335]

Article 17 complements Article 16 with specific obligations regarding the expedited disclosure of traffic data. Often, more than one service provider may be involved in the transmission of a communication. Under Article 17, service providers are to disclose sufficient data to allow identification of the path of a communication. This information is mandatory in order the preservation orders to be served to all providers.[336]

Article 18 relates to production orders, which specifically allow:

> "competent authorities to compel a person in its territory to provide specified stored computer data" or to compel an ISP to provide "subscriber information." For the purpose of this article, the term "subscriber information" means any information contained in the form of computer data or any other form that is held by a service provider, relating to subscribers of its services other than traffic or content data and by which can be established: a) the type of communication service used, the technical provisions taken thereto and the period of service; b) the subscriber's identity, postal or geographic address, telephone and other access number, billing and payment information, available on the basis of the service agreement or arrangement; c) any other information on the site of the installation of communication equipment, available on the basis of the service agreement or arrangement.

The data in question are stored or existing data, and do not include data that has not yet come into existence, such as traffic data related to future communications.

The Explanatory Report offers some guidance in respect of the definition of "subscriber information." As it is explained in paragraph 177 of the Report, the term refers to:

> any information held by the administration of a service provider relating to a subscriber to its services. Subscriber information may be contained in the form of computer data or any other form, such as paper records. As subscriber information includes forms of data other than just computer data, a special provision has been included in the article to address this type of information. "Subscriber" is intended to include a broad range of service provider clients, from persons holding paid subscriptions, to those paying on a per-use basis, to those receiving free services. It also includes information concerning persons entitled to use the subscriber's account.

Further, it has been analyzed:

---

335. European Commission, *Evidence of Potential Impacts of Options for Revising the Data Retention Directive: Current approaches to data preservation in the EU and in third countries*, Center for Strategy & Evaluation Services, Final Report – Task 2, available at: http://ec.europa.eu/dgs/home-affairs/what-we-do/policies/police-cooperation/data-retention/docs/drd_task_2_report_final_en.pdf (November 2012).

336. CoE, Cybercrime Convention Committee (T-CY), *Assessment Report Implementation of the Preservation Provisions of the Budapest Convention on Cybercrime*, T-CY (2012) 10 REV, Strasbourg, 50 (Jan. 25, 2013).

> In the course of a criminal investigation, subscriber information may be needed primarily in two specific situations. First, subscriber information is needed to identify which services and related technical measures have been used or are being used by a subscriber, such as the type of telephone service used (e.g., mobile), type of other associated services used (e.g., call forwarding, voice-mail, etc.), telephone number or other technical address (e.g., e-mail address). Second, when a technical address is known, subscriber information is needed in order to assist in establishing the identity of the person concerned. Other subscriber information, such as commercial information about billing and payment records of the subscriber may also be relevant to criminal investigations, especially where the crime under investigation involves computer fraud or other economic crimes. Therefore, subscriber information includes various types of information about the use of a service and the user of that service. With respect to the use of the service, the term means any information, other than traffic or content data, by which can be established the type of communication service used, the technical provisions related thereto, and the period of time during which the person subscribed to the service. The term "technical provisions" includes all measures taken to enable a subscriber to enjoy the communication service offered. Such provisions include the reservation of a technical number or address (telephone number, web site address or domain name, e-mail address, etc.), as well as the provision and registration of communication equipment used by the subscriber, such as telephone devices, call centers or LANs (local area networks). Subscriber information is not limited to information directly related to the use of the communication service. It also means any information, other than traffic data or content data, by which can be established the user's identity, postal or geographic address, telephone and other access number, and billing and payment information, which is available on the basis of the service agreement or arrangement between the subscriber and the service provider. It also means any other information, other than traffic data or content data, concerning the site or location where the communication equipment is installed, which is available on the basis of the service agreement or arrangement. This latter information may only be relevant in practical terms where the equipment is not portable, but knowledge as to the portability or purported location of the equipment (on the basis of the information provided according to the service agreement or arrangement) can be instrumental to an investigation.[337]

It is ambiguous whether IP addresses can be classified as "subscriber information" to which the procedural rules of Article 18 apply. As it has been noted by the CoE's Cybercrime Convention Committee, even if the term "IP address" is not used explicitly, the term "access number" in Article 18(3)(b) refers to an IP address. According to paragraph 180 of the Explanatory Report, subscriber information "also means any information, other than traffic data or content data, by which it can be established the user's identity, postal or geographic address, telephone and other access number." It is also stated in paragraph 182 of the Report that "for example, on the basis of the provision of a particular name (...) a particular associated telephone number or private email address may be requested. On the basis of a particular telephone number or email address, the name and address of the subscriber concerned may be ordered." In this context, the CoE's Cybercrime Convention Committee stressed out that it is irrelevant whether the IP address is a fixed address, assigned

337. Paragraphs 178, 179 and 180.

permanently to a single user, or a dynamic address, successively assigned to multiple users, since each of them represents an "access number."[338]

On the other hand, it could be argued that an IP address shall be classified solely as "traffic data" (Article 1(d) of the Convention) and not as "subscriber information" (Article 18(3)(b) of the Convention), since the latter is a distinct third category, other than traffic and content data, which links the electronic addresses involved with the natural or legal persons who use them, such as the names, addresses and other personal information about the owners or users of email accounts which are often held by ISPs for billing purposes.[339]

Obtaining information from service providers to identify the IP address used by a subscriber or, vice versa, to identify the IP address used by a known person, is crucial for cybercrime investigations, while subscriber information is the most sought data in international cooperation requests.[340] In its Report with the title *Rules on obtaining subscriber information*," the Cybercrime Convention Committee sustains that IP addresses might be considered both traffic data and subscriber information.

In this context, IP addresses may be considered to be subscriber information—as opposed to traffic data—if the purpose is to obtain the identification of a subscriber in relation to an IP address. Classifying IP addresses as traffic data or as subscriber data might prove to be of significant importance, since the differentiation between these two categories of data might be accompanied with different procedural rules in respect of their obtaining and processing. As it is stated in the Report, "in some countries, the interference with the rights of individuals is considered to be substantially different when obtaining subscriber information, including in relation to an IP address, in a specific criminal investigation on the one hand, and traffic data on the other" and therefore, the conditions for obtaining subscriber data might not be similar but lower than those for traffic data (e.g., the production of subscriber information can be ordered by the police or a prosecutor and not by a Court).[341]

---

338. Cybercrime Convention Committee (T-CY) T-CY Guidance Note #8, *Obtaining subscriber information for an IP address used in a specific communication within a criminal investigation*, (draft), available at: http://www.coe.int/t/dghl/cooperation/economiccrime/Source/Cybercrime/TCY/TCY%202013/T-CY%282013%2926_guidanceNote8_subscriber%20info_V10.pdf (Strasbourg, Nov. 12, 2013).

339. L. Angers, *Combating Cybercrime: National Legislation as a Prerequisite for International Cooperation*, in: Ernesto Ugo Savona, *Crime and Technology, New Frontiers for Regulation, Law enforcement and Research*, 46 (Springer 2004). Orders to produce "subscriber information" are only useful where the information is accurate. Many criminals do not use their real identities to subscribe to Internet services, or they register the services under an empty holding company. *See* Alana Maurushat, *Australia's Accession to the "Cybercrime Convention": Is the "Convention" Still Relevant in Combating Cybercrime in the Era of Botnets and Obfuscation Crime Tools?* (Mar. 31, 2011) 33(2) Uni. New South Wales Law J. 431-473 (2010); UNSW Law Research Paper No. 2011-20, available at SSRN: http://ssrn.com/abstract=1800503.

340. Cybercrime Convention Committee, *Rules on Obtaining Subscriber Information*, Report adopted by the T-CY at its 12th Plenary (Dec. 2-3, 2014), available online at: http://www.coe.int/t/dghl/cooperation/economiccrime/Source/Cybercrime/TCY/2014/T-CY%282014%2917_Report_Sub_Info_v7adopted.pdf.

341. Cybercrime Convention Committee, *ibid.*

[2] Processing of IP Address in Cybercrime Cases under the Scope of EU Law

The legal status of the IP address in EU privacy law is intrinsically linked to the general question of the legal protection of personal data in criminal investigation and proceedings. Indeed, if the IP address is considered to be personal data, then its processing shall be conducted in accordance with the general legal framework that has been established for the processing of personal data in criminal affairs.

Historically, the protection of personal data in criminal proceedings has been ominously marked by the different policies and principles of personal data protection, which have been applied in the first and third pillars. As it has already been mentioned, Directives 95/46 and 2002/58 did not apply in the processing of personal data concerning public security, defense, state security or the activities of the State in areas of criminal law since these matters were part of the European "third pillar"("Justice and Home Affairs"), until 2009.

Nevertheless, the boundaries between the first and third pillars have also appeared to be uncertain and in some instances have been strictly scrutinized by the CJEU. In this context, the Council Decision 2004/496/EC of May 17, 2004 on the conclusion of an Agreement between the European Community and the United States of America on the processing and transfer of PNR data by Air Carriers to the United States Department of Homeland Security, Bureau of Customs and Border Protection,[342] and the Commission Decision 2004/535 of 14 May 2004 on the adequate protection of personal data contained in the Passenger Name Record of air passengers transferred to the United States' Bureau of Customs and Border Protection,[343] were annulled by the Court on the grounds that the first pillar legal bases used to adopt them were inappropriate, since the decision does not concern data processing necessary for a supply of services, but data processing regarded as necessary for safeguarding public security, and for law enforcement purposes.[344]

The exclusion of personal data processing operations concerning public security, defense, state security or the activities of the State in areas of criminal law from the ambit of Directives 95/46 and 2002/58 has generated a significant asymmetry in the protection of personal data in these fields. The regulation of personal data protection safeguards in the third pillar has also been criticized as methodologically problematic. Rather than proceeding in logical order, by first establishing the general principles, the definitions and the institutions and then developing case-specific legislation, the EU has already introduced case-specific regulations (Schengen, Europol, Eurojust), while still missing any standard piece of legislation, such as the first pillar Directive 95/46.[345]

This imbalance was even more eminent after the terrorist attacks of September 11, 2001, which called for more severe and effective security measures, including the

342. OJ 2004 L 183, p. 83, and corrigendum at OJ 2005 L 255, p. 168.
343. OJ 2004 L 235/11.
344. G. González Fuster, *The Emergence of Personal Data Protection as a Fundamental Right of the EU* 220 (Springer 2014).
345. Bernd Martenczuk & Servaas van Thiel, *Justice, Liberty, Security: New Challenges for EU External Relations* 314 (VUBPRESS 2008).

massive processing of personal data.[346] Indeed, in the absence of any general third pillar EU instrument, the CoE's Convention 108,[347] continued to be the main legal instrument regulating the protection of personal data in this field.[348] Nonetheless, Convention 108 does not take into account the specific characteristics of the exchange of data by police and judicial authorities and was admittedly too broad and partly outdated.[349] In order to redress this imbalance, the Council Framework Decision 2008/977/JHA of November 27, 2008 on the protection of personal data processed in the framework of police and judicial cooperation in criminal matters was adopted.

Even so, the Framework Decision did not achieve to remedy this imbalance. One of the main reasons has been its restricted scope. The Framework Decision is not intended to cover national data processing, but applies only to inter-Member States data processing, meaning personal data that "are or have been transmitted or made available between Member States."[350] Member States are free to do as they please in their interior; some may even choose to provide "for the protection of personal data collected or processed at national level, higher safeguards than those established in this Framework Decision."[351] The limited scope and the loopholes of the Framework Decision have prepared the ground for its replacement by a new legal instrument. In this context, Directive (EU) 2016/680 of April 27, 2016 on personal data protection in criminal justice of April 27, 2016 on the protection of natural persons with regard to the processing of personal data by competent authorities for the purposes of the prevention, investigation, detection or prosecution of criminal offenses or the execution of criminal penalties, and on the free movement of such data and repealing Council Framework Decision 2008/977/JHA was voted on April 14, 2016.[352] As it is stated in the Explanatory Memorandum of the proposal of the Directive[353], it is not always easy to distinguish between purely domestic and cross-border processing, or to foresee whether certain personal data may become the object of a cross-border exchange at a later stage and, as a result, difficulties might arise for police and other competent

346. G. González Fuster, *supra* n. 344.
347. Convention for the Protection of Individuals with regard to Automatic Processing of Personal Data, Strasbourg, 28.01.1981.
348. G. González Fuster, *supra* n. 344.
349. P. De Hert & R. Bellanova, *Data Protection in the Area of Freedom, Security and Justice: A System Still to be Fully Developed?*, study requested by the European Parliament's Committee on Civil Liberties, Justice and Home Affairs (LIBE), Brussels, European Parliament, http://www.europarl.europa.eu/activities/committees/studies/download.do?language = en&file = 25213, 5 (2009).
350. Article 1.2(a).
351. Article 1.5.
352. Directive (EU) 2016/680 of the European Parliament and of the Council of 27 April 2016 on the protection of natural persons with regard to the processing of personal data by competent authorities for the purposes of the prevention, investigation, detection or prosecution of criminal offenses or the execution of criminal penalties, and on the free movement of such data, and repealing Council Framework Decision 2008/977/JHA OJ L 119, 4.5.2016, pp. 89–131.
353. Proposal for a Directive of the European Parliament and of the Council on the protection of individuals with regard to the processing of personal data by competent authorities for the purposes of prevention, investigation, detection or prosecution of criminal offenses or the execution of criminal penalties, and the free movement of such data, COM/2012/010 final – 2012/0010 (COD).

authorities in the areas of judicial cooperation in criminal matters and police cooperation. Moreover, serious interpretation issues might arise, since the Framework Decision has not provided for any mechanism or advisory group similar to the Article 29 Working Party supporting a coherent interpretation of its provisions. Furthermore, while the basic data protection principles, established since the 1960s in European data protection are also to be found in the Framework Decision, they are, nonetheless, accompanied by a series of exemptions[354] or by direct or more subtle derogations to the data protection principles,[355] such as in Article 3(1)[356] and Article 4(1)[357] and 4(2)[358] of the Framework Decision.

In this context, a basis for stronger data protection has been sought in the Recommendation No. R(87)15 of the Committee of ministers to Member States regulating the use of personal data in the police sector at CoE level.[359] In the view of WP29, the Recommendation No. R(87)15 shall be considered as the minimum required when setting out an equivalent legal framework at EU level in the sense that the Directive shall comply with the principles laid down by the Recommendation.[360]

The Recommendation sets some fundamental safeguards, such as the key principles of proportionality, purpose limitation, fairness of the processing, data accuracy and data minimization. In particular, according to Article 2.1, "the collection of personal data for police purposes should be limited to such as is necessary for the prevention of a real danger or the suppression of a specific criminal offence. Any exception to this provision should be the subject of specific national legislation."

354. Paul de Hert & Vagelis Papakonstantinou, *The Data Protection Framework Decision of 27 November 2008 Regarding Police and Judicial Cooperation in Criminal Matters – A Modest Achievement However Not the Improvement Some Have Hoped for*, 25 Computer L. & Security Rev. 409 (2009).
355. Paul de Hert & Vagelis Papakonstantinou, *ibid.*, 411.
356. Article 3.1: "further processing for another purpose shall be permitted in so far as: (a) it is not incompatible with the purposes for which the data were collected; (b) the competent authorities are authorised to process such data for such other purpose in accordance with the applicable legal provisions; and (c) processing is necessary and proportionate to that other purpose. The competent authorities may also further process the transmitted personal data for historical, statistical or scientific purposes, provided that Member States provide appropriate safeguards, such as making the data anonymous."
357. Council Framework Decision 2008/977/JHA Article 4(1) states that: "Personal data shall be rectified if inaccurate and, where this is possible and necessary, completed or updated."
358. "Personal data shall be erased or made anonymous when they are no longer required for the purposes for which they were lawfully collected or are lawfully further processed. Archiving of those data in a separate data set for an appropriate period in accordance with national law shall not be affected by this provision erased or made anonymous when they are no longer required for the purposes for which they were lawfully collected or are lawfully further processed. Archiving of those data in a separate data set for an appropriate period in accordance with national law shall not be affected by this provision."
359. Recommendation No. R(87)15 regulating the use of personal data in the police sector adopted by the Committee of Ministers of the CoE on Sep. 17, 1987 at the 410th meeting of the Ministers' Deputies. *See* http://ec.europa.eu/justice/data-protection/law/files/coe-fra-rpt-2670-en-471.pdf.
360. Opinion 03/2015 on the draft directive on the protection of individuals with regard to the processing of personal data by competent authorities for the purposes of prevention, investigation, detection or prosecution of criminal offenses or the execution of criminal penalties, and the free movement of such data, Dec. 01, 2015, 3211/15/EN, WP 233.

Furthermore, according to Article 2.3, "the collection of data by technical surveillance or other automated means should be provided for in specific provisions."

It remains to be seen whether the Directive will significantly enhance data protection in practice. The main challenge, which is highly relevant for the investigation and prosecution of cyber attacks, is how to safeguard fundamental rights and avoid mass surveillance without compromising the law enforcement efficiency. In this context, the Recital 26 of the Directive states that: "Any processing of personal data must be lawful, fair and transparent in relation to the natural persons concerned, and only processed for specific purposes laid down by law. This does not in itself prevent the law enforcement authorities from carrying out activities such as covert investigations or video surveillance. Such activities can be done for the purposes of the prevention, investigation, detection or prosecution of criminal offences or the execution of criminal penalties, including the safeguarding against and the prevention of threats to public security, as long as they are laid down by law and constitute a necessary and proportionate measure in a democratic society with due regard for the legitimate interests of the natural person concerned." The principal line of the Directive is to treat the processing of personal data for the purposes of prevention, investigation, detection or prosecution of criminal offenses or the execution of criminal penalties as a derogatory regime, which enables great flexibility for the competent authorities. This approach has been criticized by data protection defenders,[361] since the fragmentation of the legal regimes, which is expressed by an instrument of high level data protection (the Draft Regulation) and of a separate version of data protection rules (the Directive), could lead to inconsistencies in application, both due to differing provisions and, over time, due to court decisions under each instrument.[362]

Some clarifications are necessary. For example, the EU legislator has followed the Council of the European Union's proposition to enlarge the scope of application of the Directive in order to include in its scope the prevention of threats to public security.[363] In this context, it is crucial to clarify what "safeguarding against and the prevention of threats to public security" means and, more precisely to define the distinction between activities related to "public security," which fall within the scope of the Directive, and "national security," which do not.[364] This might be of great relevance for cyber attacks, if the concept of "public security" is given a broad sense, while in case of cyber attacks which strictly compromise national security the Directive would not be applicable. In

361. *See* the Opinion of the European Data protection Supervisor on the data protection reform package, Mar. 7, 2012, at: http://www.europarl.europa.eu/document/activities/cont/201205/20120524ATT45776/20120524ATT45776EN.pdf.

362. Alison Knight, EU Justice Ministers agree 'common position' for new EU data protection rules in the field of law enforcement, Oct. 13, 2015, at: https://peepbeep.wordpress.com/2015/10/13/eu-justice-ministers-agree-common-position-for-new-eu-data-protection-rules-in-the-field-of-law-enforcement/.

363. Interinstitutional File: 2012/0010 (COD), Brussels, Oct. 2, 2015. *See* http://www.statewatch.org/news/2015/oct/eu-council-dp-leas-position-12555-15.pdf. *See* Article 1 paragraph 1 of the Directive.

364. Comments of EDRI, FIPR and Panoptykon on selected key elements of the current Council text on the proposal for the Law Enforcement Data Protection Directive. *See* https://panoptykon.org/sites/default/files/leadimage-biblioteka/ledp_civilsocietyanalysisfinal_0.pdf.

order to clarify this situation, it could have been pertinent to correlate, in the framework of cyber attacks, the notion of public security with the notion of attack against critical infrastructure.

Furthermore, the European Commission proposed two legislative proposals to enhance cross-border gathering of electronic evidence: a Regulation on European Production and Preservation Orders for electronic evidence in criminal matters[365] and a Directive on the appointment of legal representatives for the purpose of gathering evidence in criminal proceedings.[366] The purpose of the proposal is to allow law enforcement authorities in one EU Member State to "seek preservation or production of data that is stored by a service provider located in another jurisdiction."[367]« In parallel, the CoE has been preparing a new protocol to the Convention on Cybercrime on cross-border access to data by law enforcement authorities.[368] Similarly, the United States, adopted the US Clarifying Lawful Use of Overseas Data (CLOUD) Act, which allows to access data stored outside of US territory while bypassing the legal safeguards of traditional international cooperation frameworks.[369]

Two new legal mechanisms will be created on the basis of the proposed Regulation: a European Production Order (EPdO) and a European Preservation Order (EPsO). Article 2(1) of the draft text of the Regulation defines an EPdO as a binding decision by an issuing authority of a Member State compelling a service provider offering services in the Union and established or represented in another Member State, to produce electronic evidence." The EPsO is defined in Article 2(2)) as "a binding decision by an issuing authority of a Member State compelling a service provider offering services in the Union and established or represented in another Member State, to preserve electronic evidence in view of a subsequent request for production." A service provider can be a natural or a legal person that offers electronic communication services, information society services and Internet domain name and IP numbering services. According to Article 2(6), the term "electronic evidence" includes noncontent data (subscriber data, access data, transactional data) and content data. In terms of the infringement of fundamental rights, the regulation distinguishes two groups of categories of data: subscriber and access data on the one hand, which are considered as less intrusive, and transactional and content data, which are considered as more significantly intrusive. This classification has an impact on the possibility of using the order, which is limited to some categories of offenses for transactional and content data,

365. Proposal for a Regulation of the European Parliament and of the Council on European Production and Preservation Orders for electronic evidence in criminal matters COM/2018/225 final - 2018/0108 (COD).
366. Proposal for a Directive of the European Parliament and of the Council laying down harmonized rules on the appointment of legal representatives for the purpose of gathering evidence in criminal proceedings COM/2018/226 final - 2018/0107 (COD).
367. *See* Sofija Voronova, Legislative Train Schedule, JD – European Production and Preservation Orders for electronic evidence in criminal matters (2017), available at: https://www.europarl.europa.eu/legislative-train/theme-area-of-justice-and-fundamental-rights/file-jd-cross-border-access-to-e-evidence-production-and-preservation-orders.
368. In June 2017, the T-CY agreed on the Terms of Reference for the preparation of the Protocol and negotiations commenced in September 2017. They are expected to be completed by December 2020. *See* https://www.coe.int/en/web/cybercrime/t-cy-drafting-group.
369. Clarifying Lawful Overseas Use of Data Act (CLOUD) Act (H.R. 4943).

whereas it is open to all offenses for subscriber and access data.[370] Specifically, issuing an EPdO for transactional or content data is limited to two groups of offenses. First, the EPdO may be issued for "offenses punishable in the issuing State by a custodial sentence of a maximum of at least three years." Second, the EPdO may be issued regardless of the severity of punishment on the national level in the cases of fraud and counterfeiting of noncash means of payment, sexual abuse and sexual exploitation of children and child pornography, attacks against information systems and terrorism.

On November 2019, the European Data Protection Supervisor (EDPS) issued its opinion on the two e-evidence proposals, by highlighting that it is necessary to establish necessary safeguards, including greater involvement of the judicial authorities in the enforcing Member State, as well as to take into consideration the case law of the CJEU and to clarify definitions of data categories in the proposed Regulation.[371] Specifically, the proposed Regulation creates artificially new categories of data which do not fit easily within the existing EU privacy legal framework. The classification of the IP address is a significant example of the conundrum that might occur by the terminology used in the proposed Regulation. In this regard, the EDPS points out that IP addresses could fall in both categories of transactional data and subscriber data, in addition to the category of access data which specifically mentions IP address. This means that IP addresses should receive different legal treatment and produced under different conditions depending on the category under which the production is requested. In this context, the EDPS recommends the amendment of the definition of subscriber data in order to further specify this category in relation to IP address, and to avoid overlap with other data categories.[372]

§2.06 INVESTIGATION AND PROSECUTION OF CYBERCRIME AND JURISDICTION

[A] The Issue

The difficulties with regard to investigation for acquiring, preserving and using electronic evidences in court are coupled with equally challenging enforcement issues due to the fact that cybercrime has often "transnational" or "international" dimensions and elements.[373] It is not rare for a cyber attack to be transnational in terms of the physical location of victims/damaged system, offenders and evidence. More specifically a crime may be regarded as "transnational" if: (a) it is committed in more than one

370. Stanislaw Tosza, The European Commission's Proposal on Cross-Border Access to E-Evidence, Overview and Critical Remarks, available at: https://eucrim.eu/articles/european-commissions-proposal-cross-border-access-e-evidence/.

371. EDPS, Opinion on Proposals regarding European Production and Preservation Orders for electronic evidence in criminal matters, Opinion 7/2019, Nov. 6, 2019. Available at: https://edps.europa.eu/sites/edp/files/publication/opinion_on_e_evidence_proposals_en.pdf.

372. EDPS, *ibid.*, p. 9.

373. Jurisdictional issues may be dealt on multiple levels (international law, national approaches etc.). In the context of this study, we discuss jurisdiction and the respective principles under the spectrum of the consequences for cybercrime enforcement and the gaps and requirements that are identified.

state; (b) it is committed in one state but a substantial part of its preparation, planning, direction or control takes place in another state;[374] (c) it is committed in one state but has substantial effects in another state.[375]

Jurisdictional issues arise where an element or substantial effect of the cybercrime offense or part of the *modus operandi* of the cybercrime offense is in another territory. Such elements may refer to "conduct," "circumstances" or "result(s)."[376] A transnational dimension existed if and when one or more of these elements occurs in, or produces substantial effects within another territorial jurisdiction.[377] Many cybercrime cases could be regarded as transnational although prima facie they are not identified as such due to failure to detect evidence in another territory.[378] Botnets used as spyware are an example of a cybercrime that has often international or transnational implications.

Walden regards the jurisdictional distinction between the initiation and the termination of an information-based criminal activity as the norm.[379] According to the findings of the United Nations Office on Drugs and Crime (UNODC) Study on Cybercrime 30%–70% of cybercrime offenses involve a transnational dimension while countries in Europe perceived the highest proportion of cybercrime acts involving a transnational element.[380] Cross-border and extraterritorial investigation is relevant not only for attacks against information systems but also for all crimes that are facilitated by the use of communications means (such as smartphone apps) or by cloud computing services (such as cloud storage platforms).

In the context of this study, the transnational dimension is examined also with reference to considerations of evidence. Technically, it is possible to collect remotely evidence that is physically located in an information system, in a state, but logically accessible and retrievable by an LEA in another state. However, such practices constitute an interference with the internal order of another sovereign state and may also affect a person's rights and interests through, for example, interference with secrecy of communications or accumulation of sanctions.

The transnational dimension itself raises issues of sovereignty and jurisdiction which gives spatial scope to the law and determines the spatial boundaries of LEAs and judiciary. While jurisdiction is dealt as synonymous to "territory," cyberspace is conceptualized in theory either as "distinct place" separated from the "real world" and

374. According to the UNODC Cybercrime Study, in many countries that have responded the questionnaire, provisions reflect the idea that the "whole" offense need not take place within the country in order to assert territorial jurisdiction as reference to elements or effects of the act, or the location of computer systems or data utilized for the offense are regarded as sufficient linkage; *supra* n. 52, 183.
375. UNODC, *Comprehensive Study on Cybercrime, supra* n. 52, 188 (2013).
376. *Ibid.*
377. *Ibid.*
378. As acknowledged by the experts drafting the CoE R 95(13) concerning problems of criminal procedural law connected with information technology, investigators were not always aware that the systems and data were located on a foreign territory, but shared a common understanding.
379. I. Walden, *Computer Crime*, in *Computer Law* 295 (C. Reed & J. Angel eds, London 2003).
380. UNODC, *Cybercrime Study, supra* n. 52, 183.

thus to be treated differently[381] or as a place connected to the offline material space that has to be viewed as a part thereof.[382] Despite the revolutionary changes ICT and Internet brought with, we should not consider cyberspace as a separate "sphere" also for the reason that criminal law[383] and its enforcement remains based on and bound with the principle of territoriality and location,[384] even if location of conduct/suspect or evidence cannot or only through immense and time-consuming effort, be identified.[385]

A major issue is whether the specific characteristics of cybercrime and its transnational borderless structure would urge to develop new and additional jurisdiction principles and arrangements to regulate the online world. As noted by Kaspersen, the question whether or not the borderless nature of cybercrime and cyberspace would bring a need for the development or adaptation of jurisdiction principles to be applied in cyberspace was answered negatively by the drafting committee of the Cybercrime Convention.[386]

Although this approach is understandable we should take into consideration that some key traditional notions, such as location, may have undergone significant changes in online environment. The determination of *locus delicti* as well as the definition of the applicable law and the relevant jurisdiction are associated with difficulties for LEAs and judicial officers by issuing warrants, drafting subpoenas and committing a case for trial.[387]

In a traditional environment, a search involves gathering evidence that has been recorded or registered in the past in tangible form. In the offline search, the precondition for obtaining legal authority to undertake a search is the existence of grounds to believe that such data exists in a particular location. Even if the "loss of location" for example in cloud environment could be conceptualized as "loss of knowledge of location" in cybercrime cases, and more specifically in cases of remote attacks against information systems, the "true data location is rarely known at the outset of an investigation or at the point at which data access may be required."[388] Moreover, it is

381. *See* about the seminal article of D.R. Johnson & D.G. Post, *Law and Borders – The Rise of Law in Cyberspace*, 48 Stanford L. Rev. 1367ff (1996). The idea of cyberspace as a "distinct place," a new topos, is quite extensively presented in B.-J. Koops & M. Goodwin, *Cyberspace, the Cloud, and Cross-Border Criminal Investigation The Limits and Possibilities of International Law* 87ff (2014).

382. *See* J.L. Goldsmith, *Against Cyberanarchy*, 65 University of Chicago L. Rev. 1199–1250 (1998).

383. In this respect, an argument of importance is that most cybercrime acts consist of virtual and physical activity. *See* H.W. Kaspersen, *Cybercrime and Internet Jurisdiction*, Discussion Paper, CoE, 40 (2009).

384. As noted by Koops and Goodwin, cyberspace is not currently understood within international law as a separate legal space with specialized rules. The consequence is that data are viewed in international law through the lens of material objects—as a physical thing—that is necessarily located somewhere; *supra* n. 381, 21.

385. This is a major problem with regard to law enforcement in cloud environments.

386. *See* H.W. Kaspersen, *supra* n. 383, 40.

387. S.W. Brenner, & B.-J Koops, *Approaches to Cyber Crime Jurisdiction*, 15(1) J. High Tech. Crime, 1 et seq. (2004).

388. UNODC, *Cybercrime Study*, *supra* n. 52, 5, 218ff. Kaspersen is of the opinion that there is no certainty whatsoever of the physical location of the data, necessary as a nexus for the execution of investigative powers within the domestic sphere or *a fortiori* within the international sphere; *see* H.W. Kaspersen, *supra* n. 383, 29.

questionable whether in offenses such as the attacks against information systems it is possible to determine a single "location" per se.

Jurisdictional issues arise both with respect to prescriptive jurisdiction, i.e., the power related to setting of rules and the enforcement jurisdiction, i.e., the ability to enforce an offense. As evidence gathering may extend beyond national territories, traditional procedures of mutual assistance are to be initiated. Transnational evidence collection is, however, subject to multiple legal requirements and restrictions as well as organizational limitations.

[B] The Principles

International law and multilateral cybercrime instruments provide for a number of bases of jurisdiction over cybercrime acts, primarily including nationality and forms of based jurisdiction. Territoriality and nationality are grounded on the sovereignty of a state that denotes the right to exercise all the functions of a state with respect to a defined physical space and frames also the forms and boundaries of international cooperation.[389]

The Cybercrime Convention and the Directive 2013/40/EC prescribe jurisdiction on the base of nationality. According to Article 22(1d) of the Budapest Convention, each Party shall establish jurisdiction when the offense is committed by one of its nationals, if the offense is punishable under criminal law where it was committed or if the offense is committed outside the territorial jurisdiction of any State. The Directive 2013/40/EC grounds jurisdiction to nationality at least in cases where the act is an offense where it was committed (Article 12).

[1] Territoriality and Jurisdictional Conflicts

As law enforcement and criminal justice matters fall within the exclusive domain of the sovereign state, criminal jurisdiction remains linked to geographical territory. It seems that various legal orders establish their jurisdiction based on location of "computer systems and/or data" used or damaged/affected or on the location where the offense was—even partly—carried out, even it was initiated or completed in another territory.[390]

The definition of territory poses additional difficulties when it comes to crimes committed against information systems, as with regard to an offender acting via web-based connection it may often not be clear in which location an act has been

389. *See* Cameron S.D. Brown, *supra* n. 174, 93. From the right of a state to sovereignty and territorial integrity and to freely determine their own political, economic, cultural and social system, derives the obligation of other States not to intervene in any form or for any reason whatsoever in the internal and external affairs of other states. *See Declaration on the Inadmissibility of Intervention in the Domestic Affairs of States*, Annex to GA resolution A/RES/20/2131 (XX), Dec. 21, 1965.

390. UNODC, *Cybercrime Study*, *supra* n. 52, 191ff.

executed.[391] It seems easier to detect the location of "effects," although in the context of cloud computing it may be proved difficult to decide about the relevant location as data, are constantly shifting from one data center to another. As in the case of traditional forms of crime, a "sufficient connection" or "genuine link" between the criminal offense and the state claiming and/or exercising jurisdiction is commonly required.[392]

As indicated above, international and regional regulatory instruments do not require all elements of the offense to occur within the territory for territorial jurisdiction to apply. Under the CoE Convention on Cybercrime a Party could assert territorial jurisdiction if both the person attacking a computer system and the victim system are located within its territory, and where the computer system attacked is within its territory, even if the attacker is not.[393] This approach has been adopted also by the Framework Decision on Attacks against information systems (Article 10) and confirmed by the Directive 2013/40/EC: Member States shall establish their jurisdiction with regard to the offenses included in the Directive where the offense has been committed in whole or in part within their territory while ensuring that they have jurisdiction where (a) the offender commits the offense when physically present on its territory, whether or not the offense is against an information system on its territory; or (b) the offense is against an information system on its territory, whether or not the offender commits the offense when physically present on its territory (Article 12).

[2] Jurisdictional Conflicts

Especially in the networked world, the territoriality of criminal law does not always correspond to territorial sovereignty as an act may be initiated in one jurisdiction and the effects thereof occur in another jurisdiction.[394] Operation of jurisdiction can result to the so-called jurisdictional conflict, i.e., more than one country assume jurisdiction over a cybercrime offense. In cases of "concurrent" jurisdiction, the European approach is focusing on cooperation or consultation between the states concerned.[395] The Framework Decision on Attacks against Information Systems not only provided for cooperation between the Member States but also it included explicitly the aim of "centralizing proceedings in a single Member State" (Article 10(4)) inviting Member States to recourse to anybody or mechanism established within the European Union for facilitating cooperation.

The Directive 2013/40/EU does not include an equivalent provision. It introduces a role for the European Commission as a point of information of the intention of a Member State to establish jurisdiction over an offense committed outside its territory (Article 10(3)), without clarifying further if the Commission will have to act as a

391. Cybercrime Convention Committee (T-CY), *supra* n. 162, 8.
392. UNODC, *Cybercrime Study*, *supra* n. 52, 196.
393. CoE Cybercrime Convention – Explanatory Report (233).
394. *See* Cameron S.D. Brown, *supra* n. 174, 61.
395. This approach is expressed in Article 22(5) of the CoE Cybercrime Convention or Article 10(4) of the Decision on Attacks against Information System.

coordinating body. In order to facilitate the coordination of prosecution of cases of attacks against information systems, the European legislator refers[396] to the application of the Council Framework Decision 2009/948/JHA of November 30, 2009 on prevention and settlement of conflict of jurisdiction in criminal proceedings. The objective of the Framework Decision is to promote a closer cooperation between the competent authorities of two or more Member States conducting criminal proceedings to prevent situations where the same person is subject to parallel criminal proceedings in different Member States in respect of the same facts. The Framework Decision sets up a model of cooperation based on information, consultation and a referral of the case to Eurojust when the competent authorities are not able to reach consensus.[397]

[C] Extraterritorial Jurisdiction

"The first and foremost restriction imposed by international law upon a State is that – failing the existence of a permissive rule to the contrary – it may not exercise its power in any form in the territory of another State."[398] As the principle of territorial jurisdiction is a deduction of territorial sovereignty, the exercising of investigation/enforcement powers is not allowed in another state, as it would impinge on its territorial sovereignty. "... In this sense jurisdiction is certainly territorial; it cannot be exercised by a State outside its territory except by virtue of a permissive rule derived from international custom or convention."[399]

Despite its predominance, the territoriality principle collides with the pressing needs of law enforcement in the digital era and virtual space where data are fragmented over, dynamically composed from, moving between or they are stored on servers in multiple jurisdictions. Another problem consists in the fact that often an agency that conducts investigation via an electronic network may not be in a position to determine whether the data set to be accessed are stored on its own territory or abroad while the increasing use of cloud computing and external hosting providers services are further complicating the situation. As the "claim of exclusive authority or jurisdiction over a defined place that was such a key part of modernity – the territorial state – is being increasingly undermined,"[400] law has come to recognize also extraterritorial jurisdiction in criminal matters. In any case, restrictions upon the sovereignty and consequently the "consent" of the other state to such a restriction cannot be presumed.[401]

396. *See* Recital 27 of the Directive 2013/40/EU.
397. *See* Recital 4 of the Council Framework Decision 2009/948/JHA. The Eurojust is regarded as particularly well suited to provide assistance in resolving conflicts of jurisdiction. Eurojust has to be informed of any case where conflicts of jurisdiction have arisen or are likely to arise and that a case can be referred to Eurojust at any moment if at least one competent authority involved in the direct consultations deems it appropriate. The referral of a case to Eurojust should be a usual step, when it has not been possible to reach consensus (Recital 14).
398. Case of the *S.S. "Lotus"* (*France v. Turkey*), PCIJ Series A, No. 10, at 18 (1927).
399. *Ibid.*
400. B.-J. Koops & M. Goodwin, *supra* n. 381, 35.
401. About an analysis of Lotus case and its significance for international law, *see* W. Friedmann, *The Uses of "General Principles" in the Development of International Law*, American J. Intl. L. 280 (1963).

Jurisdiction in International law is based upon reciprocity and—with regard to criminal proceedings—on the classic procedures of mutual legal assistance.

However, with respect to cybercrime it is highly arguable if the traditional procedure of mutual legal assistance is adequate to serve criminal investigation purposes. The issue has arisen especially with regard to the need for securing of data that relate to criminal offenses that have cross-border elements and where immediate action is required. Without an unambiguous legal ground, search and seizure extended to foreign jurisdiction could be viewed as violation of state sovereignty or international law.[402]

[D] Transborder Access to Evidence under the Cybercrime Convention

Already with the emergence of cybercrime, both scholars and cyber-investigation practitioners have recognized the challenge of extraterritorial collection of data controlled by third parties. Moreover, they have emphasized the need to move beyond the classic mutual legal assistance. The issue of cross-border access to electronic evidence was raised since the 1980s in the context of the discussions on CoE in Recommendation R(89)9 on Computer-related Crime but apparently neither the need was pressing nor the time has been evaluated as "ripe."[403] The Council of Minister's Recommendation 95(13) about the feasibility of transborder network searches reflected the common understanding that an investigative activity in international networks and/or computer systems located in a foreign territory could not be launched without prior consent of the State concerned. The Recommendation left States to negotiate the form and conditions of transborder searches.

The international community had developed longstanding methods for obtaining and providing legal assistance. These processes, however, were time consuming and often contained limitations as to what type of assistance can be obtained. The drafters of the Convention on Cybercrime discussed in detail the issue of when an investigative authority is permitted to unilaterally access data stored in another state, without seeking mutual assistance.[404]

Member States under the Cybercrime Convention accepted the transborder access to stored computer data in another state without the authorization of the latter in two situations: (1) where the data being accessed is publicly available, regardless if where the data is stored geographically, (2) where the investigative authority has accessed or received data located outside of its territory through a computer system in

402. Cybercrime Convention Committee (T-CY), *supra* n. 162, 6.

403. CoE – European Committee on Crime Problems, Computer-Related Crime, Strasbourg 1990. The Committee has recognized that there would be a "need to coordinate the investigation, prosecution and punishment" (p. 85) but it has considered that the question of the so-called direct penetration in another territory may affect the principle of sovereignty and may constitute a coercive measure and an infringement of the exclusive right of the judicial authorities to carry out investigations in their own national territory and refrained from questioning important principles of international law in this limited context (p. 88).

404. CoE, Explanatory Report to the Convention on Cybercrime, 293 (ETS 185), 2001, online available at: http://www.coe.int.

its jurisdiction, and it has obtained the lawful and voluntary consent of the person, who has lawful authority to disclose the data to the investigation through that system.

Although the provisions on national procedural law do not regulate investigation of open sources, the Cybercrime Convention contains a provision on cross-border access to open-source data. With regard to transborder access to publicly available data that is regulated by Article 32a of the Cybercrime Convention, investigating authorities are allowed to directly access information on publicly available sources such as information published on a website. Furthermore, they may download the data, take screenshots or likewise secure such data and use them as evidence without having to ask for mutual legal assistance or the permission of the State where the system hosting the data is located. As indicated in the Guidance Note on Article 32 of the Cybercrime Committee (CoE), it is commonly understood that law enforcement officials may access any data that the public may access,[405] provided that the domestic law does not limit law enforcement access and/or use of such data. This kind and base of access has been become accepted international practice[406] and—according to Cybercrime Convention Committee (T-CY)—it has raised no particular interpretation's issues.[407] However as open-source investigations often constitute an interference with the right to privacy they also have to comply with data protection legislation. Open-source investigation tools and practices used must meet general data-protection requirements and forensic reliability standards.[408]

Article 32b, the most important provision with regard to transborder access to data for the purpose of enforcement and evidence gathering, addresses the situation where a law enforcement authority accesses data stored in another State with the consent of the person lawfully authorized to disclose the data.[409] The Convention and the Explanatory Memorandum do not lay down the criteria for the person to be lawfully authorized. Both the law and other regulations, included contracts, are acceptable as basis. In any case the lawfulness will depend on the national legal framework, which can vary considerably among party states.[410] The Convention does not regulate the manner for obtaining the "voluntary consent." However, in order to serve as a legal

405. However in the Guidance it is clarified that if a part of public website, service or similar is closed to the public, then it is not considered publicly available in the meaning of Article 32a.
406. Scholars regard access to publicly available data stored in another territory as part of international customary law due to the general, worldwide use of the Internet, the often lacking knowledge of users of the physical location where data is stored as well as the low intensity of the intrusion when public data is accessed in cyberspace. *See* U. Sieber, *Straftaten und Strafverfolgung im Internet*. Gutachten C zum 69. Deutschen Juristentag. München 144–145 (2012).
407. Cybercrime Convention Committee (T-CY), *supra* n. 162.
408. For a further analysis, B.-J. Koops, *Police Investigations in Internet Open Sources: Procedural-Law Issues*, 29(6) Computer L. & Sec. Rev. 654, 663ff. (2013).
409. The Convention and the Explanatory Memorandum do not lay down the criteria for the person to be lawfully authorized. Both the law and other regulations, including contracts, are acceptable as basis.
410. B.-J. Koops & M. Goodwin, *supra* n. 381, 53.

basis, such consent should be free, informed, explicit[411] and obtained prior to the access to the data.[412]

According to the Explanatory Report (paragraph 294) a typical situation where Article 32b could be applicable is the case that a person's mail may be stored in another country by a service provider, or a person may intentionally store data in another country. These persons may retrieve the data and, provided that they have the lawful authority, they may voluntarily disclose the data to law enforcement officials or permit such officials to access the data. According to Article 32b "other situations are neither authorized, nor precluded."

Law enforcement authorities may be neither aware nor able to determine that an ongoing search extends to networks, systems and data that are located in territories of other states. In some contexts, such as the cloud computing environment, it is often not apparent, whether the connected system under search on the basis of Article 19 paragraph 2 of the Convention is indeed on the territory of the investigating LEA. Therefore in situations where it is unknown whether, or not certain that, data are stored in another territory, the LEAs may need to evaluate themselves the legitimacy of a search or other type of access in the light of domestic law, relevant international law principles or considerations of international relations.[413]

The provision of Article 32b is drafted in "permissive terms," i.e., there is no need to seek the authorities of that State on which territory data are stored. The provision does not clarify however, if the access is to notify to the other State party, "neither prohibiting it nor requiring it."[414] It is entirely in the discretion of the accessing authority if it considers it appropriate[415] to inform the accessed state, either before or after it has obtained the data sought. Although notification is not obligatory it is recommended as good practice that guarantees a certain degree of transparency.[416]

Article 32b is a measure to be applied in specific criminal investigations and proceedings within the scope of Article 14 of the Convention that regulates for the scope of procedural provisions.[417] The Convention does not prohibit States' Parties from preventing other States' Parties so accessing data stored in their territory. Such a prohibition would however be regarded as "incompatible with the spirit of the Article."[418]

411. General agreement by a person to terms and conditions of an online service used might not constitute explicit consent even if these terms and conditions indicate that data may be shared with criminal justice authorities in cases of abuse. Cybercrime Convention Committee (T-CY) T-CY Guidance Note #3, *Transborder access to data (Article 32)*, adopted by the 12th Plenary of the T-CY (Dec. 2–3, 2014), 7.
412. *See* H.W. Kaspersen, *supra* n. 383, 83.
413. Cybercrime Convention Committee (T-CY), T-CY Guidance Note #3, *supra* n. 411, 6.
414. UNODC, *Cybercrime Study*, *supra* n. 52, 218.
415. Cybercrime Convention Committee (T-CY), *supra* n. 162, 21.
416. M. Gercke, *Understanding Cybercrime: Phenomena, Challenges and Legal Response*, 278 (Geneva: ITU 2012).
417. Cybercrime Convention Committee (T-CY), T-CY Guidance Note #3, *supra* n. 411, 5.
418. UNODC, *Cybercrime Study*, *supra* n. 52, 218.

[E] Direct Contact to Service Provider

The access framework provided by Article 32b has been not very often used by law enforcement authorities.[419] It seems that instead of using the means of international judicial cooperation or this of Article 32b, LEAs prefer to obtain access via service providers or other private sector entities. Although such requests usually do not refer to content data and they allowed by the Convention,[420] the direct contact with foreign service providers has raised concerns, and it is not the type of transborder access to data that is generally encouraged or accepted in international law or policy:[421] the CoE itself discourages the "direct access directly to non-domestic ISPs and recommends to make use of make use of procedures as described in international treaties, such as the Convention on Cybercrime and the network of 24/7 law enforcement points-of-contact for urgent measures, including preservation orders/requests."[422]

Scholars questioned the compliance of this practice with the sovereignty of the foreign state.[423] This contested practice has implications especially in the case of cloud computing. Therefore, the Article 29 Data Protection Working Party recommended to adopt legislative measures to prohibit data controllers operating in the EU from disclosing personal data to a third country if so requested by a third country's judicial or administrative authority, unless this is expressly authorized by an international agreement or provided for by mutual legal assistance treaties or approved by a supervisory authority.[424]

[F] Transborder Access under the Directive 2013/40/EU

With regard to the transborder access to data for investigation purposes, the European Legislator adopted a quite different approach. There are no specific rules concerning the modes and conditions for accessing data in another state. Cooperation, coordination and approximation criminal law seem to be the main choices of the Directive 2013/40/EU on attacks against information systems as far as it concerns attacks with a cross-border dimension.

As indicated above this Directive does not govern conditions for exercising jurisdiction over any of the offenses regulated.[425] It introduces the obligation of a Member State to inform the Commission when it decides to establish jurisdiction over an offense committed outside its territory. The exchange of information is regulated in Article 13 and consists in the establishment and use of operational national point of

---

419. Cybercrime Convention Committee (T-CY), *supra* n. 162, 57.
420. According to the Cybercrime Convention Committee (T-CY), it is not always clear whether such a request may be considered a transborder measure or a domestic request if the private sector entity is delivering the service in the state of the investigating LEA, p. 57.
421. B.-J. Koops & M. Goodwin, *supra* n. 381, 58.
422. CoE, Economic Crime Division, *Guidelines for the Cooperation between Law Enforcement and Internet Service Providers against Cybercrime*, Guideline 36 (2008).
423. *See* U. Sieber, *Straftaten und Strafverfolgung im Internet.* Gutachten C zum 69. Deutschen Juristentag, 147–148 (C.H. Beck 2012), and M. Gercke, *supra* n. 416, 278 et seq.
424. Article 29 Working Party, *Opinion 05/2012 on Cloud Computing*, 22 (2012).
425. *See* Recital 21 of the Directive 2013/40/EU.

contacts and the obligation to have procedures in place for responding to urgent requests for assistance. In addition, the coordination of prosecution of cases of attacks against information systems has to be facilitated by the adequate implementation and application of Council Framework Decision 2009/948/JHA on prevention and settlement of conflict of jurisdiction in criminal proceedings, although it is questionable if its provisions may be tailored to the requirements of cybercrime.

The Framework Decision is focused on preventing situations that the same person may be subject to parallel criminal proceedings in different Member States.[426] In order to avoid the adverse consequences arising from parallel proceedings the Framework Decision considers the concentration of the proceedings in one State or the reference to Eurojust if there is no ability for reaching a consensus. The exchange of information between competent authorities and reply to requests submitted by competent authorities of another Member State are listed as obligation of Member States.

When drafting Article 32 of the Cybercrime Convention it was concluded that "the time for an overall regulation of transborder network searches had not yet come." The need for a comprehensive "and complicate" regulation had to be considered on the basis of experiences with the provided legal tools and instruments. The States which were negotiating Cybercrime Convention have avoided detailed regulation and opted for "constructive ambiguity" so that it could address different situations. The EU approach is constructed on cooperation and coordination that have to be enhanced and optimized.

From law enforcement practice cases it seems that the way for which the LEAs opted was primarily the mutual legal assistance. Even in states that allow transborder access, intrusive investigation techniques such as the "hacking" of a system or installation of surveillance tools (as keystroke loggers) are principally not permitted. Due to the difficulties of mutual legal assistance procedures practitioners sometimes proceed remotely to investigative activities on foreign territory without formal authorization. In particular, given the additional challenges of cyber-investigation, cross-border access to data has been also obtained in practice without—at least formal—permission from the foreign state in a variety of circumstances.[427]

The procedures of mutual legal assistance, although more flexible and less time consuming than in traditional mutual assistance relations, fall short of the aim to tackle the requirements in acquiring and safeguarding volatile electronic evidence. The discussion about instances in which it may be acceptable for national LEAs to act unilaterally for accessing evidences "located" in another territory has been initiated in the last years. It is recommended to further explore the cases under which unilateral actions can be agreed.[428] As the expansion of unilateral transborder access would require states to sacrifice a part of their sovereignty, concerns about the implications with jurisdiction and impact on rights and interests should be addressed. In this perspective unilateral remote access should be accomplished in a way that satisfies

426. *See* Recitals 3, 4 of the Framework Decision 2009/948/JHA on prevention and settlement of conflicts of exercise of jurisdiction in criminal proceedings.
427. About practices, *see also* Cybercrime Convention Committee (T-CY), *supra* n. 162, 32 et seq.
428. *Ibid.*, 58ff. *Also see* H.W. Kaspersen, *supra* n. 383, 89 et seq.

fundamental rights concerns (freedom of communication privacy, data protection, property rights) and rules of criminal law. It should be accompanied by procedures, provisions on enforcement and redress mechanisms. As noted by the Cybercrime Convention Committee, "no matter the urgency or importance of improving law enforcement ability to investigate and prosecute crimes facilitated by computers and the Internet, States will have to be satisfied that their interests, and the interests of their people, will be protected from undue access by other States."[429]

[G] Jurisdictional Issues and Transborder Access under the Draft Regulation on European Production and Preservation Orders for E-Evidence in Criminal Matters

During the last years it was argued that it is time to take into account that both "regular" crimes and cybercrimes may be committed across borders and consequently evidence, particularly with regard to cybercrimes, may be found anywhere in the world, making it "inevitable to have some overarching international regulations and agreements."[430] In this perspective, it had been proposed to separate judicial and enforcement jurisdiction from investigative jurisdiction to avoid "unnecessarily limiting the access to crossborder data (and electronic evidence)," the main argument being "that in the case of an investigation, the investigative jurisdiction should extend to any space where the data required for the investigation is located."[431]

The European Commission had repeatedly stressed the need for eliminating any obstacles to criminal investigation of cybercrime, including as concerns rules on access to electronic evidence. In April 2018, the European Commission presented two legislative proposals to enhance cross-border gathering of electronic evidence: a Regulation on European Production and Preservation Orders for electronic evidence in criminal matters and a Directive on the appointment of legal representatives for the purpose of gathering evidence in criminal proceedings. The Commission proposed a framework for direct and mandatory cross-border cooperation between law enforcement authorities of the Member States and service providers offering their services in the Union. According to the Proposal, enforcement jurisdiction is established irrespective of the location where the requested data is stored.[432]

The European legislators have been led to consider that "obtaining electronic evidence using judicial cooperation channels often takes a long time—longer than subsequent leads may be available. Furthermore, there is no clear framework for cooperation with service providers, while certain third-country providers accept direct

429. *See* Cybercrime Convention Committee (T-CY), *supra* n. 162, 16.
430. *See* M. Bonnici et al., *supra* n. 173.
431. *See* D. Svantesson, Preliminary Report: Law Enforcement Cross-Border Access to Data (Nov. 22, 2016). Available at SSRN: https://ssrn.com/abstract=2874238 or http://dx.doi.org/10.2139/ssrn.2874238.
432. *See* M. Böse, An assessment of the Commission's proposals on electronic evidence - STUDY Requested by the LIBE committee - Policy Department for Citizens' Rights and Constitutional Affairs Directorate General for Internal Policies of the Union, PE 604.989 (September 2018), EN, 8.

requests for noncontent data as permitted by their applicable domestic law."[433]The Draft Regulation of the European Parliament and of the Council on European production and preservation orders for electronic evidence in criminal matters[434] aims "at addressing the problems stemming from the volatile nature of e-evidence and the 'loss of location' aspect by setting new procedures for quick, efficient and effective cross-border access."[435] The draft Regulation lays down the rules under which an authority of a Member State may order a service provider offering services in the Union, to produce[436] or preserve[437] electronic evidence, regardless of the location of data.

According to the Draft-Regulation these orders can cover any category of data, e.g., subscriber, access, transactional and content data.[438] Addressee of the orders may be a service provider, defined as the natural or legal person that provides electronic communications services, Internet domain name and IP numbering services or other information society services as defined in point (b) of Article 1(1) of Directive (EU) 2015/1535. The draft Regulation provides for the obligation of the addressee to produce or preserve the requested data, without prior recognition by the Member State where the order shall be executed.

Instead of the executing Member State, the issuing Member State is assigned with the task to assess whether the conditions for the execution of the order are met. The second condition applicable to both orders refers to necessity and proportionality: However, a production order may only be issued if a similar measure would be available for the same criminal offence in a comparable domestic situation in the issuing State (Article 5(1)) while a Preservation Order may be issued where necessary and proportionate to prevent the removal, deletion or alteration of data in view of a subsequent request for production of this data via mutual legal assistance, a European Investigation Order or an EPdO (Article 6(2)).

The draft regulation provides as common conditions for issuing EPdO and European Preservation Order that they may be issued only for criminal proceedings

433. *See* Recital 8 of the Draft Regulation of the European Parliament and of the Council on European production and preservation orders for electronic evidence in criminal matters - General approach, Brussels, Jun. 11, 2019 (OR. en), 10206/19 (Interinstitutional File: 2018/0108(COD)). The present text takes into consideration the text issued by the Council of the European Union in June 2019.
434. *See* Draft Regulation of the European Parliament and of the Council on European production and preservation orders for electronic evidence in criminal matters - General approach, Brussels, Jun. 11, 2019 (OR. en), 10206/19 (Interinstitutional File: 2018/0108(COD)).
435. *See* Proposal for a Regulation of the European Parliament and of the Council on European production and preservation orders for electronic evidence in criminal matters - Policy debate. Interinstitutional File: 2018/0108(COD), Brussels, 4 October 2018, 2.
436. According to the definition included in Draft Regulation a 'European Production Order' means a binding decision by an issuing authority of a Member State compelling a service provider offering services in the Union and established or represented in another Member State, to produce electronic evidence (Article 2(1)).
437. According to the definition included in Draft Regulation a 'European Preservation Order' means a binding decision by an issuing authority of a Member State compelling a service provider offering services in the Union and established or represented in another Member State, to preserve electronic evidence in view of a subsequent request for production (Article 2(2)).
438. It is interesting to note that the Draft Regulation entails definitions of these categories of data.

(Article 3(2)).[439] With the aim to limit the scope of the instrument to more serious crimes the Draft-Regulation allows the issuing of orders for investigations that carry at least a three-year maximum sentence. However, it is noteworthy that this penalty frame is not required: (a) for terrorism related crimes and (b) the offences defined in the Articles 3–8 of the Directive 2013/40/EU on attacks against information systems. This is justified by the fact that in these cases "evidence will typically be available exclusively in electronic form, which is particularly fleeting in nature. This is the case for cyber-related crimes, even those which might not be considered serious in and of themselves but which may cause extensive or considerable damage, in particular including cases of low individual impact but high volume and overall damage. For most cases where the offence has been committed by means of an information system, applying the same threshold as for other types of offences would predominantly lead to impunity."[440]

The draft regulation is based on Article 82(1) TFEU[441] and is considered to implement the principle of mutual recognition. The goal of the Commission's proposal to establish a framework of direct cooperation between judicial and other competent authorities of the issuing Member State and private companies in another Member State has been criticized, as it "goes far beyond the well-established legislative practice and an understanding of mutual recognition of judicial decisions (Article. 82(1)2(a) TFEU) as cooperation between judicial or equivalent authorities of the MS (Article 82(1)(2)(d) TFEU)."[442]

Concerns have been raised also with regard to the principle of territorial sovereignty, that intends also at enabling the state to effectively protect the rights of its citizens. According to criticism, the Draft Regulation ignores the standard of protection under the *lex loci* and deprives the individual of the protection by the traditional framework of cross-border cooperation and the cooperation obstacles applicable to that framework. Burchard (2018) points out the risk of legal uncertainty and lack of

439. However, the explicit reference "which includes the pre-trial and the trial phase" has been deleted in the text of General Approach. The Draft Regulation should apply to criminal proceedings initiated by the issuing authority in order to localize a convict that absconded from justice to execute custodial sentences or detention orders. However, in case the sentence or detention order was rendered in absentia it should not be possible to issue an EPdO or a European Preservation Order as national law of the Member States on judgments in absentia vary considerably throughout the European Union (Recital 24b).

440. *See* Recital 32 of the Draft Regulation of the European Parliament and of the Council on European production and preservation orders for electronic evidence in criminal matters.

441. According to Article 82(1) TFEU judicial cooperation in the European Union is based on the principle of mutual recognition of judgments and judicial decisions and includes approximation of laws and regulations of the Member States in several areas that include mutual admissibility of evidence between Member States (Article 82(2,a) TFEU) and to some extent areas of serious crimes including terrorism, organized crime and cybercrime (Article 83(1) TFEU).

442. M. Böse, *supra* n. 432. M. Böse suggests that the doubts on whether Article 82(1) TFEU provides a legal basis for a mechanism of direct cooperation between law enforcement authorities and service providers find further support in Article 89 TFEU that makes EU legislation on extraterritorial operations of law enforcement authorities subject to specific requirements. According to this treaty provision, the Union may lay down the conditions and limitations under which the judicial and police authorities of the Member States (Articles 82, 87 TFEU) may operate in the territory of another Member State.

transparency, as access to providers' data will be regulated by multiple jurisdictions without the service provider or its customer being able to foresee the conditions and restrictions under the cooperation regime to be applied.[443] In any case, a clear scope of application of powers and sufficient legal authority for actions has to be defined. Bonnici et al. stress the need for electronic information/evidence exchange protocols and standards. These protocols need to have a legal basis, ideally internationally agreed and accompanied by a technical protocol for the fast transfer of the requested information exchange.[444]

At the same time the EDPS in his Opinion has underlined that certain guarantees are necessary, such as the "greater involvement of judicial authorities in the enforcing Member State." Furthermore, The EDPS has made specific recommendations on several aspects of the E-Evidence Proposals that require improvements such as the authenticity and confidentiality of orders and data transmitted, the limited preservation under European Preservation Orders, the data protection framework applicable, the rights of data subjects, data subjects benefiting from immunities and privileges, the legal representatives, the time limits to comply with EPdOs and the possibility for service providers to object to order.[445]

443. C. Burchard, *Der grenzüberschreitende Zugriff auf Clouddaten im Licht der Fundamentalprinzipien der internationalen Zusammenarbeit in Strafsachen*, in Zeitschrift für Internationale Strafrechtsdogmatik, Vol. 13, 252 (2018).
444. *See* M. Bonnici, *supra* n. 173, 232ff.
445. *See* European Data Protection Supervisor, Opinion 7/2019 – Opinion on Proposals regarding European Production and Preservation Orders for electronic evidence in criminal matters (Nov. 6, 2019).

CHAPTER 3

Prevention of Cyber Attacks

Philippe Jouglex & Tatiana-Eleni Syndinou

As any reasonable policy would manage, the regulation of acts of cybercriminality entails not only the enactment of a detailed and clear legal framework but also the construction of a preventive barrier, protecting society against the materialization of cybercrimes. In this sense, prevention should not be understood only as the sum of pedagogic and informative tools in order to increase the self-awareness of the population but also as the general risk-management legal framework, or in other words, as the means for an effective decrease of the phenomena of cybercrime rather than solely the threat of retaliation for violating the criminal rules.

Two specific offenses defined in the 2013 Directive on cyber attacks serve precisely this purpose: while they do not by themselves aim to prevent the realization of damage such as illegal system or data alteration, they work ahead in order to prevent the dissemination of the cyber attacks' technical means (section 3.01). At the same time, the role of Online Service Providers (OSPs) as major actors in terms of prevention has to be addressed, since their natural evolvement in a cybercriminality's prevention policy as "cyberspace's architects,"[1] has to be counterbalanced by issues of protection of human rights (section 3.02).

1. Susen Brenner, *Cybercrime: Re-thinking Crime Control Strategies*, in *Crimes Online*, 25 (Yvonne Jewkes (ed.), Willan Publishing 2007).

§3.01 THE OBSTACLE: CRIMES LEGISLATION

[A] Tools Used for Committing Offenses

[1] Overview of the Offense of Hacking Tools Distribution

Tools used for committing offenses can be seen by analogy as a new kind of weapon, as "cyber arms."[2] The arguments in favor of or against the free distribution of these tools are indeed very similar to the classic weapon control debate.[3] On one hand, these computer programs are just tools, by themselves inoffensive, and sometimes used in services for the general interest. On the other hand, their free circulation obviously contributes to a democratization of cybercriminal activities, as they permit everybody to become a one-day hacker without specific technical knowledge.

In the continuity of the Convention of Budapest, Article 7 of Directive 2013/40/EU, titled "tools used for committing offences," criminalizes the "intentional production, sale, procurement for use, import, distribution or otherwise making available" of these tools, when it is done "without right and with the intention that it be used to commit any of the offences referred to in Articles 3 to 6." The offense is very precise, as it does not generally cover all tools used for cyber attacks, but only two distinct categories of tools that it defines: "(a) a computer program, designed or adapted primarily for the purpose of committing any of the offences referred to in Articles 3 to 6; (b) a computer password, access code, or similar data by which the whole or any part of an information system is capable of being accessed."

A wide variety of tools can be found in the first category. Software which will automatically exploit well-known system vulnerabilities provides the basic user with the opportunity to instantly obtain illegal access to the targeted system. Indeed, in the age of standardization of IT, a single vulnerability could compromise either a huge client database or numerous client websites. Malware also belongs to this category. Automatic packages can be sold, to be inserted in online advertisement and activated with a click or, for instance, in other computer programs or smartphone application installation, for various purposes (to infect the device with a Trojan horse in order to constitute a botnet or to install a spyware able to aspire various kind of sensitive data with a keystroke logger). Viruses constitute the major part of malware. The virus itself obviously belongs to the category of: tool for committing a cybercrime offense. The offense encompasses the creation of the virus, the distribution of a virus tool kit, while the mere transmission of the virus should be dealt by the offense of illegal system interference. At least, the cracking software poses some difficulties. These computer programs use mere brute force or/and some well-known vulnerabilities of a specific encryption method, in order to crack the protection of a Wi-Fi network or of a single

2. Dorothy E. Denning, *Obstacles and Options for Cyber Arms Controls*, in *Arms Control in Cyberspace* (Heinrich Böll Foundation, Berlin, Germany, Jun. 29, 2001), available at: http://faculty.nps.edu/dedennin/publications/berlin.pdf.
3. Podins, Karlis & Czosseck, Christian, *A Vulnerability-Based Model of Cyber Weapons and Its Implications for Cyber Conflict*, European Conference on Information Warfare and Security: 198-X. Reading: Academic Conferences International Limited (July 2012).

password protected computer. They are commonly coded in Linux distribution, such as the Ophcrack Live CD. In the main website of this software, we can, for instance, read as a description that "Ophcrack is a free Windows password cracker based on rainbow tables"[4] and if it seems to fit at first sight the category of tools conceived for cybercrime activities, the issue of the intent has to be raised, as we will see below. Typically, both creators and users pretend that this program exists only to recover lost (forgotten) passwords, or to test the effectiveness of an existing password.

It has to be noted that most of the time, these tools use well-known vulnerabilities, and therefore devices with updated protection programs easily block them. For instance, the Microsoft Security Intelligence Report vol. 18 (for the second half of 2014) indicates that Microsoft recorded on a worldwide level around 20% malware encounter (which means that the malware was in fact blocked in the attempt of infecting the computer), while real infection (detected and recorded by the specific Microsoft malware remove tool) is only 1%.[5]

As regards the distribution of the hacking tool or virus, no definition is provided. It is therefore accepted that even a hyperlink's creation (with intention) has to be identified as a means of distribution of the tool.[6] This interpretation is also reinforced by the explicit reference to the notion of "making available" in Article 7. The offense covers both the distribution and the creation of the tool. This means that even the mere creation of a virus is criminalized. We can see that this offense, in this sense, is clearly related to cybercrime prevention, since at the stage of the creation there is no damage done to the individual or to society.

[2] The Three Steps of Malicious Intention

Therefore, in the first option of the hacking program, the legal framework refers to a triple, cumulative intention in order to frame the offense in very strict limits and protect the human rights involved (free speech, entrepreneur's freedom). First, the intent of creation, distribution, or acquirement has to be realized. Then it has to be proven that intent of this act of distribution will be related to future acts of cyber attacks. Finally, the tool's purpose must solely be the commitment of the cyber attack. The first intention seems to be easy enough, since it is hard to imagine how a person can negligently distribute a tool.

This triple reference to a malicious intent has some beneficial consequences, such as the exclusion of pure researchers from the offenses. It has been a concern that researchers and experts on IT need access to these tools in order to test and improve the defenses of their systems or just inform the public about new viruses, for instance.[7] In the same way, the requirement of a specific malicious purpose preserves the general IT

4. http://ophcrack.sourceforge.net/.
5. SIR Volume 18: July–December 2014, 39, available at: https://www.microsoft.com/en-us/download/details.aspx?id=46928.
6. M. Klang, *A Critical Look at the Regulation of Computer Viruses*, 11(2) Intl. J. L. & Info. 176 (Oxford University Press 2003).
7. Peter Sommer, *Criminalising Hacking Tools*, 3(2) Digital Investigation 68–72 (June 2006).

tools' possession from any judicial proceeding. The role of the specific intent's criteria as a bulwark against excessive criminalization is also expressly stated in Recital 16 of the Directive.[8]

On the other side, these strict requirements have the effect to considerably reduce the effectiveness of the offense. Let us see the example of a hacking tool's sale. The seller would protect himself by his ignorance of the final purpose of the tool. Even if a disclaimer that the tool is for educational matters only is not convincing enough by itself, the seller could argue that the buyer was only motivated by curiosity. The buyer would also be protected for the same reason: if he is arrested before using the tool, it will be difficult for the accusation to prove that indeed he bought it in order to commit a specific cyber attack.

A computer program designed to operate specific cyber attacks is most of the time based on specific known information related to system vulnerability. In other words, it is designed to exploit a specific vulnerability. In this sense, it makes sense to encompass in the same offense the tool itself, and the information from which the tool has been created. In both cases, the aim is to block the markets for software vulnerabilities and exploits. For instance, most vulnerabilities are called in practice "zero day" since it has been empirically demonstrated that when the vulnerability's existence is disclosed to the public, attacks occur on the very same day.

[3] The Black Market of Data

The offense, as we have seen above, possesses a hybrid nature, both incriminating the hacking tools' circulation and the sensitive information divulgation. It adds another layer of complexity on the debate for a better control of sensitive information together with the discussion on information theft, illegal access to information, and also the new proposal of directive about the protection of secret information,[9] which aims to harmonize on a European level the protection against divulgation of information meant to be kept silent. Technical and sensitive information are not literally trade secrets—they lack the criterion of commercial value—, but their protection could easily be compared with the proposed protection of trade secrets.

The offense expressly refers to "computer password, access code, or similar data by which the whole or any part of an information system is capable of being accessed." This offense covers a multitude of diverse situations from the credit cart pin number to

8. "(...). Even where such a tool is suitable or particularly suitable for carrying out one of the offences laid down in this Directive, it is possible that it was produced for a legitimate purpose Motivated by the need to avoid criminalisation where such tools are produced and put on the market for legitimate purposes, such as to test the reliability of information technology products or the security of information systems, apart from the general intent requirement, a direct intent requirement that those tools be used to commit one or more of the offences laid down in this Directive must be also fulfilled."
9. Proposal for a Directive of the European Parliament and of the Council on the protection of undisclosed know-how and business information (trade secrets) against their unlawful acquisition, use and disclosure, COM/2013/0813 final – 2013/0402 (COD).

the access password to online streaming services, from email's identifying information to zero-day vulnerabilities technical data.

This information is not only exploited by the hacker himself for perpetrating an illegal access to the system but also feeds a growing and very profitable black market of information,[10] which has been described as more profitable than drug dealing activities.

[B] Incitement, Aiding and Abetting and Attempt

Article 8 of Directive 2013/40/EU states that:

> 1. Member States shall ensure that the incitement, or aiding and abetting, to commit an offence referred to in Articles 3 to 7 is punishable as a criminal offence.
> 2. Member States shall ensure that the attempt to commit an offence referred to in Articles 4 and 5 is punishable as a criminal offence.

Therefore, two distinct offenses have to be analyzed: the offense of inciting or aiding and abetting cybercrime activities, which covers the entire range of cyber attacks and the offense of attempt, which only refers to illegal system interference and illegal data interference, though.

The offense of inciting or aiding and abetting, as we can see, is closely related to the offense of distributing sensitive information about a system. They share many similarities: no damage to a system is made at this point, the *actus reus* of the offense concerns mere speech and the aim is, ahead of the attack, to prevent its materialization. Therefore, they also share the same concern: a broad application of the offense would put in peril the freedom of speech. The more sensitive issue on this matter shall be the legal treatment reserved to public disclosure of system's vulnerability. It is common for IT researchers to publicly announce their findings when it concerns a widespread vulnerability, with the consequence, however, that potential hackers could learn new ways of illegal access or interference. In order to achieve a proportional balance with the freedom of expression and information, it should be accepted that specific intent to incite or aid in the committing of a specific cyber attack is required as a criteria of the offense.

As regards the attempt, it should be noted that no definition is given, which means that the European legislator leaves it to the national legislator according to his specific legal system. It creates, however, some disparities. For instance, no harmonization exists as regards the issue of voluntary withdrawal. These disparities, which have been described as "an unavoidable manifestation of the current approach to EU criminal law,"[11] certainly exceed the issue of cybercrime and call for a synthetic approach of the general principles of EU criminal law.

10. Lillian Ablon et al., *Markets for Cybercrime, Tools and Stolen Data*, Hackers' Bazaar, RAND Corporation, available at: https://www.rand.org/content/dam/rand/pubs/research_reports/RR600/RR610/RAND_RR610.pdf., 11.
11. Sarah Summers et al., *The Emergence of EU Criminal Law, Cyber Crime and the Regulation of the Information Society* 269 (Hart Publishing 2014).

For instance, the attempts of illegal access and illegal interception are not criminalized by Directive 2013/40/EU, certainly because in these cases no real harm can be done. For some State Members it means that these attempts are not illegal, whereas other State Members generally state that attempt to commit an offense can in any case be prosecuted. In such a transborder issue, wherein close collaboration between national authorities is mandatory, even the mere suspicion of a legal uncertainty may lead to great difficulties of enforcement, and it can be hoped that the European legislator will provide some clarifications on this point in the future.

§3.02 THE ROLE OF ISPs IN CYBERCRIME PREVENTION

Raising the awareness of Internet service providers (ISPs), increasing their involvement, or even establishing their liability or accountability in the fight against cybercrime, has been a growing trend for many years. Indeed, ISPs are considered the gatekeepers of the Internet, thanks to the unique place they have within the Internet's infrastructure.

In this context, where a certain involvement of ISPs in cybercrime investigation and prevention appears necessary, their conflicting role as the guardians of the privacy of their subscribers, in conjunction with human rights safeguards, is seen as a significant counterargument against such an approach. While abiding by state regulation ISPs' involvement in the fight against cybercrime is often criticized as an inappropriate interference with ISPs' freedom to conduct business and the right of freedom of expression, self-regulatory policies are also viewed with suspicion due to the lack of transparency and common standards toward the filtering of removal of illicit Internet content. Internet blocking and filtering by ISPs have proven to be a contentious form of intervention of ISPs in the fight against cybercrime, since Internet connection is protected as a component of the right of expression. In parallel, significant challenges for ISPs have also been raised by the Court of Justice of the European Union case law.

[A] ISPs as Gatekeepers of the Internet: The Debate about a More Active Role of ISPs in Cybercrime Prevention

Since ISPs have the technical capability to detect and prevent crimes and to support law enforcement agencies, an intensive discussion on the role of ISPs in cybercrime investigations has been held. Obligations discussed range from the mandatory implementation of prevention technology to voluntary support of investigation.[12] In this respect, the Council of Europe's Cybercrime Committee issued Guidelines for the

12. Marco Gercke, *Understanding Cybercrime: Phenomena, Challenges and Legal Response* 241 (ITU September 2012), available at: http://www.itu.int/ITU-D/cyb/cybersecurity/docs/Cybercrime%20legislation%20EV6.pdf. For an overview of the debate, *see* Marco Gercke, *The Role of Internet Service Providers in the Fight against Child Pornography*, Computer Law Rev. Intl. 65 et seq. (2009).

cooperation of ISPs with Law Enforcement in the fight against cybercrime, where the best regulations and self-regulations of ISPs' practices are discussed.[13]

As it is stated in a report published in 2011 by the US Institute for Homeland Security Solutions,[14] many studies have advocated that ISPs may be in a good position to cost-effectively prevent certain types of malicious cyber behavior, such as the operation of botnets on home users' and small businesses' computers.[15] To go one step further, the unique position of ISPs as the masters of the gateway through which Internet pests ("malware") enter and reenter the public computer system, i.e., the Internet, could possibly justify holding them legally accountable via an indirect tort liability regime for not stopping these pests before they spread, and also making them responsible for helping to identify individuals who are responsible for the malicious code in the first place.[16]

Nonetheless, from a legal point of view, the rhetoric about the role and the possible accountability of ISPs is not impregnable. The controversies of the ISPs safe harbor established in the EU E-Commerce Directive[17] demonstrate that it is particularly demanding to delineate the boundaries of Internet intermediaries' liability. The E-Commerce Directive sets out as a principle that intermediaries are not liable for the content of "illegal" information that they transmit, cache or host, conflicting jurisprudence at national level. However, lack of transparency on individual intermediaries' procedures and practices when taking down content, and the fragmentation of rules on notice-and-action procedures across the EU, has a negative impact on legal certainty and predictability.

Indeed, as it is stated in the Staff working document:

> some stakeholders have expressed the view that the current fragmentation and legal uncertainty have rendered the protection of property rights inefficient and are having a detrimental effect on the fight against online crime, including in areas such as the fight against hate-speech and child pornography. Others have expressed concern that not only illegal but also legal content is often taken down

---

13. Callanan & Gercke, *Study on the Cooperation between service providers and law enforcement against cybercrime – Toward common best-of-breed guidelines?*, available at: www.coe.int/cybercrime/ (2008). *See also* Marco Gercke, *The Council of Europe Guidelines for the Cooperation between LEAs and ISPs against Cybercrime*, Computer Law Review Intl. 97 et seq. (2008).
14. Brent Rowe et al., *The Role of Internet Service Providers in Cyber Security, Institute for Homeland Security Solutions*. Available online at: http://citeseerx.ist.psu.edu/viewdoc/download?doi=10.1.1.473.2323&rep=rep1&type=pdf (June 2011).
15. J. Evers, *ISPs versus the Zombies*, Cnet News.com at http://news.cnet.com/ISPs-versus-the-zombies/2100-7349_3-5793719.html (Jul. 19, 2005). Y. Huang, G. Xianjun & A. Whinston, *Defeating DDoS Attacks by Fixing the Incentive Chain*, 7(1) ACM Transactions on Internet Technology Article 5, 1-5; J. Richards, *Make Firms Bear the Cost to Improve Information Security, says Schneier*, Computer Weekly (May 22, 2007), at: http://www.computerweekly.com/Articles/2007/05/22/223959/make-firms-bear-the-cost-toimprove-information-security-says-schneier.htm.
16. Doug Lichtman & Eric Posner, *Holding Internet Service Providers Accountable*, Chicago John M. Olin Law & Economics Working Paper No. 217 (2D SERIES), (July 2004). Available at SSRN: http://ssrn.com/abstract=573502.
17. Directive 2000/31/EC of the European Parliament and of the Council of Jun. 8, 2000 on certain legal aspects of information society services, in particular electronic commerce, in the Internal Market ("Directive on E-Commerce"), OJ L 178, 17.7.2000, 1–16.

> since the ISPs, in cases of doubt as to the validity of a notice, tend to take down the information in order to ensure that they are not held liable for the content. Some also contend that it is increasingly difficult to identify clear parameters for the liability exemptions set out in the e-Commerce Directive, as the technical capabilities of online intermediaries develop and the commercial uses of the content they present become ever more sophisticated.[18]

A deeper involvement of ISPs in cybercrime prevention faces significant obstacles, such as the burden of technical costs and thorny legal questions. The exact role and competencies of ISPs in the fight against cybercrime is an intricate issue, since possible interventions of Internet intermediaries shall be scrutinized from a human rights perspective, while the regime of their liability is also at stake. Indeed, as it is stated in the United Nations Office on Drugs and Crime, Study on Cybercrime:

> that service providers should have some role in cybercrime prevention is, at the same time, both "obvious", but yet nuanced and complex – engaging issues such as service provider liability and responsibility for internet content.[19]

In the same vein, the report of the US Institute for Homeland Security Solutions states that:

> Customer contracts often specifically prevent an ISP from filtering traffic, and international connections multiply the potential legal complexities. ISPs also worry that providing more security would implicitly increase their liability (i.e., if an ISP states that they provide security and a customer is negatively affected by a security breach, the ISP could be held fully or partially liable).[20]

The question of the liability of ISPs is not exclusively raised in respect of their duties to their customers, but also in a criminal law spectrum vis-à-vis the State, such as for aiding and abetting criminal activities, as it has been demonstrated in the US by the settlement agreement of Google with the United States Department of Justice, where Google admitted to its knowledge of, and participation in, unlawful advertising, because by permitting online Canadian pharmacies to place advertisements through AdWords, it facilitated the unlawful importation of controlled pharmaceuticals into the United States.[21] Similarly, when a bulletin board is used to publish passwords to allow unauthorized access into a computer system, the operator may be liable for aiding, abetting, counseling or procuring commission of an offense, or for incitement to commit an offense if he has actually advertised that passwords are available on the bulletin board to a community of people who are likely to carry out computer hacking.[22]

---

18. Commission Staff Working document, *A Digital Single Market Strategy for Europe, – Analysis and Evidence,* Brussels, 6.5.2015, SWD 100 final, 55–56 (2015). Available online at: https://www.eccgreece.gr/wp-content/uploads/2015/06/dsm-swd_en.pdf.
19. United Nations Office on Drugs and Crime, *Comprehensive Study on Cybercrime,* Draft (February 2013).
20. Brent Rowe et al., *The Role of Internet Service Providers in Cyber Security* (Institute for Homeland Security Solutions, June 2011).
21. For the text of the non-prosecution agreement, *see* http://googlemonitor.com/wp-content/uploads/2011/05/Google%20Agreement.pdf.
22. Graham Smith, *Internet Law and Regulation* 118 (Sweet & Maxwell 2007).

Nonetheless, holding ISPs criminally responsible is subject to the classic obstacles for establishing criminal liability for corporate crimes in general, where the question of proof of the ISPs *mens rea* might be decisive. Indeed, ISPs will often not be aware of illicit contents posted by their subscribers, while the latter can modify this content without any intervention of the ISPs and they are not required to inform them for these acts.[23] Therefore, even if the E-Commerce Directive's ISPs safe harbor concerns the civil liability of online intermediaries and not the criminal one, the safe harbor could not apply anyway; since the criminal liability (for instance, for conspiracy or aiding and abetting) implies the intent of the ISPs, it encompasses by definition their actual knowledge of the civil or criminal activity of the user. Consequently, the ISPs cannot find protection against liability.

Also, while the idea of making ISPs more responsible or even legally accountable for cybersecurity purposes might be attractive, defining the legal foundations, the conditions and the scope of such a regime is certainly a complex issue, since important legal policy choices finally have to be made, such as, for example, whether an ISP's possible civil liability should be based in negligence or strict liability.[24] And yet, if such legal mechanisms are introduced in a national basis, the ubiquitous nature of Internet communications might significantly undermine the effectiveness of such legal regimes. So, even if Europe or the US establish an ideal ISP liability regime, where any cyber attack originating from a European or an American ISP can be traced, European or American Internet users would yet remain vulnerable to cyber attacks committed from computers in countries without the same, strong level of Internet regulation.[25]

[B] The Big Challenge: Balancing ISP Subscribers' Rights with Law Enforcement Objectives

Besides, ISPs appear to have two potentially conflicting roles: on the one hand, a role as the trusted stewards of their clients' personal data and private communications and, on the other hand, their emerging role as a party in possession of data which might assist in law enforcement.[26] Indeed, since gathering electronic evidence in cybercrimes is often linked to obtaining computer data from ISPs, the role of ISPs in the storage and retention of various types of data (traffic data, subscriber data, content) is substantial.

The European Convention on Cybercrime establishes specific procedural rules for obtaining such data by the ISPs. Indeed, ISPs in signatory countries would be required to respond to and comply with legal processes from other signatory countries

23. Xavier Amadei, *Standards of Liability of Internet Service Providers: A Comparative Analysis of France and the United States with a Specific Focus on Copyright, Defamation and Illicit Content*, 35 Cornell Int'l L.J. 189, at 207 (2002).
24. *See* on this issue Assaf Hamdani, *Who is Liable for Cyber Wrongs*, 87 Cornell L. Rev. 901 (2002). Available online at: http://scholarship.law.cornell.edu/clr/vol87/iss4/1.
25. Doug Lichtman & Eric Posner, *Holding Internet Service Providers Accountable*, Chicago John M. Olin Law & Economics Working Paper No. 217 (2D SERIES), (July 2004). Available at SSRN: http://ssrn.com/abstract=573502 or http://dx.doi.org/10.2139/ssrn.573502.
26. Ian Kerr & Daphne Gilbert, *The Role of ISP in the Investigation of Cybercrime*, in *Information Ethics in the Electronic Age: Current Issues in Africa and the World* 165 (Tom Mendina & Johannes J. Britz (ed.), McFarland & Company Inc 2004).

with respect to the provisions of the Cybercrime Convention, regardless of the laws of the country in which they reside.[27]

It is also important to distinguish whether the collection is about data which are already stored by the ISPs or it is real time collection of traffic or content data. While the procedural safeguards of privacy and of secrecy of communications vary depending on the type of data which are processed by ISPs, the intervention of ISPs in the fight against cybercrime marks a shift in the role of these private actors, who are now attributed certain state assigned competencies and obligations in the law enforcement process.[28]

According to Article 15 of the Cybercrime Convention, the Parties should provide some safeguards in their domestic law, in order to balance the requirements of law enforcement and the protection of human rights. Nonetheless, the Convention does not specify these conditions and safeguards, but provides for including some general criteria referring back to obligations which have been undertaken by the Parties under human rights law instruments.[29]

In this context, it shall be reminded that the European Court of Human Rights (ECtHR) has undertaken significant efforts to define the safeguards and standards governing electronic investigations and electronic surveillance. The gravity of the interference of the investigation, its purpose and its proportionality are emphasized as crucial factors to be taken into account and certain fundamental principles deriving from the Court's case law are highlighted. More precisely:

> a) a sufficient legal basis for investigation instruments is necessary b) the legal basis must be clear with regard to the subject c) the competences of the law enforcement agencies need to be foreseeable and d) surveillance of communications can be justified only in case of serious crimes.[30]

In *Weber Saravia v. Germany*, the Court held that:

> since the implementation in practice of measures of secret surveillance of communications is not open to scrutiny by the individuals concerned or the public at large, it would be contrary to the rule of law for the legal discretion granted to the executive or to a judge to be expressed in terms of an unfettered power. Consequently, the law must indicate the scope of any such discretion conferred on

27. Sylvia Mercado Kierkegaard, *Cracking Down on Cybercrime Global Response, Communications of the IIMA*: Vol. 5, Issue 1, Article 7, available at: https://scholarworks.lib.csusb.edu/ciima/vol5/iss1/7.
28. Ian Kerr and Daphne Gilbert, *supra* n. 26, 171.
29. Lorenzo Picotti & Ivan Salvadori, *National Legislation Implementing the Convention on Cybercrime – Comparative Analysis and Good Practices* 46 (Mar. 12, 2008). Available online at: http://www.coe.int/t/dghl/cooperation/economiccrime/cybercrime/cy_activity_Interface2008/567%20study2-d-version8%20provisional%20_12%20march%2008_en.pdf.
30. Cormac Callanan & Marco Gerke, *Cooperation between Law Enforcement and Internet Service Providers against Cybercrime: Towards Common Guidelines*, Council of Europe, Project on Cybercrime, 16–17 (Mar. 17, 2008). Available online at: https://www.coe.int/t/dg1/legalcooperation/economiccrime/cybercrime/Documents/Reports-Presentations/567%20prov-d-wg%20STUDY%20final%20_25%20june%202008_.pdf.

the competent authorities and the manner of its exercise with sufficient clarity to give the individual adequate protection against arbitrary interference.[31]

The possible threat of secret surveillance systems for democracy has been identified by the Court in the *Klass and others v. Germany*, where it was stressed that:

"the Court, being aware of the danger such a law poses of undermining or even destroying democracy on the ground of defending it, affirms that the Contracting States may not, in the name of the struggle against espionage and terrorism, adopt whatever measures they deem appropriate"[32] and that, "the Court must be satisfied that, whatever system of surveillance is adopted, there exist adequate and effective guarantees against abuse. This assessment has only a relative character: it depends on all the circumstances of the case, such as the nature, scope and duration of the possible measures, the grounds required for ordering such measures, the authorities competent to permit, carry out and supervise such measures, and the kind of remedy provided by the national law."[33]

The privacy implications of the perspective of a more dynamic role of ISPs in cybercrime enforcement have also been demonstrated by the controversies of the interpretation of Article 32(b) of the Cybercrime Convention. This section deals with the determination of the conditions upon which a Party is permitted to unilaterally access computer data stored in another Party without seeking mutual assistance. According to this provision, a Party may access or receive, without the authorization of another Party, stored computer data located in another Party through a computer system in its territory, if the Party obtains the lawful and voluntary consent of the person who has the lawful authority to disclose the data to the Party through that computer.

Thus, the provision of Article 32(b) addresses the situation where the Party has accessed or received data located outside of its territory through a computer system in its territory, and it has obtained the lawful and voluntary consent of the person who has lawful authority to disclose the data to the Party through that system.[34] While it has been ambiguous whether ISPs could also be considered as persons who have lawful authority to disclose the data,[35] the Council of Europe clarified the meaning of that term. After emphasizing that the respect of the rights of individuals and the interests of third parties are to be taken into account when applying the measure, the Committee determined that service providers are highly unlikely to be able to consent validly and voluntarily to disclosure of their users' data under that provision, since normally,

31. ECtHR, *Weber and Saravia against Germany*, Application No. 54934/00, Jun. 29, 2006, paragraph 94.
32. ECtHR, *Klass and others v. Germany*, Application No. 5029/71, Sep. 6, 1978, paragraph 49.
33. ECtHR, *Klass and others v. Germany*, *ibid.*, paragraph 50.
34. Convention on Cybercrime, Explanatory Report. Available online at: http://conventions.coe.int/Treaty/EN/Reports/Html/185.htm.
35. Groupe interministériel sur la lutte contre la cybercriminalité, *Protéger les internautes*, Rapport sur la cybercriminalité, at 50 (February 2014). Available online at: http://www.justice.gouv.fr/include_htm/pub/rap_cybercriminalite.pdf.

service providers will only be holders of such data, they will not control or own the data, and they will, therefore, not be in a position to give a valid consent.[36]

Similarly, Article 29 Working Party underlined that companies acting as data controllers usually do not have the "lawful authority to disclose the data" which they process. In this context:

> they can normally only disclose data upon prior presentation of a judicial authorisation/warrant or any document justifying the need to access the data and referring to the relevant legal basis for this access, presented by a national law enforcement authority according to their domestic law that will specify the purpose for which data is require.[37]

[C] Cybercrime Prevention via Internet Filtering: Precedents and Controversies

Additionally, ISPs could contribute to cybercrime prevention through active "filtering" of Internet communications or content with a view to preventing cybercrime acts in the first place.[38] By relying on intermediaries to block illicit Internet content, the administrative and technical burden of filtering on government can be reduced, whilst providing a new form of crime prevention.[39] At the same time, this policy raises important issues of accountability, due to the lack of public or governmental oversight in the implementation of such methods of control.[40]

While the ISP's role in the filtering and blocking of sites has mainly emerged in respect of cyber-enabled crimes, the use of such law enforcement techniques on *stricto sensu* cybercrimes is at stake. Definitely, Internet serves as a platform where it is possible to acquire all the necessary resources to conduct a cyber attack without having particular skills. Cybercriminal business models function on a combination of sales of various malicious products and services, with an offer of an efficient "customer care"

36. Cybercrime Convention Committee (T-CY), n. 3, Transborder access to data, Strasbourg, 7 (Nov. 5, 2013). Available online at: http://www.coe.int/t/dghl/cooperation/economiccrime/Source/Cybercrime/TCY/Guidance_Notes/T-CY%282013%297REV_GN3_transborder_V11.pdf.
37. *Article 29 Working Party's comments on the issue of direct access by third countries' law enforcement authorities to data stored in other jurisdiction, as proposed in the draft elements for an additional protocol to the Budapest Convention on Cybercrime* (Brussels, Dec. 5, 2013). Available online at: http://ec.europa.eu/justice/data-protection/article-29/documentation/other-document/files/2013/20131205_wp29_letter_to_cybercrime_committee.pdf.
38. United Nations Office on Drugs and Crime, *Comprehensive Study on Cybercrime*, Draft (February 2013). Available at: https://www.unodc.org/documents/organized-crime/UNODC_CCPCJ_EG.4_2013/CYBERCRIME_STUDY_210213.pdf.
39. M. McIntyre, *Child Abuse Images and Cleanfeeds: Assessing Internet Blocking Systems*, in *Research Handbook on Governance of the Internet* (Edward Elgar 2012).
40. Joss Wright & Yana Breindl, *Internet Filtering Trends in Liberal Democracies: French and German Regulatory Debates*, 2(2) Internet Policy. Rev. Available online at: http://policyreview.info/articles/analysis/Internet-filtering-trends-liberal-democracies-french-and-german-regulatory-debates.

to support customers in their initiatives, and social networks platforms to manage the community of clients and communicate with them rapidly.[41]

The most representative example of the implementation of filtering for cybercrime prevention purposes can be found in the respect of child pornography, while such filtering and surveillance schemes are also often found in national antiterrorist legislations. Nonetheless, as it will be demonstrated, even in those cases, where the defense of public interest goals appears to be of particular weight, the implementation of Internet filtering by ISPs has proved to be a thorny question in practice.

Using filters as a preventive measure for restricting access to illegal or harmful Internet content has proved to be controversial, even though the purposes served by such measures are not contested themselves. An illustrative example is the implementation of filters preventing access to websites containing child pornography and child abuse content.

In the European level, Article 25 of Directive 2011/93/EU on combating the sexual abuse and sexual exploitation of children and child pornography, and replacing Council Framework Decision 2004/68/JHA[42] provides that:

> 1. Member States shall take the necessary measures to ensure the prompt removal of web pages containing or disseminating child pornography hosted in their territory and to endeavor to obtain the removal of such pages hosted outside of their territory. 2. Member States may take measures to block access to web pages containing or disseminating child pornography towards the Internet users within their territory. These measures must be set by transparent procedures and provide adequate safeguards, in particular to ensure that the restriction is limited to what is necessary and proportionate, and that users are informed of the reason for the restriction. Those safeguards shall also include the possibility of judicial redress.

It is noteworthy that the Directive does not set out as a prerequisite the prior authorization of blocking by the judiciary.[43] Recitals 46 and 47 of the Directive are of particular importance on how these measures can be implemented by Member States. According to Recital (46):

> Child pornography, which constitutes child sexual abuse images, is a specific type of content which cannot be construed as the expression of an opinion. To combat it, it is necessary to reduce the circulation of child sexual abuse material by making it more difficult for offenders to upload such content onto the publicly accessible web. Action is therefore necessary to remove the content and apprehend those guilty of making, distributing or downloading child sexual abuse images. With a view to supporting the Union's efforts to combat child pornography, Member States should use their best endeavors to cooperate with third countries in seeking to secure the removal of such content from servers within their territory.

Recital 47 is more explicit, and it precisely provides that:

41. Pierluigi Paganini, *Cybercrime and the Underground Market* (Jan. 15, 2013), at: http://resources.infosecinstitute.com/cybercrime-and-the-underground-market/.
42. OJ L 335, 17.12.2011.
43. Sarah Summers et al., *supra* n. 11, 189.

> However, despite such efforts, the removal of child pornography content at its source is often not possible when the original materials are not located within the Union, either because the State where the servers are hosted is not willing to cooperate or because obtaining removal of the material from the State concerned proves to be particularly long. Mechanisms may also be put in place to block access from the Union's territory to Internet pages identified as containing or disseminating child pornography. The measures undertaken by Member States in accordance with this Directive in order to remove or, where appropriate, block websites containing child pornography could be based on various types of public action, such as legislative, non-legislative, judicial or other. In that context, this Directive is without prejudice to voluntary action taken by the Internet industry to prevent the misuse of its services or to any support for such action by Member States. Whichever basis for action or method is chosen, Member States should ensure that it provides an adequate level of legal certainty and predictability to users and service providers. Both with a view to the removal and the blocking of child abuse content, cooperation between public authorities should be established and strengthened, particularly in the interests of ensuring that national lists of websites containing child pornography material are as complete as possible and of avoiding duplication of work. Any such developments must take account of the rights of the end users and comply with existing legal and judicial procedures and the European Convention for the Protection of Human Rights and Fundamental Freedoms and the Charter of Fundamental Rights of the European Union. The Safer Internet Programme has set up a network of hotlines the goal of which is to collect information and to ensure coverage and exchange of reports on the major types of illegal content online.

Nevertheless, the European Parliament rejected a legislative proposal from the European Commission that would have imposed mandatory blocking on ISPs across the EU and left the decision to individual Member states.[44] It appears that freedom of expression and privacy concerns were among the reasons for not making obligatory the blocking of illegal websites.[45] Indeed, the adaptation of Internet blocking/filtering measures for preventing access to child sexual abuse content could imply that "users' communication and behaviours over the internet may be monitored, the retention of internet data without permission may be required, and the users may not be able to make their own connection choice to other users or to create certain connections."[46]

The dangers of the implementation of ISP blocking for fundamental rights, and more precisely on freedom of expression, have also been highlighted by the Council of Europe. For example, some Member States, under the pretext of protecting children, are blocking content related to LGBT issues, even though the ECtHR found that there is no scientific evidence that such materials have a harmful impact on the well-being of

44. United Nations Office on Drugs and Crime, *Comprehensive Study on Cybercrime*, 253.
45. For a critical overview of this change of policy, *see* Sylvia Kierkegaard, *To Block or Not to Block –European Child Porno Law in Question*, 27(6) Computer L. & Sec. Rev. 573–584 (December 2011).
46. Weixiao Wei, *Online Child Sexual Abuse Content: The Development of a Comprehensive, Transferable International Internet Notice and Takedown System*, in *Independent Report for Internet Watch Foundation*, 76 (May 2011). Available online at: https://www.iwf.org.uk/sites/default/files/inline-files/IWF%20Research%20Report_%20Development%20of%20an%20international%20internet%20notice%20and%20takedown%20syste_1.pdf.

children.[47] Moreover, the effectiveness of such measures has also been questioned. Indeed, since filtering schemes are based on blocking lists, it has been advanced that criminals will be able to check if their sites are on blocking lists and move them to other locations and, as a result, blocking risks becoming a useful tool for protecting criminal activities rather than an effective measure to fight cybercrime.[48]

On a national level, many countries, such as Finland, Sweden, Norway, Denmark, the UK, Italy, the US, Canada and New Zealand, have established self or co-regulatory blocking systems to prevent access to child abuse content.[49]

The controversies of filtering can be illustrated by the UK filtering policy, which has been based on government initiatives together with self-regulatory practices. In the UK, since the end of 2013, ISPs voluntarily agreed to apply network-level filtering.[50] The network-level filters were introduced at the persistence of the government, which said that companies could either implement them on a voluntary basis or face legislation to oblige them to do so.[51] While the main aim of the filtering has been the limitation of the distribution and viewing of child abuse content, as well as restricting adult content to children under the age of 18, filters can also block other harmful content. According to this scheme, ISP's subscribers are presented with an option to enable or disable the related Parental Controls with the "yes" option pre-selected, and if they agree they will be able to choose from a list of categories of content that they can choose to block/unblock, such as pornography, drug and tobacco offering sites, dating sites, social networks, suicide and self-harm sites, etc.[52] So, ISP customers have to "opt out" of the ISP filtering that is proposed by default in order to gain access to the blocked content or inversely to "opt-in" for accessing such content. Nonetheless, filtering schemes are questioned for their efficiency and their legality. Indeed, numerous ways to get around the filters exist, such VPNs (Virtual Private Networks), DNS patches, web proxies, alternative addresses to access the sites in question, browser extensions, and anonymous browsers.[53] Furthermore, it has been proved that filters included sites

47. *Protecting Children's Rights in the Digital World: An Ever-Growing Challenge, The Commissioner's Human Rights Comments* (Apr. 29, 2014), available at: http://www.coe.int/en/web/commissioner/-/protecting-children-s-rights-in-the-digital-world-an-ever-growing-challen-1.
48. Joe McNamee, *Internet Blocking: Crimes Should be Punished and Not Hidden*, European Digital Rights' booklet (2013). Available online at: https://edri.org/wp-content/uploads/2013/12/blocking_booklet.pdf.
49. Yana Breindl & Joss Wright, *Internet Filtering Trends in Western Liberal Democracies: French and German Regulatory Debates* (Aug. 15, 2012), available at: https://www.usenix.org/system/files/conference/foci12/breindl2012foci.pdf.
50. For a short overview, *see* Ofcom Report on Internet safety measures – Internet Service Providers, *Network Level Filtering Measures* (Jul. 22, 2014). Available online at: https://www.ofcom.org.uk/__data/assets/pdf_file/0019/27172/Internet-safety-measures-second-report.pdf. Christopher Holloway, *Content Filtering of the Internet in the UK, A Look at Where We are Now*, in: Jamie Sharpe and Richard Self, *Computers for Everyone* 84 (1st ed., 2014).
51. Andy Weir, *Overwhelming Majority of UK Broadband Users Opting Out of Porn Filters*, Neowin (Jul. 23, 2014), available at: http://www.neowin.net/news/overwhelming-majority-of-uk-broadband-users-opting-out-of-porn-filters.
52. Mark Jackson, *Big UK ISPs Clarify the Confusion over Network Level Internet Filters* (Jun. 17, 2013), at: http://www.ispreview.co.uk/index.php/2013/06/big-uk-isps-clarify-the-confusion-over-network-level-Internet-filters.html.
53. Gordon Kelly, *UK Porn Filter: 5 Reasons It Won't Work* (Jul. 27, 2013), available at: http://www.trustedreviews.com/opinions/cameron-porn-block-5-technological-reasons-it-can-t-work.

offering sexual health advice, or advice on how to deal with abusive partners, as content that needed to be blocked.[54]

Another argument is that filtering impacts net neutrality.[55] Since filters might block legitimate content, ISPs may have to establish white lists of content that will not be blocked. Nonetheless, due to the great volume of Internet content added daily, it will be much easier to include those lists major corporations which will probably have preferential treatment compared to other sites, such as, a small online gallery specializing in artistic nudes.[56] The possible conflict of the UK "porn filters" with Internet neutrality was recently raised in Europe, after the Digital Single Market legislative proposals were released in May 2015.[57] Indeed, it has been advanced that the new EU rules, which would generally ban blocking and throttling of Internet content, could put the UK "porn filter" scheme at risk, as ISPs would be barred from filtering such traffic by default, in order to enable EU citizens to have access to the same web content irrespective of the country they live in.[58]

Another illustration of the societal and legal implications of state policy imposing filtering is the German precedent of the *Zugangserschwerungsgesetz* law, which was adopted by the German Parliament on June 18, 2009 after an intense public debate. The risk of blocking web pages not containing child pornography and the fear of possible extension of filtering to other types of Internet content have been strongly advocated by the opponents of the filtering approach. Therefore, after the Federal election of 2009, the new government coalition parties distanced themselves from the *Zugangserschwerungsgesetz*. In this context, while the Act officially came into force on February 2010, the Government immediately instructed the Federal Criminal Police Office to take no action under the new Act until further notice. Furthermore, a complaint before the German Constitutional Court to declare the Act as unconstitutional was filed, but it soon became irrelevant as the Government decided to repeal the Act on April 2011.[59]

Contrary to Germany, in France, where a big debate about the effectiveness and the constitutionality or legality of Internet blocking was also held, the possibility of Internet blocking and of delisting web pages without the prior authorization of a court[60]

54. *See* http://www.newstatesman.com/future-proof/2014/01/statistical-inevitability-isp-porn-filters-blocking-wrong-stuff.
55. *See* for this argument: Joe McNamee, *supra* n. 48, where in respect of the introduction of filters for blocking of child abuse content it has been advocated that it will bring "an end to the neutrality of the Internet as Internet Service Providers (ISPs) are forced to invest in technologies that can discriminate in increasingly invasive ways between different types of content."
56. Gordon Kelly, *UK Porn Filter: 5 Reasons It Won't Work*, *supra* n. 53.
57. *See* Communication from the Commission to the European Parliament, the Council, the European Economic and Social Committee and the Committee of the Regions, *A Digital Single Market Strategy for Europe*, COM(2015) 192 final. Commission Staff Working Document, *A Digital Single Market Strategy for Europe – Analysis and Evidence*, Brussels, SWD(2015) 100 final (May 6, 2015).
58. *Legal Porn? UK Move to Block Explicit Web Content May Violate EU Law*, http://www.rt.com/uk/273826-porn-filters-eu-uk/.
59. Jenny Kortlander, *Is Filtering the New Silver Bullet in the Fight Against Child Pornography on the Internet? A Legal Study into the Experiences of Australia and Germany*, 17(7) Computer & Telecommunications L. Rev. 199–208 (2011).
60. *See* the Opinion No. 2014-3 of the National Digital Council (*Conseil National du Numérique*) where it was strongly criticized the absence of supervision by a judicial authority: Avis n°2014-3

has been activated for preventing access to websites causing acts of terrorism or glorifying such acts and to websites containing pictures or representations of minors with pornographic character.[61] Decree No. 2015-125 (*Décret n°2015-125 du 5 février 2015 relatif au blocage des sites internet*) enables the French Ministry of Interior to ask ISPs to block the access to sites hosting such content within twenty-four hours, if the host provider does not remove such content after a notification made in compliance with Article 6-1 of the Law on Confidence in Digital Economy (*Loi pour la confiance dans l'économie numérique*[62]).

Furthermore, the Decree No. 2015-253 (*Décret n°2015-253 du 4 mars 2015 relatif au déréférencement des sites internet*) provides that the Central Office for the Fight against Crime related to Information and Communication Technologies (ICTs) (*Office Central de Lutte contre la Criminalité liée aux Technologies de l'Information et de la Communication*) is empowered to order the operators of search engines or directories to implement all appropriate measures in order to remove from their result pages links to websites harboring child pornography, or websites causing acts of terrorism or which glorify such acts.

Moreover, the French law on Intelligence, which was enacted after the terrorist attacks of January 2015 against the journal *Charlie Hebdo*, is another example of the state use of ISPs in the fight against crime and more precisely against terrorism. Under the new Article L.811-2 of the French Code of Internal Security (*Code de la sécurité intérieure*), agents of the intelligence services will have the task, in France and abroad, to seek and exploit information which is of interest for the nation's security.

Various intelligence agencies are authorized to request authorization from the Prime Minister for the use of techniques of collection of data. A prior approval by the judiciary of the use of surveillance techniques is not necessary, but the law provides that, except for urgent cases, a new independent administrative authority (*Commission nationale de contrôle des techniques de renseignement (CNCTR)*) shall obligatorily give an opinion before the authorization is granted. The new Article L.821-1 of the French Code of Internal Security (*Code de la sécurité intérieure*) impels communication and ISPs to allow security agencies to install IMSI-catchers and "black boxes" on their systems in order to record metadata from all Internet and phone users in France. The data would be subject to algorithmic analysis for potentially suspicious terrorist behavior.[63]

sur l'article 9 du projet de loi renforçant les dispositions relatives à la lutte contre le terrorisme. Available online at: http://www.cnnumerique.fr/wp-content/uploads/2014/07/2014-07-15_CNNum_Avis3-2014-TerroNum.pdf.

61. The measure of Internet blocking of sites containing child pornography was established by Article 4 of the Law n° 2011-267 (*Loi n° 2011-267 du 14 mars 2011 d'orientation et de programmation pour la performance de la sécurité intérieure*), but a decree was necessary for the activation of the procedure. The measure was held to be constitutional by the French Constitutional Court: Décision n° 2011-625 DC du 10 mars 2011, available at: https://www.conseil-constitutionnel.fr/decision/2011/2011625DC.htm
62. Loi n° 2004-575 du 21 juin 2004 pour la confiance dans l'économie numérique.
63. For a description and analysis of the law, *see* Antoine Cheron, *Loi sur le renseignement: du respect des grands principes du droit à la surveillance de masse sur Internet*, at: http://www.village-justice.com/articles/Loi-sur-renseignement-respect-des,19863.html (Jun. 15, 2015).

Nonetheless, any cybercrime prevention policy measures assigned to ISPs have to be compatible with the fundamental rights safeguarded by the Charter of Fundamental Rights of the European Union, the European Convention of Human Rights (ECHR) and national Constitutions ([D][1]), while blocking and filtering measures shall also comply with the ISPs immunity regime established by the E-Commerce Directive[64] ([D][2]).

[D] The Role of ISPs in Cybercrime Prevention and Its Boundaries: An Interference with Fundamental Rights?

[1] Illegal and Harmful Criminal Content in the EU and Freedom of Expression

ISPs have a critical role for the regulation of criminal online content, since they appear to be in the ideal position for removing or blocking such content. Indeed, while going after the content provider is not always feasible; another policy is to rely on ISPs for content regulation. In this context, in Europe, a public authority can issue injunctions to national access providers or even to large foreign hosting providers as soon as they have business interests in Europe.[65]

Nevertheless, content regulation, particularly when it is accompanied by criminal sanctions, is a delicate issue,[66] since there are no common standards on how to differentiate illegal from lawful Internet content.

The question is organically linked to the interpretation of the fundamental right of freedom of expression and of its restrictions, which are dependent on societal and cultural appreciations in national jurisdictions. EU policy documents generally distinguish between illegal and harmful content. As it is stated in the Communication to the European Parliament, the Council, the Economic and Social Committee and the Committee of Regions, Illegal and harmful content on the Internet, it is crucial to differentiate illegal from harmful content, since the two categories pose different issues of principle and call for different legal and technological responses.[67]

While various legal provisions may limit the distribution of content either for the benefit of public order or the protection of individual rights (intellectual property, privacy, defamation, etc.), not all of them associate the violation of these rules with criminal sanctions. Nonetheless, a core of legal provisions about illegal criminal content apparently exists, such as child pornography, dissemination of racist material

64. Directive 2000/31/EC of the European Parliament and of the Council of Jun. 8, 2000 on certain legal aspects of information society services, in particular electronic commerce, in the Internal Market ("Directive on E-Commerce"), OJ L 178, 17/07/2000, pp. 0001–0016.
65. Benoît Frydman & Isabelle Rorive, *Regulating Internet Content through Intermediaries in Europe and the USA*, Zeitschrift für Rechtssoziologie 23, Heft 1, S. 41-59 (2002). Available online at: https://www.isys.ucl.ac.be/etudes/cours/linf2202/Frydman_&_Rorive_2002.pdf.
66. Sarah Summers et al., *supra* n. 11, 156.
67. Communication to the European Parliament, the Council, the Economic and Social Committee and the Committee of Regions, *Illegal and harmful content on the Internet*, COM(96) 487 (Brussels, Oct. 16, 1996).

or incitement to hatred or terrorism, which are obviously considered criminal.[68] On the other hand, the decision about whether certain content is harmful is deemed to depend on cultural differences,[69] and each country may reach its own conclusion in defining the borderline between what is permissible and what is not. So, as it is stated in the Communication, it is important that international activities take into consideration different ethical standards in different countries, in order to explore appropriate rules to protect people from harmful content, while safeguarding at the same time freedom of expression.[70]

The role of ISPs in cybercrime prevention and enforcement appears to be particularly delicate when ISPs, by applying self-regulatory or co-regulatory policies, are called to determine whether certain Internet content is illegal or harmful. For example, how to judge whether certain Internet content is copyright infringing or, inversely, whether it is lawful on the grounds of copyright exceptions in the ubiquitous universe of Internet? Similar considerations appear in the case of hate or racist speech, which is banned in Europe,[71] but in USA it is considered mainly as protected by the fundamental right of freedom of expression and is legal as long as it does not incite "imminent lawless action."[72]

The distinction between "only harmful" content and illegal content appears seductive at first when analyzing the liability of ISPs, but on a deeper view its superficiality leads to an impasse. Therefore, this distinction cannot be used as an appropriate criterion. It should be accepted that the right of freedom of expression has an elasticity and that its exact conceptual perimeter in any specific cases could be determined only ex post in the frame of a judiciary process and not ex ante by creating mandatory monitoring of data by ISPs.

[2] *The Internet Connection as a Component of the Right of Expression*

Cybercrime prevention and repression tools often take the form of interferences with Internet connectivity and Internet access. Since both cyber-dependent and computer enabled crimes presuppose nowadays the use of computer networks or other forms of information communications technology, Internet blocking has emerged as one of the main techniques of fighting cybercrime.

Internet blocking is widely defined and can take various forms. The principal aim of Internet blocking is that content is blocked from reaching a computer by the use of software or hardware which reviews Internet communications and concludes whether to prevent the receiving and/or display of specifically targeted content. From a

68. Sarah Summers et al., *supra* n. 11, 162.
69. *Ibid.*
70. *Ibid.*
71. *See* Framework Decision on combating certain forms and expressions of racism and xenophobia by means of criminal law. Available online at: http://eur-lex.europa.eu/legal-content/EN/TXT/?uri=URISERV:l33178.
72. MacKinnon et al., *Fostering Freedom On-line, The Role of Internet Intermediaries*, UNESCO Series on Internet Freedom 34 (UNESCO Publishing 2014). Available online at: http://unesdoc.unesco.org/images/0023/002311/231162e.pdf.

technical point of view, there are several blocking techniques whose implementation depends on the use of various identifiers, such as IP addresses, domain names and DNS, URLs, file content and filename, keywords, content signatures (hash values).

Furthermore, blocking strategies diverge depending on the level where the blocking occurs, such as the user level (when a parent or an administrator blocks a specific content) or filtering at an ISP or even a state level, where all traffic is sent through central machines which analyze incoming traffic. Blocking can target specific content included in blocking lists (of IP addresses, DNS, etc.)[73] or be based on a heuristic method, while the decision about the content to be blocked can be made with or without a human intervention.[74]

From a legal point of view, Internet blocking is certainly not anodyne, since it appears to interfere with fundamental civil and human rights, such as the freedom of expression and privacy.[75] As Internet access and connectivity are perceived as substantial democratic values in the information society and economy, a heated doctrinal and societal debate has emerged on whether Internet access shall be protected as a human right.[76] A fundamental element in this discussion has been the perception of the role and of the nature of the Internet. If the Internet is seen as a sui generis revolutionary technology with eminent importance for the contemporary world, which differs substantially and qualitatively from other means of communication, recognizing Internet access as a new human right seems justifiable and legitimate. The dynamic, non-static, character of human rights could be also seen as an argument for the recognition of new rights, such as genetic privacy, the right to a unique identity and also the right to Internet access.[77]

In this context, it has been argued that the law shall not restrict the right of the individual to a full and free access to the Internet.[78] This approach is also in line with the dogma of Internet neutrality, where the blocking, prioritizing or degrading of traffic techniques is considered illegitimate. In this context, the recent recognition by the

---

73. For example, in French law the blocking of child pornographic and terrorist content is conducted on the basis of specific lists of content to be blocked which are drawn by the Central office for the fight against crime related to ICT (OCLCTIC – *l'Office central de lutte contre la criminalité liée aux technologies de l' information et de la communication*) and sent to host providers and to ISPs. *See* Décret n° 2015-125 du 5 février 2015 relatif au blocage des sites provoquant à des actes de terrorisme ou en faisant l'apologie et des sites diffusant des images et représentations de mineurs à caractère pornographique, http://legifrance.gouv.fr/eli/decret/2015/2/5/INTX1502 813D/jo/texte.
74. Cormac Callanan et al., *Internet Blocking, Balancing Cybercrime Responses in Democratic Societies*, Open Society Institute funding Study 17 (2009).
75. Internet access interferes also more broadly with other human rights, such as political participation, employment or the right to access education. *See* S. Tully, *A Human Right to Access the Internet? Problems and Prospects*, 14(2) Human Rights L. Rev. http://hrlr.oxfordjournals.org/content/14/2/175.full#fn-93.
76. For an analysis, *see* P. De Hert & D. Kloza, *Internet (access) as a New Fundamental Right. Inflating the Current Rights Framework?*, 3(3) Eur. J. L. & Tech. (2012).
77. R. Brownsword & M. Goodwin, *Law and the Technologies of the Twenty-First Century* 225–245 (Cambridge University Press 2012).
78. A. Murray, *A Bill of Rights for the Internet* (2010), at: http://theitlawyer.blogspot.com/2010/10/bill-of-rights-for-internet.html?q = a + bill + of + rights.

European legislator of a legal dimension of the principle of Internet neutrality in a communication of the Commission of June 30, 2015[79] has a special significance.

However, the idea of a right of Internet access does not create unanimity. On the contrary, in a technologically neutral approach, Internet access is mainly considered as "an enabler of rights, not a right itself," as it has been stressed by Vinton Cerf, one of "the fathers of the Internet," in his article *Internet Access Is Not a Human Right* published in the New York Times in January 4, 2012.[80] This approach is also consistent with a more skeptical appreciation of the emergence of new human rights in general, since recognizing new rights thoughtlessly could lead to fragmentation and to the inflation of human rights, which would then decrease the value of other existing rights.[81]

Recognizing a human right to Internet access in international law is a complex issue, since such a recognition presupposes the definition of the scope and the content of such as right and its possible limitations, while another essential issue is whether such a recognition also imposes positive obligations to the states to guarantee Internet connectivity for all and to what extent. So, apart from a general positive attitude in respect of the recognition of such a right,[82] the main legal question is whether Internet access shall be recognized as an autonomous new human right, or whether it is sufficient that it is safeguarded as a component of other rights, such as the freedom of expression.

So far, Internet access has been generally acknowledged as a fundamental value that merits safeguarding and further promotion (section 3.02[D][2][a] below). Nonetheless, it is clear that it has been perceived and recognized as a component of the freedom of expression and not as a stand-alone new right (section 3.02[D][2][b] below).

[a] The Recognition of Internet Access as a Fundamental Value in the Contemporary World

The importance of the Internet and of Internet connectivity has been generally acknowledged by the international community. Various policy initiatives have been developed in this sense. For example, the United Nations Millennium Declaration guarantees that the benefits of ICTs are available to all.[83]

79. European Commission-Press release, *Commission Welcomes Agreement to End Roaming Charges and to Guarantee an Open Internet* (30 June 2015), available at: http://europa.eu/rapid/press-release_IP-15-5265_en.htm. *See also* European Commission – *Fact Sheet, Roaming Charges and Open Internet: Questions and Answers* (Jun. 30, 2015), at http://europa.eu/rapid/press-release_MEMO-15-5275_en.htm.
80. Vinton Cerf, *Internet Access Is Not a Human Right*, NY Times, (Jan. 24, 2012), at: https://www.nytimes.com/2012/01/05/opinion/internet-access-is-not-a-human-right.html.
81. *See* P. De Hert & D. Kloza, *supra* n. 76.
82. Seventy-nine per cent of interviewees from twenty-six States responded positively to the question whether Internet access is a human right. *See* 1 BBC News, *Four in Five Regard Internet Access as a Fundamental Right: Global Poll* (Mar. 8, 2010), available at: www.bbc.co.uk/pressoffice/pressreleases/stories/2010/03_march/07/poll.shtml, cited by S. Tully, *supra* n. 75.
83. GA Res 55/2, Sep. 18, 2000, A/RES/55/2 ('Millennium Declaration'). *See* Tully, *supra* n. 75.

The Report of the Special Rapporteur on the promotion and protection of the right to freedom of opinion and expression by Frank La Rue in May 2011 has been of significant importance and of great symbolic value.[84] In the Report, La Rue emphasizes the unique, interactive and transformative nature of the Internet not only to enable individuals to exercise their right to freedom of opinion and expression, as guaranteed by Article 19 of the Universal Declaration of Human Rights and the International Covenant on Civil and Political Rights,[85] but also a range of other human rights, and to promote the progress of society as a whole.

The Special Rapporteur is of the view that the arbitrary use of criminal law to sanction legitimate expression constitutes one of the gravest forms of restriction to that right. Even though La Rue acknowledges that child pornography is one of the fields where the mechanisms used to regulate and censor information on the Internet can be legitimate, he also expresses his deep concerns about the application of blocking and filtering mechanisms in order to restrict Internet access.

More specifically, the Special Rapporteur underscores that:

> States' use of blocking or filtering technologies is frequently in violation of their obligation to guarantee the right to freedom of expression, as the criteria mentioned under chapter III are not met. Firstly, the specific conditions that justify blocking are not established in law, or are provided by law but in an overly broad and vague manner, which risks content being blocked arbitrarily and excessively. Secondly, blocking is not justified to pursue aims which are listed under Article 19, paragraph 3, of the International Covenant on Civil and Political Rights, and blocking lists are generally kept secret, which makes it difficult to assess whether access to content is being restricted for a legitimate purpose. Thirdly, even where justification is provided, blocking measures constitute an unnecessary or disproportionate means to achieve the purported aim, as they are often not sufficiently targeted and render a wide range of content inaccessible beyond that which has been deemed illegal. Lastly, content is frequently blocked without the intervention of or possibility for review by a judicial or independent body.[86]

The Council of Europe has been very active in this field and adopted several Recommendations about the protection of the freedom of expression on the Internet. Although not binding, those Recommendations demonstrate a strong determination to safeguard the full enjoyment of fundamental rights on the Internet. The Recommendation on measures to promote the public service value of the Internet emphasizes the

84. United Nations, Human Rights Council, *Report of the Special Rapporteur on the Promotion and Protection of the Right to Freedom of Opinion and Expression*, Frank La Rue (May 16, 2011), at: http://www2.ohchr.org/english/bodies/hrcouncil/docs/17session/A.HRC.17.27_en.pdf.

85. The latter provides that: "(a) Everyone shall have the right to hold opinions without interference; (b)Everyone shall have the right to freedom of expression; this right shall include freedom to seek, receive and impart information and ideas of all kinds, regardless of frontiers, either orally, in writing or in print, in the form of art, or through any other media of his choice; (c) The exercise of the rights provided for in paragraph 2 of this article carries with it special duties and responsibilities. It may therefore be subject to certain restrictions, but these shall only be such as are provided by law and are necessary: (d) for respect of the rights or reputations of others; (e) or the protection of national security or of public order (ordre public), or of public health or morals."

86. Paragraphs 31, 10.

importance of access to information on the Internet and stresses that the Internet and other ICTs have high public service value, in that they serve to promote the effective exercise and enjoyment of human rights and fundamental freedoms for all who use them.[87]

In the Recommendation on the Protection and Promotion of the Universality, Integrity and Openness of the Internet, September 21, 2011[88] the Council of Europe asserts that:

> Users should have the greatest possible access to Internet-based content, applications and services of their choice, whether or not they are offered free of charge, using suitable devices of their choice. Traffic management measures which have an impact on the enjoyment of fundamental rights and freedoms, in particular the right to freedom of expression and to impart and receive information regardless of frontiers as well as the right to respect for private life, must meet the requirements of international law on the protection for freedom of expression and access to information and the right to respect for private life.

More specifically, in respect of Internet filtering and blocking measures, Members are urged to guarantee that these techniques are only introduced by the state of Conditions of Article 10 of the ECHR. In this context:

> such action by the state should only be taken if the filtering concerns specific and clearly identifiable content, a competent national authority has taken a decision on its illegality and the decision can be reviewed by an independent and impartial tribunal or regulatory body, in accordance with the requirements of Article 6 of the European Convention on Human Rights.[89]

More recently, in the Recommendation CM/Rec (2012) 3 of 4 April 2012 in the protection of human rights with regard to search engines, the Council of Europe after acknowledging that the filtering and blocking of Internet content by search engine providers entails the risk of violation of freedom of expression guaranteed by Article 10 of the Convention in respect to the rights of providers and users to distribute and access information, the Council of Europe states that "Search engine providers should not be obliged to monitor their networks and services proactively in order to detect possibly illegal content, nor should they conduct any ex ante filtering or blocking activity, unless mandated by court order or by a competent authority." While there may be legitimate requests to remove specific sources from their index, for example, in cases where other rights outweigh the right to freedom of expression and information, "de-indexing or filtering should be transparent, narrowly tailored and reviewed regularly subject to compliance with due process requirements."[90]

---

87. Recommendation CM/Rec(2007)16 of the Committee of Ministers to Member States.
88. Council of Europe, Rec CM/Rec(2011)8 of the Committee of Ministers to Member States on the *Protection and Promotion of the Universality, Integrity and Openness of the Internet*, General Principle 1.1.1 (Sep. 21, 2011).
89. Recommendation CM/Rec 6 of Mar. 28, 2008 on *Measures to Promote the Respect for Freedom of Expression and Information with Regard to Internet Filters*, available at: https://wcd.coe.int/ViewDoc.jsp?id=1266285.
90. Recommendation CM/Rec 3 of Apr. 4, 2012 *on the Protection of Human Rights with Regard to Search Engines*, available at: https://wcd.coe.int/ViewDoc.jsp?id=1929429.

The need to reconcile fundamental freedoms with other rights and legitimate interests has also been stressed by the European Parliament in its seminal Recommendation of March 26, 2009 to the Council on strengthening security and fundamental freedoms on the Internet.[91] The Recommendation affirms that the Internet gives full meaning to the definition of freedom of expression, especially in terms of the "regardless of frontiers" dimension of the Internet, that it can be an extraordinary opportunity to enhance active citizenship and that, in this respect, access to networks and contents is one of the key elements. Member States are urged to ensure that freedom of expression is not subject to arbitrary restrictions from the public and/or private sphere and to avoid all legislative or administrative measures that could have a "chilling effect" on all aspects of freedom of speech.

At the same time, it is also recognized that:

> through the freedom that it provides, the Internet has also been used as a platform for violent messages such as the ones intentionally inciting terrorist attacks, as well as for websites which can specifically incite hate-based criminal acts, and whereas cybercrime threats more broadly have increased worldwide and are endangering individuals (including children) and networks" and that "these crimes must be countered effectively and decisively, without altering the fundamental free and open nature of the Internet.

Although EU parliament's Recommendations are not binding for the Council or for Member States, national courts are bound to take those recommendations into consideration in order to decide disputes submitted to them, in particular where they are capable of casting light on the interpretation of other provisions of national or Community law.[92]

Furthermore, on May 12, 2014, the Council of the European Union adopted the EU Human Rights Guidelines on Freedom of Expression Online and Offline. One of the priority actions of the EU is promoting and respecting human rights in cyberspace and other ICTs.

In this context, nondiscriminatory access to information and freedom of expression for all individuals, both online and offline, must be ensured and protected. This aim will be achieved by, *inter alia*, promoting unhindered, uncensored and nondiscriminatory access to ICTs and online services for all, in accordance with international law, working against any attempts to block, jam, filter, censor or close down communication networks or any kind of other interference that is in violation of international law, and by providing technical support to individuals on the ground to help counter such attempts, when necessary.[93]

---

91. Recommendation of Mar. 26, 2009 to the Council on *Strengthening Security and Fundamental Freedoms on the Internet* (2008/2160(INI)), available at: http://www.europarl.europa.eu/sides/getDoc.do?pubRef=-//EP//TEXT+TA+P6-TA-2009-0194+0+DOC+XML+V0//EN.
92. Judgment of the Court (Second Chamber) of Dec. 13, 1989, *Salvatore Grimaldi v. Fonds des maladies professionnelles*, Reference for a preliminary ruling: Tribunal du travail de Bruxelles – Belgium, Case C-322/88.
93. Council of the European Union, *EU Human Rights Guidelines on Freedom of Expression Online and Offline*, paragraph 33 (May 12, 2014), at: https://eeas.europa.eu/sites/eeas/files/142549.pdf.

All the above policy recommendations and guidelines emphasize the organic link of Internet access with fundamental freedoms and mainly with the freedom of expression. While it is clear that Internet access must be fully guaranteed and that it can only be restricted under the conditions set out by international law (by law in certain, strictly defined ways and under specific circumstances), it also appears that Internet connectivity is not considered as a distinct and autonomous right itself, but it is mainly perceived as a component of the freedom of expression. This approach has also been affirmed in the case law of ECtHR (section 3.02[D][2][b] below).

[b] *The Guarantee of Internet Access as a Component of the Right of Freedom of Expression*

Article 10 of the ECHR provides that everyone has the right to freedom of expression. The right protects more than simple expression in the sense of public communication of opinion, since it expressly includes the right to hold opinions and to receive information and ideas, as well as the right to impart them.[94] Indeed, Article 10 paragraph 1 provides that this right shall include freedom to hold opinions and to receive and impart information and ideas without interference by public authority and regardless of frontiers. The limitations to freedom of expression are laid down in Article 10 paragraph 2, according to which:

> The exercise of these freedoms, since it carries with it duties and responsibilities, may be subject to such formalities, conditions, restrictions or penalties as are prescribed by law and are necessary in a democratic society, in the interests of national security, territorial integrity or public safety, for the prevention of disorder or crime, for the protection of health or morals, for the protection of the reputation or rights of others, for preventing the disclosure of information received in confidence, or for maintaining the authority and impartiality of the judiciary.

Freedom of expression is also enshrined in Article 19 of the Universal Declaration of Human Rights and the International Covenant on Civil and Political Rights. The latter provides that:

> (a) Everyone shall have the right to hold opinions without interference; (b) Everyone shall have the right to freedom of expression; this right shall include freedom to seek, receive and impart information and ideas of all kinds, regardless of frontiers, either orally, in writing or in print, in the form of art, or through any other media of his choice.

In its general Comment No. 34 of September 12, 2011, the UN Human Rights Committee considers that the generic bans on the operation of certain Internet sites is incompatible with Article 19(3). Indeed, the Comment states that:

> Any restrictions on the operation of websites, blogs or any other internet-based, electronic or other such information dissemination system, including systems to support such communication, such as internet service providers or search engines,

94. A. Nicol, G. Millar & A. Sharlad, *Media law & Human Rights* 15 (2d edn, OUP 2009).

> are only permissible to the extent that they are compatible with paragraph 3. Permissible restrictions generally should be content-specific; generic bans on the operation of certain sites and systems are not compatible with paragraph 3. It is also inconsistent with paragraph 3 to prohibit a site or an information dissemination system from publishing material solely on the basis that it may be critical of the government or the political social system espoused by the government.[95]

Furthermore, Article 11 of the Charter of the fundamental rights of the European Union provides that:

> 1. Everyone has the right to freedom of expression. This right shall include freedom to hold opinions and to receive and impart information and ideas without interference by public authority and regardless of frontiers. 2. The freedom and pluralism of the media shall be respected.[96]

While Article 19 of the Universal Declaration of Human Rights and the International Covenant on Civil and Political Rights expressly provides that the protection of freedom of expression covers not only the content of information but also the means of reception and transmission, the ECHR and the Charter of the Fundamental Rights of the European Union remain silent on this issue.

Nevertheless, the ECtHR case law solemnly and constantly affirmed that Article 10 applies not only to the content of the information but also to the means of transmission or reception, since any restriction imposed on the means necessarily interferes with the right to receive and impart information.[97] Consequently, Internet communication and electronic and Internet-based modes of expression shall be protected as any other form of expression, such as books, newspapers, pamphlets, posters, banners, radio and television.

The special and unique character of Internet communication has also been emphasized by the Court. The Internet, as a means of communication with great accessibility and capacity to store and communicate vast amounts of information, plays an important role in enhancing the public's access to news and facilitating the sharing and dissemination of information generally.[98]

In this context, while the policies governing reproduction of material from the printed media and the Internet may differ, and the latter have to be adjusted according to the technology's specific features in order to secure the protection and promotion of the rights and freedoms concerned, the Court, having regard to the role the Internet plays in the context of professional media activities and its importance for the exercise of the right of freedom of expression generally, also considered that the absence of a sufficient legal framework at the domestic level, allowing journalists to use information

95. Human Rights Committee, 102nd session, Geneva, General Comment No. 34 (Jul. 11–29, 2011), available at: http://www2.ohchr.org/english/bodies/hrc/docs/gc34.pdf.
96. Charter of the fundamental rights of the European Union, 2010/C 83/02.
97. *See, for example, Autronic AG v. Switzerland* (1990), *Öztürk v. Turkey [GC]*, No. 22479/93, §49, ECHR 1999-VI).
98. *Times Newspapers Ltd v. the United Kingdom* (Nos 1 and 2), Nos 3002/03 and 23676/03, §27, Mar. 10, 2009).

obtained from the Internet without fear of incurring sanctions, seriously hinders the exercise of the vital function of the press as a "public watchdog."[99]

The Court also recognizes that restrictions might prove necessary in the Internet context. Indeed, the coming of the Internet has not generally expanded the scope of freedom of expression, but it has rather created more opportunities for this right to enter into conflict with other rights.[100]

Accordingly, in *K.U. v. Finland* the Court held that:

> although freedom of expression and confidentiality of communications are primary considerations and users of telecommunications and Internet services must have a guarantee that their own privacy and freedom of expression will be respected, such guarantee cannot be absolute and must yield on occasion to other legitimate imperatives, such as the prevention of disorder or crime or the protection of the rights and freedoms of others.

More specifically, as concerns child pornography on the Internet, states must provide a framework allowing protection of the various interests, and it is not justified to maintain an overriding requirement of confidentiality if this prevents an effective investigation, in a case where an Internet service should have been obliged to disclose the identity of a person who had placed a sexual advertisement concerning a minor.[101]

In the same vein, a criminal conviction for the publication of a free preview webpage (not containing any age checks), freely accessible to all users, showing seriously obscene pictures and likely to be found by young people, was justified by the need to protect morals and the rights of others.[102] Furthermore, in *Neij and Sunde Kolmisoppi v. Sweden*,[103] while the condemnation of the Pirate bay founders was found by the Court to be an interference with their freedom of expression,[104] the Court ruled that, having regard to all the circumstances of the present case, in particular the nature of the information contained in the shared material and the weighty reasons for the interference with the applicants' freedom of expression, the interference was "necessary in a democratic society" within the meaning of Article 10 §2 of the Convention.

99. *Editorial Board of PravoyeDelo and Shtekel v. Ukraine* (No. 33014/05, May 5, 2011), where the Court stated that restrictions on republishing material found on Internet should be clearly provided by law, but since the Ukrainian law did not protect republishing content and because the domestic judges had refused to extend "traditional" republication news to the online environment, the sanction imposed on the journalists had not been "provided by law."
100. O. Pollicino & M. Bassini, *Free Speech, Defamation and the Limits to Freedom of Expression in the EU: A Comparative Analysis*, in *Research Handbook on EU Internet Law* 532 (A. Savin & J. Trzaskowski, Edward Elgar 2014).
101. *K.U. v. Finland*, Application No. 2872/02, Dec. 2, 2008, §§41–50.
102. *Perrin v. the United Kingdom*, cited in: *Internet: European Court of Human Rights Research Division, Case-Law of the European Court of Human Rights* (June 2001).
103. *Neij and Sunde Kolmisoppi v. Sweden*, Application No. 40397/12 (Mar. 12, 2013).
104. Indeed, the applicants had complained that their right to receive and impart information had been violated when they were convicted for other persons' use of "The Pirate Bay," since Article 10 of the Convention enshrines the right to offer an automatic service of transferring unprotected material between users, according to basic principles of communication on Internet, and within the information society and protects the right to arrange a service on the Internet which can be used for both legal and illegal purposes, without the persons responsible for the service being convicted for acts committed by the people using the service.

While it appears that a special place and significance is recognized for Internet communication in the context of Article 10 of the ECHR, the Court had for the first time the opportunity to more thoroughly analyze the scope of the protection of Internet, as a means of communication of information and ideas and the wholesale blocking of Internet content in 2012 in the landmark case *Ahmet Yıldırım v. Turkey.*[105]

The case concerned a court decision to block access to Google Sites, which hosted an Internet site whose owner was facing criminal proceedings for insulting the memory of Atatürk. As a result of the decision, access to all other sites hosted by the service was blocked. Mr. Yıldırım, a PhD student and active user of Google Sites, who publishes his academic works and evaluations on different matters on his site, complained that he was unable to access his own Internet site because of a measure ordered in the context of criminal proceedings without any connection to him or his site. He submitted that the measure infringed his right to freedom to receive and impart information and ideas.

The ECtHR affirmed that Article 10 guaranteed freedom of expression to "everyone" and applied not only to the content of information but also to the means of disseminating it. In this context, Internet access was protected in the framework of Article 10 of the Convention. The Court also slightly extended the scope of the protection by affirming that "Google sites is a module of Google allowing to facilitate the creation and sharing of a website within a group and constitutes also a means of exercising freedom of expression." Thus, in European Human Rights law, the right to have Internet access shall not only be perceived as the right to have access to the websites of others but it also comprises the right to have access to a site (in our case to "Google Sites"), which enables the users to create their own sites, which are also accessible by other users.[106]

The Court considers that, whatever its legal basis, such a measure was bound to have an influence on the accessibility of the Internet and, accordingly, engaged the responsibility of the respondent State under Article 10. Such interference would breach Article 10 unless it was prescribed by law, pursued one or more legitimate aims, and was necessary in a democratic society to achieve such aims. The Court further observes that the measure in question produced arbitrary effects and could not be said to have been aimed solely at blocking access to the offending website, since it consisted in the wholesale blocking of all the sites hosted by Google Sites. Furthermore, the judicial review procedures concerning the blocking of Internet sites are insufficient to meet the criteria for avoiding abuse, as domestic law does not provide for any safeguards to ensure that a blocking order in respect of a specific site is not used as a means of blocking access in general. Accordingly, there has been a violation of Article 10 of the Convention.

It is noteworthy that the Court in its analysis referred to comparative case law on the issue of limiting freedom on the Internet and, more specifically, to French

105. *Ahmet Yıldırım v. Turkey* (Application No. 3111/10), Dec. 18, 2012. For an analysis of the case, *see* G. Gurkkaynak, I. Yilmaz & D. Durlu, *Exploring New Frontiers in the Interface between Free Speech and Access Bans: The European Court of Human Rights' Case of Ahmet Yıldırım v. Turkey*, 5(1) Eur. J. L. & Tech. (2014).

106. J.P. Marguénaud, *La neutralisation européenne de l'effet collatéral d'une mesure de blocage d'un site Web*, Communication-Commerce Electronique, septembre 2013, 8.

Constitutional Council's decision of June 10, 2009,[107] asserting that freedom of expression must today be understood as including the right of access to the Internet. In this seminal decision, the French Constitutional Council had to rule on the compatibility of the measure of cutting off Internet access to repeated copyright infringers in the frame of the so-called graduated response strategy of the Law *Loi favorisant la diffusion et la protection de la création sur internet.*

The Constitutional Council decided that the right of each individual to connect to the Internet is an element of the freedom of communication and expression, as well as of the commerce and industry. In this decision, the Constitutional Council ruled that the Internet cannot be excluded from the scope of the constitutional protection applicable to the freedom of communication and expression, and that Internet has been considered as the contemporaneous outcome of the "right to speak, write and print freely," as defined by Article 11 of the (French) Human Rights Declaration of 1789. As the Council underlined, Internet access falls within the constitutional field of freedom of expression.[108]

Nonetheless, while it is affirmed that the freedom of expression comprises a freedom to connect to Internet, Internet access is not considered as a "fundamental right" itself.[109] The Court also stressed out that measures restricting Internet access for the protection of intellectual property cannot be taken by an administrative authority, but only by the judiciary. This was found to be particularly important in respect of the measure of cutting off Internet access, because Internet access is a component of freedom of expression and communication, which deserves a reinforced protection, since it is the safeguard for the respect of other rights.

Internet access is also at stake in another case still pending before the ECtHR, which is about the refusal by prison authorities to give a prisoner access to the Internet. In the case *Jankovskis v. Lithuania*, the applicant, a prisoner who requested information from the Ministry of Education about the possibility of enrolling at university, was subsequently informed that all relevant information was posted on an Internet website. When he addressed the prison authorities with a request for Internet access, he was informed that the rules in force did not extend to access to the Internet for prisoners.

107. Décision n° 2009-580 DC du 10 juin 2009, available at: http://www.conseil-constitutionnel.fr/decision/2009/2009-580-dc/decision-n-2009-580-dc-du-10-juin-2009.42666.html.

108. "12. Considérant qu'aux termes de l'article 11 de la Déclaration des droits de l'homme et du citoyen de 1789: 'La libre communication des pensées et des opinions est un des droits les plus précieux de l'homme: tout citoyen peut donc parler, écrire, imprimer librement, sauf à répondre de l'abus de cette liberté dans les cas déterminés par la loi'; qu'en l'état actuel des moyens de communication et eu égard au développement généralisé des services de communication au public en ligne ainsi qu'à l'importance prise par ces services pour la participation à la vie démocratique et l'expression des idées et des opinions, ce droit implique la liberté d'accéder à ces services."

109. *See* B. Ridard, *La protection constitutionnelle du droit d'accès à l'Internet, Implications juridiques de la décision "Hadopi" du Conseil constitutionnel*, Congrès mondial de l'AIDC, (December 2010) at: http://www.juridicas.unam.mx/wccl/ponencias/3/64.pdf. Jacques Rancillon, *Téléchargement illégal. Heur et malheur de la loi Création et Internet: la loi HADOPI censurée par le Conseil constitutionnel*, Revue de science criminelle et de droit pénal comparé, at 617 (2009). Iliana Boubekeur, *De la "loi HADOPI" à la "loi HADOPI 2,"* Revue Lamy Droit de l'Immatériel, n°51, at 108 (2009).

The Kaunas Regional Administrative Court dismissed the applicant's complaint on the grounds that, although the prison rules did not explicitly prohibit the use of Internet by the prisoners, the list of prohibited items included telephones and radio-communication, and that these limitations were designed to limit the prisoners' possibilities to commit new crimes. The applicant complains under Articles 10 and 14 of the Convention about the refusal to give him access to the Internet. He maintains that, by this decision, his right to receive and impart information and ideas was violated and claims that the rules in force do not extend to a ban on the use of the Internet by prisoners.[110]

[3] Site Blocking at an ISP Level in the CJEU's Case Law

The issue of site blocking and its compatibility with fundamental rights has also been raised before the Court of Justice of European Union (CJEU). In this context, the Court was called to decide on the proper balancing of the freedom of expression with other rights, mainly with intellectual property rights. In that case, certainly, the technique of dealing with that issue differs substantially with that of the ECtHR, since the CJEU deals with the specific preliminary questions submitted by the national courts and does not act as a constitutional Court of fundamental rights, despite the incorporation of the Charter into EU primary law.[111]

In this context, and given the primarily economic dimension of the EU, the question of Internet blocking is not necessarily analyzed principally under the light of the protection of freedom of expression, but also in conjunction with other rights, such as the freedom to conduct business and data protection. The most illustrative demonstrations can be found in CJEU's case law on ISP's liability for copyright infringement on the grounds of the E-commerce Directive's intermediaries' asylum,[112] while also of significant importance is the recent CJEU's ruling in the *Telecabel* case.[113]

Indeed, depending on the target of the enforcement strategy against Internet copyright infringement, different fundamental rights are at stake, and this has been naturally reflected in the CJEU's case law in the field of intellectual property rights. In claims of direct copyright infringements which were brought against individual users, the focus has been given on the reconciliation of the right to respect for private life and personal data protection with intellectual property law, since the identification of the direct infringers presupposed the disclosure of their personal data to the claimants by ISPs.

In claims against intermediaries, either on the legal grounds of secondary infringement, or in the form of injunctions against intermediaries as third parties,

110. Application No. 21575/08 by *Henrikas Jankovskis against Lithuania* lodged on Jan. 7, 2008.
111. Pollicino & Bassini, *supra* n. 100, 534.
112. Directive 2000/31/EC of the European Parliament and of the Council of Jun. 8, 2000 on certain legal aspects of information society services, in particular electronic commerce, in the Internal Market ("Directive on electronic commerce"),OJ L 178, 17/07/2000, pp. 0001–0016.
113. CJEU, *UPC Telekabel Wien GmbH v. Constantin Film Verleih GmbH, Wega Filmproduktionsgesellschaft mbH,* Case C-314/12, Judgment of Mar. 27, 2014.

copyright law clashes mainly with the freedom of ISPs to conduct business, the right of the public to receive and impart information and personal data protection.[114]

In the *Promusicae*,[115] the *Tele2*[116] and the *Bonnier Audio*[117] cases, the Court sets out as a fundamental principle of IP enforcement the proper calibration of different fundamental rights. According to the Court, each Member State has to reconcile the requirements of the protection of different fundamental rights, namely the right to respect for private life on the one hand, and the right to protection of property (including intellectual property rights) and to an effective remedy on the other. Furthermore, it stated that the authorities and courts of the Member States should ensure that they do not rely on an interpretation of their national laws in a way that would be in conflict with fundamental rights or with the other general principles of Community law, such as the principle of proportionality.

In the *Scarlet*[118] and the *Netlog*[119] cases, the Court, following the *Promusicae* case, stated that a fair balance must be struck between the protection of copyright and the fundamental rights of persons affected by such measures, since nothing in the Charter of Fundamental Rights of the European Union suggests that copyright is inviolable.[120] Installing a system for filtering all electronic communications passing through its service would infringe the fundamental rights both of the ISPs and of their customers, namely the ISP's freedom to conduct business,[121] their customers' right to protection of their personal data[122] and their customers' freedom to receive or impart information, since a filtering system would identify users' IP addresses and could lead to the blocking of lawful communications of information.[123]

Nonetheless, apart from setting the balancing of fundamental rights as a fundamental principle of IP enforcement, the Court's rulings are rather vague,[124] sparing and elliptic, since they do not provide further clarifications on how the delicate task of balancing will occur on a national level. For, example, do ISPs need to apply different

114. T. Synodinou, *Intermediaries' Liability for Online Copyright Infringement in the EU: Evolutions and Confusions*, 31(1) Computer Law & Security Report 57–67 (02/2015).
115. CJEU, *Productores de Música de España (Promusicae) v. Telefónica de España SAU*, Case C-275/06, (Jan. 29, 2008). *See* Ioannis Iglezakis, *The Legal Struggle in the EU against On Line Piracy*, in *Codification of European Copyright Law, Challenges and Perspectives* 290 (T. Synodinou ed., Kluwer Law International 2012).
116. CJEU, *LSG-Gesellschaft zur Wahrnehmung von Leistungsschutzrechten GmbH v Tele 2 Telecommunication GmbH (Tele2)*, Case C-557/07 (Feb. 19, 2009).
117. CJEU, *Bonnier Audio AB v. Perfect Communication Sweden AB (ePhone)*, Case C-461/10, (Apr. 19, 2012).
118. CJEU, *Scarlet Extended SA v. Société Belge des Auteurs, Compositeurs et Editeurs SCRL (SABAM)*, Case C-70/10 (Nov. 24, 2011).
119. CJEU, *Belgische Vereniging van Auteurs, Componisten en Uitgevers CVBA (SABAM) v. Netlog NV*, Case C-360/10 (Feb. 16, 2012).
120. *See* CJEU, *Scarlet Extended*, *supra* n. 118, at paragraph 43.
121. Article 16 of the Charter.
122. Article 8 of the Charter.
123. Article 11 of the Charter.
124. J. Griffiths, *Constitutionalising or Harmonising? The Court of Justice, the Right to Property and European Copyright Law*, 38(1) Eur. L. Rev. 74 (2013). The author notes that "In the recent copyright cases, the application of the 'fair balance' concept is vague."

tests in different situations? In respect of the disclosure of personal data, does it make a difference if it involves infringing copyright or identity theft on social media?[125]

Furthermore, the Court, which prefers to use its own normative corpus (the Charter of Fundamental Rights of the European Union instead of the ECHR),[126] focuses mainly on certain freedoms without further discussing the implications of IP enforcement for other fundamental rights, such as the confidentiality of communications.[127]

The possibility to order ISPs to prevent copyright infringements by the ordering of injunctions has also been confirmed by the CJEU. In the 2009 CJEU's Tele2 ruling, the Court clarified that access providers which merely provide users with Internet access, without offering other services such as email, FTP or file-sharing services, or exercising any control, whether de jure or de facto, over the services which users make use of, must be regarded as "intermediaries" within the meaning of Article 8(3) of the [Information Society] Directive.[128]

In *L'oreal and Others v. Ebay*,[129] the Court gave an end to the interpretative controversy whether the injunctions against the intermediaries presupposed their direct or secondary liability in tort law, when admitting that Member states shall ensure that their courts have jurisdiction to OSPs to take measures in order to prevent future infringements of intellectual property, regardless of their liability in tort law. The Court has also set out the minimum threshold in respect of this obligation. Even though the implementation of the enforcement policy via injunctions is a question of national law, those injunctions must be effective, proportionate and dissuasive and must not create barriers to legitimate trade.[130]

In the *TeleKabel* case,[131] the question of web site blocking injunctions against ISPs was put before the CJEU. The Court, in line with its ruling in the *Tele2* case, confirmed that ISPs are intermediaries in the sense of Article 8 paragraph 3 of the Infosoc Directive and, therefore, they can be ordered to block access to copyright infringing websites without necessarily having a contractual relationship to the infringing website[132] and without having to show that some of their customers actually access, on the website at issue, the protected subject matter made available to the

125. A. Tsoutsanis, *Privacy and Piracy in Cyberspace: Justice for All*, J. Intellectual Property L. & Practice Advance Access published (Oct. 24, 2013).
126. C. Castets-Renard, *Protection du droit d'auteur confrontée aux droits fondamentaux: point trop n'en faut!*, Revue Lamy Droit de l'Immatériel, n°79, 9, (2013).
127. S. Kulk & F. Zuiderveen Borgesius, *Filtering for Copyright Enforcement in Europe after the Sabam Cases*, 34(11) E.I.P.R. 791-795 (2012).
128. CJEU, *LSG v. Tele2*, *supra* n. 116, dictum.
129. CJEU, Case C-324/09 *L'Oréal and Others v. eBay* (Jul. 12, 2011).
130. M. Husovec, *Injunctions against Innocent Third Parties: The Case of Website Blocking*, 4(2) JIPITEC 117 (2012).
131. CJEU, *UPC Telekabel Wien GmbH v. Constantin Film Verleih GmbH, Wega Filmproduktionsgesellschaft mbH*, Case C-314/12, (Mar. 27, 2014).
132. *See* paragraph 35 of the judgment: "Neither the wording of Article 8(3) nor any other provision of Directive 2001/29 indicates that a specific relationship between the person infringing copyright or a related right and the intermediary is required. Furthermore, that requirement cannot be inferred from the objectives pursued by that directive, given that to admit such a requirement would reduce the legal protection afforded to the rightholders at issue, whereas the objective of that directive, as is apparent inter alia from Recital 9 in its preamble, is precisely to guarantee them a high level of protection."

public,[133] since the existence of an act of making a work available to the public presupposes only that the work was made available to the public, and it is not decisive that persons who make up that public have actually had access to that work or not.[134]

In order to give its answer, the Court first analyzes the effect of the blocking injunction on the freedom to conduct a business of the ISP and then its effects for the ISP's customers and Internet users.

In respect of the balancing of copyright protection with the freedom to conduct a business, the Court states that an injunction that leaves it to the ISP to determine its means does not seem to infringe the very substance of the freedom of an ISP, since such an injunction enables the ISP to choose to put in place measures which are best adapted to the resources and abilities available to him and which are compatible with the other obligations and challenges which he will encounter in the exercise of his activity.

Moreover, such an injunction allows its addressee to avoid liability by proving that he has taken all reasonable measures.[135]

Furthermore, when choosing these measures, the ISP has to take into consideration the fundamental rights of Internet users, and more precisely, he must ensure compliance with the fundamental right of Internet users to freedom of information.

The formula that has been enshrined by the Court is accompanied with procedural safeguards aiming to comfort both the position of the ISP and of Internet users. As regards ISPs, in accordance with the principle of legal certainty, it must be possible for the addressee of an injunction to maintain before the court, once the implementing measures which he has taken are known and before any decision imposing a penalty on him is adopted, that the measures taken were indeed those which could be expected of him in order to prevent the proscribed result.[136] In respect of Internet users, the national procedural rules must provide a possibility for Internet users to assert their rights before the court once the implementing measures taken by the ISP are known.[137]

In respect of copyright, the Court recognizes that it is possible that the enforcement of an injunction such as that in the main proceedings will not lead to a complete cessation of the infringements of the intellectual property right of the persons concerned. Nonetheless, the measures which are taken by the addressee of an injunction must be sufficiently effective to ensure genuine protection of the fundamental right at issue, that is to say that they must have the effect of preventing unauthorized access to the protected subject matter or, at least, of making it difficult to achieve and of seriously discouraging Internet users who are using the services of the addressee of that injunction from accessing the subject matter made available to them.

133. *See* paragraph 36 of the judgment: "Nor is the conclusion reached by the Court in paragraph 30 of this judgment invalidated by the assertion that, in order to obtain the issue of an injunction against an Internet service provider, the holders of a copyright or of a related right must show that some of the customers of that provider actually access, on the website at issue, the protected subject-matter made available to the public without the agreement of the rightholders."
134. Paragraph 40 of the judgment.
135. Paragraph 53 of the judgment.
136. Paragraph 54 of the judgment.
137. Paragraph 57 of the judgment.

Therefore, the Court has established various safety keys in order to limit the availability of ISPs injunctions. The requirement of the effectivity of the measure and the application of the principle of proportionality act in this direction. However, the principle stands clear: by operating with a certain judicial activism, the court bypasses the intermediary's safe harbor with various direct and indirect consequences in terms of cybercrime's policy.

First, it appears that certain legal tools of cybercrime prevention are legitimate, provided that they comply with human rights. In other words, it rehabilitates the ISPs as actors and protagonists in the fight against cybercrime. Second, the conjunction between the installation of reasonable measures and the avoidance of any civil liability would lead the ISPs to operate more reasonably in terms of self-regulation, whereas the safe harbor system only gave them a wild card to act. However, some issues still have to be raised.

For example, could this legal framework be applied under the same terms to other kinds of intermediaries, such as the OSPs? We can refer, for instance, to the discontent of some video uploaders about Facebook's policy: while on YouTube each video possesses a unique identification process that helps to prevent copyright infringement, no such system exists in the new Facebook video system. It should be noted that Article 15 of the E-commerce Directive forbids a State member to impose a general duty of control of the content to online intermediaries.[138]

In the CJEU's judgment, in the case *Scarlet v. Sabam,*[139] the Court had the opportunity to explain that this rule leads to the rejection of the "take down, stay down" theory.[140] In other words, it cannot be imposed to OSPs to generally control the content. This means that an injunction to block content related to cybercriminal activities would apply only to existing content. To the contrary, the injunction cannot be interpreted or applied in a way to force the OSPs to ensure that any future upload will be automatically blocked.

In conclusion, the implication of intermediaries, not only in the process of identification of the cybercriminals, but also in the prevention stage (for instance via the automatic blocking of virus traps on websites) should be more exploited. Copyright law enforcement tools offer here a model of responsible system linked to safeguards.

138. "1. Member States shall not impose a general obligation on providers, when providing the services covered by Articles 12, 13 and 14, to monitor the information which they transmit or store, nor a general obligation actively to seek facts or circumstances indicating illegal activity. 2. Member States may establish obligations for information society service providers promptly to inform the competent public authorities of alleged illegal activities undertaken or information provided by recipients of their service or obligations to communicate to the competent authorities, at their request, information enabling the identification of recipients of their service with whom they have storage agreements."

139. Judgment of the Court (Third Chamber) of Nov. 24, 2011, *Scarlet Extended SA v. Société belge des auteurs, compositeurs et éditeurs SCRL (SABAM)*, C-70/10.

140. Indeed, no matter how specific the content being targeted, a duty to prevent reuploads signifies that a host provider shall monitor all uploads on an ongoing basis to be sure to catch re-uploads. This is an obligation to monitor similar to the filtering that the *Sabam* judgment rejected. *See Cases Wrestle with Role of Online Intermediaries in Fighting Copyright Infringement* (Jun. 26, 2012), available at: https://cdt.org/insight/cases-wrestle-with-role-of-online-intermediaries-in-fighting-copyright-infringement/.

From national experiences (like this of the child abuse content in the UK), it can be deduced that an optimal form of intervention in this domain should foster on incitement to autoregulation, meaning that the authorities should specify to the ISPs the various forms of possible interventions compatible with the protection of human rights.

CHAPTER 4
Legal Consequences of Cybercrime

Tatiana-Eleni Synodinou & Lilian Mitrou

§4.01 THE REGIME OF SECURITY AND DATA BREACH NOTIFICATION

[A] Security and Data Breach Notification as a Compliance and Transparency Tool

There were recently many serious security breach incidents that highlighted the need to reinforce the security of systems and information.[1] According to the findings of European Commission's online public consultation on "Improving network and information security in the EU," 57% of respondents had experienced security incidents over the previous year that had a serious impact on their activities.[2] The high profile incidents of personal data loss across Europe have prompted a wide discussion with regard to the level of security and the ways it could be enhanced.[3] Security threats are rapidly emerging as one of the most critical issues for policy makers and legislators.

However, security of information and information systems is a difficult field as ensuring security requires responding to multiple challenges. Cybersecurity is inherently multidisciplinary: legal framework, technical security measures, policies and strategies are interrelated. As it became clear that the growing number of attacks and respectively security breaches may be a structural problem for the European society, European policy makers have tried to identify and introduce measures that aim at boosting security through regulation, such as the penalization of attacks, and also

1. V. Reding, *The EU Data Protection Reform 2012 – Making Europe the Standard Setter for Modern Data Protection Rules in the Digital Age*, Speech 12/26 (2012).
2. Proposal for a Directive of the European Parliament and of the Council Concerning Measures to Ensure a High Common Level of Network and Information Security Across the Union 2, COM(2013) 48 final (Feb. 7, 2013) – Explanatory Memorandum.
3. ENISA, *Data breach notifications in the EU*, 8 (2011), available online at: https://www.enisa.europa.eu/activities/identity-and-trust/library/deliverables/dbn.

through understanding, management and mitigation of risks. An area of quite significant regulatory attention has been the introduction of binding disclosure obligations after a security breach.

Disclosure obligations can be categorized in security incidents notification and (personal) data breach notification. As "incident" is defined as "any circumstance or event having an actual adverse effect on security."[4] However, this term needs to be interpreted and clarified in relation to the notion of "security" meant as "the ability of a network and information system to resist, at a given level of confidence, accident or malicious action that compromise the availability, authenticity, integrity and confidentiality of stored or transmitted data or the related services offered by or accessible via that network and information system."[5]

In the European context as personal data breach is understood as "... a breach of security leading to the accidental or unlawful destruction, loss, alteration, unauthorized disclosure of, or access to, personal data transmitted, stored or otherwise processed in connection with the provision of a publicly available electronic communications service in the Community."[6]

After USA, this trend has obtained the attention of the European legislator[7] and became a significant reform topic. Data breach notification has initially been considered as "consumer privacy phenomenon." Due to the increasing number and complexity of attacks against information systems, security and data breach notification are viewed as a remedy and a means to address the multifaceted problems of inadequate information security measures in organizations, the rapid increase of attacks, including identity theft crimes, and personal data protection.[8]

Breach notification can support affected entities and individuals to mitigate the harm caused by the breach. Organizations are compelled to suggest measures to limit and/or reduce the damage. Breach notification regimes do have also a preempting function: Due to the increased scrutiny of their activity and their possible liability, organizations are expected to respond more effectively and rigorously to threats and breaches.[9] Especially entities holding personally identifiable information (personal

4. Definition as laid down in Article 3(4) of the Draft NIS Directive (Proposal for a Directive of the European Parliament and of the Council concerning measures to ensure a high common level of network and information security across the Union).
5. Proposal for a Directive of the European Parliament and of the Council concerning measures to ensure a high common level of network and information security across the Union. Article 3(2) The European Data Protection Supervisor (EDPS) considers this term as needing further clarification as it is not clear whether an attack on an information system should be considered an incident if the attacker does not succeed in compromising its security. EDPS, Opinion on a "Cyber Security Strategy of the European Union: an Open, Safe and Secure Cyberspace," and on the Commission proposal for a Directive concerning measures to ensure a high common level of network and information security across the Union.
6. Article 2(i), Directive 2009/136/EC.
7. F. Bisogni, *Evaluating Data Breach Notification Laws. What Do the Numbers Tell Us?* 2015 TPRC | 43rd Research Conference on Communications, Information and Internet Policy, George Mason University School of Law (2015).
8. M. Burdon, B. Lane & P. von Nessen, *Data Breach Notification Law in the EU and Australia – Where to Now?*, 28(3) Computer L. & Security Rev. 296 (2012).
9. P.M. Schwartz & E.J. Janger, *Notification of Data Security Breaches*, Michigan Law Rev. 105 at 936 (2007).

data) are encouraged to better protect that information. As security of information systems are in some cases foreseen and imposed by the law the breach notification can enhance the impact of mandatory security obligations[10] and ensure compliance with them.

The disclosure of a security breach imposes a "reputational cost" on the entity that has experienced the "breach." As reputation is a valuable asset for any organization, the potential negative publicity could serve as an incentive to identify and implement more effective security measures.[11] This would increase the security costs and budgets, but in Europe it seems to be supported also for the reason that it is believed to drive forward the market for data security technology.[12] The notification requirement may increase the situational awareness inside the organizations that allows a better evaluation of security risks.[13]

The notification of breaches to individuals, in case that they are affected thereby reinforces their right to information, which is a fundamental principle of the EU legal framework.[14] Furthermore, security breach notification legislation is related to the idea/approach of "governance through transparency" or "regulation through disclosure"[15] which itself should raise the level of accountability. Accountability involves committing to legal and ethical obligations, policies, procedures and mechanisms as well as explaining and demonstrating implementation to internal and external stakeholders and remedying any failure to act properly.

[B] The USA Breach Notification Model

California was the first that enacted the data breach legislation in Civil Code (§ 1729.98), becoming the basis for further legislative developments in USA.[16] Currently, forty-seven states, the District of Columbia, Guam, Puerto Rico and the Virgin Islands

10. J. Winn, *Are Better Security Breach Notification Laws Possible*, 24 Berkeley Tech. L.J. 1133 (2009).
11. *See* S. Esayas, *Breach Notification Requirements under the European Union Legal Framework: Convergence, Conflicts, and Complexity in Compliance*, 31 J. Marshall J. Info. Tech. & Privacy L 323 (2014).
12. About this aspect, *see* ENISA, *Recommendations for a Methodology of the Assessment of Severity of Personal Data Breaches*, Working document (2013).
13. As noted by Kulikova et al., incident information disclosure constitutes an essential part of crisis communications, which can "reduce and contain harm, provide specific information to stakeholders, initiate and enhance recovery, manage image and perceptions of blame and responsibility." *See* O. Kulikova et al., *Cyber Crisis Management: A Decision-Support Framework for Disclosing Security Incident Information*, in *Cyber Security (CyberSecurity), 2012 International Conference IEEE* 104 (December 2012).
14. S. Esayas, *Breach Notification Requirements Under the European Union Legal Framework: Convergence, Conflicts, and Complexity in Compliance*, 31 J. Marshall J. Info. Tech. & Privacy L 323 (2014).
15. These development are associated with the community's "right to know" regulation laws, which was developed in order to improve the efficacy of environmental laws. S. Esayas, *ibid.*, 319, with further references.
16. M. Bisogni, *Evaluating Data Breach Notification Laws. What Do the Numbers Tell Us?* TPRC, 2013. Also P. Schwartz & E.J. Janger, *Notification of Data Security Breaches*, Michigan L. Rev. 105 at 915 (2007).

have enacted legislation requiring private, governmental or educational entities to notify individuals of security breaches of information involving personally identifiable information.

In general, the legislators consider as breach the unauthorized acquisition of data. Addressees of the security breach obligations are businesses, data/information brokers, government entities, etc. The laws define specific requirements with regard to notification (e.g., timing or method of notice, who must be notified) as well as exemptions from the notification requirements (e.g., for encrypted information).[17] However individuals lack meaningful and efficient remedies against companies for the exposure of their information resulting from a data breach.[18] The judgment of the Court (7th Cir. 2007) in *Pisciotta v. Old National Bancorp* has demonstrated that consumers in general do not have a cause of action: Plaintiffs sought compensation after their personal information was taken from the Old National Bancorp website, but the Court held that "without more than allegations of increased risk of future identity theft, the plaintiffs have not suffered a harm that the law is prepared to remedy."[19]

In order to face this problem and introduce a national data breach notification requirement, instead of the patchwork system currently implemented at the state level, federal legislation has been proposed: the Data Accountability and Trust Act, introduced in 2009, provided for more specific notification requirements and for fairly excessive fines for noncomplying with the law. The Federal Trade Commission (FTC) should play a key role as it was charged with the specification of the law by issuing regulations on storing and the disposal of personal information. These proposals have been criticized mainly with reference to increasing regulatory burdens put on critical infrastructure companies.[20]

In 2015, a new bill has been introduced in Senate: The Data Security and Breach Notification Act establishes procedures to be followed in the event of an information security breach. Entities that discover a breach will have to notify the FTC[21] and affected individuals while setting forth requirements with regard to methods of notification and timeliness. Entities will be exempted from notification obligation if they reasonably conclude that there is no reasonable risk of identity theft, fraud or other unlawful conduct. The Bill establishes a presumption that there is no such risk for

17. National Conference of State Legislatures. Information and reference to the state laws available at: http://www.ncsl.org/research/telecommunications-and-informationtechnology/security-breach-notification-laws.aspx.
18. S.J. Rancourt, *Hacking, Theft, and Corporate Negligence: Making the Case for Mandatory Encryption of Personal Information*, 18 Tex. Wesleyan L. Rev. 186 (2011).
19. *See, e.g., Pisciotta v. Old National Bancorp*, 499 F.3d 629, 639.
20. L. Bonner, *Cyber Risk: How the 2011 Sony Data Breach and the Need for Cyber Risk Insurance Policies Should Direct the Federal Response to Rising Data Breaches*, 40 Wash. U. J. L. & Pol'y 266 et seq. (2012).
21. Unless the covered entity has already notified a federal entity designated by the Department of Homeland Security (DHS) to receive such information. However the Bill directs DHS to designate a federal entity that covered entities would be required to notify if a security breach involves: (1) the personal information of more than 10,000 individuals, (2) a database containing the personal information of more than 1 million individuals, (3) federal government databases, or (4) the personal information of federal employees or contractors known to be involved in national security or law enforcement.

encrypted data. For concealing security breaches that result in economic harm of at least USD 1,000 to an individual the Bill provides for criminal penalties of a fine, imprisonment for up to five years, or both. Finally the Bill charges the FTC with the promulgation of regulations on security policies and procedures for the treatment and protection of personal information that commercial entities, nonprofit and for-profit corporations, estates, trusts, cooperatives and other specified entities that own or possess data containing personal information have to comply with.[22]

[C] The Current European Framework

The breach notification has become a reform topic and policy tool in the European Union in the first review phase of the Telecom Package. Both the Framework Directive (2002/21/EC)[23] and the e-Privacy Directive (2002/58/EC)[24] imposed security obligations to electronic communication sector operators, but it did not require them to notify security and/or data breaches. The introduction of the European data breach notification requirements reflected the shift of the European policy toward a multifaceted approach for increasing the level of security and fostering trust among citizens in how their data is being dealt with, in a secured and protected.

[1] The Electronic Communications Sector: The e-Privacy Directive

The Directive 2009/136/EC that amended the e-Privacy Directive introduced a framework for the reporting of data breaches to regulatory authorities and the potential notification of personal data breaches to affected individuals. The disclosure of data breaches forms a part of the security obligation that the European legislator compelled to telecommunication providers. The reporting of breaches relates to the obligation under Article 4(1), which requires providers to take the appropriate technical and organizational measures to safeguard the security of its services, if necessary in conjunction with the provider of the public communications network with respect to network security with the aim to ensure a level of security appropriate to the risk presented. To this effect, it is important to identify proactively the risks that may affect the security of services and network and have an appropriate risk management framework in place.[25] Directive 2009/136 has enhanced the security to be provided by

22. *See* the report in the website of USA Congress available at: https://www.congress.gov/bill/114th-congress/senate-bill/177.
23. Directive 2002/21/EC of the European Parliament and of the Council of Mar. 7, 2002 on a common regulatory framework for electronic communications networks and services (Framework Directive).
24. Directive 2002/58/EC of the European Parliament and of the Council of 12 July 2002 concerning the processing of personal data and the protection of privacy in the electronic communications sector (Directive on privacy and electronic communications (e-Privacy Directive).
25. Article 29 Data Protection Working Party, Opinion 03/2014 on Personal Data Breach Notification, 4.

specifying the obligation with regard to security of data[26] and by requiring the implementation of a security policy.

In case of a particular risk of a breach of the security of the network, the provider of a publicly available electronic communications service must inform the subscribers concerning such risk and, where the risk lies outside the scope of the measures to be taken by the service provider, of any possible remedies, including an indication of the likely costs involved (Article 4(2)). The provision does not give further instructions about the kinds of security risks to be notified, but in any case the use of the term "particular" risks seems to imply certain level of significance to be further determined by the national regulatory bodies.[27]

The provisions concerning data breach notification are quite detailed in comparison with security obligations. In the case of a personal data breach, the provider of publicly available electronic communications services shall, without undue delay, notify the personal data breach to the competent national authority. The first issue has been the determination of data breach events, thus the criteria vary from country to country depending also on the understanding of security event and/or incident.[28]

While the competent authority is to be informed about all breaches subscribers and/or individuals concerned are to be informed[29] about data breaches that pose an adverse effect to their personal data or the privacy of the individual. This Directive does not define strictly what is meant with "adversely affected," but Recital 61 provides an indication of the type of situations will be deemed to create a sufficient risk for individuals and consequently require a notification:

> breach should be considered as adversely affecting the data or privacy of a subscriber or individual where it could result in, for example, identity theft or fraud, physical harm, significant humiliation or damage to reputation in connection with the provision of publicly available communications services in the Community.[30]

It is clear that the European legislator understands as harm not only the pure economic loss arising for example from identity theft but also wider social harms mainly in the form of reputation damage caused from the unauthorized release of her information.

---

26. According to the amended provision organizational and technical security measures shall (a) ensure that personal data can be accessed only by authorized personnel for legally authorized purposes and (b) protect personal data stored or transmitted against accidental or unlawful destruction, accidental loss or alteration, and unauthorized or unlawful storage, processing, access or disclosure.
27. S. Esayas, *supra*, 333 ff.
28. While for example Spain distinguished between a security threat and mismanagement that does not violate security protocols, Ireland and other countries applied a broad definition of security incidents.
29. According to Article 29 DPWP Opinion notification to subscribers and individuals affected should not be dependent on the notification of the personal data breach to the competent national authority.
30. Article 29 DPWP proposes in Opinion 3/2014 a nonexhaustive list of examples where data subjects should be notified.

In dubio, Article 29 DPWP favors the notification as it states that the data controller should err on the side of caution and proceed with notification. Article 4(3) also contains a general exception to subscriber or individual notification if the provider can demonstrate to the satisfaction of the competent authority that it has implemented appropriate technological protection measures to render the data unintelligible to any person who is not authorized to access it and those measures were applied to the data concerned by the security breach. The use of "technological protection measures" as a general exception has raised criticism.[31] However, it seems that the Data Protection Authorities do not have serious concerns with regard to this exception as they regard that its ratio is that appropriate measures may reduce the residual privacy risks on the data subject to a negligible level.[32]

With regard to the scope and the content of notification, the e-Privacy Directive leaves national legislators a large degree of interpretation. The Directive specifies neither the form nor the substance of notification providing, however, that a notification to subscribers or individuals should at least include the nature of the breach, relevant contact points to gain further information and the recommendation of further measures to mitigate adverse effects of the breach. Moreover, providers are required to maintain an inventory of data breaches that includes the material facts, the effects of the breach and remedial action taken that is provided to national regulators. This requirement ensures the transparency and allows the assessment of this notification model while enabling national authorities to verify compliance with the law. National authorities have the power to audit providers, and in case they do not comply with notification requirements, to impose appropriate sanctions.

[2] Notification under the Framework Directive

Reporting on security breaches is provided also in the Framework Directive. Initially the 2002/21 Framework Directive contained no clear requirement for breach notification. Such a requirement has been introduced by its amendment, Directive 2009/140/EC that states that Member States have to ensure that undertakings providing public communications networks or publicly available electronic communications services shall notify the competent national regulatory authority of a breach of security or loss of integrity that has had a significant impact on the operation of networks or services (Article 13(a)(3)).

The Directive does not contain any definition of "security breach" and "loss of integrity" although Recital 44 of the Directive 2009/140/EC sheds some light with the reference to "system complexity, technical failure or human mistake, accidents or attacks may all have consequences for the functioning and availability of the physical infrastructures that deliver important services to EU citizens, including e-Government services." Both the wording and the overall scope and aim of the Framework Directive

31. M. Burdon, R. Low & J. Reid, *If Its Encrypted Its Secure! The Viability of US State-Based Encryption Exemptions*, Paper presented at the IEEE International Symposium on Technology and Society, University of Wollongong, (Jun. 7–9, 2010).
32. *See* Article 29 DPWP 3/2014.

derives that a breach under Article 13(a)(3) essentially focuses on breaches that effect the performance functionality or continuity of the network or service.[33] The Directive defines neither what is meant under "significant impact on the operations of the network or services."

In contrast to the e-Privacy Directive, it is not required to notify affected individuals. However, the national regulatory authority concerned may inform the public or require the undertakings to do so, where it determines that disclosure of the breach is in the public interest. The Directive does not include provisions with regard to timeframes, content and procedures leaving their determination to national legislators.

[3] Notification under the Regulation 611/2013

The European legislator was oriented to the use of guidelines to assist the harmonization by providing for broad ranging powers for both national data protection authorities and the Commission regarding the development of binding guidelines in relation to personal data breaches.[34] Although the wide room of maneuver left to national legislators seemed to be a conscious choice of the e-Privacy Directive,[35] major concerns have been expressed with regard to the different transposition and implementation of the data breach notification regime into Member States.

The Commission considered necessary to adopt technical implementing measures as different national requirements in this regard may lead to legal uncertainty, more complex and cumbersome procedures and significant administrative costs for providers operating cross-border.[36] In order to deal with this inconsistency and concerns with regard to the interpretation of some vague terms, such as the "undue delay," the EU passed the Regulation 611/2013, which complemented the existing rules and harmonized data breach notification requirements by public electronic communications service providers, including both traditional telecom providers such as telephony companies and Internet Service Providers (ISPs).

The notification of personal data breaches under the e-Privacy Directive is replaced by the Regulation 611/2013. Under this Regulation, every breach has to be notified and brought to the attention of the competent national authorities regardless of its significance within twenty-four hours[37] after the detection[38] of the data breach.

---

33. S. Esayas, *supra*, 326 et seq.
34. According to Burdon et al. continued monitoring and development across the EU Member States should provide support for the uniform application that could face many of the difficulties arising from the fragmented approach of US state-based legislatures. Mark Burdon, Bill Lane, Paul von Nessen & Jason Reid, *Australian Data Breach Notification: Avoiding the State/Federal Overlap* (Paper presented at the 5th International Conference on Legal, Security and Privacy Issues in IT Law, Barcelona, 2010).
35. *See* M. Burdon, B. Lane & P. von Nessen, *ibid.*, 305.
36. Commission Regulation (EU) No. 611/2013 of 24 June 2013 on the measures applicable to the notification of personal data breaches under Directive 2002/58/EC of the European Parliament and of the Council on privacy and electronic communications. Recital 4.
37. It is possible for the provider to delay the notification to the subscriber or individual if it may put at the risk the proper investigation of the personal data breach such as criminal investigation or

However, this general notification regime should not prevent the competent national authority concerned from prioritizing the investigation of certain breaches in the way it sees fit in accordance with the applicable law, and to take steps as necessary to avoid over- or under-reporting of personal data breaches.[39]

With regard to the notification to subscriber and/or individual, providers have to notify them where the personal data breach is likely to adversely affect the personal data or privacy of a subscriber or individual. This Regulation provides in Article 3(2) the circumstances to be taken into consideration when assessing the impact of the breach on personal data and/or privacy of subscribers and/or individuals concerned.

These criteria refer first to the nature the nature and content of the personal data. The Regulation contains (Article 3(2)(a)) an indicative list which comprises financial information, special categories of data referred in Article 8(1) of the Data Protection Directive (racial or ethnic origin, political opinions, religious or philosophical beliefs, trade-union membership and the processing of data concerning health or sex life), location data, Internet log files, web browsing histories, email data and itemized call lists. Providers also have to take into account the likely consequences of the personal data breach for the subscriber or individual concerned, in particular where the breach could result in identity theft or fraud, physical harm, psychological distress, humiliation or damage to reputation as well as the circumstances of the personal data breach, in particular where the data has been stolen or when the provider knows that the data are in the possession of an unauthorized third party.

The Regulation provides derogation from notifying the breach to a subscriber or individual concerned if the provider has demonstrated to the satisfaction of the competent national authority that it has implemented appropriate technological protection measures, and that those measures were applied to the data concerned by the security breach. The Commission refrained from setting out specific technological protection measures that justify derogation from the obligation to notify as it would be impossible to keep pace with technological advances. However, the Commission is charged with the publication of an indicative list of such specific technological protection measures according to current practices.[40] In this Regulation, reference is made to encryption and hash function.

other personal data breaches and agreement should be reach with the competent national authority on the delay until the competent national authority considers it possible to notify the personal data breach (Article 3(5) and Recital 13).

38. According to Article 2(2) of the Regulation No. 611/2013, detection of a personal data breach shall be deemed to have taken place when the provider has acquired sufficient awareness that a security incident has occurred that led to personal data being compromised, in order to make a meaningful notification as required under this Regulation.
39. Commission Regulation (EU) No. 611/2013, Recital 6.
40. Commission Regulation (EU) No. 611/2013, Recital 16.

[D] The Future: A Comprehensive Notification Regime?

[1] The General Data Protection Regulation (GDPR)

The increasing number of serious data breach incidents and the need to reinforce both the security of information systems and the trust of consumers have led the European Commission to propose a general obligation for data controllers to notify data breaches. The Commission considered also the concerns stated by ENISA and Article 29 Data Protection Working Party[41] with regard to the fragmentation of a potential EU wide notification scheme and especially the limited scope of coverage involving telecommunications service providers only as well as the implementation of different technological protection measures as an exception to notification.[42]

The GDPR[43] seems to heed to such quest and extends the personal data breach notifications beyond the electronic communications sector to controllers and, to certain extent, processors. It is worthy to be noted that the breach notification requirement under Regulation 611/2013 is essentially similar to the scheme in GDPR,[44] reflecting the legislator's intent of harmonizing notification requirements regarding personal data across sectors.

In the GDPR European legislators have extended the notification requirement beyond the electronic communications sector, while taking into consideration that "a personal data breach may, if not addressed in an appropriate and timely manner, result in physical, material or non-material damage to natural persons ...." (Recital 85). According to Article 29 Data Protection Working Party, breaches can be categorized according to the following three well-known information security principles: "Confidentiality breach"—where there is an unauthorized or accidental disclosure of, or access to, personal data; "Integrity breach"—where there is an unauthorised or accidental alteration of personal data; "Availability breach"—where there is an accidental or unauthorised loss of access to, or destruction of, personal data. [45]The GDPR defines a "personal data breach" as "a breach of security leading to the accidental or

41. Article 29 Data Protection Working Party, Working Document 01/2011 on the current EU personal data breach framework and recommendations for future policy developments (WP 168, 2011). *See also* Opinion 03/2014 on Personal Data Breach Notification http://ec.europa.eu/justice/data-protection/article29/documentation/opinion-recommendation/files/2014/wp213_en.pdf.
42. M. Burdon, B. Lane & P. von Nessen, *Data Breach Notification Law in the EU and Australia – Where to Now?*, 28(3) Computer Law and Security Rev. 299 et seq. (2012).
43. Articles 33-34 of Regulation (EU) No. 2016/679 of the European Parliament and of the Council of 27 April 2016 on the protection of natural persons with regard to the processing of personal data and on the free movement of such data, and repealing Directive 95/46/EC (General Data Protection Regulation), OJ L 119, 4.5.2016, p. 1–88.
44. *See the* Commission Regulation 611/2013, 2013 OJ L 173 2, 3 (EU), where it is referred that the Regulation is fully consistent with the proposed measure under the draft Data Protection Regulation.
45. *See* Article 29 Data Protection Working Party, Guidelines on Personal data breach notification under Regulation 2016/679, adopted on 3 October 2017, last Revised and adopted on 6 February 2018, p. 7.

unlawful destruction, loss, alteration, unauthorized disclosure of, or access to, personal data transmitted, stored or otherwise processed."

However, although the initial Commission draft (2012) and the Regulation 611/2013 require the notification to competent authorities regardless of the impact and significance of the breach, the GDPR—adopting the risk-based approach[46]—limits the breaches to be notified only to those which are likely to result in a high risk for the rights and freedoms of individuals, such as discrimination, identity theft or fraud, financial loss, unauthorized reversal of pseudonymization, damage to the reputation, loss of confidentiality of data protected by professional secrecy or any other significant economic or social disadvantage.[47]

The breach has to be notified to the supervisory authority without undue delay and, where feasible, not later than seventy-two hours after having become aware of it and in case of delay the reasons therefore. Without undue delay, the personal data breach is to be communicated also to data subject(s), while it is required to ascertain whether all appropriate technological protection and organizational measures have been implemented to establish immediately whether a personal data breach has taken place and to inform promptly the supervisory authority and the data subject (Recital 87). The communication should contain the nature of the personal data breach including where possible, the categories and approximate number of data subjects concerned and the categories and approximate number of personal data records concerned, the likely consequences as well as the measures taken (or proposed to be taken) in order to address the breach. With regard to data subject the communication should include recommendations for the natural person concerned to mitigate potential adverse effect (Recital 86).

The communication to the data subjects concerned is not required if the controller has implemented appropriate technological protection measures, and that those measures were applied to the data affected by the personal data breach. Such technological protection measures should include those that render the data unintelligible to any person who is not authorized to access it, in particular though encryption. The other exemptions from notification to data subjects limit significantly the scope of notification obligation: the data controller is not obliged to communicate the breach also if: (a) he has taken subsequent measures that ensure that the high risk for the rights and freedoms of data subjects is no longer likely to materialize; (b) the notification would involve disproportionate effort, in particular owing to the number of

46. A common view emerged during the discussions on the GDPR in the Council was that the risk inherent in certain data processing operations should be a main criterion for calibrating the data protection obligations. Where the data protection risks are higher, more detailed obligations would be necessary and where it is comparably lower, the level of prescriptiveness can and should be reduced proposals to implement a strengthened risk-based approach in the text of the Regulation At the Council of March 2013, there was a large agreement on the need to reduce burdens on enterprises, in particular regarding small and medium-sized enterprises and the drafting of the Regulation was based on the risk-based approach, inter alia, by further developing criteria for enabling the controller and processor to distinguish risk levels.
47. *See* Article 31(1) and Recital 67 of the Draft GDPR (text of General Approach - 9565/15 - Jun. 11, 2015). However, the European Parliament in its First Reading has voted for the Commission's initial proposal that did not include this restriction.

cases involved. In such case, there shall instead be a public communication or similar measure whereby the data subjects are informed in an equally effective manner; or (c) the notification would adversely affect a substantial public interest. This is the case for example if an early disclosure could unnecessarily hamper the investigation of the circumstances of a personal data breach (Recital 88).[48]

According to the European Data Protection Supervisor, (high) risk should be assessed on the basis of an objective assessment, considering both the likelihood and severity of the adverse effect to the rights and freedoms of data subjects.[49] As recommended by the WP29 in the respective guidelines, the factors to be taken into account when assessing the risks are: (a) type of breach; (b) nature, sensitivity and volume of personal data; (c) ease of identification of individuals; (d) severity of consequences for individuals; (e) special characteristics of the individual; (f) special characteristics of the data controller; (g) the number of affected individuals.[50]

Security breach notification legislation is related to the approach of "governance through transparency" or "regulation through disclosure" and is associated with the community's "right to know" laws, which was developed in order to improve the efficacy of environmental laws.[51] The aim of GDPR legislators was to bring transparency in data breaches and their handling and consequently to reduce the number, the frequency and the implications of data breaches.[52] Transparency in its turn should raise the level of accountability. Accountability involves committing to legal and ethical obligations, policies, procedures and mechanisms as well as explaining and demonstrating implementation to internal and external stakeholders and remedying any failure to act properly. According to the GDPR (art 5 (2)), data controllers shall be responsible for, and be able to demonstrate compliance with the principles of data protection and the law.

[2] The NIS Directive

Breach notification requirements are inserted also in the so-called NIS Directive. Directive 2016/1148 on security of network and information systems (the NIS Directive) is the first horizontal legislation undertaken at European Union level for the

48. *See* Karyda M. and Mitrou L., *Data Breach Notification: Issues and Challenges for Security Management*, MCIS 2016, Pafos-Cyprus 4-6/9/2016.
49. European Data Protection Supervisor, Guidelines on personal data breach notification, Draft November 2018.
50. Article 29 Data Protection Working Party, Guidelines on Personal data breach notification under Regulation 2016/679 adopted on Oct. 3, 2017, last revised and adopted on 6 Feb. 6, 2018.
51. *See* Esayas S., *Breach Notification Requirements Under the European Union Legal Framework: Convergence, Conflicts, and Complexity in Compliance*, 31, J. Marshall J. Info. Tech. & Privacy L (2014), p. 319 with further references.
52. *See* Shastri et al. who note that the GDPR's impact has been swift and clear. Just in the first eight months (May 2018–January 2019), regulators have received 41,502 data breach notifications. This number is in stark contrast from the pre-GDPR era, with reports of 945 worldwide data breaches in the first half of 2018. *See* Shastri S, Wasserman M., Chidambaram V., *The Seven Sins of Personal-Data Processing Systems under GDPR*, accepted for publication at USENIX HotCloud 2019.

protection of network and information systems across the Union[53] and the improvement of cybersecurity. Adopting security measures and incident reporting obligations form key obligations of operators of essential services and digital service providers.

These requirements have to be perceived with regard to the aims of this Directive,[54] i.e., the prevention of disruptions and attacks and the response thereto. Incident reporting is regarded as a prominent feature for ensuring a common level of security in the EU related also to risk management practices. The reporting of security incident is introduced as means for obtaining of timely information about the occurrence, type and time for response to an incident of particular nature and also for facilitating a culture of collaboration between the private and the public sector.

Article 16 of NIS Directive requires Member States to ensure that public administrations and Data Service Providers[55] notify to the competent authority incidents having a significant impact on the security of the core services they provide.[56] We should emphasize that the Proposal for NIS Directive did not provide any guidance on the thresholds to be applied on the "incidents that have a significant impact on the security." Article 16(4) of the Directive provides that in order to determine whether the impact of an incident is substantial, the following parameters in particular that should be taken into account are: (a) the number of users affected by the incident, in particular users relying on the service for the provision of their own services; (b) the duration of the incident; (c) the geographical spread with regard to the area affected by the incident; (d) the extent of the disruption of the functioning of the service; (e) the extent of the impact on economic and societal activities.

After consulting the digital service provider concerned, the competent authority or the CSIRT may inform the public about individual incidents or require the digital service provider to do so, where public awareness is necessary in order to prevent an incident or to deal with an ongoing incident, or where disclosure of the incident is otherwise in the public interest. In order to ensure transparency and raise awareness the competent authority shall once a year, submit a summary report to the cooperation network on the notifications received and the action taken. Notification shall not

53. *See* D. Markopoulou, V. Papakonstantinou and P. deHert, *The New EU Cybersecurity Framework: The NIS Directive, ENISA's Role and the General Data Protection Regulation*, 35(6) Computer Law & Security Review: The International Journal of Technology Law and Practice, https://doi.org/10.1016/j.clsr.2019.06.007.
54. The Draft Directive is currently the subject of ongoing discussions (trilogies) between the European Parliament, the Commission and the Council.
55. The notion of Digital Service Providers includes any legal person that provides a digital service and more specifically an online market place, an online search engine, or a cloud computing service. The notification requirements should according to the initial draft be applicable to all "market operators providing services in the European Union." The Draft Directive did not specify what is meant under this term: addressed are operators of critical infrastructures and providers of information society services, the indicative list including e-commerce platforms, Internet payment gateways, Social networks, Search engines, Cloud computing services, and application stores. However, the amendment of the European Parliament limited the wide scope of the initial draft by exempting information society service providers and public administration.
56. As incident' is defined in the NIS Directive (Article 4(7)) any event having an actual adverse effect on the security of network and information systems.

expose the notifying party to increased liability. The exclusion of individuals' notification has been criticized also due to the use of the (vague) term of "public interest."[57]

Due to the wide scope of the NIS Directive, there is a risk that the requirements imposed overlap with the provisions of the GDPR. A security incident may in many cases result to a personal data breach. The European legislator tries to tackle this issue by referring to the need of cooperation between the (NIS) competent authorities and the data protection authorities on all relevant matters to face personal data breaches resulting from incidents. At the same time Member States are invited to implement the obligation to notify security incidents in a way that minimizes the administrative burden in case the security incident is also a personal data breach in line with the GDPR (Recital 31).[58] Overlaps may result also between the notification regime under the NIS and the notification requirements provided by the Framework Directive.[59]

§4.02 CYBERCRIME AS A TOOL FOR COMMITTING OTHER OFFENSES

[A] Sociology of Hacking: The Enemy from Within

What is a hacker? Who is a hacker? Although it was not called "hacking," the earliest identified events of technological mischief date back to 1878, when teenagers working for Bell Telephone Company as switchboard operators purposefully misdirected and detached telephone calls and eavesdropped on telephone conversations.[60]

The term "hacker" was first devised nearly one century later at the Massachusetts Institute of Technology (MIT) in the 1950s and 1960s, to define the very skillful activity of academic computer programmers searching for the most elegant and concise programming solution to any given problem.[61] A "hack" has always been a kind of shortcut or modification—a way to bypass or rework the standard operation of an object or system.[62] Nowadays, the term "hacker" is almost exclusively used to describe a person who has an unauthorized illicit access to a computer system. In this context, while hackers were in the past seen as "technological wizards" and "computer virtuosos," the term is now used to describe "electronic vandals."[63]

57. R. Wong, *Data Security Breaches and Privacy in Europe* 44 (Springer 2013).
58. In his Opinion about the NIS Directive, the European Data Protection Supervisor asked for a further and clearer analysis of interaction and articulation between the current and future data protection legal frameworks with the Cybersecurity Directive. The EDPS raised also several questions on the relationship between the security obligations within the NIS Directive and that they should ensure to be within the personal data protection framework.
59. *See* S. Esayas, *supra*, 356.
60. Slatalla, Michelle, *A Brief History of Hacking*, Online, Discovery Communications (Oct. 28, 2003). http://tlc.discovery.com/convergence/hackers/articles/history.html.
61. Levy, *Hackers: Heroes of the Computer Revolution* (New York: Bantam DoubledayDell 1984).
62. Zuley Clarke, James Clawson, Maria Cordell, *A Brief History of Hacking* (November 2003), available at: http://steel.lcc.gatech.edu/~mcordell/lcc6316/Hacker%20Group%20Project%20FINAL.pdf.
63. S.W. Kleinknecht, *Hacking Hackers: Ethnographic Insights into the Hacker Subculture-Definition, Ideology and Argot*, Thesis, (McMaster University 2003), available at: https://macsphere.mcmaster.ca/bitstream/11375/10956/1/fulltext.pdf.

Cyber threats and cyber attacks[64] are often associated with a mythical hacker profile, where the perpetrator is sensationally regarded as a highly skilled deviant youth who has an unhealthy association with computers.[65] As Huss notes, "the prototypical computer crime story presents a hacker who is a maladjusted, teenage, computer genius who is a thrill seeker that breaks into a military computer system and brings humanity to the brink of World War III."[66] Therefore, a dominant social perception about hackers is that they are marginal external perpetrators who have contravened the legal conventions of society.[67]

In this context, the motivation of monetary gain appears to be less important than other motivations for hacking, such as having an adventurous online life compared to a boring offline life, or gaining peer recognition from other hackers.[68] In more than one way, hackers are seen as a digital version of the mythical pirates of Hollywood.

Nonetheless, the true profile of the hacker is much more complex than this sensationalistic representation. Cyber attacks are often conducted by government agents and not by deviant techno freaks, while, contrary to what many ordinary people tend to believe, cyber threats are often designed and executed by insiders in governments and private companies. Furthermore, although many in the general public tend to believe that hackers are loners and antisocial, social science research indicates that hackers operate within a collective subculture where individuals share information with one another.[69]

An important classification of hackers is that between outsiders and insiders. Persons employed by government agencies or by the private sector which cause a damage to the network are used to be called "insiders," while hackers not employed by the state or the industry are called "outsiders."[70] In his 1978 book *Crime by Computer*, Donn Parker estimated that 95% of cyber attacks were committed by authorized users of the system.[71] This was mainly due to the fact that in the pre-Internet era it was difficult for outsiders to have access to the system, while in the increasingly global and

64. Cyber threat is a potential for deliberate attack or an inadvertent compromise of an organization's mission, while cyber attack is a deliberate attempt to compromise an organization's mission. For these definitions, *see* National Security Research Division, Richard C. Brackney, Robert H. Anderson, *Understanding the Insider Threat*, Proceedings of a March 2004 Workshop, Prepared for the Advanced Research and Development Activity. Available online at: http://www.rand.org/content/dam/rand/pubs/conf_proceedings/2005/RAND_CF196.pdf (2004).
65. Reid Skibell, *The Myth of the Computer Hacker*, 5(3) Information, Communication & Society (2002).
66. S.T. Huss, *Hackers: Practices, Motivations, and Identity*, Master's Thesis (University of Tennessee, Knoxville 1998).
67. S.W. Kleinknecht, *supra*.
68. Tim Jordan & Paul Taylor, *A Sociology of Hackers* (Blackwell Publisher 1998), available at: http://www.yorku.ca/kitzmann/hackers.pdf.
69. Thomas J. Holt, et al., *Examining the Social Networks of Malware Writers and Hackers*, 6(1) Intl. J. Cyber Criminology (IJCC) ISSN: 0974 – 2891, 891–903 (January–June 2012).
70. Thomas J. Holt & Bernadette Hlubik Schell, *Hackers and Hacking: A Reference Handbook*, at 23 (ABC-CLIO 2013).
71. *See* Steven Bellovin, *The Insider Attack Problem Nature and Scope*, in *Insider Attack and Cyber Security: Beyond the Hacker* (Salvatore J. Stolfo et al., Springer 2008).

interconnected modern environment, isolation is no longer an option.[72] The insider threat, thus the threat coming from an "organizational trusted agent" inside the firewall, is considered to be the greatest threat for information security.[73]

Nonetheless, much of the press coverage still focuses on outsider attacks for various reasons. Insider attacks are not easily discovered and, unlike external attacks, are probably not likely to be reported to the authorities.[74] Insider attacks can have disastrous consequences: suspension of operations, loss of confidential information and intellectual property, reputational harm, reducing investor and customer confidence.[75]

A well-known example of insider threat is insider sabotage, which has a long history in the US. One of the most prominent precedents of insider sabotage took place in the US in 1996, at Omega Engineering. Tom Lloyd, the creator of the company's network, who had been fired three weeks before the attack, planted a logic bomb in the firm's network. The server went down and took nearly every program down along with it, destroying any means of finding them and causing millions of dollars of loss to the company.[76]

Since then, the examples of insider attacks in various forms are numerous. Both private companies and governments are candidates to be the targets of these attacks. In this context, some of possibly the worst intelligence disasters in US history came from insiders. Robert Hanssen was an FBI Supervisory Special Agent who, over the course of twenty-two years, gave the Soviet Union and Russia vast quantities of documents and computer diskettes filled with national security information.[77] Hanssen was paid USD 1.4 million by the Russians for his espionage. Although the motives of Hanssen remain uncertain, they seem to have included ego gratification, disgruntlement with FBI employment and financial need.[78]

Most recently, Bradley Manning, a US intelligence army analyst who had access to the Department of Defense's Secret Internet Protocol Router Network (SIPRNet) accessed about 260,000 classified diplomatic cables from the network and delivered it to Wiki leaks.[79] Finally, the most spectacular insider leak is undoubtedly the Edward

72. Merrill Warkentin & Robert Willison, *Behavioral and Policy Issues in Information Systems Security: the Insider Threat*, 18 Eur. J. Info. Systems 101–105 (2009).
73. Merrill Warkentin & Robert Willison, *ibid.*
74. *Top Five Insider Attacks of the Decade*, linux.com, (Jan. 13, 2011), available at: https://www.linux.com/news/technology-feature/security/397143-top-five-insider-attacks-of-the-decade.
75. David M. Upton & Sadie Creese, *The Danger from Within*, Harvard Business Review (September 2014), available at: https://hbr.org/2014/09/the-danger-from-within.
76. Sharon Gaudin, *Case Study of Insider Sabotage: The Tim Lloyd/Omega Case*, XVI(3) Computer Security Journal (2000), available online at: http://130.18.86.27/faculty/warkentin/SecurityPapers/Robert/Others/Gaudin2000_CSJ16_3_Sabotage.pdf.
77. National Security Research Division, Richard C. Brackney, Robert H. Anderson, *Understanding the Insider Threat*, Proceedings of a March 2004 Workshop, Prepared for the Advanced Research and Development Activity (2004), available at: http://www.rand.org/content/dam/rand/pubs/conf_proceedings/2005/RAND_CF196.pdf.
78. Dale L. June, *Terrorism and Homeland Security: Perspectives, Thoughts, and Opinions* 90 (CRC Press, Taylor and Francis Group, 2010).
79. Kevin Poulsen & Kim Zetter, *US Intelligence Analyst Arrested in Wikileaks Video Prob*, Wired.com (2010), available at: http://www.wired.com/2010/06/leak/.

Snowden case, who has proved to be the ultimate insider attacker[80] by providing Wiki Leaks with numerous government confidential data.[81]

The taxonomy of insider hackers is rich and not exhaustive. An insider can be an employee, a student or a member of the "host institution," someone who has a business relationship with the target (contractors,[82] subcontractors, technicians, etc.), a person who is authorized to enter the network in order to perform specific actions (such as a bank customer) or a person to whom an insider has given access (e.g., by revealing his credentials), a former authorized member of the network (such as a former employee) who uses credentials which were not revoked or credentials which have been secretly created for hacking purposes.[83]

Moreover, the motivations of insiders are various and divergent. Insiders' motivations can range from "innocent action," "fun," "technical challenge," "criminal intentions," to "espionage," or a mixture of each of these factors.[84] Insiders might be driven by the innocent curiosity to surpass or test the limits and the weaknesses of the system or even by less innocent incentives, such as revenge, greed, boredom or by the purpose of attracting attention and fame.[85] While the acts of insiders will often be intention-based and willful (such as data theft, data destruction, sabotage), the source of the threat can also be an unintentional or accidental action of a trusted agent which will enable an external perpetrator to enter the system, such as when forgetting to change passwords or leaving the workstation without logging off.[86]

While the comprehensive classification of insider threats and insider attackers is not easy, two main types of insider attackers appear to exist: malicious insiders and exploited or unintentional insiders.[87]

Malicious insiders, who deliberately steal data or attack the system, generally cause the most significant harms. Their motives are diverse, ranging from financial to ideological.[88] In this respect, two subcategories of malicious insiders often attract

80. Kim Zetter, *NSA Whistleblower: The Ultimate Insider Attack*, Wired.com (Sep. 06, 2013), available at: http://www.wired.com/2010/06/leak/.
81. Jeffrey Hunker & Christian W. Probst, *Insiders and Insider Threats an Overview of Definitions and Mitigation Techniques*, 2.1 J. Wireless Mobile Networks, Ubiquitous Computing, and Dependable Applications 24-27 (2011).
82. Consider, for example, the case of leaked British bank accounts from call centers in India. *See Indian call centers selling U.K.'s secrets*, available at: http://www.siliconindia.com/shownews/Indian_call_centers_selling_UKs_secrets-nid-28560-cid-2.html.
83. Charles Pfleeger, *Reflections on the Insider Threat*, in *Insider Attack and Cyber Security: Beyond the Hacker* (Salvatore J. Stolfo, et al.), *supra*, 6.
84. Jeffrey Hunker & Christian Probst, *Insiders and Insider Threats, An Overview of Definitions and Mitigation Techniques*, 2(1) J. Wireless Mobile Networks, Ubiquitous Computing, and Dependable Applications, 4-27 (2011), available at: http://citeseerx.ist.psu.edu/viewdoc/download?doi=10.1.1.465.7490&rep=rep1&type=pdf.
85. Charles Pfleeger, *Reflections on the Insider Threat*, *supra*.
86. Merrill Warkentin & Robert Willison, *Behavioral and Policy Issues in Information Systems Security: The Insider Threat*, 18 Eur. J. Info. Systems, 101-105 (2009).
87. Russell Miller & Merritt Maxim, *Have to Trust Someone....Don't I?, Dealing with Insider Threats to Cyber-security*, CA Technologies, Security Management, White Paper, (January 2015), available at: https://docs.broadcom.com/docs-and-downloads/content/dam/ca/us/files/white-paper/dealing-with-insider-threats-to-cyber-security.pdf.
88. Mark Maybury, Penny Chase, Brant Cheikes, Dick Brackney, Sara Matzner Brad Wood Tom Longstaff and Tom Hetherington, Brad Wood, Conner Sibley and Jack Marin, Tom Longstaff,

attention: the "traitors" and the "zealots." While the "traitor" is a person with a malicious intent to damage, destroy or sell out the organization, the "zealot" is an insider who believes strongly in the rightness of one position or feels the organization is on the wrong side of a certain issue.[89]

Exploited or unintentional insiders are unconsciously exploited by external parties. Unintentional insider threats are described as:

> (1) a current or former employee, contractor, or business partner (2) who has or had authorized access to an organization's network, system, or data and who, (3) through action or inaction without malicious intent, (4) unwittingly causes harm or substantially increases the probability of future serious harm to the confidentiality, integrity, or availability of the organization's resources or assets, including information, information systems, or financial systems.[90]

These cyber threats often result from phishing and other social engineering cases, specifically those involving malware.[91] Downloading shareware, disabling virus protection software, or using unapproved CDs, can all provide the assistance a hacker needs to penetrate a system. Subsequently, the unintentional or careless user becomes the unwitting associate of the attacker.

In this respect, the 2013 Verizon Data Breach Report concludes that 47% of malware was downloaded through email attachments, 48% of hacking took place with stolen credentials, 77% of social engineering takes places through phishing, and 79% of social engineering takes place through emails.[92] This phenomenon is also related to some progress in terms of IT security. While no system can be declared as ultimately secure, from a competent IT engineer point of view, the most vulnerable part of the system always constitutes the "human element."[93]

One of the most well-known cyber attacks in Europe via the use of phishing was the attack made by cyber jihadists against the French television channel TV5 in April 2015. The cyber attackers blocked transmissions and hijacked the channel's website, as well as its Facebook and Twitter accounts. The attack started with a "phishing" email that was sent to all journalists of TV5 on January 2015. The "hackers" were first informed on one or more employees of the channel, using Google, social networks and other means (such as the Skype accounts of journalists who interviewed jihadists in order to retrieve the IP address of their workstations). Then, they sent an email to their

---

Analysis and Detection of Malicious Insiders, Conference paper (March 2005), available at: https://www.mitre.org/sites/default/files/pdf/05_0207.pdf.

89. Hayden, Michael, *The Insider Threat to U.S. Government Information Systems*, National Security Agency/Central Security Service Fort George G Meade MD (July 1999), available at: https://apps.dtic.mil/dtic/tr/fulltext/u2/a406622.pdf.
90. CERT *Insider Threat Team, Unintentional Insider Threats: A Review of Phishing and Malware Incidents by Economic Sector*, (07/2014), available t: http://repository.cmu.edu/cgi/viewcontent.cgi?article = 1799&context = sei.
91. *See* Jeremy R. Strozer, Matthew L. Collins & Tracy Cassidy, *Unintentional Insider Threats: A Review of Phishing and Malware Incidents by Economic Sector* (CERT, July 2014).
92. Verizon, *2013 Data Breach Investigations Report* (Verizon, 2013), available at: http://www.verizonenterprise.com/resources/reports/rp_data-breach-investigations-report-2013_en_xg.pdf.
93. Denis Besnard & Budi Arief, *Computer Security Impaired by Legitimate Users*, 23(3) Computers & Security 253–264 (May 2004).

targets, inviting them to download a file attachment, which was actually a Trojan. After that, they were able to install key loggers and malware. These tools have helped the cyber attackers to recover the credentials and the passwords which were necessary for the "takeover" of the social networks accounts of TV5 Monde.[94]

In the US, the cyber attack on the retail chain Target in 2013, where the attackers stole the payment card numbers of some 40 million customers and the personal data of roughly 70 million, cost the company USD 162 million.[95] What is less well known is that, although the attackers were outsiders, they succeeded to access the company's systems by using the credentials of an insider: one of the company's vendors.[96]

From a legal point of view, the identification of the motivations and the actions or inactions of outsiders and insiders and the determination of the techniques which are used for hacking are important when considering the criminal penalties the attacker faces. Indeed, when the attack takes place via phishing or identity theft, there is cumulative application of several criminal offenses. Furthermore, while hackers are often described to specific communities with a particular collective identity, it is difficult to establish the aggravating factor of being member or being associated to a criminal or terrorist organization for imposing heavier criminal sentences.

For example, is it possible to classify Anonymous, which is generally described as a loosely associated international network of activist and hacktivist entities, but often called by the press as "cyber terrorists,"[97] as a criminal or a terrorist organization? The question has been raised when Anonymous claimed to have operated numerous successful cyber attacks against Israeli websites. Hamas is considered a terrorist organization not only by Israel but also by the EU, the USA and other countries. So, could Anonymous also be considered a terrorist organization—or a supporter of a terrorist organization—by association?[98]

According to Article 2(1) of the Framework Decision on combating terrorism,[99] "terrorist group" shall mean: a structured group of more than two persons, established over a period of time and acting in concert to commit terrorist offenses. "'Structured group' shall mean a group that is not randomly formed for the immediate commission of an offence and that does not need to have formally defined roles for its members, continuity of its membership or a developed structure." This definition appears to exclude groups randomly formed to immediately commit an offense.[100]

94. Fabien Soyez, *Cyberattaque contre TV5 Monde, ou le b.a.-ba du hacker débutant*, Cnet France (Apr. 14, 2015), available at: http://www.cnetfrance.fr/news/cyberattaque-contre-tv5-monde-ou-le-ba-ba-du-hacker-debutant-39817950.htm.
95. Dan Worth, *Target takes $162m hit from cyber attack data breach*, V3 (Feb. 26, 2015), available at: http://www.v3.co.uk/v3-uk/news/2397099/target-takes-usd162m-hit-from-cyber attack-data-breach.
96. David Upton & Sadie Creese, *The Danger from Within*, *supra*.
97. *See* https://en.wikipedia.org/wiki/Anonymous_%28group%29.
98. Clint Arizmendi, *Blurring the Lines Between Hacktivism and Terrorism, Are the Anonymous Hacktivists, Cyber Combatants or Criminals?*, blogsofwar.com (2012), available at: http://www.blogsofwar.com/2012/11/26/guest-post-blurring-the-lines-between-hacktivism-and-terrorism.
99. Council Framework Decision of Jun. 13, 2002 on combating terrorism, OJ L 164, 22/06/2002, p. 3-7.
100. Sara Summers et al., *The Emergence of EU Criminal Law, Cyber Crime and the Regulation of the Information Society* 250 (Hart Publishing 2014).

The question is delicate, but the absence of a group structure and the nonprofit driven nature of hacktivist cyber attacks by members of groups such as Anonymous hinder their qualification as an organized criminal group.[101]

Furthermore, the classification of such groups as terrorist groups depends essentially on the definition of "terrorism" in national jurisdictions worldwide. Here too, the old maxim, "One man's terrorist is another man's freedom fighter" is still alive.[102] For example, the terrorism definition in the UK Terrorism Act of 2010 is significantly broad, and it can encompass politically motivated acts that are designed to seriously interfere with or disrupt electronic systems, while encouraging terrorism or disseminating terrorist information is also punished (*see* section 2(3) of the UK Terrorism Act 2006).[103]

In this context, in *R. v. Mohammed Gul,*[104] a law student in the UK was condemned for having disseminated terrorist publications, and more precisely for having uploaded on YouTube videos of attacks by members of Al-Qaeda, the Taliban and other proscribed groups on military targets in Chechnya, and on the Coalition forces in Iraq and in Afghanistan, accompanied by commentaries praising the bravery and martyrdom of those carrying out the attacks. Nonetheless, it has to be noticed that the EU Framework Decision on combating terrorism[105] establishes a definition of terrorism which is one of the broadest nationally and supranationally.[106]

101. According to Article 2(a) of the United Nations Convention against Transnational Organized Crime (UNTOC), an organized criminal group is "a group of three or more persons that was not randomly formed; existing for a period of time; acting in concert with the aim of committing at least one crime punishable by at least four years' incarceration; in order to obtain, directly or indirectly, a financial or other material benefit." *See also* Article 1(1) of the Framework Decision 2008/841/JHA "on the fight against organised crime": "'criminal organization' means a structured association, established over a period of time, of more than two persons acting in concert with a view to committing offences which are punishable by deprivation of liberty or a detention order of a maximum of at least four years or a more serious penalty, to obtain, directly or indirectly, a financial or other material benefit."
102. Serge Krasavin, *What Is Cyber-terrorism?* (last access 2015), available at: http://www.crime-research.org/library/Cyber-terrorism.htm.
103. Keiran Hardy & George Williams, *What Is Cyberterrorism?, Computer and Internet Technology in Legal Definitions of Terrorism,* in *Cyberterrorism: Understanding, Assessment, and Response* 6-7 (Tom Chen, Lee Jarvis & Stuart Macdonald eds, Springer 2014).
104. *R v. Gul,* 2013 UKSC 64, Oct. 23, 2013, available at: https://www.supremecourt.uk/cases/docs/uksc-2012-0124-judgment.pdf. *See* Kimberley Trapp, *R v. Mohammed Gul, Are You a Terrorist if You Support the Syrian Insurgency?* (Mar. 14, 2012), available at: http://www.ejiltalk.org/r-v-mohammed-gul-are-you-a-terrorist-if-you-support-the-syrian-insurgency/; Antonio Coco, *Crocodile Tears, The UK Supreme Court's Broad Definition of Terrorism in R. v. Mohammed Gul* (Nov. 18, 2013), available at: http://www.ejiltalk.org/crocodile-tears-the-uk-supreme-courts-broad-definition-of-terrorism-in-r-v-mohammed-gul/.
105. *See* Article 1 of the Council Framework Decision of 13 Jun. 2002 on combating terrorism, OJ L 164, 22/06/2002, p. 3–7.
106. Sara Summers et al., *The Emergence of EU Criminal Law, Cyber Crime and the Regulation of the Information Society, supra.*

[B] Cybercrime as a Parallel Economy

Cybercrime is often profit-driven and has turned into an immense and lucrative business. Cyber attackers monetize compromised computers and networks via various means, such as the theft of personal or confidential data, blackmail through Distributed-Denial-of-Service (DDoS) attacks, hacking for hire, spamming, search engine poisoning and click fraud.[107]

The underground economy of cybercrime is flourishing. Two main factors contribute to this. "First, the potential gains from cyber attacks are increasing with the growth of importance of the Internet, and, secondly, malefactors' expected costs (e.g., the penalties and the likelihood of being apprehended and prosecuted) are frequently lower compared with traditional crimes."[108] As is stated in a report sponsored by the RAND Corporation's National Security Research Division in 2014, "the hacker market, once a varied landscape of discrete, ad hoc networks of individuals initially motivated by little more than ego and notoriety, has emerged as a playground of financially driven, highly organized, and sophisticated groups."[109]

Cybercrime black markets function on basic principles similar to offline markets, where suppliers (sellers), buyers and intermediaries can be found. They are also subject to the normal microeconomic fluctuations of supply and demand.[110] Nonetheless, cybercrime black markets appear to have their own hierarchies and specialized roles for those who participate in them: administrators, subject-matter experts with specialized knowledge of particular areas (root kit creators, malware writers, data traffickers, cryptanalysts, etc.), intermediaries, brokers and vendors (spammers, botnet owners, virtual money mule services, etc.) and the general members (buyers and observers).[111]

In this chain of trade and exchanges, digital cryptocurrencies appear to play a substantial role thanks to the near anonymity and the security of transactions they provide. Indeed, digital currencies, and more precisely cryptocurrencies, appear to act as a powerful fuel fostering the development of cybercrime economy. Whereas there is no uniform definition of digital currencies, some of their traits can be identified in juxtaposition with real money or electronic money. According to the European Central Bank,[112] digital currency can be divided into two basic types: (1) Electronic money schemes, whose units are traditional currency and (2) virtual currencies (such as

107. *See* B. Krebs, *The Scrap Value of a Hacked pc*, The Washington Post (2009), at: http://voices.washingtonpost.com/securityfix/2009/05/the_scrap_value_of_a_hacked_pc.html; Y. Namestnikov, *The Economics of Botnets* (July 2009), available at: http://www.viruslist.com/en/analysis?pubid=204792068.
108. Alvaro A. Cardenas et al., *An Economic Map of Cybercrime*, Working Paper (2009), available at: http://chess.eecs.berkeley.edu/pubs/772/cardenas_2009.pdf.
109. Lillian Ablon, Martin C. Libicki & Andrea A. Golay, *Markets for Cybercrime Tools and Stolen Data*, Hacker's Bazaar, RAND Corporation's National Security Research Division (2014), available at: http://www.rand.org/content/dam/rand/pubs/research_reports/RR600/RR610/RAND_RR610.pdf.
110. *Ibid.*
111. *Ibid.*, 5-6.
112. *See Virtual currency schemes* (October 2012), available at: https://www.ecb.europa.eu/pub/pdf/other/virtualcurrencyschemes201210en.pdf.

Linden dollars, Bitcoins, etc.), whose units are "invented currency." While electronic money are linked to traditional money formats and, therefore, have a legal foundation, digital currencies are unregulated and not supervised by any authority.[113]

Cryptocurrencies, which are a subcategory of digital currencies, offer a medium of exchange using cryptography to verify the exchange of funds and regulate the making of new units of currency.[114] Cryptocurrencies allow for the validation of transactions without the need for a trusted third party, such as a bank.

The near anonymity often provided to the users of cryptocurrencies, such as Bitcoin, that results in making it extremely difficult to trace the transitions and users, renders cryptocurrencies attractive to the black market, money laundering and the exchange of cybercrime generated income. For instance, in 2012, it was assessed that 4.5–9% of all transactions of all Bitcoin exchanges in the world were for drug sales on (the now defunct website) Silk Road.[115] In 2012, the FBI estimated that Bitcoin will continue to attract cybercriminals for transferring, laundering or stealing funds and as a means for donating money to groups participating in illegal activities, such as hacktivists, while cybercriminals will have an incentive to steal them, because it is possible to convert bitcoins to real money.[116]

While the economic gain from cybercrime is an undeniable reason for the booming of cybercrime, it might also somehow act as the Achilles' heel for cyber criminals. In this context, a follow-the-money approach in cybercrime law enforcement might be decisive. Certainly, following the money trail of cybercrime requires the cooperation of financial institutions.[117] Furthermore, tracking the cyber attackers through their economic gains is also a thorny task in practice. For instance, tracking the Pay pal accounts of fraudsters might be only the beginning of the investigation, since the accounts might have been opened with the use of stolen IDs, while at the same time the illegal activity might have been conducted with a stolen Wi-Fi connection.[118]

Even though cryptocurrencies appear as an ideal tool for underground cybercrime black markets, in some cases it is still possible to trace the cybercriminal who makes use of them. Cryptocurrency can ultimately be converted to flat currency

113. Raj Samani, *Digital Laundry, An Analysis of Online Currencies, and their Use in Cybercrime*, at: http://www.mcafee.com/us/resources/white-papers/wp-digital-laundry.pdf.
114. Monty Raphael QC, Bitcoin, *Cybercrime and Future Regulation*, IBA Annual Conference, Tokyo (October 2014), available at: http://www.petersandpeters.com/wp-content/uploads/2014/10/Bitcoin-Cybercrime-and-Future-Regulation.pdf.
115. Monty Raphael QC, *Bitcoin, Cybercrime and Future Regulation, ibid.*; Nicolas Christin, *Traveling the Silk Road: A Measurement Analysis of a Large Anonymous Online Marketplace*, Carnegie Mellon University CyLab Report 12-018 (Jul. 30, 2012, revised Nov. 28, 2012).
116. FBI Intelligence Assessment, *Bitcoin Virtual Currency: Unique Features Present Distinct Challenges for Deterring Illicit Activity* (Apr. 24, 2012), available at: http://cryptome.org/2012/05/fbi-bitcoin.pdf.
117. Felicia Donovan & Kristyn Bernier, *Cyber Crime Fighters: Tales from the Trenches* (Pearson Education, 2009).
118. Scott J. Shackelford, *Managing Cyber Attacks*, in *International Law, Business, and Relations: In Search of Cyber Peace* 15 (Cambridge University Press 2014).

through various intermediaries such as an "exchanger,"[119] and this "cashing out" could enable law enforcement to link funds to a specific person or account.[120] Besides, since most of them are based on a decentralized peer-to-peer network, the transactions are permanently stored on an online public ledger and, thus, are visible to all on the system.[121] Law enforcement agencies can constantly observe and investigate these public logs and can trace transactions since all these data are public, and freely accessible, by design.[122]

Even though the transactions are recorded only as addresses, which are not necessarily linked to anyone's identity, there are techniques available to help link users to their addresses. In this context, cryptocurrencies are rather "pseudonymous" instead of anonymous, and as a matter of policy, authorities should apply personal data legal protection rules when investigating such data. For example, "if the identity of some wallet owners is known, it is theoretically possible to use these known nodes in the system to build a 'transaction graph' that tracks each particular cryptocurrency and, by doing so, one could expose the identity of owners of unknown wallets with which the known wallets transacted."[123]

Transaction graph analysis, which aims to link Bitcoin transactions to the holders of the virtual currency by allowing transactional relationships between these holders to be mapped, might be the first crucial step for such identifications. Then, other publicly available information linking bitcoin addresses to their identities (e.g., businesses accepting bitcoin may place a QR code near a cash register or on a website), together with the set of IP addresses of the computers that announce new bitcoin transactions, are complementary sources of potentially deanonymizing information.[124]

119. Erik R. Barnett, *Back to the Future: Criminal Organizations Exploit Another New Technology, Crypto-Currencies* (2014), available at: http://www.observatoire-fic.com/back-to-the-future-criminal-organizations-exploit-another-new-technology-crypto-currencies/#sthash.mwHSqIL4.dpuf.
120. *Ibid.*
121. *Ibid.*
122. Jason Weistein, *How Can Law Enforcement Leverage the Blockchain in Investigations?, A Backgrounder for Policymakers* (May 12, 2015), available at: https://coincenter.org/2015/05/how-can-law-enforcement-leverage-the-blockchain-in-investigations/.
123. Omri Marian, *A Conceptual Framework for the Regulation of Cryptocurrencies*, 82 U Chi L Rev Dialogue 53 (2015), available at: https://lawreview.uchicago.edu/page/conceptual-framework-regulation-cryptocurrencies.
124. Adam Ludwin, *How Anonymous is Bitcoin? A Backgrounder for Policymakers* (Jan. 20, 2015), available at: https://coincenter.org/2015/01/anonymous-bitcoin/.

Conclusion

Cyber attacks raise many interrelated and complex issues. Answering the question of illegality, thus making a distinction between legal and illegal activities (legal access or not, legal interference or not), does not sufficiently address this complexity.

The substantive hypothesis of this book lies in the idea that the legal phenomenon of cyber attack does not simply constitute a subcategory of cyber criminality, but that it should be studied as an independent legal institution, in the sense that specific legal issues related strictly to cyber attacks have gradually emerged. In this context, and given the spread and the constant rise of cyber attack incidents, the legal framework of cyber attacks merits a special and detailed analysis.

One of the areas most urgently requiring clarifications is the classification of attacks that have been reduced to criminal offenses, which presupposes a common understanding of the definitions used to ensure a consistent approach and taxonomy. Technical terms used by the legislator, such as "information systems," "security," "attacks," and "threats" delineate (albeit vaguely) the legally protected good(s), the means of crime and, ultimately, which conduct is punishable. The meaning of these terms, as well as of the surrounding concepts, is inherent to understanding the objects and/or protected legal interests and addressing the issues raised. The provisions of the Directive 2013/40/EU (and the Cybercrime Convention) rely more on the underlying conduct rather than the technical mechanisms for commission of crime, in order to enable law enforcement to deal with forms of cybercriminality not foreseen or fully appreciated at the time of their adoption.

At the same time, the legal framework, both at the international and the European level, highlights and fosters the need for enhanced cooperation. Besides, law enforcement is strongly related to the intricate issues of digital forensics and, particularly, with the processing of personal data as evidence. Therefore, this book's perspective has been multifold.

First, we have analyzed the specific legal offenses related to cyber attacks and the relevant legal framework, with emphasis on the legal technicalities and the intricacies of the specific legal provisions. In this context, European regulation is bound in great part by the provisions of the Budapest Convention. In some cases, e.g., in respect of the crime of illegal access to an information system, the scope of the crime is defined with more precise criteria, such as the additional prerequisite of the violation of a security measure. In other instances, the scope of application of cyber attacks is enlarged in order to encompass new types of attacks. For instance, this is the case of the offense of illegal interference, which today undoubtedly encompasses DDoS attacks. In a similar fashion, the European Directive slightly modifies the offense of dissemination of tools created for hacking purposes, adding additional safeguards for the protection of the legitimate interests of researchers and network administrators.

However, the core provisions and definitions used in the EU legal framework on cyber attacks and, primarily, the definition of the concept of information system have been directly inherited from the Budapest Convention. The major question is, therefore, to ascertain whether the Convention, which was enacted fifteen years ago, is still able to ensure an acceptable level of protection against cyber attacks. The same objectives which convinced the European legislator to modernize the 2005 legal framework with the adoption of a new Directive certainly apply to the Budapest Convention. At the same time, the creation of a high level of protection in association with a high level of cooperation inside the European Union should be completed with similar efforts on a global scale. Consequently, it is argued that a substantial effort at a political level should be made to urge the Council of Europe to take the initiative and consider revising the Budapest Convention. This international perspective should include a way to deal with the growing phenomenon of State involvement in cyber attacks, for instance, with the development of judicial mechanisms of international criminal law able to directly condemn rogue States for their association to such acts.

Second, we illustrated and scrutinized the technical, legal and social phenomenon of cyber attacks in a broader sense, taking into consideration all the legal issues related to the application of the legal provisions, the prevention of cyber attacks and the challenges of law enforcement.

In this context, the question of electronic evidence was discussed: whether, to what extent and how, digital traces and computer data can be treated as evidence that has to be extracted, gathered, considered and evaluated in compliance to fundamental evidentiary principles. It has been considered that digital evidence must have all the attributes of conventional evidence: any tool, method or procedure used during an investigation has also to meet strict standards (authenticity, integrity, continuity, reliability). Thus, we have presented the specific challenges posed with regard to digital forensics (fragility, vulnerability and transience of many forms of digital evidences) with emphasis on cloud forensics and smartphone forensics. Smartphones characterized as a "treasure trove of evidence" reveal/highlight the discussion about forensic readiness, i.e., the incorporation of design requirements in devices, aiming at ensuring availability and admissibility of data produced for potential future uses. The expansion of judicial investigation into proactive investigative actions and the increasing overlap between law enforcement and the intelligence community have been further accelerated by rapid technological developments and the expansion of devices' use in everyday life. Being an intrusive approach, forensic readiness has to comply not only with data protection and communication secrecy but also with (the principles of) the rule of law.

Jurisdictional issues present some of the greatest challenges to combating cybercrime. One particular challenge when investigating attacks against information systems is that evidence gathering often transcends national jurisdictions. Cybercrime and, more specifically, attacks against information systems often have "transnational" or "international" dimensions and elements. Despite the borderless and virtual nature of the Internet, criminal law and enforcement remain bound with territoriality. Cyber-investigation requirements are still largely dependent on classic mutual assistance procedures or dubious practices of informal direct access to data retained by Internet Service Providers (ISPs). It has become commonplace to suggest that due to the globalization of information flows and the deterritorialization of cyber attacks, mutual assistance schemes are inadequate. A major issue is whether the specific characteristics of cyber attacks and their transnational borderless nature would urge the legislator to develop new and additional jurisdiction principles and arrangements to regulate and facilitate law enforcement. The approximation of substantial law in this field is a first step toward harmonized approaches with respect to procedural law and new forms of judicial cooperation.

Furthermore, a strong focus has been given on secondary, but strongly relevant questions, such as the legal status of the IP address as evidence and, possibly, as the primary manner of identification of cyber attackers and the role of ISPs in the prevention of cyber attacks and more broadly in cybercrime prevention and prosecution. The role of ISPs, regarded as gate-keepers and long-arm collectors of enforcement information, has been emphasized, as data retention and communication surveillance by private players has become a key tool of criminal law enforcement.

Even if the processing of personal data for crime prevention and investigation purposes is subject to specific rules that take into account the needs of law enforcement, the essential dilemma between privacy and security is still dominant and the proper balance has to be found. Fundamental rights to anonymity, privacy and personal data protection run counter to a systematic, preventive tracing of data trails left by users while surfing the Internet. Leaving the delicate exercise of the specific balancing of those interests to national jurisdictions has been a source of inconsistency which has negatively impacted cross-border cooperation in cybercrime cases. The Directive on the protection of individuals with regard to the processing of personal data for the purposes of prevention, investigation, detection or prosecution of criminal offenses or the execution of criminal penalties is expected to enhance consistency of data protection in the field of law enforcement by enhancing mutual trust between the police and judicial authorities of different Member States and by facilitating the free flow of data and cooperation between police and judicial authorities.

The doctrinal and jurisprudential ambiguity surrounding the legal status of the IP address is an ideal example of the intricacies related to the investigation and prosecution of cyber attacks. Although an IP address is a number, it has a dual nature; it is information with an identifying ability and a constituent part of communication.

Given the detrimental personal and financial consequences of cyber attacks, the fight against cyber attacks is generally received by public opinion as one of those issues where the necessities of law enforcement might justify more intrusive methods of investigation. Nonetheless, even if cyber attacks, akin to cyber child pornography, trigger public outrage more intensively than Internet copyright infringement, the entire philosophical and legal edifice of data protection could lose its coherence and collapse if the law admits restrictions of fundamental rights à la carte, depending on the kind of cybercrime activities.

In this context, the issue of the role of ISPs is also pertinent. The idea of transforming ISPs as guardians of the law in cyberspace is certainly seductive. Various means of implementing such an idea exist. Filtering Internet pests (e.g., malware), which can facilitate or enable an attack against an information system at a later stage, at an ISP level, is an idea which is increasingly gaining support, given that the advancement of technology has reduced the degree of performance degradation caused by extended filtering which has been criticized in the past. Filtering at an ISP level requires an in-depth control of the packets (deep packet inspection) by the ISPs in order to prevent the spread of illegal or harmful content. Therefore, the whole mechanism of filtering itself implies the implementation of a generalized control over Internet content, which is contrary to the current legal regime applicable to ISPs. Furthermore, the compatibility of such regimes with fundamental rights is also at stake.

It should be noted that the book opts for a horizontal approach and advances the idea that Internet copyright enforcement tools could serve as a model of responsible ISP intervention in the fight against cybercrime. First, it appears that certain legal tools of cybercrime prevention could be legitimate, provided that they comply with human rights and, more specifically, with the safeguards developed by case law in respect of Internet copyright infringements. Second, the conjunction between the installation of reasonable measures and the avoidance of any civil liability would lead the ISPs to operate more reasonably in terms of self-regulation, whereas the E-Commerce Directive's safe harbor system only give them a wild card to act. Even so, the idea that surveillance is delegated to ISPs is still controversial.

In conclusion, the mechanisms for regulating cyber attacks in the European legal framework, as described in detail in this study, are definitely very classic: definition of a catalog of specific offenses, regulation of the criminal procedure, enhancement of police and judicial cooperation. However, the specificity and novelty of the phenomenon of cyber attacks should lead to more innovative approaches. The direct implication of ISPs and the generalization of data breach notifications are good examples of new ways to regulate the attacks with an emphasis on prevention. Security and data breach notification requirements may contribute to compliance with security requirements, thus pre-empting cyber attacks and mitigating their effects. Due to the increased transparency scrutiny of their activity and their possible liability, organizations are expected to understand and assess cybersecurity risks and respond more effectively and rigorously to threats and breaches. Other more technical mechanisms could be added. As it has already been analyzed, DDoS attacks are based mostly on the use of botnets. Should not the police have the power to directly disrupt zombie networks? We have also seen that malware, ransomware and other cyber attacks are nowadays strictly related to economic purposes, based on the technology of crypto-currencies. Therefore, new implementations of the "follow the money" approach should be enacted in order, for instance, to proceed to the direct confiscation or to the deletion of crypto-currency wallets.

Appendices

APPENDIX I

Directive 2013/40/EU on attacks against information systems and replacing Council Framework Decision 2005/222/JHA

THE EUROPEAN PARLIAMENT AND THE COUNCIL OF THE EUROPEAN UNION, Having regard to the Treaty on the Functioning of the European Union, and in particular Article 83(1) thereof, Having regard to the proposal from the European Commission, After transmission of the draft legislative act to the national parliaments, Having regard to the opinion of the European Economic and Social Committee,[1] Acting in accordance with the ordinary legislative procedure,[2]
Whereas:

(1) The objectives of this Directive are to approximate the criminal law of the Member States in the area of attacks against information systems by establishing minimum rules concerning the definition of criminal offences and the relevant sanctions and to improve cooperation between competent authorities, including the police and other specialised law enforcement services of the Member States, as well as the competent specialised Union agencies and bodies, such as Eurojust, Europol and its European Cyber Crime Centre, and the European Network and Information Security Agency (ENISA).

(2) Information systems are a key element of political, social and economic interaction in the Union. Society is highly and increasingly dependent on such systems. The smooth operation and security of those systems in the Union is vital for the development of the internal market and of a competitive and innovative economy. Ensuring an appropriate level of

1. OJ C 218, 23.7.2011, p. 130.
2. Position of the European Parliament of 4 July 2013 (not yet published in the Official Journal) and decision of the Council of 22 July 2013.

protection of information systems should form part of an effective comprehensive framework of prevention measures accompanying criminal law responses to cybercrime.

(3) Attacks against information systems, and, in particular, attacks linked to organised crime, are a growing menace in the Union and globally, and there is increasing concern about the potential for terrorist or politically motivated attacks against information systems which form part of the critical infrastructure of Member States and of the Union. This constitutes a threat to the achievement of a safer information society and of an area of freedom, security, and justice, and therefore requires a response at Union level and improved cooperation and coordination at international level.

(4) There are a number of critical infrastructures in the Union, the disruption or destruction of which would have a significant cross-border impact. It has become apparent from the need to increase the critical infrastructure protection capability in the Union that the measures against cyber attacks should be complemented by stringent criminal penalties reflecting the gravity of such attacks. Critical infrastructure could be understood to be an asset, system or part thereof located in Member States, which is essential for the maintenance of vital societal functions, health, safety, security, economic or social well-being of people, such as power plants, transport networks or government networks, and the disruption or destruction of which would have a significant impact in a Member State as a result of the failure to maintain those functions.

(5) There is evidence of a tendency towards increasingly dangerous and recurrent large-scale attacks conducted against information systems which can often be critical to Member States or to particular functions in the public or private sector. This tendency is accompanied by the development of increasingly sophisticated methods, such as the creation and use of so-called 'botnets', which involves several stages of a criminal act, where each stage alone could pose a serious risk to public interests. This Directive aims, *inter alia*, to introduce criminal penalties for the creation of botnets, namely, the act of establishing remote control over a significant number of computers by infecting them with malicious software through targeted cyber attacks. Once created, the infected network of computers that constitute the botnet can be activated without the computer users' knowledge in order to launch a large-scale cyber attack, which usually has the capacity to cause serious damage, as referred to in this Directive. Member States may determine what constitutes serious damage according to their national law and practice, such as disrupting system services of significant public importance, or causing major financial cost or loss of personal data or sensitive information.

(6) Large-scale cyber attacks can cause substantial economic damage both through the interruption of information systems and communication and through the loss or alteration of commercially important confidential information or other data. Particular attention should be paid to raising the

awareness of innovative small and medium-sized enterprises to threats relating to such attacks and their vulnerability to such attacks, due to their increased dependence on the proper functioning and availability of information systems and often limited resources for information security.

(7) Common definitions in this area are important in order to ensure a consistent approach in the Member States to the application of this Directive.

(8) There is a need to achieve a common approach to the constituent elements of criminal offences by introducing common offences of illegal access to an information system, illegal system interference, illegal data interference, and illegal interception.

(9) Interception includes, but is not necessarily limited to, the listening to, monitoring or surveillance of the content of communications and the procuring of the content of data either directly, through access and use of the information systems, or indirectly through the use of electronic eavesdropping or tapping devices by technical means.

(10) Member States should provide for penalties in respect of attacks against information systems. Those penalties should be effective, proportionate and dissuasive and should include imprisonment and/or fines.

(11) This Directive provides for criminal penalties at least for cases which are not minor. Member States may determine what constitutes a minor case according to their national law and practice. A case may be considered minor, for example, where the damage caused by the offence and/or the risk to public or private interests, such as to the integrity of a computer system or to computer data, or to the integrity, rights or other interests of a person, is insignificant or is of such a nature that the imposition of a criminal penalty within the legal threshold or the imposition of criminal liability is not necessary.

(12) The identification and reporting of threats and risks posed by cyber attacks and the related vulnerability of information systems is a pertinent element of effective prevention of, and response to, cyber attacks and to improving the security of information systems. Providing incentives to report security gaps could add to that effect. Member States should endeavour to provide possibilities for the legal detection and reporting of security gaps.

(13) It is appropriate to provide for more severe penalties where an attack against an information system is committed by a criminal organization, as defined in Council Framework Decision 2008/841/JHA of 24 October 2008 on the fight against organised crime,[3] where a cyber attack is conducted on a large scale, thus affecting a significant number of information systems, including where it is intended to create a botnet, or where a cyber attack causes serious damage, including where it is carried out through a botnet. It is also appropriate to provide for more severe penalties where an attack

3. OJ L 300, 11.11.2008, p. 42.

is conducted against a critical infrastructure of the Member States or of the Union.

(14) Setting up effective measures against identity theft and other identity-related offences constitutes another important element of an integrated approach against cybercrime. Any need for Union action against this type of criminal behaviour could also be considered in the context of evaluating the need for a comprehensive horizontal Union instrument.

(15) The Council Conclusions of 27 to 28 November 2008 indicated that a new strategy should be developed with the Member States and the Commission, taking into account the content of the 2001 Council of Europe Convention on Cybercrime. That Convention is the legal framework of reference for combating cybercrime, including attacks against information systems. This Directive builds on that Convention. Completing the process of ratification of that Convention by all Member States as soon as possible should be considered to be a priority.

(16) Given the different ways in which attacks can be conducted, and given the rapid developments in hardware and software, this Directive refers to tools that can be used in order to commit the offences laid down in this Directive. Such tools could include malicious software, including those able to create botnets, used to commit cyber attacks. Even where such a tool is suitable or particularly suitable for carrying out one of the offences laid down in this Directive, it is possible that it was produced for a legitimate purpose Motivated by the need to avoid criminalisation where such tools are produced and put on the market for legitimate purposes, such as to test the reliability of information technology products or the security of information systems, apart from the general intent requirement, a direct intent requirement that those tools be used to commit one or more of the offences laid down in this Directive must be also fulfilled.

(17) This Directive does not impose criminal liability where the objective criteria of the offences laid down in this Directive are met but the acts are committed without criminal intent, for instance where a person does not know that access was unauthorised or in the case of mandated testing or protection of information systems, such as where a person is assigned by a company or vendor to test the strength of its security system. In the context of this Directive, contractual obligations or agreements to restrict access to information systems by way of a user policy or terms of service, as well as labour disputes as regards the access to and use of information systems of an employer for private purposes, should not incur criminal liability where the access under such circumstances would be deemed unauthorised and thus would constitute the sole basis for criminal proceedings. This Directive is without prejudice to the right of access to information as laid down in national and Union law, while at the same time it may not serve as a justification for unlawful or arbitrary access to information.

(18) Cyber attacks could be facilitated by various circumstances, such as where the offender has access to security systems inherent in the affected

information systems within the scope of his or her employment. In the context of national law, such circumstances should be taken into account in the course of criminal proceedings as appropriate.

(19) Member States should provide for aggravating circumstances in their national law in accordance with the applicable rules established by their legal systems on aggravating circumstances. They should ensure that those aggravating circumstances are available for judges to consider when sentencing offenders. It remains within the discretion of the judge to assess those circumstances together with the other facts of the particular case.

(20) This Directive does not govern conditions for exercising jurisdiction over any of the offences referred to herein, such as a report by the victim in the place where the offence was committed, a denunciation from the State of the place where the offence was committed, or the non-prosecution of the offender in the place where the offence was committed.

(21) In the context of this Directive, States and public bodies remain fully bound to guarantee respect for human rights and fundamental freedoms, in accordance with existing international obligations.

(22) This Directive strengthens the importance of networks, such as the G8 or the Council of Europe's network of points of contact available on a 24 hour, seven-day-a-week basis. Those points of contact should be able to deliver effective assistance thus, for example, facilitating the exchange of relevant information available and the provision of technical advice or legal information for the purpose of investigations or proceedings concerning criminal offences relating to information systems and associated data involving the requesting Member State. In order to ensure the smooth operation of the networks, each contact point should have the capacity to communicate with the point of contact of another Member State on an expedited basis with the support, *inter alia*, of trained and equipped personnel. Given the speed with which large-scale cyber attacks can be carried out, Member States should be able to respond promptly to urgent requests from this network of contact points. In such cases, it may be expedient that the request for information be accompanied by telephone contact in order to ensure that the request is processed swiftly by the requested Member State and that feedback is provided within eight hours.

(23) Cooperation between public authorities on the one hand, and the private sector and civil society on the other, is of great importance in preventing and combating attacks against information systems. It is necessary to foster and improve cooperation between service providers, producers, law enforcement bodies and judicial authorities, while fully respecting the rule of law. Such cooperation could include support by service providers in helping to preserve potential evidence, in providing elements helping to identify offenders and, as a last resort, in shutting down, completely or partially, in accordance with national law and practice, information systems or functions that have been compromised or used for illegal purposes. Member States should also consider setting up cooperation and partnership

networks with service providers and producers for the exchange of information in relation to the offences within the scope of this Directive.

(24) There is a need to collect comparable data on the offences laid down in this Directive. Relevant data should be made available to the competent specialised Union agencies and bodies, such as Europol and ENISA, in line with their tasks and information needs, in order to gain a more complete picture of the problem of cybercrime and network and information security at Union level and thereby to contribute to formulating a more effective response. Member States should submit information on the modus operandi of the offenders to Europol and its European Cybercrime Centre for the purpose of conducting threat assessments and strategic analyses of cybercrime in accordance with Council Decision 2009/371/JHA of 6 April 2009 establishing the European Police Office (Europol).[4] Providing information can facilitate a better understanding of present and future threats and thus contribute to more appropriate and targeted decision-making on combating and preventing attacks against information systems.

(25) The Commission should submit a report on the application of this Directive and make necessary legislative proposals which could lead to broadening its scope, taking into account developments in the field of cybercrime. Such developments could include technological developments, for example those enabling more effective enforcement in the area of attacks against information systems or facilitating prevention or minimising the impact of such attacks. For that purpose, the Commission should take into account the available analyses and reports produced by relevant actors and, in particular, Europol and ENISA.

(26) In order to fight cybercrime effectively, it is necessary to increase the resilience of information systems by taking appropriate measures to protect them more effectively against cyber attacks. Member States should take the necessary measures to protect their critical infrastructure from cyber attacks, as part of which they should consider the protection of their information systems and associated data. Ensuring an adequate level of protection and security of information systems by legal persons, for example in connection with the provision of publicly available electronic communications services in accordance with existing Union legislation on privacy and electronic communication and data protection, forms an essential part of a comprehensive approach to effectively counteracting cybercrime. Appropriate levels of protection should be provided against reasonably identifiable threats and vulnerabilities in accordance with the state of the art for specific sectors and the specific data processing situations. The cost and burden of such protection should be proportionate to the likely damage a cyber attack would cause to those affected. Member States are encouraged to provide for relevant measures incurring liabilities

4. OJ L 121, 15.5.2009, p. 37.

in the context of their national law in cases where a legal person has clearly not provided an appropriate level of protection against cyber attacks.

(27) Significant gaps and differences in Member States' laws and criminal procedures in the area of attacks against information systems may hamper the fight against organised crime and terrorism, and may complicate effective police and judicial cooperation in this area. The transnational and borderless nature of modern information systems means that attacks against such systems have a cross-border dimension, thus underlining the urgent need for further action to approximate criminal law in this area. In addition, the coordination of prosecution of cases of attacks against information systems should be facilitated by the adequate implementation and application of Council Framework Decision 2009/948/JHA of 30 November 2009 on prevention and settlement of conflict of jurisdiction in criminal proceedings.[5] Member States, in cooperation with the Union, should also seek to improve international cooperation relating to the security of information systems, computer networks and computer data. Proper consideration of the security of data transfer and storage should be given in any international agreement involving data exchange.

(28) Improved cooperation between the competent law enforcement bodies and judicial authorities across the Union is essential in an effective fight against cybercrime. In this context, stepping up the efforts to provide adequate training to the relevant authorities in order to raise the understanding of cybercrime and its impact, and to foster cooperation and the exchange of best practices, for example via the competent specialised Union agencies and bodies, should be encouraged. Such training should, *inter alia*, aim at raising awareness about the different national legal systems, the possible legal and technical challenges of criminal investigations, and the distribution of competences between the relevant national authorities.

(29) This Directive respects human rights and fundamental freedoms and observes the principles recognised in particular by the Charter of Fundamental Rights of the European Union and the European Convention for the Protection of Human Rights and Fundamental Freedoms, including the protection of personal data, the right to privacy, freedom of expression and information, the right to a fair trial, the presumption of innocence and the rights of the defence, as well as the principles of legality and proportionality of criminal offences and penalties. In particular, this Directive seeks to ensure full respect for those rights and principles and must be implemented accordingly.

(30) The protection of personal data is a fundamental right in accordance with Article 16(1) TFEU and Article 8 of the Charter on Fundamental Rights of the European Union. Therefore, any processing of personal data in the

5. OJ L 328, 15.12.2009, p. 42.

context of the implementation of this Directive should fully comply with the relevant Union law on data protection.

(31) In accordance with Articles 1 and 2 of the Protocol on the position of Denmark annexed to the Treaty on European Union and to the Treaty on the Functioning of the European Union, Denmark is not taking part in the adoption of this Directive and is not bound by it or subject to its application.

(32) In accordance with Article 3 of the Protocol on the position of the United Kingdom and Ireland in respect of the Area of Freedom, Security and Justice, annexed to the Treaty on European Union and to the Treaty on the Functioning of the European Union, those Member States have notified their wish to take part in the adoption and application of this Directive.

(33) Since the objectives of this Directive, namely to subject attacks against information systems in all Member States to effective, proportionate and dissuasive criminal penalties and to improve and encourage cooperation between judicial and other competent authorities, cannot be sufficiently achieved by the Member States, and can therefore, by reason of their scale or effects, be better achieved at Union level, the Union may adopt measures in accordance with the principle of subsidiarity as set out in Article 5 of the Treaty on European Union. In accordance with the principle of proportionality, as set out in that Article, this Directive does not go beyond what is necessary in order to achieve those objectives.

(34) This Directive aims to amend and expand the provisions of Council Framework Decision 2005/222/JHA of 24 February 2005 on attacks against information systems.[6] Since the amendments to be made are of substantial number and nature, Framework Decision 2005/222/JHA should, in the interests of clarity, be replaced in its entirety in relation to Member States participating in the adoption of this Directive,

HAVE ADOPTED THIS DIRECTIVE:

Article 1

Subject matter

This Directive establishes minimum rules concerning the definition of criminal offences and sanctions in the area of attacks against information systems. It also aims to facilitate the prevention of such offences and to improve cooperation between judicial and other competent authorities.

Article 2

Definitions

For the purposes of this Directive, the following definitions shall apply:

6. OJ L 69, 16.3.2005, p. 67.

(a) 'information system' means a device or group of inter-connected or related devices, one or more of which, pursuant to a programme, automatically processes computer data, as well as computer data stored, processed, retrieved or transmitted by that device or group of devices for the purposes of its or their operation, use, protection and maintenance;
(b) 'computer data' means a representation of facts, information or concepts in a form suitable for processing in an information system, including a programme suitable for causing an information system to perform a function;
(c) 'legal person' means an entity having the status of legal person under the applicable law, but does not include States or public bodies acting in the exercise of State authority, or public international organizations;
(d) 'without right' means conduct referred to in this Directive, including access, interference, or interception, which is not authorised by the owner or by another right holder of the system or of part of it, or not permitted under national law.

Article 3

Illegal access to information systems

Member States shall take the necessary measures to ensure that, when committed intentionally, the access without right, to the whole or to any part of an information system, is punishable as a criminal offence where committed by infringing a security measure, at least for cases which are not minor.

Article 4

Illegal system interference

Member States shall take the necessary measures to ensure that seriously hindering or interrupting the functioning of an information system by inputting computer data, by transmitting, damaging, deleting, deteriorating, altering or suppressing such data, or by rendering such data inaccessible, intentionally and without right, is punishable as a criminal offence, at least for cases which are not minor.

Article 5

Illegal data interference

Member States shall take the necessary measures to ensure that deleting, damaging, deteriorating, altering or suppressing computer data on an information system, or rendering such data inaccessible, intentionally and without right, is punishable as a criminal offence, at least for cases which are not minor.

Article 6

Illegal interception

Member States shall take the necessary measures to ensure that intercepting, by technical means, non-public transmissions of computer data to, from or within an information system, including electromagnetic emissions from an information system carrying such computer data, intentionally and without right, is punishable as a criminal offence, at least for cases which are not minor.

Article 7

Tools used for committing offences

Member States shall take the necessary measures to ensure that the intentional production, sale, procurement for use, import, distribution or otherwise making available, of one of the following tools, without right and with the intention that it be used to commit any of the offences referred to in Articles 3 to 6, is punishable as a criminal offence, at least for cases which are not minor:

(a) a computer programme, designed or adapted primarily for the purpose of committing any of the offences referred to in Articles 3 to 6;
(b) a computer password, access code, or similar data by which the whole or any part of an information system is capable of being accessed.

Article 8

Incitement, aiding and abetting and attempt

1. Member States shall ensure that the incitement, or aiding and abetting, to commit an offence referred to in Articles 3 to 7 is punishable as a criminal offence.
2. Member States shall ensure that the attempt to commit an offence referred to in Articles 4 and 5 is punishable as a criminal offence.

Article 9

Penalties

1. Member States shall take the necessary measures to ensure that the offences referred to in Articles 3 to 8 are punishable by effective, proportionate and dissuasive criminal penalties.
2. Member States shall take the necessary measures to ensure that the offences referred to in Articles 3 to 7 are punishable by a maximum term of imprisonment of at least two years, at least for cases which are not minor.

3. Member States shall take the necessary measures to ensure that the offences referred to in Articles 4 and 5, when committed intentionally, are punishable by a maximum term of imprisonment of at least three years where a significant number of information systems have been affected through the use of a tool, referred to in Article 7, designed or adapted primarily for that purpose.
4. Member States shall take the necessary measures to ensure that offences referred to in Articles 4 and 5 are punishable by a maximum term of imprisonment of at least five years where:
   (a) they are committed within the framework of a criminal organization, as defined in Framework Decision 2008/841/JHA, irrespective of the penalty provided for therein;
   (b) they cause serious damage; or
   (c) they are committed against a critical infrastructure information system.
5. Member States shall take the necessary measures to ensure that when the offences referred to in Articles 4 and 5 are committed by misusing the personal data of another person, with the aim of gaining the trust of a third party, thereby causing prejudice to the rightful identity owner, this may, in accordance with national law, be regarded as aggravating circumstances, unless those circumstances are already covered by another offence, punishable under national law.

Article 10

Liability of legal persons

1. Member States shall take the necessary measures to ensure that legal persons can be held liable for offences referred to in Articles 3 to 8, committed for their benefit by any person, acting either individually or as part of a body of the legal person, and having a leading position within the legal person, based on one of the following:
   (a) a power of representation of the legal person;
   (b) an authority to take decisions on behalf of the legal person;
   (c) an authority to exercise control within the legal person.
2. Member States shall take the necessary measures to ensure that legal persons can be held liable where the lack of supervision or control by a person referred to in paragraph 1 has allowed the commission, by a person under its authority, of any of the offences referred to in Articles 3 to 8 for the benefit of that legal person.
3. The liability of legal persons under paragraphs 1 and 2 shall not exclude criminal proceedings against natural persons who are perpetrators or inciters of, or accessories to, any of the offences referred to in Articles 3 to 8.

Article 11

Sanctions against legal persons

1. Member States shall take the necessary measures to ensure that a legal person held liable pursuant to Article 10(1) is punishable by effective, proportionate and dissuasive sanctions, which shall include criminal or non-criminal fines and which may include other sanctions, such as:
   (a) exclusion from entitlement to public benefits or aid;
   (b) temporary or permanent disqualification from the practice of commercial activities;
   (c) placing under judicial supervision;
   (d) judicial winding-up;
   (e) temporary or permanent closure of establishments which have been used for committing the offence.
2. Member States shall take the necessary measures to ensure that a legal person held liable pursuant to Article 10(2) is punishable by effective, proportionate and dissuasive sanctions or other measures.

Article 12

Jurisdiction

1. Member States shall establish their jurisdiction with regard to the offences referred to in Articles 3 to 8 where the offence has been committed:
   (a) in whole or in part within their territory; or
   (b) by one of their nationals, at least in cases where the act is an offence where it was committed.
2. When establishing jurisdiction in accordance with point (a) of paragraph 1, a Member State shall ensure that it has jurisdiction where:
   (a) the offender commits the offence when physically present on its territory, whether or not the offence is against an information system on its territory; or
   (b) the offence is against an information system on its territory, whether or not the offender commits the offence when physically present on its territory.
3. A Member State shall inform the Commission where it decides to establish jurisdiction over an offence referred to in Articles 3 to 8 committed outside its territory, including where:
   (a) the offender has his or her habitual residence in its territory; or
   (b) the offence is committed for the benefit of a legal person established in its territory.

Article 13
Exchange of information

1. For the purpose of exchanging information relating to the offences referred to in Articles 3 to 8, Member States shall ensure that they have an operational national point of contact and that they make use of the existing network of operational points of contact available 24 hours a day and seven days a week. Member States shall also ensure that they have procedures in place so that for urgent requests for assistance, the competent authority can indicate, within eight hours of receipt, at least whether the request will be answered, and the form and estimated time of such an answer.
2. Member States shall inform the Commission of their appointed point of contact referred to in paragraph 1. The Commission shall forward that information to the other Member States and competent specialised Union agencies and bodies.
3. Member States shall take the necessary measures to ensure that appropriate reporting channels are made available in order to facilitate the reporting of the offences referred to in Article 3 to 6 to the competent national authorities without undue delay.

Article 14
Monitoring and statistics

1. Member States shall ensure that a system is in place for the recording, production and provision of statistical data on the offences referred to in Articles 3 to 7.
2. The statistical data referred to in paragraph 1 shall, as a minimum, cover existing data on the number of offences referred to in Articles 3 to 7 registered by the Member States, and the number of persons prosecuted for and convicted of the offences referred to in Articles 3 to 7.
3. Member States shall transmit the data collected pursuant to this Article to the Commission. The Commission shall ensure that a consolidated review of the statistical reports is published and submitted to the competent specialised Union agencies and bodies.

Article 15
Replacement of Framework Decision 2005/222/JHA

Framework Decision 2005/222/JHA is hereby replaced in relation to Member States participating in the adoption of this Directive, without prejudice to the obligations of the Member States relating to the time limit for transposition of the Framework Decision into national law.

In relation to Member States participating in the adoption of this Directive, references to the Framework Decision 2005/222/JHA shall be construed as references to this Directive.

Article 16

Transposition

1. Member States shall bring into force the laws, regulations and administrative provisions necessary to comply with this Directive by 4 September 2015.
2. Member States shall transmit to the Commission the text of the measures transposing into their national law the obligations imposed on them under this Directive.
3. When Member States adopt those measures, they shall contain a reference to this Directive or shall be accompanied by such a reference on the occasion of their official publication. The methods of making such a reference shall be laid down by the Member States.

Article 17

Reporting

The Commission shall, by 4 September 2017, submit a report to the European Parliament and the Council, assessing the extent to which the Member States have taken the necessary measures in order to comply with this Directive, accompanied, if necessary, by legislative proposals. The Commission shall also take into account the technical and legal developments in the field of cybercrime, particularly with regard to the scope of this Directive.

Article 18

Entry into force

This Directive shall enter into force on the twentieth day following that of its publication in the *Official Journal of the European Union*.

Article 19

Addressees

This Directive is addressed to the Member States in accordance with the Treaties.
Done at Brussels, 12 August 2013.
For the European Parliament
The President
M. SCHULZ

For the Council
The President
L. LINKEVIČIUS

Appendix II

Convention on Cybercrime

Budapest, 23.XI.2001

Preamble

The Member States of the Council of Europe and the other States signatory hereto,

Considering that the aim of the Council of Europe is to achieve a greater unity between its members;

Recognising the value of fostering co-operation with the other States parties to this Convention;

Convinced of the need to pursue, as a matter of priority, a common criminal policy aimed at the protection of society against cybercrime, *inter alia*, by adopting appropriate legislation and fostering international co-operation;

Conscious of the profound changes brought about by the digitalisation, convergence and continuing globalisation of computer networks;

Concerned by the risk that computer networks and electronic information may also be used for committing criminal offences and that evidence relating to such offences may be stored and transferred by these networks;

Recognising the need for co-operation between States and private industry in combating cybercrime and the need to protect legitimate interests in the use and development of information technologies;

Believing that an effective fight against cybercrime requires increased, rapid and well-functioning international co-operation in criminal matters;

Convinced that the present Convention is necessary to deter action directed against the confidentiality, integrity and availability of computer systems, networks and computer data as well as the misuse of such systems, networks and data by providing for the criminalisation of such conduct, as described in this Convention, and the adoption of powers sufficient for effectively combating such criminal offences, by facilitating their detection, investigation and prosecution at both the domestic and international levels and by providing arrangements for fast and reliable international co-operation;

Mindful of the need to ensure a proper balance between the interests of law enforcement and respect for fundamental human rights as enshrined in the 1950 Council of

Europe Convention for the Protection of Human Rights and Fundamental Freedoms, the 1966 United Nations International Covenant on Civil and Political Rights and other applicable international human rights treaties, which reaffirm the right of everyone to hold opinions without interference, as well as the right to freedom of expression, including the freedom to seek, receive, and impart information and ideas of all kinds, regardless of frontiers, and the rights concerning the respect for privacy;

Mindful also of the right to the protection of personal data, as conferred, for example, by the 1981 Council of Europe Convention for the Protection of Individuals with regard to Automatic Processing of Personal Data;

Considering the 1989 United Nations Convention on the Rights of the Child and the 1999 International Labour Organization Worst Forms of Child Labour Convention;

Taking into account the existing Council of Europe conventions on co-operation in the penal field, as well as similar treaties which exist between Council of Europe Member States and other States, and stressing that the present Convention is intended to supplement those conventions in order to make criminal investigations and proceedings concerning criminal offences related to computer systems and data more effective and to enable the collection of evidence in electronic form of a criminal offence;

Welcoming recent developments which further advance international understanding and co-operation in combating cybercrime, including action taken by the United Nations, the OECD, the European Union and the G8;

Recalling Committee of Ministers Recommendations No. R (85) 10 concerning the practical application of the European Convention on Mutual Assistance in Criminal Matters in respect of letters rogatory for the interception of telecommunications, No. R (88) 2 on piracy in the field of copyright and neighbouring rights, No. R (87) 15 regulating the use of personal data in the police sector, No. R (95) 4 on the protection of personal data in the area of telecommunication services, with particular reference to telephone services, as well as No. R (89) 9 on computer-related crime providing guidelines for national legislatures concerning the definition of certain computer crimes and No. R (95) 13 concerning problems of criminal procedural law connected with information technology;

Having regard to Resolution No. 1 adopted by the European Ministers of Justice at their 21st Conference (Prague, 10 and 11 June 1997), which recommended that the Committee of Ministers support the work on cybercrime carried out by the European Committee on Crime Problems (CDPC) in order to bring domestic criminal law provisions closer to each other and enable the use of effective means of investigation into such offences, as well as to Resolution No. 3 adopted at the 23rd Conference of the European Ministers of Justice (London, 8 and 9 June 2000), which encouraged the negotiating parties to pursue their efforts with a view to finding appropriate solutions to enable the largest possible number of States to become parties to the Convention and acknowledged the need for a swift and efficient system of international co-operation, which duly takes into account the specific requirements of the fight against cybercrime;

Having also regard to the Action Plan adopted by the Heads of State and Government of the Council of Europe on the occasion of their Second Summit (Strasbourg, 10 and 11 October 1997), to seek common responses to the development of the new information technologies based on the standards and values of the Council of Europe;

Have agreed as follows:

Chapter I – Use of terms
Article 1 – Definitions

For the purposes of this Convention:

a “computer system” means any device or a group of interconnected or related devices, one or more of which, pursuant to a program, performs automatic processing of data;
b “computer data” means any representation of facts, information or concepts in a form suitable for processing in a computer system, including a program suitable to cause a computer system to perform a function;
c “service provider” means:
  I any public or private entity that provides to users of its service the ability to communicate by means of a computer system, and
  ii any other entity that processes or stores computer data on behalf of such communication service or users of such service.
d “traffic data” means any computer data relating to a communication by means of a computer system, generated by a computer system that formed a part in the chain of communication, indicating the communication’s origin, destination, route, time, date, size, duration, or type of underlying service.

Chapter II – Measures to be taken at the national level
Section 1 – Substantive criminal law

Title 1 – Offences against the confidentiality, integrity and availability of computer data and systems

Article 2 – Illegal access

Each Party shall adopt such legislative and other measures as may be necessary to establish as criminal offences under its domestic law, when committed intentionally, the access to the whole or any part of a computer system without right. A Party may require that the offence be committed by infringing security measures, with the intent of obtaining computer data or other dishonest intent, or in relation to a computer system that is connected to another computer system.

Article 3 – Illegal interception

Each Party shall adopt such legislative and other measures as may be necessary to establish as criminal offences under its domestic law, when committed intentionally, the interception without right, made by technical means, of non-public transmissions of computer data to, from or within a computer system, including electromagnetic emissions from a computer system carrying such computer data. A Party may require that the offence be committed with dishonest intent, or in relation to a computer system that is connected to another computer system.

Article 4 – Data interference

1 Each Party shall adopt such legislative and other measures as may be necessary to establish as criminal offences under its domestic law, when committed intentionally, the damaging, deletion, deterioration, alteration or suppression of computer data without right.
2 A Party may reserve the right to require that the conduct described in paragraph 1 result in serious harm.

Article 5 – System interference

Each Party shall adopt such legislative and other measures as may be necessary to establish as criminal offences under its domestic law, when committed intentionally, the serious hindering without right of the functioning of a computer system by inputting, transmitting, damaging, deleting, deteriorating, altering or suppressing computer data.

Article 6 – Misuse of devices

1 Each Party shall adopt such legislative and other measures as may be necessary to establish as criminal offences under its domestic law, when committed intentionally and without right:
 a the production, sale, procurement for use, import, distribution or otherwise making available of:
  i a device, including a computer program, designed or adapted primarily for the purpose of committing any of the offences established in accordance with Articles 2 through 5;
  ii a computer password, access code, or similar data by which the whole or any part of a computer system is capable of being accessed, with intent that it be used for the purpose of committing any of the offences established in Articles 2 through 5; and
 b the possession of an item referred to in paragraphs a.i or ii above, with intent that it be used for the purpose of committing any of the offences established in Articles 2 through 5. A Party may require by law that a number of such items be possessed before criminal liability attaches.
2 This article shall not be interpreted as imposing criminal liability where the production, sale, procurement for use, import, distribution or otherwise making available or possession referred to in paragraph 1 of this article is not for the purpose of committing an offence established in accordance

with Articles 2 through 5 of this Convention, such as for the authorised testing or protection of a computer system.

3 Each Party may reserve the right not to apply paragraph 1 of this article, provided that the reservation does not concern the sale, distribution or otherwise making available of the items referred to in paragraph 1 a.ii of this article.

Title 2 – Computer-related offences

Article 7 – Computer-related forgery

Each Party shall adopt such legislative and other measures as may be necessary to establish as criminal offences under its domestic law, when committed intentionally and without right, the input, alteration, deletion, or suppression of computer data, resulting in inauthentic data with the intent that it be considered or acted upon for legal purposes as if it were authentic, regardless whether or not the data is directly readable and intelligible. A Party may require an intent to defraud, or similar dishonest intent, before criminal liability attaches.

Article 8 – Computer-related fraud

Each Party shall adopt such legislative and other measures as may be necessary to establish as criminal offences under its domestic law, when committed intentionally and without right, the causing of a loss of property to another person by:

a any input, alteration, deletion or suppression of computer data,

b any interference with the functioning of a computer system, with fraudulent or dishonest intent of procuring, without right, an economic benefit for oneself or for another person.

Title 3 – Content-related offences

Article 9 – Offences related to child pornography

1 Each Party shall adopt such legislative and other measures as may be necessary to establish as criminal offences under its domestic law, when committed intentionally and without right, the following conduct:

a producing child pornography for the purpose of its distribution through a computer system;

b offering or making available child pornography through a computer system;

c distributing or transmitting child pornography through a computer system;

d procuring child pornography through a computer system for oneself or for another person;

e possessing child pornography in a computer system or on a computer-data storage medium.

2 For the purpose of paragraph 1 above, the term "child pornography" shall include pornographic material that visually depicts:
a a minor engaged in sexually explicit conduct;
b a person appearing to be a minor engaged in sexually explicit conduct;
c realistic images representing a minor engaged in sexually explicit conduct.

3 For the purpose of paragraph 2 above, the term "minor" shall include all persons under 18 years of age. A Party may, however, require a lower age-limit, which shall be not less than 16 years.

4 Each Party may reserve the right not to apply, in whole or in part, paragraphs 1, sub-paragraphs d and e, and 2, sub-paragraphs b and c.

Title 4 – Offences related to infringements of copyright and related rights

Article 10 – Offences related to infringements of copyright and related rights

1 Each Party shall adopt such legislative and other measures as may be necessary to establish as criminal offences under its domestic law the infringement of copyright, as defined under the law of that Party, pursuant to the obligations it has undertaken under the Paris Act of 24 July 1971 revising the Bern Convention for the Protection of Literary and Artistic Works, the Agreement on Trade-Related Aspects of Intellectual Property Rights and the WIPO Copyright Treaty, with the exception of any moral rights conferred by such conventions, where such acts are committed wilfully, on a commercial scale and by means of a computer system.

2 Each Party shall adopt such legislative and other measures as may be necessary to establish as criminal offences under its domestic law the infringement of related rights, as defined under the law of that Party, pursuant to the obligations it has undertaken under the International Convention for the Protection of Performers, Producers of Phonograms and Broadcasting Organizations (Rome Convention), the Agreement on Trade-Related Aspects of Intellectual Property Rights and the WIPO Performances and Phonograms Treaty, with the exception of any moral rights conferred by such conventions, where such acts are committed wilfully, on a commercial scale and by means of a computer system. 3 A Party may reserve the right not to impose criminal liability under paragraphs 1 and 2 of this article in limited circumstances, provided that other effective remedies are available and that such reservation does not derogate from the Party's international obligations set forth in the international instruments referred to in paragraphs 1 and 2 of this article.

Title 5 – Ancillary liability and sanctions

Article 11 – Attempt and aiding or abetting

1 Each Party shall adopt such legislative and other measures as may be necessary to establish as criminal offences under its domestic law, when committed intentionally, aiding or abetting the commission of any of the offences established in accordance with Articles 2 through 10 of the present Convention with intent that such offence be committed.
2 Each Party shall adopt such legislative and other measures as may be necessary to establish as criminal offences under its domestic law, when committed intentionally, an attempt to commit any of the offences established in accordance with Articles 3 through 5, 7, 8, and 9.1.a and c of this Convention.
3 Each Party may reserve the right not to apply, in whole or in part, paragraph 2 of this article.

Article 12 – Corporate liability

1 Each Party shall adopt such legislative and other measures as may be necessary to ensure that legal persons can be held liable for a criminal offence established in accordance with this Convention, committed for their benefit by any natural person, acting either individually or as part of an organ of the legal person, who has a leading position within it, based on:
a a power of representation of the legal person;
b an authority to take decisions on behalf of the legal person;
c an authority to exercise control within the legal person.
2 In addition to the cases already provided for in paragraph 1 of this article, each Party shall take the measures necessary to ensure that a legal person can be held liable where the lack of supervision or control by a natural person referred to in paragraph 1 has made possible the commission of a criminal offence established in accordance with this Convention for the benefit of that legal person by a natural person acting under its authority.
3 Subject to the legal principles of the Party, the liability of a legal person may be criminal, civil or administrative.
4 Such liability shall be without prejudice to the criminal liability of the natural persons who have committed the offence.

Article 13 – Sanctions and measures

1 Each Party shall adopt such legislative and other measures as may be necessary to ensure that the criminal offences established in accordance with

Articles 2 through 11 are punishable by effective, proportionate and dissuasive sanctions, which include deprivation of liberty.

2 Each Party shall ensure that legal persons held liable in accordance with Article 12 shall be subject to effective, proportionate and dissuasive criminal or non-criminal sanctions or measures, including monetary sanctions.

Section 2 – Procedural law

Title 1 - Common provisions

Article 14 – Scope of procedural provisions

1 Each Party shall adopt such legislative and other measures as may be necessary to establish the powers and procedures provided for in this section for the purpose of specific criminal investigations or proceedings.

2 Except as specifically provided otherwise in Article 21, each Party shall apply the powers and procedures referred to in paragraph 1 of this article to:

a the criminal offences established in accordance with Articles 2 through 11 of this Convention;

b other criminal offences committed by means of a computer system; and

c the collection of evidence in electronic form of a criminal offence.

3 a Each Party may reserve the right to apply the measures referred to in Article 20 only to offences or categories of offences specified in the reservation, provided that the range of such offences or categories of offences is not more restricted than the range of offences to which it applies the measures referred to in Article 21. Each Party shall consider restricting such a reservation to enable the broadest application of the measure referred to in Article 20.

b Where a Party, due to limitations in its legislation in force at the time of the adoption of the present Convention, is not able to apply the measures referred to in Articles 20 and 21 to communications being transmitted within a computer system of a service provider, which system:

i is being operated for the benefit of a closed group of users, and

ii does not employ public communications networks and is not connected with another computer system, whether public or private, that Party may reserve the right not to apply these measures to such communications. Each Party shall consider restricting such a reservation to enable the broadest application of the measures referred to in Articles 20 and 21.

Article 15 – Conditions and safeguards

1 Each Party shall ensure that the establishment, implementation and application of the powers and procedures provided for in this Section are subject to conditions and safeguards provided for under its domestic law, which shall provide for the adequate protection of human rights and liberties, including rights arising pursuant to obligations it has undertaken under the 1950 Council of Europe Convention for the Protection of Human Rights and Fundamental Freedoms, the 1966 United Nations International Covenant on Civil and Political Rights, and other applicable international human rights instruments, and which shall incorporate the principle of proportionality.
2 Such conditions and safeguards shall, as appropriate in view of the nature of the procedure or power concerned, *inter alia*, include judicial or other independent supervision, grounds justifying application, and limitation of the scope and the duration of such power or procedure.
3 To the extent that it is consistent with the public interest, in particular the sound administration of justice, each Party shall consider the impact of the powers and procedures in this section upon the rights, responsibilities and legitimate interests of third parties.

Title 2 – Expedited preservation of stored computer data

Article 16 – Expedited preservation of stored computer data

1 Each Party shall adopt such legislative and other measures as may be necessary to enable its competent authorities to order or similarly obtain the expeditious preservation of specified computer data, including traffic data, that has been stored by means of a computer system, in particular where there are grounds to believe that the computer data is particularly vulnerable to loss or modification.
2 Where a Party gives effect to paragraph 1 above by means of an order to a person to preserve specified stored computer data in the person's possession or control, the Party shall adopt such legislative and other measures as may be necessary to oblige that person to preserve and maintain the integrity of that computer data for a period of time as long as necessary, up to a maximum of ninety days, to enable the competent authorities to seek its disclosure. A Party may provide for such an order to be subsequently renewed.
3 Each Party shall adopt such legislative and other measures as may be necessary to oblige the custodian or other person who is to preserve the computer data to keep confidential the undertaking of such procedures for the period of time provided for by its domestic law.
4 The powers and procedures referred to in this article shall be subject to Articles 14 and 15.

Article 17 – Expedited preservation and partial disclosure of traffic data

1 Each Party shall adopt, in respect of traffic data that is to be preserved under Article 16, such legislative and other measures as may be necessary to:
a ensure that such expeditious preservation of traffic data is available regardless of whether one or more service providers were involved in the transmission of that communication; and
b ensure the expeditious disclosure to the Party's competent authority, or a person designated by that authority, of a sufficient amount of traffic data to enable the Party to identify the service providers and the path through which the communication was transmitted.
2 The powers and procedures referred to in this article shall be subject to Articles 14 and 15.

Title 3 – Production order
Article 18 – Production order

1 Each Party shall adopt such legislative and other measures as may be necessary to empower its competent authorities to order:
a a person in its territory to submit specified computer data in that person's possession or control, which is stored in a computer system or a computer data storage medium; and
b a service provider offering its services in the territory of the Party to submit subscriber information relating to such services in that service provider's possession or control.
2 The powers and procedures referred to in this article shall be subject to Articles 14 and 15.
3 For the purpose of this article, the term "subscriber information" means any information contained in the form of computer data or any other form that is held by a service provider, relating to subscribers of its services other than traffic or content data and by which can be established:
a the type of communication service used, the technical provisions taken thereto and the period of service;
b the subscriber's identity, postal or geographic address, telephone and other access number, billing and payment information, available on the basis of the service agreement or arrangement;
c any other information on the site of the installation of communication equipment, available on the basis of the service agreement or arrangement.

Title 4 – Search and seizure of stored computer data

Article 19 – Search and seizure of stored computer data

1 Each Party shall adopt such legislative and other measures as may be necessary to empower its competent authorities to search or similarly access:
   a a computer system or part of it and computer data stored therein; and
   b a computer-data storage medium in which computer data may be stored in its territory.

2 Each Party shall adopt such legislative and other measures as may be necessary to ensure that where its authorities search or similarly access a specific computer system or part of it, pursuant to paragraph 1.a, and have grounds to believe that the data sought is stored in another computer system or part of it in its territory, and such data is lawfully accessible from or available to the initial system, the authorities shall be able to expeditiously extend the search or similar accessing to the other system.

3 Each Party shall adopt such legislative and other measures as may be necessary to empower its competent authorities to seize or similarly secure computer data accessed according to paragraphs 1 or 2. These measures shall include the power to:
   a seize or similarly secure a computer system or part of it or a computer-data storage medium;
   b make and retain a copy of those computer data;
   c maintain the integrity of the relevant stored computer data;
   d render inaccessible or remove those computer data in the accessed computer system.

4 Each Party shall adopt such legislative and other measures as may be necessary to empower its competent authorities to order any person who has knowledge about the functioning of the computer system or measures applied to protect the computer data therein to provide, as is reasonable, the necessary information, to enable the undertaking of the measures referred to in paragraphs 1 and 2.

5 The powers and procedures referred to in this article shall be subject to Articles 14 and 15.

Title 5 – Real-time collection of computer data

Article 20 – Real-time collection of traffic data

1 Each Party shall adopt such legislative and other measures as may be necessary to empower its competent authorities to:
   a collect or record through the application of technical means on the territory of that Party, and
   b compel a service provider, within its existing technical capability:

i to collect or record through the application of technical means on the territory of that Party; or

ii to co-operate and assist the competent authorities in the collection or recording of, traffic data, in real-time, associated with specified communications in its territory transmitted by means of a computer system.

2 Where a Party, due to the established principles of its domestic legal system, cannot adopt the measures referred to in paragraph 1.a, it may instead adopt legislative and other measures as may be necessary to ensure the real-time collection or recording of traffic data associated with specified communications transmitted in its territory, through the application of technical means on that territory.

3 Each Party shall adopt such legislative and other measures as may be necessary to oblige a service provider to keep confidential the fact of the execution of any power provided for in this article and any information relating to it.

4 The powers and procedures referred to in this article shall be subject to Articles 14 and 15.

Article 21 – Interception of content data

1 Each Party shall adopt such legislative and other measures as may be necessary, in relation to a range of serious offences to be determined by domestic law, to empower its competent authorities to:

a collect or record through the application of technical means on the territory of that Party, and

b compel a service provider, within its existing technical capability:

i to collect or record through the application of technical means on the territory of that Party, or

ii to co-operate and assist the competent authorities in the collection or recording of, content data, in real-time, of specified communications in its territory transmitted by means of a computer system.

2 Where a Party, due to the established principles of its domestic legal system, cannot adopt the measures referred to in paragraph 1.a, it may instead adopt legislative and other measures as may be necessary to ensure the real-time collection or recording of content data on specified communications in its territory through the application of technical means on that territory.

3 Each Party shall adopt such legislative and other measures as may be necessary to oblige a service provider to keep confidential the fact of the execution of any power provided for in this article and any information relating to it.

4 The powers and procedures referred to in this article shall be subject to Articles 14 and 15.

Section 3 – Jurisdiction

Article 22 – Jurisdiction

1 Each Party shall adopt such legislative and other measures as may be necessary to establish jurisdiction over any offence established in accordance with Articles 2 through 11 of this Convention, when the offence is committed:
  a in its territory; or
  b on board a ship flying the flag of that Party; or
  c on board an aircraft registered under the laws of that Party; or
  d by one of its nationals, if the offence is punishable under criminal law where it was committed or if the offence is committed outside the territorial jurisdiction of any State.

2 Each Party may reserve the right not to apply or to apply only in specific cases or conditions the jurisdiction rules laid down in paragraphs 1.b through 1.d of this article or any part thereof.

3 Each Party shall adopt such measures as may be necessary to establish jurisdiction over the offences referred to in Article 24, paragraph 1, of this Convention, in cases where an alleged offender is present in its territory and it does not extradite him or her to another Party, solely on the basis of his or her nationality, after a request for extradition.

4 This Convention does not exclude any criminal jurisdiction exercised by a Party in accordance with its domestic law.

5 When more than one Party claims jurisdiction over an alleged offence established in accordance with this Convention, the Parties involved shall, where appropriate, consult with a view to determining the most appropriate jurisdiction for prosecution.

Chapter III – International co-operation

Section 1 – General principles

Title 1 – General principles relating to international co-operation

Article 23 – General principles relating to international co-operation

The Parties shall co-operate with each other, in accordance with the provisions of this chapter, and through the application of relevant international instruments on international co-operation in criminal matters, arrangements agreed on the basis of uniform or reciprocal legislation, and domestic laws, to the widest extent possible for the purposes of investigations or proceedings concerning criminal offences related to computer systems and data, or for the collection of evidence in electronic form of a criminal offence.

Title 2 – Principles relating to extradition

Article 24 – Extradition

1 a This article applies to extradition between Parties for the criminal offences established in accordance with Articles 2 through 11 of this Convention, provided that they are punishable under the laws of both Parties concerned by deprivation of liberty for a maximum period of at least one year, or by a more severe penalty.

b Where a different minimum penalty is to be applied under an arrangement agreed on the basis of uniform or reciprocal legislation or an extradition treaty, including the European Convention on Extradition (ETS No. 24), applicable between two or more parties, the minimum penalty provided for under such arrangement or treaty shall apply.

2 The criminal offences described in paragraph 1 of this article shall be deemed to be included as extraditable offences in any extradition treaty existing between or among the Parties. The Parties undertake to include such offences as extraditable offences in any extradition treaty to be concluded between or among them.

3 If a Party that makes extradition conditional on the existence of a treaty receives a request for extradition from another Party with which it does not have an extradition treaty, it may consider this Convention as the legal basis for extradition with respect to any criminal offence referred to in paragraph 1 of this article.

4 Parties that do not make extradition conditional on the existence of a treaty shall recognise the criminal offences referred to in paragraph 1 of this article as extraditable offences between themselves.

5 Extradition shall be subject to the conditions provided for by the law of the requested Party or by applicable extradition treaties, including the grounds on which the requested Party may refuse extradition.

6 If extradition for a criminal offence referred to in paragraph 1 of this article is refused solely on the basis of the nationality of the person sought, or because the requested Party deems that it has jurisdiction over the offence, the requested Party shall submit the case at the request of the requesting Party to its competent authorities for the purpose of prosecution and shall report the final outcome to the requesting Party in due course. Those authorities shall take their decision and conduct their investigations and proceedings in the same manner as for any other offence of a comparable nature under the law of that Party.

7 a Each Party shall, at the time of signature or when depositing its instrument of ratification, acceptance, approval or accession, communicate to the Secretary General of the Council of Europe the name and address of each authority responsible for making or receiving requests for extradition or provisional arrest in the absence of a treaty.

b The Secretary General of the Council of Europe shall set up and keep updated a register of authorities so designated by the Parties. Each Party shall ensure that the details held on the register are correct at all times.

Title 3 - General principles relating to mutual assistance

Article 25 – General principles relating to mutual assistance

1 The Parties shall afford one another mutual assistance to the widest extent possible for the purpose of investigations or proceedings concerning criminal offences related to computer systems and data, or for the collection of evidence in electronic form of a criminal offence.
2 Each Party shall also adopt such legislative and other measures as may be necessary to carry out the obligations set forth in Articles 27 through 35.
3 Each Party may, in urgent circumstances, make requests for mutual assistance or communications related thereto by expedited means of communication, including fax or e-mail, to the extent that such means provide appropriate levels of security and authentication (including the use of encryption, where necessary), with formal confirmation to follow, where required by the requested Party. The requested Party shall accept and respond to the request by any such expedited means of communication.
4 Except as otherwise specifically provided in articles in this chapter, mutual assistance shall be subject to the conditions provided for by the law of the requested Party or by applicable mutual assistance treaties, including the grounds on which the requested Party may refuse co-operation. The requested Party shall not exercise the right to refuse mutual assistance in relation to the offences referred to in Articles 2 through 11 solely on the ground that the request concerns an offence which it considers a fiscal offence.
5 Where, in accordance with the provisions of this chapter, the requested Party is permitted to make mutual assistance conditional upon the existence of dual criminality, that condition shall be deemed fulfilled, irrespective of whether its laws place the offence within the same category of offence or denominate the offence by the same terminology as the requesting Party, if the conduct underlying the offence for which assistance is sought is a criminal offence under its laws.

Article 26 – Spontaneous information

1 A Party may, within the limits of its domestic law and without prior request, forward to another Party information obtained within the framework of its own investigations when it considers that the disclosure of such information might assist the receiving Party in initiating or carrying out investigations or

proceedings concerning criminal offences established in accordance with this Convention or might lead to a request for co-operation by that Party under this chapter.

2 Prior to providing such information, the providing Party may request that it be kept confidential or only used subject to conditions. If the receiving Party cannot comply with such request, it shall notify the providing Party, which shall then determine whether the information should nevertheless be provided. If the receiving Party accepts the information subject to the conditions, it shall be bound by them.

Title 4 – Procedures pertaining to mutual assistance requests in the absence of applicable international agreements

Article 27 –Procedures pertaining to mutual assistance requests in the absence of applicable international agreements

1 Where there is no mutual assistance treaty or arrangement on the basis of uniform or reciprocal legislation in force between the requesting and requested Parties, the provisions of paragraphs 2 through 9 of this article shall apply. The provisions of this article shall not apply where such treaty, arrangement or legislation exists, unless the Parties concerned agree to apply any or all of the remainder of this article in lieu thereof.

2 a Each Party shall designate a central authority or authorities responsible for sending and answering requests for mutual assistance, the execution of such requests or their transmission to the authorities competent for their execution.

b The central authorities shall communicate directly with each other;

c Each Party shall, at the time of signature or when depositing its instrument of ratification, acceptance, approval or accession, communicate to the Secretary General of the Council of Europe the names and addresses of the authorities designated in pursuance of this paragraph;

d The Secretary General of the Council of Europe shall set up and keep updated a register of central authorities designated by the Parties. Each Party shall ensure that the details held on the register are correct at all times.

3 Mutual assistance requests under this article shall be executed in accordance with the procedures specified by the requesting Party, except where incompatible with the law of the requested Party.

4 The requested Party may, in addition to the grounds for refusal established in Article 25, paragraph 4, refuse assistance if:

a the request concerns an offence which the requested Party considers a political offence or an offence connected with a political offence, or

b it considers that execution of the request is likely to prejudice its sovereignty, security, *ordre public* or other essential interests.

5 The requested Party may postpone action on a request if such action would prejudice criminal investigations or proceedings conducted by its authorities.
6 Before refusing or postponing assistance, the requested Party shall, where appropriate after having consulted with the requesting Party, consider whether the request may be granted partially or subject to such conditions as it deems necessary.
7 The requested Party shall promptly inform the requesting Party of the outcome of the execution of a request for assistance. Reasons shall be given for any refusal or postponement of the request. The requested Party shall also inform the requesting Party of any reasons that render impossible the execution of the request or are likely to delay it significantly.
8 The requesting Party may request that the requested Party keep confidential the fact of any request made under this chapter as well as its subject, except to the extent necessary for its execution. If the requested Party cannot comply with the request for confidentiality, it shall promptly inform the requesting Party, which shall then determine whether the request should nevertheless be executed.
9 a In the event of urgency, requests for mutual assistance or communications related thereto may be sent directly by judicial authorities of the requesting Party to such authorities of the requested Party. In any such cases, a copy shall be sent at the same time to the central authority of the requested Party through the central authority of the requesting Party.
b Any request or communication under this paragraph may be made through the International Criminal Police Organization (Interpol).
c Where a request is made pursuant to sub-paragraph a. of this article and the authority is not competent to deal with the request, it shall refer the request to the competent national authority and inform directly the requesting Party that it has done so.
d Requests or communications made under this paragraph that do not involve coercive action may be directly transmitted by the competent authorities of the requesting Party to the competent authorities of the requested Party.
e Each Party may, at the time of signature or when depositing its instrument of ratification, acceptance, approval or accession, inform the Secretary General of the Council of Europe that, for reasons of efficiency, requests made under this paragraph are to be addressed to its central authority.

Article 28 – Confidentiality and limitation on use

1 When there is no mutual assistance treaty or arrangement on the basis of uniform or reciprocal legislation in force between the requesting and the requested Parties, the provisions of this article shall apply. The provisions of this article shall not apply where such treaty, arrangement or legislation exists,

unless the Parties concerned agree to apply any or all of the remainder of this article in lieu thereof.

2 The requested Party may make the supply of information or material in response to a request dependent on the condition that it is:
   a kept confidential where the request for mutual legal assistance could not be complied with in the absence of such condition, or
   b not used for investigations or proceedings other than those stated in the request.

3 If the requesting Party cannot comply with a condition referred to in paragraph 2, it shall promptly inform the other Party, which shall then determine whether the information should nevertheless be provided. When the requesting Party accepts the condition, it shall be bound by it.

4 Any Party that supplies information or material subject to a condition referred to in paragraph 2 may require the other Party to explain, in relation to that condition, the use made of such information or material.

Section 2 – Specific provisions

Title 1 – Mutual assistance regarding provisional measures

Article 29 – Expedited preservation of stored computer data

1 A Party may request another Party to order or otherwise obtain the expeditious preservation of data stored by means of a computer system, located within the territory of that other Party and in respect of which the requesting Party intends to submit a request for mutual assistance for the search or similar access, seizure or similar securing, or disclosure of the data.

2 A request for preservation made under paragraph 1 shall specify:
   a the authority seeking the preservation;
   b the offence that is the subject of a criminal investigation or proceedings and a brief summary of the related facts;
   c the stored computer data to be preserved and its relationship to the offence;
   d any available information identifying the custodian of the stored computer data or the location of the computer system;
   e the necessity of the preservation; and
   f that the Party intends to submit a request for mutual assistance for the search or similar access, seizure or similar securing, or disclosure of the stored computer data.

3 Upon receiving the request from another Party, the requested Party shall take all appropriate measures to preserve expeditiously the specified data in accordance with its domestic law. For the purposes of responding to a request, dual criminality shall not be required as a condition to providing such preservation.

4 A Party that requires dual criminality as a condition for responding to a request for mutual assistance for the search or similar access, seizure or similar

securing, or disclosure of stored data may, in respect of offences other than those established in accordance with Articles 2 through 11 of this Convention, reserve the right to refuse the request for preservation under this article in cases where it has reasons to believe that at the time of disclosure the condition of dual criminality cannot be fulfilled.

5 In addition, a request for preservation may only be refused if:
  a the request concerns an offence which the requested Party considers a political offence or an offence connected with a political offence, or
  b the requested Party considers that execution of the request is likely to prejudice its sovereignty, security, *ordre public* or other essential interests.

6 Where the requested Party believes that preservation will not ensure the future availability of the data or will threaten the confidentiality of or otherwise prejudice the requesting Party's investigation, it shall promptly so inform the requesting Party, which shall then determine whether the request should nevertheless be executed.

7 Any preservation effected in response to the request referred to in paragraph 1 shall be for a period not less than sixty days, in order to enable the requesting Party to submit a request for the search or similar access, seizure or similar securing, or disclosure of the data. Following the receipt of such a request, the data shall continue to be preserved pending a decision on that request.

Article 30 – Expedited disclosure of preserved traffic data

1 Where, in the course of the execution of a request made pursuant to Article 29 to preserve traffic data concerning a specific communication, the requested Party discovers that a service provider in another State was involved in the transmission of the communication, the requested Party shall expeditiously disclose to the requesting Party a sufficient amount of traffic data to identify that service provider and the path through which the communication was transmitted.

2 Disclosure of traffic data under paragraph 1 may only be withheld if:
  a the request concerns an offence which the requested Party considers a political offence or an offence connected with a political offence; or
  b the requested Party considers that execution of the request is likely to prejudice its sovereignty, security, *ordre public* or other essential interests.

Title 2 – Mutual assistance regarding investigative powers

Article 31 – Mutual assistance regarding accessing of stored computer data

1 A Party may request another Party to search or similarly access, seize or similarly secure, and disclose data stored by means of a computer system located within the territory of the requested Party, including data that has been preserved pursuant to Article 29.
2 The requested Party shall respond to the request through the application of international instruments, arrangements and laws referred to in Article 23, and in accordance with other relevant provisions of this chapter.
3 The request shall be responded to on an expedited basis where:
a there are grounds to believe that relevant data is particularly vulnerable to loss or modification; or
b the instruments, arrangements and laws referred to in paragraph 2 otherwise provide for expedited co-operation.

Article 32 –Trans-border access to stored computer data with consent or where publicly available

A Party may, without the authorisation of another Party:

a access publicly available (open source) stored computer data, regardless of where the data is located geographically; or
b access or receive, through a computer system in its territory, stored computer data located in another Party, if the Party obtains the lawful and voluntary consent of the person who has the lawful authority to disclose the data to the Party through that computer system.

Article 33 – Mutual assistance regarding the real-time collection of traffic data

1 The Parties shall provide mutual assistance to each other in the real-time collection of traffic data associated with specified communications in their territory transmitted by means of a computer system. Subject to the provisions of paragraph 2, this assistance shall be governed by the conditions and procedures provided for under domestic law.
2 Each Party shall provide such assistance at least with respect to criminal offences for which real-time collection of traffic data would be available in a similar domestic case.

Article 34 – Mutual assistance regarding the interception of content data

The Parties shall provide mutual assistance to each other in the real-time collection or recording of content data of specified communications transmitted by means of a computer system to the extent permitted under their applicable treaties and domestic laws.

Title 3 – 24/7 Network

Article 35 – 24/7 Network

1 Each Party shall designate a point of contact available on a twenty-four hour, seven-day-a-week basis, in order to ensure the provision of immediate assistance for the purpose of investigations or proceedings concerning criminal offences related to computer systems and data, or for the collection of evidence in electronic form of a criminal offence. Such assistance shall include facilitating, or, if permitted by its domestic law and practice, directly carrying out the following measures:
  a the provision of technical advice;
  b the preservation of data pursuant to Articles 29 and 30;
  c the collection of evidence, the provision of legal information, and locating of suspects.

2 a A Party's point of contact shall have the capacity to carry out communications with the point of contact of another Party on an expedited basis.
  b If the point of contact designated by a Party is not part of that Party's authority or authorities responsible for international mutual assistance or extradition, the point of contact shall ensure that it is able to co-ordinate with such authority or authorities on an expedited basis.

3 Each Party shall ensure that trained and equipped personnel are available, in order to facilitate the operation of the network.

Chapter IV – Final provisions

Article 36 – Signature and entry into force

1 This Convention shall be open for signature by the Member States of the Council of Europe and by non-Member States which have participated in its elaboration.

2 This Convention is subject to ratification, acceptance or approval. Instruments of ratification, acceptance or approval shall be deposited with the Secretary General of the Council of Europe.

3 This Convention shall enter into force on the first day of the month following the expiration of a period of three months after the date on which five States, including at least three Member States of the Council of Europe, have

expressed their consent to be bound by the Convention in accordance with the provisions of paragraphs 1 and 2.

4 In respect of any signatory State which subsequently expresses its consent to be bound by it, the Convention shall enter into force on the first day of the month following the expiration of a period of three months after the date of the expression of its consent to be bound by the Convention in accordance with the provisions of paragraphs 1 and 2.

Article 37 – Accession to the Convention

1 After the entry into force of this Convention, the Committee of Ministers of the Council of Europe, after consulting with and obtaining the unanimous consent of the Contracting States to the Convention, may invite any State which is not a member of the Council and which has not participated in its elaboration to accede to this Convention. The decision shall be taken by the majority provided for in Article 20.d. of the Statute of the Council of Europe and by the unanimous vote of the representatives of the Contracting States entitled to sit on the Committee of Ministers.

2 In respect of any State acceding to the Convention under paragraph 1 above, the Convention shall enter into force on the first day of the month following the expiration of a period of three months after the date of deposit of the instrument of accession with the Secretary General of the Council of Europe.

Article 38 – Territorial application

1 Any State may, at the time of signature or when depositing its instrument of ratification, acceptance, approval or accession, specify the territory or territories to which this Convention shall apply.

2 Any State may, at any later date, by a declaration addressed to the Secretary General of the Council of Europe, extend the application of this Convention to any other territory specified in the declaration. In respect of such territory the Convention shall enter into force on the first day of the month following the expiration of a period of three months after the date of receipt of the declaration by the Secretary General.

3 Any declaration made under the two preceding paragraphs may, in respect of any territory specified in such declaration, be withdrawn by a notification addressed to the Secretary General of the Council of Europe. The withdrawal shall become effective on the first day of the month following the expiration of a period of three months after the date of receipt of such notification by the Secretary General.

Article 39 – Effects of the Convention

1 The purpose of the present Convention is to supplement applicable multilateral or bilateral treaties or arrangements as between the Parties, including the provisions of:
- the European Convention on Extradition, opened for signature in Paris, on 13 December 1957 (ETS No. 24);
- the European Convention on Mutual Assistance in Criminal Matters, opened for signature in Strasbourg, on 20 April 1959 (ETS No. 30);
- the Additional Protocol to the European Convention on Mutual Assistance in Criminal Matters, opened for signature in Strasbourg, on 17 March 1978 (ETS No. 99).

2 If two or more Parties have already concluded an agreement or treaty on the matters dealt with in this Convention or have otherwise established their relations on such matters, or should they in future do so, they shall also be entitled to apply that agreement or treaty or to regulate those relations accordingly. However, where Parties establish their relations in respect of the matters dealt with in the present Convention other than as regulated therein, they shall do so in a manner that is not inconsistent with the Convention's objectives and principles.

3 Nothing in this Convention shall affect other rights, restrictions, obligations and responsibilities of a Party.

Article 40 – Declarations

By a written notification addressed to the Secretary General of the Council of Europe, any State may, at the time of signature or when depositing its instrument of ratification, acceptance, approval or accession, declare that it avails itself of the possibility of requiring additional elements as provided for under Articles 2, 3, 6 paragraph 1.b, 7, 9 paragraph 3, and 27, paragraph 9.e.

Article 41 – Federal clause

1 A federal State may reserve the right to assume obligations under Chapter II of this Convention consistent with its fundamental principles governing the relationship between its central government and constituent States or other similar territorial entities provided that it is still able to co-operate under Chapter III.

2 When making a reservation under paragraph 1, a federal State may not apply the terms of such reservation to exclude or substantially diminish its obligations to provide for measures set forth in Chapter II. Overall, it shall provide for a broad and effective law enforcement capability with respect to those measures.

3 With regard to the provisions of this Convention, the application of which comes under the jurisdiction of constituent States or other similar territorial entities, that are not obliged by the constitutional system of the federation to take legislative measures, the federal government shall inform the competent authorities of such States of the said provisions with its favourable opinion, encouraging them to take appropriate action to give them effect.

Article 42 – Reservations

By a written notification addressed to the Secretary General of the Council of Europe, any State may, at the time of signature or when depositing its instrument of ratification, acceptance, approval or accession, declare that it avails itself of the reservation(s) provided for in Article 4, paragraph 2, Article 6, paragraph 3, Article 9, paragraph 4, Article 10, paragraph 3, Article 11, paragraph 3, Article 14, paragraph 3, Article 22, paragraph 2, Article 29, paragraph 4, and Article 41, paragraph 1. No other reservation may be made.

Article 43 – Status and withdrawal of reservations

1 A Party that has made a reservation in accordance with Article 42 may wholly or partially withdraw it by means of a notification addressed to the Secretary General of the Council of Europe. Such withdrawal shall take effect on the date of receipt of such notification by the Secretary General. If the notification states that the withdrawal of a reservation is to take effect on a date specified therein, and such date is later than the date on which the notification is received by the Secretary General, the withdrawal shall take effect on such a later date.

2 A Party that has made a reservation as referred to in Article 42 shall withdraw such reservation, in whole or in part, as soon as circumstances so permit.

3 The Secretary General of the Council of Europe may periodically enquire with Parties that have made one or more reservations as referred to in Article 42 as to the prospects for withdrawing such reservation(s).

Article 44 – Amendments

1 Amendments to this Convention may be proposed by any Party, and shall be communicated by the Secretary General of the Council of Europe to the member States of the Council of Europe, to the non-Member States which have participated in the elaboration of this Convention as well as to any State which has acceded to, or has been invited to accede to, this Convention in accordance with the provisions of Article 37.

2 Any amendment proposed by a Party shall be communicated to the European Committee on Crime Problems (CDPC), which shall submit to the Committee of Ministers its opinion on that proposed amendment.
3 The Committee of Ministers shall consider the proposed amendment and the opinion submitted by the CDPC and, following consultation with the non-Member States Parties to this Convention, may adopt the amendment.
4 The text of any amendment adopted by the Committee of Ministers in accordance with paragraph 3 of this article shall be forwarded to the Parties for acceptance.
5 Any amendment adopted in accordance with paragraph 3 of this article shall come into force on the thirtieth day after all Parties have informed the Secretary General of their acceptance thereof.

Article 45 – Settlement of disputes

1 The European Committee on Crime Problems (CDPC) shall be kept informed regarding the interpretation and application of this Convention.
2 In case of a dispute between Parties as to the interpretation or application of this Convention, they shall seek a settlement of the dispute through negotiation or any other peaceful means of their choice, including submission of the dispute to the CDPC, to an arbitral tribunal whose decisions shall be binding upon the Parties, or to the International Court of Justice, as agreed upon by the Parties concerned.

Article 46 – Consultations of the Parties

1 The Parties shall, as appropriate, consult periodically with a view to facilitating:
   a the effective use and implementation of this Convention, including the identification of any problems thereof, as well as the effects of any declaration or reservation made under this Convention;
   b the exchange of information on significant legal, policy or technological developments pertaining to cybercrime and the collection of evidence in electronic form;
   c consideration of possible supplementation or amendment of the Convention.
2 The European Committee on Crime Problems (CDPC) shall be kept periodically informed regarding the result of consultations referred to in paragraph 1.
3 The CDPC shall, as appropriate, facilitate the consultations referred to in paragraph 1 and take the measures necessary to assist the Parties in their efforts to supplement or amend the Convention. At the latest three years after the present Convention enters into force, the European Committee on Crime

Problems (CDPC) shall, in co-operation with the Parties, conduct a review of all of the Convention's provisions and, if necessary, recommend any appropriate amendments.

4 Except where assumed by the Council of Europe, expenses incurred in carrying out the provisions of paragraph 1 shall be borne by the Parties in the manner to be determined by them.
5 The Parties shall be assisted by the Secretariat of the Council of Europe in carrying out their functions pursuant to this article.

Article 47 – Denunciation

1 Any Party may, at any time, denounce this Convention by means of a notification addressed to the Secretary General of the Council of Europe.
2 Such denunciation shall become effective on the first day of the month following the expiration of a period of three months after the date of receipt of the notification by the Secretary General.

Article 48 – Notification

The Secretary General of the Council of Europe shall notify the Member States of the Council of Europe, the non-Member States which have participated in the elaboration of this Convention as well as any State which has acceded to, or has been invited to accede to, this Convention of:

a any signature;
b the deposit of any instrument of ratification, acceptance, approval or accession;
c any date of entry into force of this Convention in accordance with Articles 36 and 37;
d any declaration made under Article 40 or reservation made in accordance with Article 42;
e any other act, notification or communication relating to this Convention. In witness whereof the undersigned, being duly authorised thereto, have signed this Convention.

Done at Budapest, this 23rd day of November 2001, in English and in French, both texts being equally authentic, in a single copy which shall be deposited in the archives of the Council of Europe. The Secretary General of the Council of Europe shall transmit certified copies to each Member State of the Council of Europe, to the non-Member States which have participated in the elaboration of this Convention, and to any State invited to accede to it.

APPENDIX III

Directive (EU) 2016/1148 of the European Parliament and of the Council of 6 July 2016 concerning measures for a high common level of security of network and information systems across the Union

THE EUROPEAN PARLIAMENT AND THE COUNCIL OF THE EUROPEAN UNION,
Having regard to the Treaty on the Functioning of the European Union, and in particular Article 114 thereof,
Having regard to the proposal from the European Commission,
After transmission of the draft legislative act to the national parliaments,
Having regard to the opinion of the European Economic and Social Committee ([1]),
Acting in accordance with the ordinary legislative procedure ([2]),
Whereas:

(1) Network and information systems and services play a vital role in society. Their reliability and security are essential to economic and societal activities, and in particular to the functioning of the internal market.

(2) The magnitude, frequency and impact of security incidents are increasing, and represent a major threat to the functioning of network and information systems. Those systems may also become a target for deliberate harmful actions intended to damage or interrupt the operation of the systems. Such incidents can impede the pursuit of economic activities, generate substantial financial losses, undermine user confidence and cause major damage to the economy of the Union.

(3) Network and information systems, and primarily the internet, play an essential role in facilitating the cross-border movement of goods, services and people. Owing to that transnational nature, substantial disruptions of

those systems, whether intentional or unintentional and regardless of where they occur, can affect individual Member States and the Union as a whole. The security of network and information systems is therefore essential for the smooth functioning of the internal market.

(4) Building upon the significant progress within the European Forum of Member States in fostering discussions and exchanges on good policy practices, including the development of principles for European cyber-crisis cooperation, a Cooperation Group, composed of representatives of Member States, the Commission, and the European Union Agency for Network and Information Security ('ENISA'), should be established to support and facilitate strategic cooperation between the Member States regarding the security of network and information systems. For that group to be effective and inclusive, it is essential that all Member States have minimum capabilities and a strategy ensuring a high level of security of network and information systems in their territory. In addition, security and notification requirements should apply to operators of essential services and to digital service providers to promote a culture of risk management and ensure that the most serious incidents are reported.

(5) The existing capabilities are not sufficient to ensure a high level of security of network and information systems within the Union. Member States have very different levels of preparedness, which has led to fragmented approaches across the Union. This results in an unequal level of protection of consumers and businesses, and undermines the overall level of security of network and information systems within the Union. Lack of common requirements on operators of essential services and digital service providers in turn makes it impossible to set up a global and effective mechanism for cooperation at Union level. Universities and research centres have a decisive role to play in spurring research, development and innovation in those areas.

(6) Responding effectively to the challenges of the security of network and information systems therefore requires a global approach at Union level covering common minimum capacity building and planning requirements, exchange of information, cooperation and common security requirements for operators of essential services and digital service providers. However, operators of essential services and digital service providers are not precluded from implementing security measures that are stricter than those provided for under this Directive.

(7) To cover all relevant incidents and risks, this Directive should apply to both operators of essential services and digital service providers. However, the obligations on operators of essential services and digital service providers should not apply to undertakings providing public communication networks or publicly available electronic communication services within the meaning of Directive 2002/21/EC of the European Parliament and of the Council ([3]), which are subject to the specific security and integrity requirements laid down in that Directive, nor should they apply to trust service

providers within the meaning of Regulation (EU) No 910/2014 of the European Parliament and of the Council ([4]), which are subject to the security requirements laid down in that Regulation.

(8) This Directive should be without prejudice to the possibility for each Member State to take the necessary measures to ensure the protection of the essential interests of its security, to safeguard public policy and public security, and to allow for the investigation, detection and prosecution of criminal offences. In accordance with Article 346 of the Treaty on the Functioning of the European Union (TFEU), no Member State is to be obliged to supply information the disclosure of which it considers to be contrary to the essential interests of its security. In this context, Council Decision 2013/488/EU ([5]) and non-disclosure agreements, or informal non-disclosure agreements such as the Traffic Light Protocol, are of relevance.

(9) Certain sectors of the economy are already regulated or may be regulated in the future by sector-specific Union legal acts that include rules related to the security of network and information systems. Whenever those Union legal acts contain provisions imposing requirements concerning the security of network and information systems or notifications of incidents, those provisions should apply if they contain requirements which are at least equivalent in effect to the obligations contained in this Directive. Member States should then apply the provisions of such sector-specific Union legal acts, including those relating to jurisdiction, and should not carry out the identification process for operators of essential services as defined by this Directive. In this context, Member States should provide information to the Commission on the application of such *lex specialis* provisions. In determining whether the requirements on the security of network and information systems and the notification of incidents contained in sector-specific Union legal acts are equivalent to those contained in this Directive, regard should only be had to the provisions of relevant Union legal acts and their application in the Member States.

(10) In the water transport sector, security requirements for companies, ships, port facilities, ports and vessel traffic services under Union legal acts cover all operations, including radio and telecommunication systems, computer systems and networks. Part of the mandatory procedures to be followed includes the reporting of all incidents and should therefore be considered as *lex specialis*, in so far as those requirements are at least equivalent to the corresponding provisions of this Directive.

(11) When identifying operators in the water transport sector, Member States should take into account existing and future international codes and guidelines developed in particular by the International Maritime Organisation, with a view to providing individual maritime operators with a coherent approach.

(12) Regulation and supervision in the sectors of banking and financial market infrastructures is highly harmonised at Union level, through the use of

primary and secondary Union law and standards developed together with the European supervisory authorities. Within the banking union, the application and the supervision of those requirements are ensured by the single supervisory mechanism. For Member States that are not part of the banking union, this is ensured by the relevant banking regulators of Member States. In other areas of financial sector regulation, the European System of Financial Supervision also ensures a high degree of commonality and convergence in supervisory practices. The European Securities Markets Authority also plays a direct supervision role for certain entities, namely credit-rating agencies and trade repositories.

(13) Operational risk is a crucial part of prudential regulation and supervision in the sectors of banking and financial market infrastructures. It covers all operations including the security, integrity and resilience of network and information systems. The requirements in respect of those systems, which often exceed the requirements provided for under this Directive, are set out in a number of Union legal acts, including: rules on access to the activity of credit institutions and the prudential supervision of credit institutions and investment firms, and rules on prudential requirements for credit institutions and investment firms, which include requirements concerning operational risk; rules on markets in financial instruments, which include requirements concerning risk assessment for investment firms and for regulated markets; rules on OTC derivatives, central counterparties and trade repositories, which include requirements concerning operational risk for central counterparties and trade repositories; and rules on improving securities settlement in the Union and on central securities depositories, which include requirements concerning operational risk. Furthermore, requirements for notification of incidents are part of normal supervisory practice in the financial sector and are often included in supervisory manuals. Member States should consider those rules and requirements in their application of *lex specialis*.

(14) As noted by the European Central Bank in its opinion of 25 July 2014 ([6]), this Directive does not affect the regime under Union law for the Eurosystem's oversight of payment and settlement systems. It would be appropriate for the authorities responsible for such oversight to exchange experiences on matters concerning security of network and information systems with the competent authorities under this Directive. The same consideration applies to non-euro area members of the European System of Central Banks exercising such oversight of payment and settlement systems on the basis of national laws and regulations.

(15) An online marketplace allows consumers and traders to conclude online sales or service contracts with traders, and is the final destination for the conclusion of those contracts. It should not cover online services that serve only as an intermediary to third-party services through which a contract can ultimately be concluded. It should therefore not cover online services that compare the price of particular products or services from different

traders, and then redirect the user to the preferred trader to purchase the product. Computing services provided by the online marketplace may include processing of transactions, aggregations of data or profiling of users. Application stores, which operate as online stores enabling the digital distribution of applications or software programmes from third parties, are to be understood as being a type of online marketplace.

(16) An online search engine allows the user to perform searches of, in principle, all websites on the basis of a query on any subject. It may alternatively be focused on websites in a particular language. The definition of an online search engine provided in this Directive should not cover search functions that are limited to the content of a specific website, irrespective of whether the search function is provided by an external search engine. Neither should it cover online services that compare the price of particular products or services from different traders, and then redirect the user to the preferred trader to purchase the product.

(17) Cloud computing services span a wide range of activities that can be delivered according to different models. For the purposes of this Directive, the term 'cloud computing services' covers services that allow access to a scalable and elastic pool of shareable computing resources. Those computing resources include resources such as networks, servers or other infrastructure, storage, applications and services. The term 'scalable' refers to computing resources that are flexibly allocated by the cloud service provider, irrespective of the geographical location of the resources, in order to handle fluctuations in demand. The term 'elastic pool' is used to describe those computing resources that are provisioned and released according to demand in order to rapidly increase and decrease resources available depending on workload. The term 'shareable' is used to describe those computing resources that are provided to multiple users who share a common access to the service, but where the processing is carried out separately for each user, although the service is provided from the same electronic equipment.

(18) The function of an internet exchange point (IXP) is to interconnect networks. An IXP does not provide network access or act as a transit provider or carrier. Nor does an IXP provide other services unrelated to interconnection, although this does not preclude an IXP operator from providing unrelated services. An IXP exists to interconnect networks that are technically and organisationally separate. The term 'autonomous system' is used to describe a technically stand-alone network.

(19) Member States should be responsible for determining which entities meet the criteria of the definition of operator of essential services. In order to ensure a consistent approach, the definition of operator of essential services should be coherently applied by all Member States. To that end, this Directive provides for the assessment of the entities active in specific sectors and subsectors, the establishment of a list of essential services, the consideration of a common list of cross-sectoral factors to determine

whether a potential incident would have a significant disruptive effect, a consultation process involving relevant Member States in the case of entities providing services in more than one Member State, and the support of the Cooperation Group in the identification process. In order to ensure that possible changes in the market are accurately reflected, the list of identified operators should be reviewed regularly by Member States and updated when necessary. Finally, Member States should submit to the Commission the information necessary to assess the extent to which this common methodology has allowed a consistent application of the definition by Member States.

(20) In the process of identification of operators of essential services, Member States should assess, at least for each subsector referred to in this Directive, which services have to be considered as essential for the maintenance of critical societal and economic activities, and whether the entities listed in the sectors and subsectors referred to in this Directive and providing those services meet the criteria for the identification of operators. When assessing whether an entity provides a service which is essential for the maintenance of critical societal or economic activities, it is sufficient to examine whether that entity provides a service that is included in the list of essential services. Furthermore, it should be demonstrated that provision of the essential service is dependent on network and information systems. Finally, when assessing whether an incident would have a significant disruptive effect on the provision of the service, Member States should take into account a number of cross-sectoral factors, as well as, where appropriate, sector-specific factors.

(21) For the purposes of identifying operators of essential services, establishment in a Member State implies the effective and real exercise of activity through stable arrangements. The legal form of such arrangements, whether through a branch or a subsidiary possessing legal personality, is not the determining factor in this respect.

(22) It is possible that entities operating in the sectors and subsectors referred to in this Directive provide both essential and non-essential services. For example, in the air transport sector, airports provide services which might be considered by a Member State to be essential, such as the management of the runways, but also a number of services which might be considered as non-essential, such as the provision of shopping areas. Operators of essential services should be subject to the specific security requirements only with respect to those services which are deemed to be essential. For the purpose of identifying operators, Member States should therefore establish a list of the services which are considered as essential.

(23) The list of services should contain all services provided in the territory of a given Member State that fulfil the requirements under this Directive. Member States should be able to supplement the existing list by including new services. The list of services should serve as a reference point for Member States, allowing for identification of operators of essential ser

vices. Its purpose is to identify the types of essential services in any given sector referred to in this Directive, thus distinguishing them from non-essential activities for which an entity active in any given sector might be responsible. The list of services established by each Member State would serve as further input in the assessment of the regulatory practice of each Member State with a view to ensuring the overall level of consistency of the identification process amongst Member States.

(24) For the purposes of the identification process, where an entity provides an essential service in two or more Member States, those Member States should engage in bilateral or multilateral discussions with each other. This consultation process is intended to help them to assess the critical nature of the operator in terms of cross-border impact, thereby allowing each Member State involved to present its views regarding the risks associated with the services provided. The Member States concerned should take into account each other's views in this process, and should be able to request the assistance of the Cooperation Group in this regard.

(25) As a result of the identification process, Member States should adopt national measures to determine which entities are subject to obligations regarding the security of network and information systems. This result could be achieved by adopting a list enumerating all operators of essential services or by adopting national measures including objective quantifiable criteria, such as the output of the operator or the number of users, which make it possible to determine which entities are subject to obligations regarding the security of network and information systems. The national measures, whether already existing or adopted in the context of this Directive, should include all legal measures, administrative measures and policies allowing for the identification of operators of essential services under this Directive.

(26) In order to give an indication of the importance, in relation to the sector concerned, of the identified operators of essential services, Member States should take into account the number and the size of those operators, for example in terms of market share or of the quantity produced or carried, without being obliged to divulge information which would reveal which operators have been identified.

(27) In order to determine whether an incident would have a significant disruptive effect on the provision of an essential service, Member States should take into account a number of different factors, such as the number of users relying on that service for private or professional purposes. The use of that service can be direct, indirect or by intermediation. When assessing the impact that an incident could have, in terms of its degree and duration, on economic and societal activities or public safety, Member States should also assess the time likely to elapse before the discontinuity would start to have a negative impact.

(28) In addition to the cross-sectoral factors, sector-specific factors should also be considered in order to determine whether an incident would have a

significant disruptive effect on the provision of an essential service. With regard to energy suppliers, such factors could include the volume or proportion of national power generated; for oil suppliers, the volume per day; for air transport, including airports and air carriers, rail transport and maritime ports, the proportion of national traffic volume and the number of passengers or cargo operations per year; for banking or financial market infrastructures, their systemic importance based on total assets or the ratio of those total assets to GDP; for the health sector, the number of patients under the provider's care per year; for water production, processing and supply, the volume and number and types of users supplied, including, for example, hospitals, public service organisations, or individuals, and the existence of alternative sources of water to cover the same geographical area.

(29) To achieve and maintain a high level of security of network and information systems, each Member State should have a national strategy on the security of network and information systems defining the strategic objectives and concrete policy actions to be implemented.

(30) In view of the differences in national governance structures and in order to safeguard already existing sectoral arrangements or Union supervisory and regulatory bodies, and to avoid duplication, Member States should be able to designate more than one national competent authority responsible for fulfilling the tasks linked to the security of the network and information systems of operators of essential services and digital service providers under this Directive.

(31) In order to facilitate cross-border cooperation and communication and to enable this Directive to be implemented effectively, it is necessary for each Member State, without prejudice to sectoral regulatory arrangements, to designate a national single point of contact responsible for coordinating issues related to the security of network and information systems and cross-border cooperation at Union level. Competent authorities and single points of contact should have the adequate technical, financial and human resources to ensure that they can carry out the tasks assigned to them in an effective and efficient manner and thus achieve the objectives of this Directive. As this Directive aims to improve the functioning of the internal market by creating trust and confidence, Member State bodies need to be able to cooperate effectively with economic actors and to be structured accordingly.

(32) Competent authorities or the computer security incident response teams ('CSIRTs') should receive notifications of incidents. The single points of contact should not receive directly any notifications of incidents unless they also act as a competent authority or a CSIRT. A competent authority or a CSIRT should however be able to task the single point of contact with forwarding incident notifications to the single points of contact of other affected Member States.

(33) To ensure the effective provision of information to the Member States and to the Commission, a summary report should be submitted by the single point of contact to the Cooperation Group, and should be anonymised in order to preserve the confidentiality of the notifications and the identity of operators of essential services and digital service providers, as information on the identity of the notifying entities is not required for the exchange of best practice in the Cooperation Group. The summary report should include information on the number of notifications received, as well as an indication of the nature of the notified incidents, such as the types of security breaches, their seriousness or their duration.

(34) Member States should be adequately equipped, in terms of both technical and organisational capabilities, to prevent, detect, respond to and mitigate network and information system incidents and risks. Member States should therefore ensure that they have well-functioning CSIRTs, also known as computer emergency response teams ('CERTs'), complying with essential requirements to guarantee effective and compatible capabilities to deal with incidents and risks and ensure efficient cooperation at Union level. In order for all types of operators of essential services and digital service providers to benefit from such capabilities and cooperation, Member States should ensure that all types are covered by a designated CSIRT. Given the importance of international cooperation on cybersecurity, CSIRTs should be able to participate in international cooperation networks in addition to the CSIRTs network established by this Directive.

(35) As most network and information systems are privately operated, cooperation between the public and private sectors is essential. Operators of essential services and digital service providers should be encouraged to pursue their own informal cooperation mechanisms to ensure the security of network and information systems. The Cooperation Group should be able to invite relevant stakeholders to the discussions where appropriate. To encourage effectively the sharing of information and of best practice, it is essential to ensure that operators of essential services and digital service providers who participate in such exchanges are not disadvantaged as a result of their cooperation.

(36) ENISA should assist the Member States and the Commission by providing expertise and advice and by facilitating the exchange of best practice. In particular, in the application of this Directive, the Commission should, and Member States should be able to, consult ENISA. To build capacity and knowledge among Member States, the Cooperation Group should also serve as an instrument for the exchange of best practice, discussion of capabilities and preparedness of the Member States and, on a voluntary basis, to assist its members in evaluating national strategies on the security of network and information systems, building capacity and evaluating exercises relating to the security of network and information systems.

(37) Where appropriate, Member States should be able to use or adapt existing organisational structures or strategies when applying this Directive.

(38) The respective tasks of the Cooperation Group and of ENISA are interdependent and complementary. In general, ENISA should assist the Cooperation Group in the execution of its tasks, in line with the objective of ENISA set out in Regulation (EU) No 526/2013 of the European Parliament and the Council ([7]), namely to assist the Union institutions, bodies, offices and agencies and the Member States in implementing the policies necessary to meet the legal and regulatory requirements of network and information system security under existing and future legal acts of the Union. In particular, ENISA should provide assistance in those areas that correspond to its own tasks, as set out in Regulation (EU) No 526/2013, namely analysing network and information system security strategies, supporting the organisation and running of Union exercises relating to the security of network and information systems, and exchanging information and best practice on awareness-raising and training. ENISA should also be involved in the development of guidelines for sector-specific criteria for determining the significance of the impact of an incident.

(39) In order to promote advanced security of network and information systems, the Cooperation Group should, where appropriate, cooperate with relevant Union institutions, bodies, offices and agencies, to exchange know-how and best practice, and to provide advice on security aspects of network and information systems that might have an impact on their work, while respecting existing arrangements for the exchange of restricted information. In cooperating with law enforcement authorities regarding the security aspects of network and information systems that might have an impact on their work, the Cooperation Group should respect existing channels of information and established networks.

(40) Information about incidents is increasingly valuable to the general public and businesses, particularly small and medium-sized enterprises. In some cases, such information is already provided via websites at the national level, in the language of a specific country and focusing mainly on incidents and occurrences with a national dimension. Given that businesses increasingly operate across borders and citizens use online services, information on incidents should be provided in an aggregated form at Union level. The secretariat of the CSIRTs network is encouraged to maintain a website or to host a dedicated page on an existing website, where general information on major incidents that have occurred across the Union is made available to the general public, with a specific focus on the interests and needs of businesses. CSIRTs participating in the CSIRTs network are encouraged to provide on a voluntary basis the information to be published on that website, without including confidential or sensitive information.

(41) Where information is considered to be confidential in accordance with Union and national rules on business confidentiality, such confidentiality should be ensured when carrying out the activities and fulfilling the objectives set by this Directive.

(42) Exercises which simulate real-time incident scenarios are essential for testing Member States' preparedness and cooperation regarding the security of network and information systems. The CyberEurope cycle of exercises coordinated by ENISA with the participation of the Member States is a useful tool for testing and drawing up recommendations on how incident-handling at Union level should improve over time. Considering that the Member States are not currently under any obligation to either plan or participate in exercises, the creation of the CSIRTs network under this Directive should enable Member States to participate in exercises on the basis of accurate planning and strategic choices. The Cooperation Group set up under this Directive should discuss the strategic decisions regarding exercises, in particular but not exclusively as regards the regularity of the exercises and the design of the scenarios. ENISA should, in accordance with its mandate, support the organisation and running of Union-wide exercises by providing its expertise and advice to the Cooperation Group and the CSIRTs network.

(43) Given the global nature of security problems affecting network and information systems, there is a need for closer international cooperation to improve security standards and information exchange, and to promote a common global approach to security issues.

(44) Responsibilities in ensuring the security of network and information systems lie, to a great extent, with operators of essential services and digital service providers. A culture of risk management, involving risk assessment and the implementation of security measures appropriate to the risks faced, should be promoted and developed through appropriate regulatory requirements and voluntary industry practices. Establishing a trustworthy level playing field is also essential to the effective functioning of the Cooperation Group and the CSIRTs network, to ensure effective cooperation from all Member States.

(45) This Directive applies only to those public administrations which are identified as operators of essential services. Therefore, it is the responsibility of Member States to ensure the security of network and information systems of public administrations not falling within the scope of this Directive.

(46) Risk-management measures include measures to identify any risks of incidents, to prevent, detect and handle incidents and to mitigate their impact. The security of network and information systems comprises the security of stored, transmitted and processed data.

(47) Competent authorities should retain the ability to adopt national guidelines concerning the circumstances in which operators of essential services are required to notify incidents.

(48) Many businesses in the Union rely on digital service providers for the provision of their services. As some digital services could be an important resource for their users, including operators of essential services, and as such users might not always have alternatives available, this Directive

should also apply to providers of such services. The security, continuity and reliability of the type of digital services referred to in this Directive are of the essence for the smooth functioning of many businesses. A disruption of such a digital service could prevent the provision of other services which rely on it and could thus have an impact on key economic and societal activities in the Union. Such digital services might therefore be of crucial importance for the smooth functioning of businesses that depend on them and, moreover, for the participation of such businesses in the internal market and cross-border trade across the Union. Those digital service providers that are subject to this Directive are those that are considered to offer digital services on which many businesses in the Union increasingly rely.

(49) Digital service providers should ensure a level of security commensurate with the degree of risk posed to the security of the digital services they provide, given the importance of their services to the operations of other businesses within the Union. In practice, the degree of risk for operators of essential services, which are often essential for the maintenance of critical societal and economic activities, is higher than for digital service providers. Therefore, the security requirements for digital service providers should be lighter. Digital service providers should remain free to take measures they consider appropriate to manage the risks posed to the security of their network and information systems. Because of their cross-border nature, digital service providers should be subject to a more harmonised approach at Union level. Implementing acts should facilitate the specification and implementation of such measures.

(50) While hardware manufacturers and software developers are not operators of essential services, nor are they digital service providers, their products enhance the security of network and information systems. Therefore, they play an important role in enabling operators of essential services and digital service providers to secure their network and information systems. Such hardware and software products are already subject to existing rules on product liability.

(51) Technical and organisational measures imposed on operators of essential services and digital service providers should not require a particular commercial information and communications technology product to be designed, developed or manufactured in a particular manner.

(52) Operators of essential services and digital service providers should ensure the security of the network and information systems which they use. These are primarily private network and information systems managed by their internal IT staff or the security of which has been outsourced. The security and notification requirements should apply to the relevant operators of essential services and digital service providers regardless of whether they perform the maintenance of their network and information systems internally or outsource it.

(53) To avoid imposing a disproportionate financial and administrative burden on operators of essential services and digital service providers, the requirements should be proportionate to the risk presented by the network and information system concerned, taking into account the state of the art of such measures. In the case of digital service providers, those requirements should not apply to micro- and small enterprises.

(54) Where public administrations in Member States use services offered by digital service providers, in particular cloud computing services, they might wish to require from the providers of such services additional security measures beyond what digital service providers would normally offer in compliance with the requirements of this Directive. They should be able to do so by means of contractual obligations.

(55) The definitions of online marketplaces, online search engines and cloud computing services in this Directive are for the specific purpose of this Directive, and without prejudice to any other instruments.

(56) This Directive should not preclude Member States from adopting national measures requiring public-sector bodies to ensure specific security requirements when they contract cloud computing services. Any such national measures should apply to the public-sector body concerned and not to the cloud computing service provider.

(57) Given the fundamental differences between operators of essential services, in particular their direct link with physical infrastructure, and digital service providers, in particular their cross-border nature, this Directive should take a differentiated approach with respect to the level of harmonisation in relation to those two groups of entities. For operators of essential services, Member States should be able to identify the relevant operators and impose stricter requirements than those laid down in this Directive. Member States should not identify digital service providers, as this Directive should apply to all digital service providers within its scope. In addition, this Directive and the implementing acts adopted under it should ensure a high level of harmonisation for digital service providers with respect to security and notification requirements. This should enable digital service providers to be treated in a uniform way across the Union, in a manner proportionate to their nature and the degree of risk which they might face.

(58) This Directive should not preclude Member States from imposing security and notification requirements on entities that are not digital service providers within the scope of this Directive, without prejudice to Member States' obligations under Union law.

(59) Competent authorities should pay due attention to preserving informal and trusted channels of information-sharing. Publicity of incidents reported to the competent authorities should duly balance the interest of the public in being informed about threats against possible reputational and commercial damage for the operators of essential services and digital service providers reporting incidents. In the implementation of the notification obligations,

competent authorities and the CSIRTs should pay particular attention to the need to keep information about product vulnerabilities strictly confidential, prior to the release of appropriate security fixes.

(60) Digital service providers should be subject to light-touch and reactive *ex post* supervisory activities justified by the nature of their services and operations. The competent authority concerned should therefore only take action when provided with evidence, for example by the digital service provider itself, by another competent authority, including a competent authority of another Member State, or by a user of the service, that a digital service provider is not complying with the requirements of this Directive, in particular following the occurrence of an incident. The competent authority should therefore have no general obligation to supervise digital service providers.

(61) Competent authorities should have the necessary means to perform their duties, including powers to obtain sufficient information in order to assess the level of security of network and information systems.

(62) Incidents may be the result of criminal activities the prevention, investigation and prosecution of which is supported by coordination and cooperation between operators of essential services, digital service providers, competent authorities and law enforcement authorities. Where it is suspected that an incident is related to serious criminal activities under Union or national law, Member States should encourage operators of essential services and digital service providers to report incidents of a suspected serious criminal nature to the relevant law enforcement authorities. Where appropriate, it is desirable that coordination between competent authorities and law enforcement authorities of different Member States be facilitated by the European Cybercrime Centre (EC3) and ENISA.

(63) Personal data are in many cases compromised as a result of incidents. In this context, competent authorities and data protection authorities should cooperate and exchange information on all relevant matters to tackle any personal data breaches resulting from incidents.

(64) Jurisdiction in respect of digital service providers should be attributed to the Member State in which the digital service provider concerned has its main establishment in the Union, which in principle corresponds to the place where the provider has its head office in the Union. Establishment implies the effective and real exercise of activity through stable arrangements. The legal form of such arrangements, whether through a branch or a subsidiary with a legal personality, is not the determining factor in this respect. This criterion should not depend on whether the network and information systems are physically located in a given place; the presence and use of such systems do not, in themselves, constitute such main establishment and are therefore not criteria for determining the main establishment.

(65) Where a digital service provider not established in the Union offers services within the Union, it should designate a representative. In order to deter

mine whether such a digital service provider is offering services within the Union, it should be ascertained whether it is apparent that the digital service provider is planning to offer services to persons in one or more Member States. The mere accessibility in the Union of the digital service provider's or an intermediary's website or of an email address and of other contact details, or the use of a language generally used in the third country where the digital service provider is established, is insufficient to ascertain such an intention. However, factors such as the use of a language or a currency generally used in one or more Member States with the possibility of ordering services in that other language, or the mentioning of customers or users who are in the Union, may make it apparent that the digital service provider is planning to offer services within the Union. The representative should act on behalf of the digital service provider and it should be possible for competent authorities or the CSIRTs to contact the representative. The representative should be explicitly designated by a written mandate of the digital service provider to act on the latter's behalf with regard to the latter's obligations under this Directive, including incident reporting.

(66) Standardisation of security requirements is a market-driven process. To ensure a convergent application of security standards, Member States should encourage compliance or conformity with specified standards so as to ensure a high level of security of network and information systems at Union level. ENISA should assist Member States through advice and guidelines. To this end, it might be helpful to draft harmonised standards, which should be done in accordance with Regulation (EU) No 1025/2012 of the European Parliament and of the Council ([8]).

(67) Entities falling outside the scope of this Directive may experience incidents having a significant impact on the services they provide. Where those entities consider that it is in the public interest to notify the occurrence of such incidents, they should be able to do so on a voluntary basis. Such notifications should be processed by the competent authority or the CSIRT where such processing does not constitute a disproportionate or undue burden on the Member States concerned.

(68) In order to ensure uniform conditions for the implementation of this Directive, implementing powers should be conferred on the Commission to lay down the procedural arrangements necessary for the functioning of the Cooperation Group and the security and notification requirements applicable to digital service providers. Those powers should be exercised in accordance with Regulation (EU) No 182/2011 of the European Parliament and of the Council ([9]). When adopting implementing acts related to the procedural arrangements necessary for the functioning of the Cooperation Group, the Commission should take the utmost account of the opinion of ENISA.

(69) When adopting implementing acts on the security requirements for digital service providers, the Commission should take the utmost account of the opinion of ENISA and should consult interested stakeholders. Moreover,

the Commission is encouraged to take into account the following examples: as regards security of systems and facilities: physical and environmental security, security of supplies, access control to network and information systems and integrity of network and information systems; as regards incident handling: incident-handling procedures, incident detection capability, incident reporting and communication; as regards business continuity management: service continuity strategy and contingency plans, disaster recovery capabilities; and as regards monitoring, auditing and testing: monitoring and logging policies, exercise contingency plans, network and information systems testing, security assessments and compliance monitoring.

(70) In the implementation of this Directive, the Commission should liaise as appropriate with relevant sectoral committees and relevant bodies set up at Union level in the fields covered by this Directive.

(71) The Commission should periodically review this Directive, in consultation with interested stakeholders, in particular with a view to determining the need for modification in the light of changes to societal, political, technological or market conditions.

(72) The sharing of information on risks and incidents within the Cooperation Group and the CSIRTs network and the compliance with the requirements to notify incidents to the national competent authorities or the CSIRTs might require processing of personal data. Such processing should comply with Directive 95/46/EC of the European Parliament and the Council ([10]) and Regulation (EC) No 45/2001 of the European Parliament and of the Council ([11]). In the application of this Directive, Regulation (EC) No 1049/2001 of the European Parliament and of the Council ([12]) should apply as appropriate.

(73) The European Data Protection Supervisor was consulted in accordance with Article 28(2) of Regulation (EC) No 45/2001 and delivered an opinion on 14 June 2013 ([13]).

(74) Since the objective of this Directive, namely to achieve a high common level of security of network and information systems in the Union, cannot be sufficiently achieved by the Member States but can rather, by reason of the effects of the action, be better achieved at Union level, the Union may adopt measures, in accordance with the principle of subsidiarity as set out in Article 5 of the Treaty on European Union. In accordance with the principle of proportionality as set out in that Article, this Directive does not go beyond what is necessary in order to achieve that objective.

(75) This Directive respects the fundamental rights, and observes the principles, recognised by the Charter of Fundamental Rights of the European Union, in particular the right to respect for private life and communications, the protection of personal data, the freedom to conduct a business, the right to property, the right to an effective remedy before a court and the right to be heard. This Directive should be implemented in accordance with those rights and principles,

HAVE ADOPTED THIS DIRECTIVE:

CHAPTER I

GENERAL PROVISIONS

Article 1

Subject matter and scope

1. This Directive lays down measures with a view to achieving a high common level of security of network and information systems within the Union so as to improve the functioning of the internal market.
2. To that end, this Directive:
   (a) lays down obligations for all Member States to adopt a national strategy on the security of network and information systems;
   (b) creates a Cooperation Group in order to support and facilitate strategic cooperation and the exchange of information among Member States and to develop trust and confidence amongst them;
   (c) creates a computer security incident response teams network ('CSIRTs network') in order to contribute to the development of trust and confidence between Member States and to promote swift and effective operational cooperation;
   (d) establishes security and notification requirements for operators of essential services and for digital service providers;
   (e) lays down obligations for Member States to designate national competent authorities, single points of contact and CSIRTs with tasks related to the security of network and information systems.
3. The security and notification requirements provided for in this Directive shall not apply to undertakings which are subject to the requirements of Articles 13a and 13b of Directive 2002/21/EC, or to trust service providers which are subject to the requirements of Article 19 of Regulation (EU) No 910/2014.
4. This Directive applies without prejudice to Council Directive 2008/114/EC ([14]) and Directives 2011/93/EU ([15]) and 2013/40/EU ([16]) of the European Parliament and of the Council.
5. Without prejudice to Article 346 TFEU, information that is confidential pursuant to Union and national rules, such as rules on business confidentiality, shall be exchanged with the Commission and other relevant authorities only where such exchange is necessary for the application of this Directive. The information exchanged shall be limited to that which is relevant and proportionate to the purpose of such exchange. Such exchange of information shall preserve the confidentiality of that information and protect the security and commercial interests of operators of essential services and digital service providers.
6. This Directive is without prejudice to the actions taken by Member States to safeguard their essential State functions, in particular to safeguard national

security, including actions protecting information the disclosure of which Member States consider contrary to the essential interests of their security, and to maintain law and order, in particular to allow for the investigation, detection and prosecution of criminal offences.

7. Where a sector-specific Union legal act requires operators of essential services or digital service providers either to ensure the security of their network and information systems or to notify incidents, provided that such requirements are at least equivalent in effect to the obligations laid down in this Directive, those provisions of that sector-specific Union legal act shall apply.

Article 2

Processing of personal data

1. Processing of personal data pursuant to this Directive shall be carried out in accordance with Directive 95/46/EC.
2. Processing of personal data by Union institutions and bodies pursuant to this Directive shall be carried out in accordance with Regulation (EC) No 45/2001.

Article 3

Minimum harmonisation

Without prejudice to Article 16(10) and to their obligations under Union law, Member States may adopt or maintain provisions with a view to achieving a higher level of security of network and information systems.

Article 4

Definitions

For the purposes of this Directive, the following definitions apply:

(1) 'network and information system' means:
  (a) an electronic communications network within the meaning of point (a) of Article 2 of Directive 2002/21/EC;
  (b) any device or group of interconnected or related devices, one or more of which, pursuant to a program, perform automatic processing of digital data; or
  (c) digital data stored, processed, retrieved or transmitted by elements covered under points (a) and (b) for the purposes of their operation, use, protection and maintenance;

(2) 'security of network and information systems' means the ability of network and information systems to resist, at a given level of confidence, any action that compromises the availability, authenticity, integrity or confidentiality of stored or transmitted or processed data or the related services offered by, or accessible via, those network and information systems;
(3) 'national strategy on the security of network and information systems' means a framework providing strategic objectives and priorities on the security of network and information systems at national level;
(4) 'operator of essential services' means a public or private entity of a type referred to in Annex II, which meets the criteria laid down in Article 5(2);
(5) 'digital service' means a service within the meaning of point (b) of Article 1(1) of Directive (EU) 2015/1535 of the European Parliament and of the Council ([17]) which is of a type listed in Annex III;
(6) 'digital service provider' means any legal person that provides a digital service;
(7) 'incident' means any event having an actual adverse effect on the security of network and information systems;
(8) 'incident handling' means all procedures supporting the detection, analysis and containment of an incident and the response thereto;
(9) 'risk' means any reasonably identifiable circumstance or event having a potential adverse effect on the security of network and information systems;
(10) 'representative' means any natural or legal person established in the Union explicitly designated to act on behalf of a digital service provider not established in the Union, which may be addressed by a national competent authority or a CSIRT instead of the digital service provider with regard to the obligations of that digital service provider under this Directive;
(11) 'standard' means a standard within the meaning of point (1) of Article 2 of Regulation (EU) No 1025/2012;
(12) 'specification' means a technical specification within the meaning of point (4) of Article 2 of Regulation (EU) No 1025/2012;
(13) 'internet exchange point (IXP)' means a network facility which enables the interconnection of more than two independent autonomous systems, primarily for the purpose of facilitating the exchange of internet traffic; an IXP provides interconnection only for autonomous systems; an IXP does not require the internet traffic passing between any pair of participating autonomous systems to pass through any third autonomous system, nor does it alter or otherwise interfere with such traffic;
(14) 'domain name system (DNS)' means a hierarchical distributed naming system in a network which refers queries for domain names;
(15) 'DNS service provider' means an entity which provides DNS services on the internet;
(16) 'top-level domain name registry' means an entity which administers and operates the registration of internet domain names under a specific top-level domain (TLD);

(17) 'online marketplace' means a digital service that allows consumers and/or traders as respectively defined in point (a) and in point (b) of Article 4(1) of Directive 2013/11/EU of the European Parliament and of the Council ([18]) to conclude online sales or service contracts with traders either on the online marketplace's website or on a trader's website that uses computing services provided by the online marketplace;

(18) 'online search engine' means a digital service that allows users to perform searches of, in principle, all websites or websites in a particular language on the basis of a query on any subject in the form of a keyword, phrase or other input, and returns links in which information related to the requested content can be found;

(19) 'cloud computing service' means a digital service that enables access to a scalable and elastic pool of shareable computing resources.

Article 5

Identification of operators of essential services

1. By 9 November 2018, for each sector and subsector referred to in Annex II, Member States shall identify the operators of essential services with an establishment on their territory.
2. The criteria for the identification of the operators of essential services, as referred to in point (4) of Article 4, shall be as follows:
   (a) an entity provides a service which is essential for the maintenance of critical societal and/or economic activities;
   (b) the provision of that service depends on network and information systems; and
   (c) an incident would have significant disruptive effects on the provision of that service.
3. For the purposes of paragraph 1, each Member State shall establish a list of the services referred to in point (a) of paragraph 2.
4. For the purposes of paragraph 1, where an entity provides a service as referred to in point (a) of paragraph 2 in two or more Member States, those Member States shall engage in consultation with each other. That consultation shall take place before a decision on identification is taken.
5. Member States shall, on a regular basis, and at least every two years after 9 May 2018, review and, where appropriate, update the list of identified operators of essential services.
6. The role of the Cooperation Group shall be, in accordance with the tasks referred to in Article 11, to support Member States in taking a consistent approach in the process of identification of operators of essential services.
7. For the purpose of the review referred to in Article 23 and by 9 November 2018, and every two years thereafter, Member States shall submit to the Commission the information necessary to enable the Commission to assess the implementation of this Directive, in particular the consistency of

Member States' approaches to the identification of operators of essential services. That information shall include at least:

(a) national measures allowing for the identification of operators of essential services;
(b) the list of services referred to in paragraph 3;
(c) the number of operators of essential services identified for each sector referred to in Annex II and an indication of their importance in relation to that sector;
(d) thresholds, where they exist, to determine the relevant supply level by reference to the number of users relying on that service as referred to in point (a) of Article 6(1) or to the importance of that particular operator of essential services as referred to in point (f) of Article 6(1).

In order to contribute to the provision of comparable information, the Commission, taking the utmost account of the opinion of ENISA, may adopt appropriate technical guidelines on parameters for the information referred to in this paragraph.

Article 6

Significant disruptive effect

1. When determining the significance of a disruptive effect as referred to in point (c) of Article 5(2), Member States shall take into account at least the following cross-sectoral factors:
   (a) the number of users relying on the service provided by the entity concerned;
   (b) the dependency of other sectors referred to in Annex II on the service provided by that entity;
   (c) the impact that incidents could have, in terms of degree and duration, on economic and societal activities or public safety;
   (d) the market share of that entity;
   (e) the geographic spread with regard to the area that could be affected by an incident;
   (f) the importance of the entity for maintaining a sufficient level of the service, taking into account the availability of alternative means for the provision of that service.
2. In order to determine whether an incident would have a significant disruptive effect, Member States shall also, where appropriate, take into account sector-specific factors.

CHAPTER II

NATIONAL FRAMEWORKS ON THE SECURITY OF NETWORK AND INFORMATION SYSTEMS

Article 7

National strategy on the security of network and information systems

1. Each Member State shall adopt a national strategy on the security of network and information systems defining the strategic objectives and appropriate policy and regulatory measures with a view to achieving and maintaining a high level of security of network and information systems and covering at least the sectors referred to in Annex II and the services referred to in Annex III. The national strategy on the security of network and information systems shall address, in particular, the following issues:
   (a) the objectives and priorities of the national strategy on the security of network and information systems;
   (b) a governance framework to achieve the objectives and priorities of the national strategy on the security of network and information systems, including roles and responsibilities of the government bodies and the other relevant actors;
   (c) the identification of measures relating to preparedness, response and recovery, including cooperation between the public and private sectors;
   (d) an indication of the education, awareness-raising and training programmes relating to the national strategy on the security of network and information systems;
   (e) an indication of the research and development plans relating to the national strategy on the security of network and information systems;
   (f) a risk assessment plan to identify risks;
   (g) a list of the various actors involved in the implementation of the national strategy on the security of network and information systems.
2. Member States may request the assistance of ENISA in developing national strategies on the security of network and information systems.
3. Member States shall communicate their national strategies on the security of network and information systems to the Commission within three months from their adoption. In so doing, Member States may exclude elements of the strategy which relate to national security.

Article 8

National competent authorities and single point of contact

1. Each Member State shall designate one or more national competent authorities on the security of network and information systems ('competent authority'), covering at least the sectors referred to in Annex II and the services referred to in Annex III. Member States may assign this role to an existing authority or authorities.
2. The competent authorities shall monitor the application of this Directive at national level.
3. Each Member State shall designate a national single point of contact on the security of network and information systems ('single point of contact'). Member States may assign this role to an existing authority. Where a Member State designates only one competent authority, that competent authority shall also be the single point of contact.
4. The single point of contact shall exercise a liaison function to ensure cross-border cooperation of Member State authorities and with the relevant authorities in other Member States and with the Cooperation Group referred to in Article 11 and the CSIRTs network referred to in Article 12.
5. Member States shall ensure that the competent authorities and the single points of contact have adequate resources to carry out, in an effective and efficient manner, the tasks assigned to them and thereby to fulfil the objectives of this Directive. Member States shall ensure effective, efficient and secure cooperation of the designated representatives in the Cooperation Group.
6. The competent authorities and single point of contact shall, whenever appropriate and in accordance with national law, consult and cooperate with the relevant national law enforcement authorities and national data protection authorities.
7. Each Member State shall notify to the Commission without delay the designation of the competent authority and single point of contact, their tasks, and any subsequent change thereto. Each Member State shall make public its designation of the competent authority and single point of contact. The Commission shall publish the list of designated single points of contacts.

Article 9

Computer security incident response teams (CSIRTs)

1. Each Member State shall designate one or more CSIRTs which shall comply with the requirements set out in point (1) of Annex I, covering at least the sectors referred to in Annex II and the services referred to in Annex III,

responsible for risk and incident handling in accordance with a well-defined process. A CSIRT may be established within a competent authority.

2. Member States shall ensure that the CSIRTs have adequate resources to effectively carry out their tasks as set out in point (2) of Annex I.

   Member States shall ensure the effective, efficient and secure cooperation of their CSIRTs in the CSIRTs network referred to in Article 12.
3. Member States shall ensure that their CSIRTs have access to an appropriate, secure, and resilient communication and information infrastructure at national level.
4. Member States shall inform the Commission about the remit, as well as the main elements of the incident-handling process, of their CSIRTs.
5. Member States may request the assistance of ENISA in developing national CSIRTs.

Article 10

Cooperation at national level

1. Where they are separate, the competent authority, the single point of contact and the CSIRT of the same Member State shall cooperate with regard to the fulfilment of the obligations laid down in this Directive.
2. Member States shall ensure that either the competent authorities or the CSIRTs receive incident notifications submitted pursuant to this Directive. Where a Member State decides that CSIRTs shall not receive notifications, the CSIRTs shall, to the extent necessary to fulfil their tasks, be granted access to data on incidents notified by operators of essential services, pursuant to Article 14(3) and (5), or by digital service providers, pursuant to Article 16(3) and (6).
3. Member States shall ensure that the competent authorities or the CSIRTs inform the single points of contact about incident notifications submitted pursuant to this Directive.

   By 9 August 2018, and every year thereafter, the single point of contact shall submit a summary report to the Cooperation Group on the notifications received, including the number of notifications and the nature of notified incidents, and the actions taken in accordance with Article 14(3) and (5) and Article 16(3) and (6).

CHAPTER III

COOPERATION

Article 11

Cooperation Group

1. In order to support and facilitate strategic cooperation and the exchange of information among Member States and to develop trust and confidence, and with a view to achieving a high common level of security of network and information systems in the Union, a Cooperation Group is hereby established.

   The Cooperation Group shall carry out its tasks on the basis of biennial work programmes as referred to in the second subparagraph of paragraph 3.
2. The Cooperation Group shall be composed of representatives of the Member States, the Commission and ENISA.

   Where appropriate, the Cooperation Group may invite representatives of the relevant stakeholders to participate in its work.

   The Commission shall provide the secretariat.
3. The Cooperation Group shall have the following tasks:
   (a) providing strategic guidance for the activities of the CSIRTs network established under Article 12;
   (b) exchanging best practice on the exchange of information related to incident notification as referred to in Article 14(3) and (5) and Article 16(3) and (6);
   (c) exchanging best practice between Member States and, in collaboration with ENISA, assisting Member States in building capacity to ensure the security of network and information systems;
   (d) discussing capabilities and preparedness of the Member States, and, on a voluntary basis, evaluating national strategies on the security of network and information systems and the effectiveness of CSIRTs, and identifying best practice;
   (e) exchanging information and best practice on awareness-raising and training;
   (f) exchanging information and best practice on research and development relating to the security of network and information systems;
   (g) where relevant, exchanging experiences on matters concerning the security of network and information systems with relevant Union institutions, bodies, offices and agencies;
   (h) discussing the standards and specifications referred to in Article 19 with representatives from the relevant European standardisation organisations;
   (i) collecting best practice information on risks and incidents;
   (j) examining, on an annual basis, the summary reports referred to in the second subparagraph of Article 10(3);

(k) discussing the work undertaken with regard to exercises relating to the security of network and information systems, education programmes and training, including the work done by ENISA;
(l) with ENISA's assistance, exchanging best practice with regard to the identification of operators of essential services by the Member States, including in relation to cross-border dependencies, regarding risks and incidents;
(m) discussing modalities for reporting notifications of incidents as referred to in Articles 14 and 16.

By 9 February 2018 and every two years thereafter, the Cooperation Group shall establish a work programme in respect of actions to be undertaken to implement its objectives and tasks, which shall be consistent with the objectives of this Directive.

4. For the purpose of the review referred to in Article 23 and by 9 August 2018, and every year and a half thereafter, the Cooperation Group shall prepare a report assessing the experience gained with the strategic cooperation pursued under this Article.
5. The Commission shall adopt implementing acts laying down procedural arrangements necessary for the functioning of the Cooperation Group. Those implementing acts shall be adopted in accordance with the examination procedure referred to in Article 22(2).

For the purposes of the first subparagraph, the Commission shall submit the first draft implementing act to the committee referred to in Article 22(1) by 9 February 2017.

Article 12

CSIRTs network

1. In order to contribute to the development of confidence and trust between the Member States and to promote swift and effective operational cooperation, a network of the national CSIRTs is hereby established.
2. The CSIRTs network shall be composed of representatives of the Member States' CSIRTs and CERT-EU. The Commission shall participate in the CSIRTs network as an observer. ENISA shall provide the secretariat and shall actively support the cooperation among the CSIRTs.
3. The CSIRTs network shall have the following tasks:
   (a) exchanging information on CSIRTs' services, operations and cooperation capabilities;
   (b) at the request of a representative of a CSIRT from a Member State potentially affected by an incident, exchanging and discussing non-commercially sensitive information related to that incident and associated risks; however, any Member State's CSIRT may refuse to

contribute to that discussion if there is a risk of prejudice to the investigation of the incident;

(c) exchanging and making available on a voluntary basis non-confidential information concerning individual incidents;

(d) at the request of a representative of a Member State's CSIRT, discussing and, where possible, identifying a coordinated response to an incident that has been identified within the jurisdiction of that same Member State;

(e) providing Member States with support in addressing cross-border incidents on the basis of their voluntary mutual assistance;

(f) discussing, exploring and identifying further forms of operational co-operation, including in relation to:
   (i) categories of risks and incidents;
   (ii) early warnings;
   (iii) mutual assistance;
   (iv) principles and modalities for coordination, when Member States respond to cross-border risks and incidents;

(g) informing the Cooperation Group of its activities and of the further forms of operational cooperation discussed pursuant to point (f), and requesting guidance in that regard;

(h) discussing lessons learnt from exercises relating to the security of network and information systems, including from those organised by ENISA;

(i) at the request of an individual CSIRT, discussing the capabilities and preparedness of that CSIRT;

(j) issuing guidelines in order to facilitate the convergence of operational practices with regard to the application of the provisions of this Article concerning operational cooperation.

4. For the purpose of the review referred to in Article 23 and by 9 August 2018, and every year and a half thereafter, the CSIRTs network shall produce a report assessing the experience gained with the operational cooperation, including conclusions and recommendations, pursued under this Article. That report shall also be submitted to the Cooperation Group.
5. The CSIRTs network shall lay down its own rules of procedure.

Article 13

International cooperation

The Union may conclude international agreements, in accordance with Article 218 TFEU, with third countries or international organisations, allowing and organising their participation in some activities of the Cooperation Group. Such agreements shall take into account the need to ensure adequate protection of data.

CHAPTER IV

SECURITY OF THE NETWORK AND INFORMATION SYSTEMS OF OPERATORS OF ESSENTIAL SERVICES

Article 14

Security requirements and incident notification

1. Member States shall ensure that operators of essential services take appropriate and proportionate technical and organisational measures to manage the risks posed to the security of network and information systems which they use in their operations. Having regard to the state of the art, those measures shall ensure a level of security of network and information systems appropriate to the risk posed.
2. Member States shall ensure that operators of essential services take appropriate measures to prevent and minimise the impact of incidents affecting the security of the network and information systems used for the provision of such essential services, with a view to ensuring the continuity of those services.
3. Member States shall ensure that operators of essential services notify, without undue delay, the competent authority or the CSIRT of incidents having a significant impact on the continuity of the essential services they provide. Notifications shall include information enabling the competent authority or the CSIRT to determine any cross-border impact of the incident. Notification shall not make the notifying party subject to increased liability.
4. In order to determine the significance of the impact of an incident, the following parameters in particular shall be taken into account:
   (a) the number of users affected by the disruption of the essential service;
   (b) the duration of the incident;
   (c) the geographical spread with regard to the area affected by the incident.
5. On the basis of the information provided in the notification by the operator of essential services, the competent authority or the CSIRT shall inform the other affected Member State(s) if the incident has a significant impact on the continuity of essential services in that Member State. In so doing, the competent authority or the CSIRT shall, in accordance with Union law or national legislation that complies with Union law, preserve the security and commercial interests of the operator of essential services, as well as the confidentiality of the information provided in its notification.

   Where the circumstances allow, the competent authority or the CSIRT shall provide the notifying operator of essential services with relevant information regarding the follow-up of its notification, such as information that could support the effective incident handling.

   At the request of the competent authority or the CSIRT, the single point of contact shall forward notifications as referred to in the first subparagraph to single points of contact of other affected Member States.
6. After consulting the notifying operator of essential services, the competent authority or the CSIRT may inform the public about individual incidents,

where public awareness is necessary in order to prevent an incident or to deal with an ongoing incident.

7. Competent authorities acting together within the Cooperation Group may develop and adopt guidelines concerning the circumstances in which operators of essential services are required to notify incidents, including on the parameters to determine the significance of the impact of an incident as referred to in paragraph 4.

Article 15

Implementation and enforcement

1. Member States shall ensure that the competent authorities have the necessary powers and means to assess the compliance of operators of essential services with their obligations under Article 14 and the effects thereof on the security of network and information systems.
2. Member States shall ensure that the competent authorities have the powers and means to require operators of essential services to provide:
   (a) the information necessary to assess the security of their network and information systems, including documented security policies;
   (b) evidence of the effective implementation of security policies, such as the results of a security audit carried out by the competent authority or a qualified auditor and, in the latter case, to make the results thereof, including the underlying evidence, available to the competent authority.

   When requesting such information or evidence, the competent authority shall state the purpose of the request and specify what information is required.
3. Following the assessment of information or results of security audits referred to in paragraph 2, the competent authority may issue binding instructions to the operators of essential services to remedy the deficiencies identified.
4. The competent authority shall work in close cooperation with data protection authorities when addressing incidents resulting in personal data breaches.

CHAPTER V

SECURITY OF THE NETWORK AND INFORMATION SYSTEMS OF DIGITAL SERVICE PROVIDERS

Article 16

Security requirements and incident notification

1. Member States shall ensure that digital service providers identify and take appropriate and proportionate technical and organisational measures to manage the risks posed to the security of network and information systems which they use in the context of offering services referred to in Annex III within the

Union. Having regard to the state of the art, those measures shall ensure a level of security of network and information systems appropriate to the risk posed, and shall take into account the following elements:

(a) the security of systems and facilities;
(b) incident handling;
(c) business continuity management;
(d) monitoring, auditing and testing;
(e) compliance with international standards.

2. Member States shall ensure that digital service providers take measures to prevent and minimise the impact of incidents affecting the security of their network and information systems on the services referred to in Annex III that are offered within the Union, with a view to ensuring the continuity of those services.

3. Member States shall ensure that digital service providers notify the competent authority or the CSIRT without undue delay of any incident having a substantial impact on the provision of a service as referred to in Annex III that they offer within the Union. Notifications shall include information to enable the competent authority or the CSIRT to determine the significance of any cross-border impact. Notification shall not make the notifying party subject to increased liability.

4. In order to determine whether the impact of an incident is substantial, the following parameters in particular shall be taken into account:

(a) the number of users affected by the incident, in particular users relying on the service for the provision of their own services;
(b) the duration of the incident;
(c) the geographical spread with regard to the area affected by the incident;
(d) the extent of the disruption of the functioning of the service;
(e) the extent of the impact on economic and societal activities.

The obligation to notify an incident shall only apply where the digital service provider has access to the information needed to assess the impact of an incident against the parameters referred to in the first subparagraph.

5. Where an operator of essential services relies on a third-party digital service provider for the provision of a service which is essential for the maintenance of critical societal and economic activities, any significant impact on the continuity of the essential services due to an incident affecting the digital service provider shall be notified by that operator.

6. Where appropriate, and in particular if the incident referred to in paragraph 3 concerns two or more Member States, the competent authority or the CSIRT shall inform the other affected Member States. In so doing, the competent authorities, CSIRTs and single points of contact shall, in accordance with Union law, or national legislation that complies with Union law, preserve the digital service provider's security and commercial interests as well as the confidentiality of the information provided.

7. After consulting the digital service provider concerned, the competent authority or the CSIRT and, where appropriate, the authorities or the CSIRTs of other

Member States concerned may inform the public about individual incidents or require the digital service provider to do so, where public awareness is necessary in order to prevent an incident or to deal with an ongoing incident, or where disclosure of the incident is otherwise in the public interest.

8. The Commission shall adopt implementing acts in order to specify further the elements referred to in paragraph 1 and the parameters listed in paragraph 4 of this Article. Those implementing acts shall be adopted in accordance with the examination procedure referred to in Article 22(2) by 9 August 2017.
9. The Commission may adopt implementing acts laying down the formats and procedures applicable to notification requirements. Those implementing acts shall be adopted in accordance with the examination procedure referred to in Article 22(2).
10. Without prejudice to Article 1(6), Member States shall not impose any further security or notification requirements on digital service providers.
11. Chapter V shall not apply to micro- and small enterprises as defined in Commission Recommendation 2003/361/EC ([19]).

Article 17

Implementation and enforcement

1. Member States shall ensure that the competent authorities take action, if necessary, through *ex post* supervisory measures, when provided with evidence that a digital service provider does not meet the requirements laid down in Article 16. Such evidence may be submitted by a competent authority of another Member State where the service is provided.
2. For the purposes of paragraph 1, the competent authorities shall have the necessary powers and means to require digital service providers to:
   (a) provide the information necessary to assess the security of their network and information systems, including documented security policies;
   (b) remedy any failure to meet the requirements laid down in Article 16.
3. If a digital service provider has its main establishment or a representative in a Member State, but its network and information systems are located in one or more other Member States, the competent authority of the Member State of the main establishment or of the representative and the competent authorities of those other Member States shall cooperate and assist each other as necessary. Such assistance and cooperation may cover information exchanges between the competent authorities concerned and requests to take the supervisory measures referred to in paragraph 2.

Article 18

Jurisdiction and territoriality

1. For the purposes of this Directive, a digital service provider shall be deemed to be under the jurisdiction of the Member State in which it has its main establishment. A digital service provider shall be deemed to have its main establishment in a Member State when it has its head office in that Member State.
2. A digital service provider that is not established in the Union, but offers services referred to in Annex III within the Union, shall designate a representative in the Union. The representative shall be established in one of those Member States where the services are offered. The digital service provider shall be deemed to be under the jurisdiction of the Member State where the representative is established.
3. The designation of a representative by the digital service provider shall be without prejudice to legal actions which could be initiated against the digital service provider itself.

CHAPTER VI

STANDARDISATION AND VOLUNTARY NOTIFICATION

Article 19

Standardisation

1. In order to promote convergent implementation of Article 14(1) and (2) and Article 16(1) and (2), Member States shall, without imposing or discriminating in favour of the use of a particular type of technology, encourage the use of European or internationally accepted standards and specifications relevant to the security of network and information systems.
2. ENISA, in collaboration with Member States, shall draw up advice and guidelines regarding the technical areas to be considered in relation to paragraph 1 as well as regarding already existing standards, including Member States' national standards, which would allow for those areas to be covered.

Article 20

Voluntary notification

1. Without prejudice to Article 3, entities which have not been identified as operators of essential services and are not digital service providers may notify, on a voluntary basis, incidents having a significant impact on the continuity of the services which they provide.

2. When processing notifications, Member States shall act in accordance with the procedure set out in Article 14. Member States may prioritise the processing of mandatory notifications over voluntary notifications. Voluntary notifications shall only be processed where such processing does not constitute a disproportionate or undue burden on Member States concerned.

   Voluntary notification shall not result in the imposition upon the notifying entity of any obligations to which it would not have been subject had it not given that notification.

CHAPTER VII

FINAL PROVISIONS

Article 21

Penalties

Member States shall lay down the rules on penalties applicable to infringements of national provisions adopted pursuant to this Directive and shall take all measures necessary to ensure that they are implemented. The penalties provided for shall be effective, proportionate and dissuasive. Member States shall, by 9 May 2018, notify the Commission of those rules and of those measures and shall notify it, without delay, of any subsequent amendment affecting them.

Article 22

Committee procedure

1. The Commission shall be assisted by the Network and Information Systems Security Committee. That committee shall be a committee within the meaning of Regulation (EU) No 182/2011.
2. Where reference is made to this paragraph, Article 5 of Regulation (EU) No 182/2011 shall apply.

Article 23

Review

1. By 9 May 2019, the Commission shall submit a report to the European Parliament and to Council, assessing the consistency of the approach taken by Member States in the identification of the operators of essential services.
2. The Commission shall periodically review the functioning of this Directive and report to the European Parliament and to the Council. For this purpose and with a view to further advancing the strategic and operational cooperation, the

Commission shall take into account the reports of the Cooperation Group and the CSIRTs network on the experience gained at a strategic and operational level. In its review, the Commission shall also assess the lists contained in Annexes II and III, and the consistency in the identification of operators of essential services and services in the sectors referred to in Annex II. The first report shall be submitted by 9 May 2021.

Article 24

Transitional measures

1. Without prejudice to Article 25 and with a view to providing Member States with additional possibilities for appropriate cooperation during the period of transposition, the Cooperation Group and the CSIRTs network shall begin to perform the tasks set out in Articles 11(3) and 12(3) respectively by 9 February 2017.
2. For the period from 9 February 2017 to 9 November 2018, and for the purposes of supporting Member States in taking a consistent approach in the process of identification of operators of essential services, the Cooperation Group shall discuss the process, substance and type of national measures allowing for the identification of operators of essential services within a specific sector in accordance with the criteria set out in Articles 5 and 6. The Cooperation Group shall also discuss, at the request of a Member State, specific draft national measures of that Member State, allowing for the identification of operators of essential services within a specific sector in accordance with the criteria set out in Articles 5 and 6.
3. By 9 February 2017 and for the purposes of this Article, Member States shall ensure appropriate representation in the Cooperation Group and the CSIRTs network.

Article 25

Transposition

1. Member States shall adopt and publish, by 9 May 2018, the laws, regulations and administrative provisions necessary to comply with this Directive. They shall immediately inform the Commission thereof.

   They shall apply those measures from 10 May 2018.

   When Member States adopt those measures, they shall contain a reference to this Directive or shall be accompanied by such a reference on the occasion of their official publication. The methods of making such reference shall be laid down by Member States.

2. Member States shall communicate to the Commission the text of the main provisions of national law which they adopt in the field covered by this Directive.

Article 26

Entry into force

This Directive shall enter into force on the twentieth day following that of its publication in the *Official Journal of the European Union*.

Article 27

Addressees

This Directive is addressed to the Member States.
Done at Strasbourg, 6 July 2016.

APPENDIX IV

Directive (EU) 2019/713 of the European Parliament and of the Council of 17 April 2019 on combating fraud and counterfeiting of non-cash means of payment and replacing Council Framework Decision 2001/413/JHA

THE EUROPEAN PARLIAMENT AND THE COUNCIL OF THE EUROPEAN UNION,
Having regard to the Treaty on the Functioning of the European Union, and in particular Article 83(1) thereof,
Having regard to the proposal from the European Commission,
After transmission of the draft legislative act to the national parliaments,
Having regard to the opinion of the European Economic and Social Committee,
Acting in accordance with the ordinary legislative procedure,
Whereas:

(1) Fraud and counterfeiting of non-cash means of payment are threats to security, as they represent a source of income for organised crime and are therefore enablers for other criminal activities such as terrorism, drug trafficking and trafficking in human beings.
(2) Fraud and counterfeiting of non-cash means of payment also represent obstacles to the digital single market, as they erode consumers' trust and cause direct economic loss.
(3) Council Framework Decision 2001/413/JHA needs to be updated and complemented in order to include further provisions on offences in particular with regard to computer-related fraud, and on penalties, prevention, assistance to victims and cross-border cooperation.

(4) Significant gaps and differences in Member States' laws in the areas of fraud and of counterfeiting of non-cash means of payment can obstruct the prevention, detection and sanctioning of those types of crime and other serious and organised crimes related to and enabled by them, and make police and judicial cooperation more complicated and therefore less effective, with negative consequences for security.

(5) Fraud and counterfeiting of non-cash means of payment have a significant cross-border dimension, accentuated by an increasing digital component, which underlines the need for further action to approximate criminal legislation in the areas of fraud and of counterfeiting of non-cash means of payment.

(6) Recent years have brought not only an exponential increase in the digital economy, but also a proliferation of innovation in many areas, including payment technologies. New payment technologies involve the use of new types of payment instruments, which, while creating new opportunities for consumers and businesses, also increase opportunities for fraud. Consequently, the legal framework must remain relevant and up-to-date against the background of those technological developments, on the basis of a technology-neutral approach.

(7) Fraud is not only used to fund criminal groups, but also limits the development of the digital single market and makes citizens more reluctant to make online purchases.

(8) Common definitions in the areas of fraud and of counterfeiting of non-cash means of payment are important to ensure a consistent approach in Member States' application of this Directive and to facilitate information exchange and cooperation between competent authorities. The definitions should cover new types of non-cash payment instruments which allow for transfers of electronic money and virtual currencies. The definition of non-cash payment instruments should acknowledge that a non-cash payment instrument may consist of different elements acting together, for example a mobile payment application and a corresponding authorisation (e.g. a password). Where this Directive uses the concept of a non-cash payment instrument, it should be understood that the instrument puts the holder or user of the instrument in a position to actually enable a transfer of money or monetary value or to initiate a payment order. For example, unlawfully obtaining a mobile payment application without the necessary authorisation should not be considered as an unlawful obtainment of a non-cash payment instrument as it does not actually enable the user to transfer money or monetary value.

(9) This Directive should apply to non-cash payment instruments only insofar as the instrument's payment function is concerned.

(10) This Directive should cover virtual currencies only insofar as they can be commonly used for making payments. The Member States should be encouraged to ensure in their national law that future currencies of a virtual nature issued by their central banks or other public authorities will enjoy

the same level of protection against fraudulent offences as non-cash means of payment in general. Digital wallets that allow the transfer of virtual currencies should be covered by this Directive to the same extent as non-cash payment instruments. The definition of the term 'digital means of exchange' should acknowledge that digital wallets for transferring virtual currencies may provide, but do not necessarily provide, the features of a payment instrument and should not extend the definition of a payment instrument.

(11) Sending fake invoices to obtain payment credentials should be considered as an attempt at unlawful appropriation within the scope of this Directive.

(12) By using criminal law to give legal protection primarily to payment instruments that make use of special forms of protection against imitation or abuse, the intention is to encourage operators to provide such special forms of protection to payment instruments issued by them.

(13) Effective and efficient criminal law measures are essential to protect non-cash means of payment against fraud and counterfeiting. In particular, a common criminal law approach is needed as regards the constituent elements of criminal conduct that contribute to or prepare the way for the actual fraudulent use of a non-cash means of payment. Conduct such as the collection and possession of payment instruments with the intention to commit fraud, through, for instance, phishing, skimming or directing or redirecting payment service users to imitation websites, and their distribution, for example by selling credit card information on the internet, should thus be made a criminal offence in its own right without requiring the actual fraudulent use of a non-cash means of payment. Such criminal conduct should therefore cover circumstances where possession, procurement or distribution does not necessarily lead to fraudulent use of such payment instruments. However, where this Directive criminalises possession or holding, it should not criminalise mere omission. This Directive should not sanction the legitimate use of a payment instrument, including and in relation to the provision of innovative payment services, such as services commonly developed by fintech companies.

(14) With regard to the criminal offences referred to in this Directive, the concept of intent applies to all elements constituting those criminal offences in accordance with national law. It is possible for the intentional nature of an act, as well as any knowledge or purpose required as an element of an offence, to be inferred from objective, factual circumstances. Criminal offences which do not require intent should not be covered by this Directive.

(15) This Directive refers to classical forms of conduct, like fraud, forgery, theft and unlawful appropriation that had already been shaped by national law before the era of digitalisation. The extended scope of this Directive with regard to non-corporeal payment instruments therefore requires the definition of equivalent forms of conduct in the digital sphere, complementing and reinforcing Directive 2013/40/EU of the European Parliament and of

the Council. The unlawful obtainment of a non-corporeal non-cash payment instrument should be a criminal offence, at least when it involves the commission of one of the offences referred to in Articles 3 to 6 of Directive 2013/40/EU or the misappropriation of a non-corporeal non-cash payment instrument. 'Misappropriation' should be understood to mean the action of a person entrusted with a non-corporeal non-cash payment instrument, to knowingly use the instrument without the right to do so, to his own benefit or to the benefit of another. The procurement for fraudulent use of such an unlawfully obtained instrument should be punishable without it being necessary to establish all the factual elements of the unlawful obtainment and without requiring a prior or simultaneous conviction for the predicate offence which led to the unlawful obtainment.

(16) This Directive also refers to tools which can be used in order to commit the offences referred to in it. Given the need to avoid criminalisation where such tools are produced and placed on the market for legitimate purposes and, though they could be used to commit criminal offences, are therefore not in themselves a threat, criminalisation should be limited to those tools which are primarily designed or specifically adapted for the purpose of committing the offences referred to in this Directive.

(17) The sanctions and penalties for fraud and counterfeiting of non-cash means of payment should be effective, proportionate and dissuasive throughout the Union. This Directive is without prejudice to the individualisation and application of penalties and execution of sentences in accordance with the circumstances of the case and the general rules of national criminal law.

(18) As this Directive provides for minimum rules, Member States are free to adopt or maintain more stringent criminal law rules with regard to fraud and counterfeiting of non-cash means of payment, including a broader definition of offences.

(19) It is appropriate to provide for more severe penalties where a crime is committed in the framework of a criminal organisation, as defined in Council Framework Decision 2008/841/JHA. Member States should not be obliged to provide for specific aggravating circumstances where national law provides for separate criminal offences and this may lead to more severe sanctions. When an offence referred to in this Directive has been committed in conjunction with another offence referred to in this Directive by the same person, and one of those offences de facto constitutes a necessary element of the other, a Member State may, in accordance with general principles of national law, provide that such conduct is regarded as an aggravating circumstance to the main offence.

(20) Jurisdictional rules should ensure that the offences referred to in this Directive are prosecuted effectively. In general, offences are best dealt with by the criminal justice system of the country in which they occur. Each Member State should therefore establish jurisdiction over offences committed on its territory and over offences committed by its nationals. Member

States may also establish jurisdiction over offences that cause damage in their territory. They are strongly encouraged to do so.

(21) Recalling the obligations under Council Framework Decision 2009/948/JHA and Council Decision 2002/187/JHA, competent authorities are encouraged in cases of conflicts of jurisdiction to use the possibility of conducting direct consultations with the assistance of the European Union Agency for Criminal Justice Cooperation (Eurojust).

(22) Given the need for special tools to effectively investigate fraud and counterfeiting of non-cash means of payment, and their relevance to effective international cooperation between national authorities, investigative tools that are typically used for cases involving organised crime or other serious crime should be available to competent authorities in all Member States, if and to the extent that the use of those tools is appropriate and commensurate with the nature and gravity of the offences as defined in national law. In addition, law enforcement authorities and other competent authorities should have timely access to relevant information in order to investigate and prosecute the offences referred to in this Directive. Member States are encouraged to allocate adequate human and financial resources to the competent authorities in order to properly investigate and prosecute the offences referred to in this Directive.

(23) National authorities investigating or prosecuting offences referred to in this Directive should be empowered to cooperate with other national authorities within the same Member State and their counterparts in other Member States.

(24) In many cases, criminal activities are behind incidents that should be notified to the relevant national competent authorities under Directive (EU) 2016/1148 of the European Parliament and of the Council. Such incidents may be suspected to be of a criminal nature even if there is insufficient evidence of a criminal offence at that stage. In such a context, relevant operators of essential services and digital service providers should be encouraged to share the reports required under Directive (EU) 2016/1148 with law enforcement authorities so as to form an effective and comprehensive response and to facilitate attribution and accountability by the perpetrators for their actions. In particular, promoting a safe, secure and more resilient environment requires systematic reporting of incidents of a suspected serious criminal nature to law enforcement authorities. Moreover, when relevant, computer security incident response teams designated under Directive (EU) 2016/1148 should be involved in law enforcement investigations with a view to providing information, as considered appropriate at national level, and also to providing specialist expertise on information systems.

(25) Major security incidents as referred to in Directive (EU) 2015/2366 of the European Parliament and of the Council may be of criminal origin. Where relevant, payment service providers should be encouraged to share with law enforcement authorities the reports they are required to submit to the

competent authority in their home Member State under Directive (EU) 2015/2366.

(26) A number of instruments and mechanisms exist at Union level to enable the exchange of information among national law enforcement authorities for the purposes of investigating and prosecuting crimes. To facilitate and speed up cooperation among national law enforcement authorities and make sure that those instruments and mechanisms are used to the fullest extent, this Directive should strengthen the importance of the operational points of contact introduced by Framework Decision 2001/413/JHA. It should be possible for Member States to decide to make use of the existing networks of operational points of contact, such as the one set up in Directive 2013/40/EU. The points of contact should provide effective assistance, for example by facilitating the exchange of relevant information and the provision of technical advice or legal information. To ensure the network runs smoothly, each point of contact should be able to communicate quickly with the point of contact in another Member State. Given the significant trans-border dimension of crimes covered by this Directive and in particular the volatile nature of electronic evidence, Member States should be able to deal promptly with urgent requests from the network and provide feedback within eight hours. In very urgent and serious cases, Member States should inform the European Union Agency for Law Enforcement Cooperation (Europol).

(27) Reporting crime to public authorities without undue delay is of great importance in combating fraud and counterfeiting of non-cash means of payment, as it is often the starting point of criminal investigations. Measures should be taken to encourage reporting by natural and legal persons, in particular financial institutions, to law enforcement and judicial authorities. Those measures can be based on various types of action, including legislative acts containing obligations to report suspected fraud, or non-legislative actions, such as setting up or supporting organisations or mechanisms favouring the exchange of information, or awareness raising. Any such measure that involves processing of the personal data of natural persons should be carried out in accordance with Regulation (EU) 2016/679 of the European Parliament and of the Council. In particular, any transmission of information for the purposes of preventing and combating offences relating to fraud and counterfeiting of non-cash means of payment should comply with the requirements laid down in that Regulation, notably the lawful grounds for processing.

(28) In order to facilitate the prompt and direct reporting of crime, the Commission should carefully assess the establishment of effective online fraud-reporting systems by Member States and standardised reporting templates at Union level. Such systems could facilitate the reporting of non-cash fraud which often takes place online, thereby strengthening support for victims, the identification and analysis of cybercrime threats and the work and cross-border cooperation of national competent authorities.

(29) The offences referred to in this Directive often have a cross-border nature. Therefore, combating these offences relies on close cooperation between the Member States. Member States are encouraged to ensure, to the extent appropriate, effective application of mutual recognition and legal assistance instruments in relation to the offences covered by this Directive.

(30) Investigation and prosecution of all types of fraud and counterfeiting of non-cash means of payment, including those involving small amounts of money, are particularly important in order to combat them effectively. Reporting obligations, information exchange and statistical reports are efficient ways to detect fraudulent activities, especially similar activities that involve small amounts of money when considered separately.

(31) Fraud and counterfeiting of non-cash means of payment can result in serious economic and non-economic consequences for its victims. Where such fraud involves, for example, identity theft, its consequences are often aggravated because of reputational and professional damage, damage to an individual's credit rating and serious emotional harm. Member States should adopt assistance, support and protection measures aimed to mitigate those consequences.

(32) Often a considerable amount of time can pass before victims find out that they have suffered a loss from fraud and counterfeiting offences. During that time a spiral of interlinked crimes might develop, thereby aggravating the negative consequences for the victims.

(33) Natural persons who are victims of fraud related to non-cash means of payment have rights conferred under Directive 2012/29/EU of the European Parliament and of the Council ([11]). Member States should adopt measures of assistance and support to such victims which build on the measures required by that Directive but respond more directly to the specific needs of victims of fraud related to identity theft. Such measures should include, in particular, the provision of a list of dedicated institutions covering different aspects of identity-related crime and victim support, specialised psychological support and advice on financial, practical and legal matters, as well as assistance in receiving available compensation. Member States should be encouraged to set up a single national online information tool to facilitate access to assistance and support for victims. Specific information and advice on protection against the negative consequences of such crime should be offered to legal persons as well.

(34) This Directive should provide for the right for legal persons to access information in accordance with national law about the procedures for making complaints. This right is necessary in particular for small and medium-sized enterprises and should contribute to creating a friendlier business environment for small and medium-sized enterprises. Natural persons already benefit from this right under Directive 2012/29/EU.

(35) Member States should, with the assistance of the Commission, establish or strengthen policies to prevent fraud and counterfeiting of non-cash means of payment and measures to reduce the risk of such offences occurring by

means of information and awareness-raising campaigns. In this context, Member States could develop and keep up to date a permanent online awareness-raising tool with practical examples of fraudulent practices, in a format that is easy to understand. That tool could be linked to or be part of the single national online information tool for victims. Member States could also put in place research and education programmes. Special attention should be paid to the needs and interests of vulnerable persons. Member States are encouraged to ensure that sufficient funding is made available for such campaigns.

(36) It is necessary to collect statistical data on fraud and counterfeiting of non-cash payment instruments. Member States should therefore be obliged to ensure that an adequate system is in place for the recording, production and provision of existing statistical data on the offences referred to in this Directive.

(37) This Directive aims to amend and expand the provisions of Framework Decision 2001/413/JHA. Since the amendments to be made are substantial in number and nature, Framework Decision 2001/413/JHA should, in the interests of clarity, be replaced in its entirety for the Member States bound by this Directive.

(38) In accordance with Articles 1 and 2 of Protocol No 21 on the position of the United Kingdom and Ireland in respect of the area of freedom, security and justice, annexed to the Treaty on European Union (TEU) and to the Treaty on the Functioning of the European Union (TFEU), and without prejudice to Article 4 of that Protocol, those Member States are not taking part in the adoption of this Directive and are not bound by it or subject to its application.

(39) In accordance with Articles 1 and 2 of Protocol No 22 on the position of Denmark annexed to TEU and to TFEU, Denmark is not taking part in the adoption of this Directive and is not bound by it or subject to its application.

(40) Since the objectives of this Directive, namely to subject fraud and counterfeiting of non-cash means of payment to effective, proportionate and dissuasive criminal penalties and to improve and encourage cross-border cooperation both between competent authorities and between natural and legal persons and competent authorities, cannot be sufficiently achieved by the Member States, but can rather, by reason of their scale or effects, be better achieved at Union level, the Union may adopt measures in accordance with the principle of subsidiarity as set out in Article 5 TEU. In accordance with the principle of proportionality as set out in that Article, this Directive does not go beyond what is necessary in order to achieve those objectives.

(41) This Directive respects fundamental rights and observes the principles recognised in particular by the Charter of Fundamental Rights of the European Union, including the right to liberty and security, the respect for private and family life, the protection of personal data, the freedom to conduct a business, the right to property, the right to an effective remedy

and to a fair trial, the presumption of innocence and right of defence, the principles of the legality and proportionality of criminal offences and penalties, as well as the right not to be tried or punished twice in criminal proceedings for the same criminal offence. This Directive seeks to ensure full respect for those rights and principles and should be implemented accordingly,

HAVE ADOPTED THIS DIRECTIVE:

TITLE I

SUBJECT MATTER AND DEFINITIONS

Article 1

Subject matter

This Directive establishes minimum rules concerning the definition of criminal offences and sanctions in the areas of fraud and counterfeiting of non-cash means of payment. It facilitates the prevention of such offences, and the provision of assistance to and support for victims.

Article 2

Definitions

For the purpose of this Directive, the following definitions apply:

(a) 'non-cash payment instrument' means a non-corporeal or corporeal protected device, object or record, or a combination thereof, other than legal tender, and which, alone or in conjunction with a procedure or a set of procedures, enables the holder or user to transfer money or monetary value, including through digital means of exchange;
(b) 'protected device, object or record' means a device, object or record safeguarded against imitation or fraudulent use, for example through design, coding or signature;
(c) 'digital means of exchange' means any electronic money as defined in point (2) of Article 2 of Directive 2009/110/EC of the European Parliament and of the Council ([12]) or virtual currency;
(d) 'virtual currency' means a digital representation of value that is not issued or guaranteed by a central bank or a public authority, is not necessarily attached to a legally established currency and does not possess a legal status of a currency or money, but is accepted by natural or legal persons as a means of exchange, and which can be transferred, stored and traded electronically;
(e) 'information system' means information system as defined in point (a) of Article 2 of Directive 2013/40/EU;
(f) 'computer data' means computer data as defined in point (b) of Article 2 of Directive 2013/40/EU;

(g) 'legal person' means an entity having legal personality under the applicable law, except for states or public bodies in the exercise of state authority and for public international organisations.

TITLE II
OFFENCES

Article 3
Fraudulent use of non-cash payment instruments

Member States shall take the necessary measures to ensure that, when committed intentionally, the following conduct is punishable as a criminal offence:

(a) the fraudulent use of a stolen or otherwise unlawfully appropriated or obtained non-cash payment instrument;
(b) the fraudulent use of a counterfeit or falsified non-cash payment instrument.

Article 4
Offences related to the fraudulent use of corporeal non-cash payment instruments

Member States shall take the necessary measures to ensure that, when committed intentionally, the following conduct is punishable as a criminal offence:

(a) the theft or other unlawful appropriation of a corporeal non-cash payment instrument;
(b) the fraudulent counterfeiting or falsification of a corporeal non-cash payment instrument;
(c) the possession of a stolen or otherwise unlawfully appropriated, or of a counterfeit or falsified corporeal non-cash payment instrument for fraudulent use;
(d) the procurement for oneself or another, including the receipt, appropriation, purchase, transfer, import, export, sale, transport or distribution of a stolen, counterfeit or falsified corporeal non-cash payment instrument for fraudulent use.

Article 5
Offences related to the fraudulent use of non-corporeal non-cash payment instruments

Member States shall take the necessary measures to ensure that, when committed intentionally, the following conduct is punishable as a criminal offence:

(a) the unlawful obtainment of a non-corporeal non-cash payment instrument, at least when this obtainment has involved the commission of one of the offences referred to in Articles 3 to 6 of Directive 2013/40/EU, or misappropriation of a non-corporeal non-cash payment instrument;
(b) the fraudulent counterfeiting or falsification of a non-corporeal non-cash payment instrument;
(c) the holding of an unlawfully obtained, counterfeit or falsified non-corporeal non-cash payment instrument for fraudulent use, at least if the unlawful origin is known at the time of the holding of the instrument;
(d) the procurement for oneself or another, including the sale, transfer or distribution, or the making available, of an unlawfully obtained, counterfeit or falsified non-corporeal non-cash payment instrument for fraudulent use.

Article 6

Fraud related to information systems

Member States shall take the necessary measures to ensure that performing or causing a transfer of money, monetary value or virtual currency and thereby causing an unlawful loss of property for another person in order to make an unlawful gain for the perpetrator or a third party is punishable as a criminal offence, when committed intentionally by:

(a) without right, hindering or interfering with the functioning of an information system;
(b) without right, introducing, altering, deleting, transmitting or suppressing computer data.

Article 7

Tools used for committing offences

Member States shall take the necessary measures to ensure that producing, procurement for oneself or another, including the import, export, sale, transport or distribution, or making available a device or an instrument, computer data or any other means primarily designed or specifically adapted for the purpose of committing any of the offences referred to in points (a) and (b) of Article 4, in points (a) and (b) of Article 5 or in Article 6, at least when committed with the intention that these means be used, is punishable as a criminal offence.

Article 8

Incitement, aiding and abetting and attempt

1. Member States shall take the necessary measures to ensure that inciting or aiding and abetting an offence referred to in Articles 3 to 7 is punishable as a criminal offence.
2. Member States shall take the necessary measures to ensure that an attempt to commit an offence referred to in Article 3, in point (a), (b) or (d) of Article 4, in point (a) or (b) of Article 5 or in Article 6 is punishable as a criminal offence. With regard to point (d) of Article 5, Member States shall take the necessary measures to ensure that at least the attempted fraudulent procurement of an unlawfully obtained, counterfeit or falsified non-corporeal non-cash payment instrument for oneself or another is punishable as a criminal offence.

Article 9

Penalties for natural persons

1. Member States shall take the necessary measures to ensure that the offences referred to in Articles 3 to 8 are punishable by effective, proportionate and dissuasive criminal penalties.
2. Member States shall take the necessary measures to ensure that the offences referred to in Article 3, in points (a) and (b) of Article 4 and in points(a) and (b) of Article 5 are punishable by a maximum term of imprisonment of at least two years.
3. Member States shall take the necessary measures to ensure that the offences referred to in points (c) and (d) of Article 4 and in points (c) and (d) of Article 5 are punishable by a maximum term of imprisonment of at least one year.
4. Member States shall take the necessary measures to ensure that the offence referred to in Article 6 is punishable by a maximum term of imprisonment of at least three years.
5. Member States shall take the necessary measures to ensure that the offence referred to in Article 7 is punishable by a maximum term of imprisonment of at least two years.
6. Member States shall take the necessary measures to ensure that the offences referred to in Articles 3 to 6 are punishable by a maximum term of imprisonment of at least five years if they are committed within the framework of a criminal organisation, as defined in Framework Decision 2008/841/JHA, irrespective of the penalty provided for in that Decision.

Article 10
Liability of legal persons

1. Member States shall take the necessary measures to ensure that legal persons can be held liable for offences referred to in Articles 3 to 8 committed for their benefit by any person, acting either individually or as part of an organ of the legal person, and having a leading position within the legal person, based on one of the following:
   (a) a power of representation of the legal person;
   (b) an authority to take decisions on behalf of the legal person;
   (c) an authority to exercise control within the legal person.
2. Member States shall take the necessary measures to ensure that legal persons can be held liable where the lack of supervision or control by a person referred to in paragraph 1 has made possible the commission of any of the offences referred to in Articles 3 to 8 for the benefit of the legal person by a person under its authority.
3. Liability of legal persons pursuant to paragraphs 1 and 2 shall not exclude criminal proceedings against natural persons who are perpetrators or inciters of, or accessories to, any of the offences referred to in Articles 3 to 8.

Article 11
Sanctions for legal persons

Member States shall take the necessary measures to ensure that a legal person held liable pursuant to Article 10(1) or (2) is subject to effective, proportionate and dissuasive sanctions, which shall include criminal or non-criminal fines and which may include other sanctions, such as:

(a) exclusion from entitlement to public benefits or aid;
(b) temporary exclusion from access to public funding, including tender procedures, grants and concessions;
(c) temporary or permanent disqualification from the practice of commercial activities;
(d) placing under judicial supervision;
(e) judicial winding-up;
(f) temporary or permanent closure of establishments which have been used for committing the offence.

TITLE III

JURISDICTION AND INVESTIGATION

Article 12

Jurisdiction

1. Each Member State shall take the necessary measures to establish its jurisdiction over the offences referred to in Articles 3 to 8 where one or more of the following apply:
   (a) the offence is committed in whole or in part on its territory;
   (b) the offender is one of its nationals.
2. For the purposes of point (a) of paragraph 1, an offence shall be considered to have been committed in whole or in part on the territory of a Member State where the offender commits the offence when physically present on that territory and irrespective of whether the offence is committed using an information system on that territory.
3. A Member State shall inform the Commission where it decides to establish jurisdiction over an offence referred to in Articles 3 to 8 committed outside its territory, including where:
   (a) the offender has his or her habitual residence in its territory;
   (b) the offence is committed for the benefit of a legal person established in its territory;
   (c) the offence is committed against one of its nationals or a person who is a habitual resident in its territory.

Article 13

Effective investigations and cooperation

1. Member States shall take the necessary measures to ensure that investigative tools, such as those which are used in countering organised crime or in other serious crime cases, are effective, proportionate to the crime committed and available to the persons, units or services responsible for investigating or prosecuting the offences referred to in Articles 3 to 8.
2. Member States shall take the necessary measures to ensure that, where national law obliges natural and legal persons to submit information regarding offences referred to in Articles 3 to 8, such information reaches the authorities investigating or prosecuting those offences without undue delay.

TITLE IV

EXCHANGE OF INFORMATION AND REPORTING OF CRIME

Article 14

Exchange of information

1. For the purpose of exchanging information relating to the offences referred to in Articles 3 to 8, Member States shall ensure that they have an operational national point of contact available 24 hours a day, seven days a week. Member States shall also ensure that they have procedures in place so that urgent requests for assistance are promptly dealt with and the competent authority replies within eight hours of receipt, by at least indicating whether the request will be answered and the form of such an answer and the estimated time within which it will be sent. Member States may decide to make use of the existing networks of operational points of contact.
2. Member States shall inform the Commission, Europol and Eurojust of their appointed point of contact referred to in paragraph 1. They shall update that information as necessary. The Commission shall forward that information to the other Member States.

Article 15

Reporting of crime

1. Member States shall take the necessary measures to ensure that appropriate reporting channels are made available in order to facilitate reporting of the offences referred to in Articles 3 to 8 to law enforcement authorities and other competent national authorities without undue delay.
2. Member States shall take the necessary measures to encourage financial institutions and other legal persons operating in their territory to report suspected fraud to law enforcement authorities and other competent authorities without undue delay, for the purpose of detecting, preventing, investigating or prosecuting offences referred to in Articles 3 to 8.

Article 16

Assistance and support to victims

1. Member States shall ensure that natural and legal persons who have suffered harm as a result of any of the offences referred to in Articles 3 to 8 being committed by misusing personal data, are:

(a) offered specific information and advice on how to protect themselves against the negative consequences of the offences, such as reputational damage; and
(b) provided with a list of dedicated institutions that deal with different aspects of identity-related crime and victim support.

2. Member States are encouraged to set up single national online information tools to facilitate access to assistance and support for natural or legal persons who have suffered harm as a result of the offences referred to in Articles 3 to 8 being committed by misusing personal data.
3. Member States shall ensure that legal persons that are victims of the offences referred to in Articles 3 to 8 of this Directive are offered the following information without undue delay after their first contact with a competent authority:
   (a) the procedures for making complaints with regard to the offence and the victim's role in such procedures;
   (b) the right to receive information about the case in accordance with national law;
   (c) the available procedures for making complaints if the competent authority does not respect the victim's rights in the course of criminal proceedings;
   (d) the contact details for communications about their case.

Article 17

Prevention

Member States shall take appropriate action, including through the internet, such as information and awareness-raising campaigns and research and education programmes, aimed to reduce overall fraud, raise awareness and reduce the risk of becoming a victim of fraud. Where appropriate, Member States shall act in cooperation with stakeholders.

Article 18

Monitoring and statistics

1. By 31 August 2019, the Commission shall establish a detailed programme for monitoring the outputs, results and impacts of this Directive. The monitoring programme shall set out the means by which and the intervals at which the necessary data and other evidence will be collected. It shall specify the action to be taken by the Commission and by the Member States in collecting, sharing and analysing the data and other evidence.
2. Member States shall ensure that a system is in place for the recording, production and provision of anonymised statistical data measuring the

reporting, investigative and judicial phases involving the offences referred to in Articles 3 to 8.

3. The statistical data referred to in paragraph 2 shall, as a minimum, cover existing data on the number of offences referred to in Articles 3 to 8 registered by the Member States and on the number of persons prosecuted for and convicted of the offences referred to in Articles 3 to 7.
4. Member States shall transmit the data collected pursuant to paragraphs 1, 2 and 3 to the Commission on an annual basis. The Commission shall ensure that a consolidated review of the statistical reports is published each year and submitted to the competent specialised Union agencies and bodies.

Article 19

Replacement of Framework Decision 2001/413/JHA

Framework Decision 2001/413/JHA is replaced with regard to the Member States bound by this Directive, without prejudice to the obligations of those Member States with regard to the date for transposition of that Framework Decision into national law. With regard to Member States bound by this Directive, references to Framework Decision 2001/413/JHA shall be construed as references to this Directive.

Article 20

Transposition

1. Member States shall bring into force the laws, regulations and administrative provisions necessary to comply with this Directive by 31 May 2021. They shall immediately inform the Commission thereof.

   When Member States adopt those measures, they shall contain a reference to this Directive or shall be accompanied by such a reference on the occasion of their official publication. The methods of making such reference shall be laid down by Member States.
2. Member States shall communicate to the Commission the text of the measures of national law which they adopt in the field covered by this Directive.

Article 21

Evaluation and reporting

1. The Commission shall, by 31 May 2023, submit a report to the European Parliament and to the Council, assessing the extent to which the Member States have taken the necessary measures to comply with this Directive.

Member States shall provide the Commission with the necessary information for the preparation of that report.

2. The Commission shall, by 31 May 2026, carry out an evaluation of the impact of this Directive on combating fraud and counterfeiting of non-cash means of payment, as well as on fundamental rights, and submit a report to the European Parliament and to the Council. Member States shall provide the Commission with necessary information for the preparation of that report.
3. In the context of the evaluation referred to in paragraph 2 of this Article, the Commission shall also report on the necessity, feasibility and effectiveness of creating national secure online systems to allow victims to report any of the offences referred to in Articles 3 to 8, as well as of establishing a standardised Union reporting template to serve as a basis for Member States.

Article 22
Entry into force

This Directive shall enter into force on the twentieth day following that of its publication in the *Official Journal of the European Union*.
This Directive is addressed to the Member States in accordance with the Treaties.
Done at Strasbourg, 17 April 2019.

Bibliography

Ablon, L. et al. *Markets for Cybercrime Tools and Stolen Data*, Hacker's Bazaar, RAND Corporation's National Security Research Division (2014), at: http://www.rand.org/content/dam/rand/pubs/research_reports/RR600/RR610/RAND_RR610.pdf.

ACPO. *ACPO Good Practice Guide for Digital Evidence* (2011), at: http://www.acpo.police.uk/documents/crime/2011/201110-cba-digital-evidence-v5.pdf.

Amadei, X. *Standards of Liability of Internet Service Providers: A Comparative Analysis of France and the United States with a Specific Focus on Copyright, Defamation and Illicit Content*, 35 Cornell Int'l L.J. 189 (2002).

Angers, L. *Combating Cybercrime: National Legislation as a Prerequisite for International Cooperation*, in *Crime and Technology, New Frontiers for Regulation, Law enforcement and Research* (Ernesto Ugo Savona (ed.), Springer 2004).

Article 29 Data Protection Working Party. *Working Document 01/2011 on the Current EU Personal Data Breach Framework and Recommendations for Future Policy Developments* (WP 168, 2011).

Article 29 Working Group. *Opinion 04/2014 on Surveillance of Electronic Communications for Intelligence and National Security Purposes*. WP 215 (10 April 2014).

Article 29 Working Party. *Opinion 05/2012 on Cloud Computing* (2012).

Article 29 Working Party. *Opinion 1/2008 on Data Protection Issues Related to Search Engines*, WP 148, available at: http://ec.europa.eu/justice/policies/privacy/docs/wpdocs/2008/wp148_en.pdf (April 4, 2008).

Article 29 Working Party. *Opinion 1/2009 on the Proposals Amending Directive 2002/58/EC on Privacy and Electronic Communications*, available at: http://ec.europa.eu/justice_home/fsj/privacy/docs/wpdocs/2009/wp159_en.pdf.

Article 29 Working Party. *Opinion 4/2007 on the Concept of Personal Data*. WP 136, June 20, 2007, available at: http://ec.europa.eu/justice/policies/privacy/docs/wpdocs/2007/wp136_en.pdf.

Ashworth, A. *Sentencing and Criminal Justice* (Cambridge University Press 2010).

Balboni, P. *Data Protection and Data Security Issues Related to Cloud Computing in the EU*, TILBURG University legal Studies Working Paper series, accessible at http://ssrn.com/abstract=1661437 (2010).

Barnett, E.R. *Back to the Future: Criminal Organizations Exploit Another New Technology, Crypto-Currencies* (2014), at: http://www.observatoire-fic.com/back-to-the-future-criminal-organizations-exploit-another-new-technology-crypto-currencies/#sthash.mwHSqIL4.dpuf.

Bellovin, S. *The Insider Attack Problem Nature and Scope*, in *Insider Attack and Cyber Security: Beyond the Hacker* (Salvatore J. Stolfo, Steven M. Bellovin, Shlomo Hershkop, Angelos D. Keromytis, Sara Sinclair, Sean Smith (eds), Springer, 2008).

Bisogni, F. *Evaluating Data Breach Notification Laws. What Do the Numbers Tell Us?* 2015 TPRC | 43rd Research Conference on Communications (Information and Internet Policy, George Mason University School of Law, 2015).

Blackwell, C. *An Investigative Framework for Incident Analysis.* In *Advances in Digital Forensics* (G. Peterson & S. Shenoi (eds), Springer 2011).

Bonner, L. *Cyber Risk: How the 2011 Sony Data Breach and the Need for Cyber Risk Insurance Policies Should Direct the Federal Response to Rising Data Breaches*, 40 Wash. U. J. L. & Pol'y (2012).

Boubekeur, I. *De la "loi HADOPI" à la "loi HADOPI 2"*, Revue Lamy Droit de l'Immatériel, n°51 (2009).

Breindl, Y. & Wright J. *Internet Filtering Trends in Western Liberal Democracies: French and German Regulatory Debates* (August 15, 2012), at: https://www.usenix.org/system/files/conference/foci12/breindl2012foci.pdf.

Brenner, S. *Cybercrime: Re-thinking Crime Control Strategies*, in *Crimes Online*, 25 (Yvonne Jewkes (ed.), Willan Publishing 2007).

Brenner, S.W. & Koops, B.-J. *Approaches to Cyber Crime Jurisdiction.* 15(1) J. High Technology Crime (2004).

Broadway, J. Turnbull, B. & Slay, J. *Improving the Analysis of Lawfully Intercepted Network Packet Data Captured for Forensic Analysis.* In The Third International Conference on Availability, Reliability and Security (2008).

Brown, C.S.D. *Investigating and Prosecuting Cyber Crime: Forensic Dependencies and Barriers to Justice.* 9(1) Intrl. J. Cyber Criminology 83 (January–June 2015).

Brownsword, R. & Goodwin, M. *Law and the Technologies of the Twenty-First Century*, 225–245 (Cambridge University Press 2012).

Burdon, M., Lane, B. & von Nessen, P. *Data Breach Notification Law in the EU and Australia – Where to Now?*, 28(3) Computer Law & Security Rev. 296 (2012).

Burdon, M., Low, R. & Reid, J. *If its Encrypted its Secure! The Viability of US State-Based Encryption Exemptions*, Paper presented at the IEEE International Symposium on Technology and Society, University of Wollongong, (Jun. 7–9, 2010).

Burdon, M., et al. 'Australian Data Breach Notification: Avoiding the State/Federal Overlap.' (Paper presented at the 5th International Conference on Legal, Security and Privacy Issues in IT Law, Barcelona, 2010).

Cahen, M. *L'adresse IP est-elle une donnée personnelle?*, available at: http://www.net-iris.fr/blog-juridique/13-murielle-cahen/20455/adresse-ip-est-elle-une-donnee-personnelle (2015).

Callanan, C. & Gerke, M. *Cooperation between Law Enforcement and Internet Service Providers against Cybercrime: Towards Common Guidelines*, Council of Europe, Project on Cybercrime, 16–17 (Mar. 17, 2008).

Callanan, C. et al. *Internet Blocking, Balancing Cybercrime Responses in Democratic Societies*, Open Society Institute funding Study (2009).

Caprioli, É. *Données à caractère personnel et sécurité de l'information*, Communication Commerce Electronique, 46–47 (July 2015).

Capriolli, A. *Absence d'intention de nuire et requête automatisée et répétitive*, Communication Commerce électronique n° 11, comm. 109 (November 2011).

Cardenas, A. et al. An Economic Map of Cybercrime, working paper (2009), available at: http://chess.eecs.berkeley.edu/pubs/772/cardenas_2009.pdf.

Carrier, B.D. Risks of Live Digital Forensic Analysis. *Communications of the ACM*, 49(2), 56 et seq (2006). *See also* ENISA, *Electronic Evidence – A Basic Guide for First Responders* that recommends that documentation and explanation of gathering steps and actions taken gains in importance (p. 7).

Casey, E. *Error, Uncertainty, and Loss in Digital Evidence*, 1(2) Intrl. J. Digital Evidence (2002).

Casey, E. *Digital Evidence and Computer Crime: Forensic Science, Computers and the Internet* (Elsevier 2011).

Castets-Renard, C. *Droit de l'Internet: Droit français et européen* (Montchrestien, Lextenso editions, 2012).

Castets-Renard, C. *Protection du droit d'auteur confrontée aux droits fondamentaux: point trop n'en faut !*. Revue Lamy Droit de l'Immatériel, n°79, 9 (2013).

Cheron, A. *Loi sur le renseignement: du respect des grands principes du droit à la surveillance de masse sur Internet*, at: http://www.village-justice.com/articles/Loi-sur-renseignement-respect-des,19863.html (June 15, 2015).

Christin, N. *Traveling the Silk Road: A Measurement Analysis of a Large Anonymous Online Marketplace*, Carnegie Mellon University CyLab Report 12-018 (July 30, 2012, revised November 28, 2012).

Clarke, Z., Clawson, J. & Cordell, M. *A Brief History of Hacking* (November 2003), available at: http://steel.lcc.gatech.edu/~mcordell/lcc6316/Hacker%20Group%20Project%20FINAL.pdf.

Clough, J. *The Council of Europe Convention on Cybercrime: Defining 'Crime' in a Digital World*, 23 Criminal Law Forum 375 (2012).

Commission Report to the Council on Article 12 of the Council Framework Decision of 24 February 2005 on attacks against information systems (COM(2008) 448 final).

Commission Staff Working document. *A Digital Single Market Strategy for Europe, – Analysis and Evidence*, Brussels, 6.5.2015, SWD 100 final, 55–56 (2015), available at: http://ec.europa.eu/priorities/digital-single-market/docs/dsm-swd_en.pdf.

Communication of March 31, 2011 from the Commission to the European Parliament, the Council, the European Economic and Social Committee and the Committee of the Regions on Critical Information Infrastructure Protection 'Achievements and next steps: towards global cyber-security' (COM(2011) 163 final).

Communication to the European Parliament, the Council, the Economic and Social Committee and the Committee of Regions. *Illegal and Harmful Content on the Internet*, COM(96) 487 (Brussels, October 16, 1996).

Council of Europe, Cybercrime Convention Committee (T-CY). *Assessment Report Implementation of the Preservation Provisions of the Budapest Convention on Cybercrime*, T-CY (2012) 10 REV, Strasbourg, 50 (January 25, 2013).

Council of Europe. *Problems of Criminal Procedural Law Connected with Information Technology*. Recommendation No. R(95)13 and Explanatory Memorandum, Legal Issues, (1998).

Council of Europe, Rec CM/Rec(2011)8 of the Committee of Ministers to Member States on the *Protection and Promotion of the Universality, Integrity and Openness of the Internet*, General Principle 1.1.1 (September 21, 2011).

Cybercrime Convention Committee (T-CY). Ad-hoc-group on Jurisdiction and Transborder Access to Data, *Transborder access and jurisdiction: What are the options?*, Report adopted by T-CY, 9 (December 6, 2012).

Cybercrime Convention Committee. *Rules on Obtaining Subscriber Information*, Report adopted by the T-CY at its 12th Plenary (December 2–3, 2014), available at: http://www.coe.int/t/dghl/cooperation/economiccrime/Source/Cybercrime/TCY/2014/TCY%282014%2917_Report_Sub_Info_v7adopted.pdf.

CYBEX. *The Admissibility of Electronic Evidence in Court – Fighting against High-Tech Crime – Study*, available at: www.cybex.es (2006).

Dale, J. L., *Terrorism and Homeland Security: Perspectives, Thoughts, and Opinions*, 90 (CRC Press, Taylor and Francis Group, 2010).

Dittrich, D., Leder, F. & Werner, T. *A Case Study in Ethical Decision Making Regarding Remote Mitigation of Botnets, Financial Cryptography and Data Security*, IFCA/Springer-Verlarg Berlin Heidelberg, 216 (2010).

De Hert, P. & Bellanova, R. *Data Protection in the Area of Freedom, Security and Justice: A System Still To Be Fully Developed?*, Study requested by the European Parliament's Committee on Civil Liberties, Justice and Home Affairs (LIBE), Brussels, European Parliament, available at: http://www.europarl.europa.eu/activities/committees/studies/download.do?language = en&file = 25213 (2009).

De Hert, P. & Kloza, D. *Internet (access) as a New Fundamental Right. Inflating the Current Rights Framework?*, 3(3) Eur. J. Law & Tech. (2012).

De Herta, P. & Papakonstantinou, V. *The Data Protection Framework Decision of 27 November 2008 Regarding Police and Judicial Cooperation in Criminal Matters – A Modest Achievement However Not the Improvement Some Have Hoped for*, 25 Computer Law & Security Rev. 409 (2009).

De Lecomte F. & Lemaitre M.-H. *Inconnue juridique à cette adresse (IP), Ou les affres du débat autour de la qualification de donnée à caractère personnel de l'adresse IP*, Expertises, (May 2008).

Denning D.E. *Obstacles and Options for Cyber Arms Controls*, in *Arms Control in Cyberspace*, (Heinrich Böll Foundation, Berlin, Germany, June 29, 2001), available at: http://faculty.nps.edu/dedennin/publications/berlin.pdf.

Dix A. in: Bullesbach, Gijrath, Poullet, Prins, *Concise European IT Law* (2nd edn 2010).

Donovan, F. & Bernier K. *Cyber Crime Fighters: Tales from the Trenches* (Pearson Education 2009).

Edwards, L. *Dawn of the Death of Distributed Denial of Service: How to Kill Zombies*, 24 Cardozo Arts & Ent LJ 23 (2006).

ENISA. *Cloud Computing Benefits, Risks and Recommendations for Information Security*, 45 (2009).

ENISA. *Data Breach Notifications in the EU.* (2011), available at: https://www.enisa.europa.eu/activities/identity-and-trust/library/deliverables/dbn.

Esayas, S. *Breach Notification Requirements under the European Union Legal Framework: Convergence, Conflicts, and Complexity in Compliance*, 31 J. Marshall J. Info. Tech. & Privacy L 323 (2014).

European Commission – *Fact Sheet, Roaming Charges and Open Internet: Questions and Answers*, (June 30, 2015), at http://europa.eu/rapid/press-release_MEMO-15-5275_en.htm.

European Commission. *Cybersecurity Strategy of the European Union: An Open, Safe and Secure Cyberspace.* Joint Communication to the European Parliament, the Council, The European Economic and Social Committee and the Committee of the Regions (2013).

European Commission. *Evidence of Potential Impacts of Options for Revising the Data Retention Directive: Current approaches to data preservation in the EU and in third countries.* Center for Strategy & Evaluation Services, Final Report – Task 2, available at: http://ec.europa.eu/dgs/home-affairs/what-we-do/policies/police-cooperation/data-retention/docs/drd_task_2_report_final_en.pdf (November 2012).

Evers, J. *ISPs versus the Zombies*, Cnet News.com at http://news.cnet.com/ISPs-versus-the-zombies/2100-7349_3-5793719.html (Jul. 19, 2005).

FBI Intelligence Assessment. *Bitcoin Virtual Currency: Unique Features Present Distinct Challenges for Deterring Illicit Activity* (April 24, 2012), at: http://cryptome.org/2012/05/fbi-bitcoin.pdf.

Frayssinet, J. in: Lucas, Frayssinet, Deveze, *Droit de l'informatique et de l'Internet* (PUF 2001).

Frydman B. & Rorive, I. *Regulating Internet Content through Intermediaries in Europe and the USA*, Zeitschrift für Rechtssoziologie 23, Heft 1, S. 41-59 (2002), available at: http://www.philodroit.be/IMG/pdf/regulating_20Internet_20through_20intermediaries-2.pdf.

Gonzales, A.R., Schofield Regina, B. & Hagy David, W. *US. Department of Justice, Special Report on Investigations Involving the Internet and Computer Networks*, January 2007, at: https://www.ncjrs.gov/pdffiles1/nij/210798.pdf.

Garfinkel, S.L. & McCarrin, M. *Can We Sniff Wi-Fi?: Implications of Joffe v. Google, Security & Privacy*. IEEE, (2014).

Gaudin, S. *Case Study of Insider Sabotage: The Tim Lloyd/Omega Case*, Computer Security Journal, Volume XVI, Number 3, (2000), available at: http://www.craigchamberlain.com/library/insider/Case%20Study%20of%20Insider%20Sabotage.pdf.

Georgiades, E. et al. *Crisis on Impact: Responding to Cyber Attacks on Critical Information Infrastructures,* 30 J. Marshall J. Info. Tech. & Privacy L. 31 (2013).
Gercke, M. *The Council of Europe Guidelines for the Cooperation between LEAs and ISPs against Cybercrime,* Computer Law Rev. Intrl. (2008).
Gercke, M. *The Role of Internet Service Providers in the Fight Against Child Pornography,* Computer Law Rev. Intrl. (2009).
Gercke, M. *Understanding Cybercrime: Phenomena, Challenges and Legal Response* (ITU, September 2012).
Gershowitz, A. *The iPhone Meets the Fourth Amendment,* available at: http://works.bepress.com/adam_gershowitz/3 (2008).
Goldsmith, J.L. *Against Cyberanarchy.* 65 Uni. Chicago Law Rev., 1199–1250 (1998).
González Fuster, G. *The Emergence of Personal Data Protection as a Fundamental Right of the EU,* 220 (Springer 2014).
Gordon, S. & Ford, R. *On the Definition and Classification of Cybercrime,* 2(1) J. Computer Virology 13–20 (August 2006).
Graux, X. *New Directive on Attacks against Information Systems.* time.lex, http://www.timelex.eu/en/blog/detail/new-directive-on-attacks-against-information-systems (October 16, 2013).
Griffiths, J. *Constitutionalising or Harmonising? The Court of Justice, the Right to Property and European Copyright Law,* 38(1) Eur. Law Rev. 74 (2013).
Groupe interministériel sur la lutte contre la cybercriminalité. *Protéger les internautes,* Rapport sur la cybercriminalité, at 50 (February 2014), available at: http://www.justice.gouv.fr/include_htm/pub/rap_cybercriminalite.pdf.
Gruodyte, E. & Bilius, M. *Investigating Cybercrimes: Theoretical and Practical Issues.* In *Regulating e-Technologies in the European Union – Normative Realities and Trends,* 229, (T. Kerikmae (Ed.) 2014).
Gurkkaynak, G., Yilmaz, I. & Durlu, D. *Exploring New Frontiers in the Interface between Free Speech and Access Bans: The European Court of Human Rights' Case of Ahmet Yıldırım v. Turkey,* 5(1) Eur. J. Law & Tech. (2014).
Hamdani, A. *Who is Liable for Cyber Wrongs.* 87 Cornell L. Rev. 901 (2002). Available on line at: http://scholarship.law.cornell.edu/clr/vol87/iss4/1.
Hammond, A. & Richard, J.A. *Afterword: Securing Freedom. Obama and the World: New Directions,* US Foreign Policy 303 (2014).
Hansman, S. & Hunt, R. *A Taxonomy of Network and Computer Attacks.* Computers & Security, 24(1) 31–43 (2005).
Hardy Keiran & Williams George. *What is Cyberterrorism?, Computer and Internet Technology in Legal Definitions of Terrorism.* In *Cyberterrorism: Understanding, Assessment, and Response,* 6–7 (Tom Chen, Lee Jarvis, Stuart Macdonald (ed.), Springer 2014).
Hathaway, O. & Crootof, R. *The Law of Cyber Attack,* Faculty Scholarship Series Paper 3852, http://digitalcommons.law.yale.edu/fss_papers/3852 (2012).
Hayden, M. *The Insider Threat to U.S. Government Information Systems.* National Security Agency/Central Security Service Fort George G Meade MD (July 1999), available at: http://oai.dtic.mil/oai/oai?verb=getRecord&metadataPrefix=html&identifier=ADA406622.

Helmbrecht, U. *ENISA at the Service of the EU's Cyber Security, SEDE Speech*, European Parliament Brussels, (March 16th, 2015).

Herrera-Flanigan, J. & Ghosh, S. *Criminal Regulations*, in *Cybercrimes: A Multidisciplinary Analysis* (Ghosh S. & E. Turrini (eds), Springer 2011).

Hoar, Sean B. *Identity Theft: The Crime of the New Millennium*, 80 Or. L. Rev. 1423 (2001).

Hoe, C., Kantarcioglu, M. & Bensoussan, A. *A Game Theoretical Analysis of Lemonizing Cybercriminal Black Markets*, 7638 Computer Science Volume, 60–77 (2012).

Holt Thomas, J. & Hlubik Schell Bernadette. *Hackers and Hacking: A Reference Handbook*. at 23 (ABC-CLIO 2013).

Holt Thomas, J. et al. *Examining the Social Networks of Malware Writers and Hackers*, 6(1) International Journal of Cyber Criminology (IJCC) ISSN: 0974 - 2891, 891–903 (January–June 2012).

Huang, Y., Xianjun, G. & Whinston, A. *Defeating DDoS Attacks by Fixing the Incentive Chain*, 7(1) ACM Transactions on Internet Technology Article 5, 1-5.

Hunker Jeffrey & Probst Christian, *Insiders and Insider Threats, An Overview of Definitions and Mitigation Techniques*, 2(1) Journal of Wireless Mobile Networks, Ubiquitous Computing, and Dependable Applications 4–27 (2011), available at: http://citeseerx.ist.psu.edu/viewdoc/download?doi = 10.1.1.465.7490& rep = rep1&type = pdf.

Hunker J. & Probst C.W. *Insiders and Insider Threats An Overview of Definitions and Mitigation Techniques*, 2.1 Journal of Wireless Mobile Networks, Ubiquitous Computing, and Dependable Applications 4–27 (2011).

Hunton & Williams LLP. *German Court Asks European Court of Justice if IP Addresses are Personal Data*. Privacy and Information Security Law Blog, at: https://www.huntonprivacyblog.com/ 2014/11/articles/german-court-asks-european-court-justice-ip-addresses-personal data/ (November 6, 2014).

Husovec, M. *Injunctions against Innocent Third Parties: The Case of Website Blocking*, 2 JIPITEC, 117 (2012).

Huss, S.T. *Hackers: Practices, Motivations, and Identity*. Master's Thesis (University of Tennessee, Knoxville 1998).

Iglezakis, I. *The Legal Struggle in the EU against On Line Piracy*, in *Codification of European Copyright Law, Challenges and Perspectives* 290 (T. Synodinou ed., Kluwer Law International 2012) *The Legal Struggle in the EU against On Line Piracy*, in *Codification of European Copyright Law, Challenges and Perspectives* 290 (T. Synodinou ed., Kluwer Law International 2012).

Jackson, M. *Big UK ISPs Clarify the Confusion over Network Level Internet Filters* (Jun. 17, 2013), at: http://www.ispreview.co.uk/index.php/2013/06/big-uk-isps-clarify-the-confusion-over-network-level-Internet-filters.html.

Jansen, W. & Ayers, R. *Guidelines on Cell Phone Forensics*. NIST Special Publication 800: 101 (2007).

Jensen, E. *Sovereignty and Neutrality in Cyber Conflict* (Symposium: cyber attacks: international cybersecurity in the 21st century), 35 Fordham Int'l L.J. 815, 3, (2012).

Johnson D.R. & Post, D.G. *Law and Borders – The Rise of Law in Cyberspace*, 48 Stanford Law Rev., 1367ff (1996).

Jordan, T. & Taylor, P. *A Sociology of Hackers* (Blackwell Publisher 1998), available at: http://www.yorku.ca/kitzmann/hackers.pdf.

Joyner, C. & Lotrionte, C. *Information Warfare as International Coercion: Elements of a Legal Framework*, 12 Eur. J. Int'l L. 825, 842 (2001).

Jurich, J. *Cyberwar and Customary International Law: The Potential of a "Bottom-up" Approach to an International Law of Information Operations*, 9 Chi. J. Int'l L. 275 (2008).

Kaiafa-Gbanti, M. *Criminalizing Attacks against Information Systems in the EU – The Anticipated Impact of the European Legal Instruments on the Greek Legal Order*, 20 Eur. J. Crime Crim. L. & Crim. Just., 59 (2012).

Karyda, M. & Mitrou, L. *Internet Forensics: Legal and Technical Issues*, *WDFIA*, International, Workshop on Digital Forensics and Incident Analysis, International 2007, 3 (2007).

Kaspersen, H.W. *Cybercrime and Internet Jurisdiction*, Discussion Paper, Council of Europe, 40 (2009).

Kazdagli, M. et al. *Morpheus: Benchmarking Computational Diversity in Mobile Malware*, Proceedings of the Third Workshop on Hardware and Architectural Support for Security and Privacy (ACM, 2014).

Kelly, G. *UK Porn Filter: 5 Reasons It Won't Work* (Jul. 27, 2013), at: http://www.trustedreviews.com/opinions/cameron-porn-block-5-technological-reasons-it-can-t-work.

Kerr, I. & Gilbert, D. *The Role of ISP in the Investigation of Cybercrime*. In *Information Ethics in the Electronic Age: Current Issues in Africa and the World*, 165 (Tom Mendina & Johannes J. Britz (ed.), McFarland & Company Inc, 2004).

Keyser, M. *The Council of Europe Convention on Cybercrime*, 12 J. Transnational Law & Policy 311 (2003).

Kierkegaard, S. *To Block or Not to Block –European Child Porno Law in Question*, 27(6) Computer Law & Security Rev., 573–584 (December 2011).

Kierkegaard, S.M. *Cracking Down on Cybercrime Global Response*, 5(1) Communications of the IIMA, 59 (2005), available at: http://www.iima.org/CIIMA/CIIMA%205.1%2059%20Kirkegaard-7.pdf.

Klang, M. *A Critical Look at the Regulation of Computer Viruses*, 11(2) Intrl. J. Law & Info., 176 (Oxford University Press 2003).

Kleinknecht, S.W. *Hacking Hackers: Ethnographic Insights into the Hacker Subculture-Definition, Ideology and Argot*, Thesis (McMaster University 2003), available at: https://macsphere.mcmaster.ca/bitstream/11375/10956/1/fulltext.pdf.

Koops, B.-J. & Goodwin, M. *Cyberspace, the Cloud, and Cross-Border Criminal Investigation the Limits and Possibilities of International Law*, 87ff (2014).

Koops, B.-J. *Police Investigations in Internet Open Sources: Procedural-Law Issues*, 29(6) Computer Law & Security Rev., 654, 663ff. (2013).

Koops, B.-J. *Should ICT Regulation be Technology-Neutral?*. In *Starting Points for ICT Regulation. Deconstructing Prevalent Policy One-Liners* (B.-J. Koops, M. Lips, C.

Prins & M. Schellekens (eds), IT & Law Series, Vol. 9, The Hague, 2006), 77-108, available at SSRN: http://ssrn.com/abstract=918746.

Kortlander, J. *Is Filtering the New Silver Bullet in the Fight against Child Pornography on the Internet? A Legal Study into the Experiences of Australia and Germany*, 17(7) Computer & Telecommunications Law Rev. 199–208 (2011).

Krasavin, S. *What is Cyber-Terrorism?* (last access 2015), available at: http://www.crime-research.org/library/Cyber-terrorism.htm.

Kulikova, O., Heil, R., van den Berg, J. & Pieters, W. *Cyber Crisis Management: A Decision-Support Framework for Disclosing Security Incident Information.* In *Cyber Security (CyberSecurity), 2012 International Conference IEEE* 104 (December 2012).

Kulk, S. & Zuiderveen Borgesius, F. *Filtering for Copyright Enforcement in Europe after the Sabam Cases*, 34(11) E.I.P.R. 791–795 (2012).

Lalas E., Mitrou, L. & Lambrinoudakis, C. *ProCAVE: Privacy-Preserving Collection and Authenticity Validation of Online Evidence.* in Proc. of the 10th International Conference on Trust, Privacy & Security in Digital Business (TRUSTBUS-2013), 137-148 (Springer (LNCS 8058) Czech Republic, August 2013).

Le Stanc, C. *Du "Hacking" considéré comme un des beaux arts et de l'opportun renforcement de sa répression.* Communication Commerce électronique n° 4, chron. 10 (April 2002).

Le Stanc, C. Communication Commerce électronique n° 1, Janvier 2002, comm. 5.

Leeson, P. & Coyne, C. *The Economics of Computer Hacking*, 1 J.L. Econ. & Pol'y 511 (2005).

Levin, A., Goodrick, P. & Ilkina, P. *Securing Cyberspace: A Comparative Review of Strategies Worldwide*, Privacy and Cyber crime institute (Ryerson University 2013).

Leroux, O. *Legal Admissibility of Electronic Evidence*, 18(2) International Review of Law Computers and Technology, 193 (2004).

Levy, Hackers. *Heroes of the Computer Revolution* (Bantam DoubledayDell 1984).

Lichtman, D. & Posner, E. *Holding Internet Service Providers Accountable*, Chicago John M. Olin Law & Economics Working Paper No. 217, (2D SERIES), July 2004, available at SSRN: http://ssrn.com/abstract=573502 or http://dx.doi.org/10.2139/ssrn.573502.

Lotrionte, C. *State Sovereignty and Self-defense in Cyberspace: A Normative Framework for Balancing Legal Rights (Symposium: International Law and the Internet: Adapting Legal Frameworks in Response to Online Warfare and Revolutions Fueled by Social Media)*, 26 Emory Int'l L. Rev. 825, 1 (2012).

Lynn, W. *Defending a New Domain: The Pentagon's Cyberstrategy.* 89(5) Foreign Affairs, available at: www.foreignaffairs.com/articles/66552/william-j-lynn-iii/defending-a-new-domain (2010).

MacEwan, N. *The Computer Misuse Act 1990: Lessons from Its Past and Predictions for Its Future*, 12 Crim. L.R. 2008, 955–967 (2008).

MacKinnon, R. et al. *Fostering Freedom On-line, The Role of Internet Intermediaries*, Unesco Series on Internet Freedom, at 34 (UNESCO Publishing, 2014), available at: http://unesdoc.unesco.org/images/0023/002311/231162e.pdf.

Marangos, N., Rizomiliotis, P. & Mitrou, L. *Digital Forensics in the Cloud Computing Era*, First International Workshop on Management and Security Technologies for Cloud Computing, IEEE 779 (2012).

Marble, J.L. et al. *The Human Factor in Cybersecurity: Robust & Intelligent Defense*, Cyber Warfare. Springer International Publishing, 173–206 (2015).

Marguénaud, J.P. *La neutralisation européenne de l'effet collatéral d'une mesure de blocage d'un site Web*. Communication-Commerce Electronique, 8 (September 2013).

Marian, O. *A Conceptual Framework for the Regulation of Cryptocurrencies*. 82 U Chi L Rev Dialogue 53 (2015), available at: https://lawreview.uchicago.edu/page/conceptual-framework-regulation-cryptocurrencies.

Marion, N. *The Council of Europe's Cyber Crime Treaty: An Exercise in Symbolic Legislation*, 4(1&2) Intrl J. Cyber Criminology, 700 (January–July 2010/July–December 2010).

Martenczuk, B. & van Thiel, S. *Justice, Liberty, Security: New Challenges for EU External Relations* (VUBPRESS 2008).

Maurushat, A. *Australia's Accession to the "Cybercrime Convention": Is the "Convention" Still Relevant in Combating Cybercrime in the Era of Botnets and Obfuscation Crime Tools?* 33(2) University of New South Wales Law J., 431–473 (2010); UNSW Law Research Paper No. 2011-20, available at SSRN: http://ssrn.com/abstract = 1800503.

Maybury, M. et al. *Analysis and Detection of Malicious Insiders*, Conference paper (March 2005), available at: http://oai.dtic.mil/oai/oai?verb = getRecord&metadataPrefix = html&identifier = ADA456356.

McGrayne, S.B. *The Theory that Would Not Die: How Bayes' Rule Cracked the Enigma Code, Hunted Down Russian Submarines, & Emerged Triumphant from Two Centuries of Controversy* (Yale University Press 2011).

McIntyre, M. *Child Abuse Images and Cleanfeeds: Assessing Internet Blocking Systems*, in *Research Handbook on Governance of the Internet* (Edward Elgar 2012).

McNamee, J. *Internet Blocking Crimes Should Be Punished and Not Hidden*, European Digital Rights's booklet (2013), available at: https://edri.org/wp-content/uploads/2013/12/blocking_booklet.pdf.

Mell, P. & Grance, T. *The NIST Definition of Cloud Computing*. National Institute of Standards and Technology, accessible at http://www.*csrc.nist.gov/groups/SNS/cloud-computing/cloud-def-v15.doc* (2009).

Miller, R. & Merritt, M., *Have to Trust Someone .... Don't I?, Dealing with Insider Threats to Cyber-Security*, CA Technologies, Security Management, White Paper (January 2015), available at: http://www.ca.com/us/ ~ /media/Files/whitepapers/dealing-with-insider-threats-to-cyber-security.pdf.

Mitrakas, A. & Zaitch, D. *Law, Cybercrime and Digital Forensics: Trailing Digital Suspects*. In *Digital Crime and Forensic Science in Cyberspace*, 267 et seq. (Kanelis P Kiountouzis, E., Kolokotronis, N., Drakoulis, M. (eds) London 2006).

Morrissey, S. *IOS Forensic Analysis: For IPhone, IPad and IPod Touch*, Apress 71 (2010).

Munz, M. & Mette, M. *Are Dynamic IP Addresses "Personal Data"? German Federal Court of Justice Seeks Advice from the European Court of Justice*, available at:

http://www.whitecase.com/articles/122014/are-dynamic-ip-addresses-person al-data/#.VJBgzsnLJpk. (December 2014).

Murray, A. *A Bill of Rights for the Internet* (2010), available at: http://theitlawyer.blogspot.com/2010/10/bill-of-rights-for-Internet.html.

Mylonas, A. et al. *Dynamic Evidence Acquisition for Smartphone Forensics*, in *Proc. of the 27 th IFIP International Information Security and Privacy Conference*, Springer (IFIP AICT376), Greece (June 2012).

Mylonas, A. et al. *Smartphone Sensor Data as Digital Evidence*. Computers & Security (Special Issue: Cybercrime in the Digital Economy), 66, Vol. 38 (2013).

Mylonas, A. et al. *Smartphone Forensics: A Proactive Investigation Scheme for Evidence Acquisition*. In *Information Security and Privacy Research*, 249 (Springer Berlin Heidelberg 2012).

National Security Research Division, Richard C. Brackney & Robert H. Anderson. *Understanding the Insider Threat*, Proceedings of a March 2004 Workshop, Prepared for the Advanced Research and Development Activity, available at: http://www.rand.org/content/dam/rand/pubs/conf_proceedings/2005/RAND_CF196.pdf. (2004).

NATO Cooperative Cyber Defence Centre of Excellence. *Ten Rules for Cyber Security* (Talinn 2011).

Nicol, A., Millar, G. & Sharlad, A. *Media Law & Human Rights* (2nd edn, OUP 2009).

Nieman, A. *Cyberforensics: Bridging the Law/Technology Divide*. (1) J. Info., Law & Tech. (JILT), 19 (2009).

OECD. *Computer Viruses and Other Malicious Software: A Threat to the Internet Economy*. (OECD Publishing 2009).

OECD. *Guidelines for the Security of Information Systems and Networks: Towards a Culture of Security*. (OECD Publishing 2002).

OECD. *Policy Guidance on Online Identity Theft*. (OECD Publishing 2008).

OECD. *Recommendation of the Council on Digital Security Risk Management for Economic and Social Prosperity*. (October 1, 2015).

Orin, S. Kerr. *Cybercrime's Scope: Interpreting "Access" and "Authorization" in Computer Misuse Statutes*, 78 New York University Law Rev. 1596 (2003).

Ottis, R. *Proceedings of the 10th European Conference on Information Warfare and Security*, 233 (Academic Publishing Limited 2011).

Paganini, P. *Cybercrime and the Underground Market*. (January 15, 2013), avail able at: http://resources.infosecinstitute.com/cybercrime-and-the-underground-market/.

Pedro, M., Freitasa, F. & Gonçalvesa, N. *Illegal Access to Information Systems and the Directive 2013/40/EU, International Review of Law*, 29(1) Computers & Technology 50–62 (2015).

Pichan A., Lazarescu, M. & Teng Soh, S. *Cloud Forensics: Technical Challenges, Solutions and Comparative Analysis*, 13 Digital Investigation 38 (2015).

Picotti, L. & Salvadori, I. *National Legislation Implementing the Convention on Cybercrime -Comparative Analysis and Good Practices*, 46 (March 12, 2008), available at: http://www.coe.int/t/dghl/cooperation/economiccrime/cyber

crime/cy_activity_Interface2008/567%20study2-d-version8%20provisional%20_12%20march%2008_en.pdf.

Pipyros, K. et al. *A Cyber Attack Evaluation Methodology*. In Proceedings of the 13th European conference on Cyber Warfare and Security, 264–270 (2014).

Pipyros, K., Mitrou, L., Gritzalis, D. and Apostolopoulos, T. *Cyberoperations and International Humanitarian Law: A Review of Obstacles in Applying International Law Rules in Cyber Warfare*, 24(1) Information and Computer Security, pp. 38-52, (2016) https://doi.org/10.1108/ICS-12-2014-0081.

Podins, K. & Czosseck, C. *A Vulnerability-Based Model of Cyber Weapons and its Implications for Cyber Conflict*, European Conference on Information Warfare and Security: 198-X. Reading: Academic Conferences International Limited (Jul 2012).

Pollicino, O. & Bassini, M. *Free Speech, Defamation and the Limits to Freedom of Expression in the EU: A Comparative Analysis*. In *Research Handbook on EU Internet Law*, at 532 (A. Savin & J. Trzaskowski (ed.), Edward Elgar 2014).

Poulsen Kevin & Zetter Kim. *US Intelligence Analyst Arrested in Wikileaks Video Prob*, Wired.com (2010), available at: http://www.wired.com/2010/06/leak/.

Rainer, K., Turban, E. & Potter, R. *Introduction to Information Systems*, 6 (Wiley 2007).

Rancillon, J. *Téléchargement illégal. Heur et malheur de la loi Création et Internet: la loi HADOPI censurée par le Conseil constitutionnel*. Revue de science criminelle et de droit pénal comparé, at 617 (2009).

Rancourt, S.J. *Hacking, Theft, and Corporate Negligence: Making the Case for Mandatory Encryption of Personal Information*. 18 Tex.Wesleyan L. Rev. 186 (2011).

RAND Europe. *Handbook of Legislative Procedures of Computer and Network Misuse in EU Countries – Study for the European Commission* (Directorate-General Information Society 2002).

Reding, V. *The EU Data Protection Reform 2012 – Making Europe the Standard Setter for Modern Data Protection Rules in the Digital Age*, Speech 12/26 (2012).

Reid, M. *United States v. Jones: Big Brother and the "Common Good" versus the Fourth Amendment and Your Right to Privacy*, available at: http://works.bepress.com/melanie_reid/9; (2012).

Richards, J. *Make Firms Bear the Cost to Improve Information Security, says Schneier*, Computer Weekly (May 22, 2007), available at: http://www.computerweekly.com/Articles/2007/05/22/223959/make-firms-bear-the-cost-toimprove-information-security-says-schneier.htm.

Ridard, B. *La protection constitutionnelle du droit d'accès à l'Internet, Implications juridiques de la décision "Hadopi" du Conseil constitutionnel*, Congrès mondial de l'AIDC, (December 2010), available at: http://www.juridicas.unam.mx/wccl/ponencias/3/64.pdf.

Roberts, L.D. *Cyber Identity Theft*. In *Cyber Crime: Concepts, Methodologies, Tools and Applications*, 21–36 (Hershey 2012).

Robinson, N. et al. *Comparative Study on Legislative and Non Legislative Measures to Combat Identity Theft and Identity Related Crime: Final Report*, TR-982-EC, available at ec.europa.eu/dgs/home-affairs/e.../rand_study_tr-982-ec_en.pdf (June 2011).

Rosier, K. in: Bullesbach, Gijrath, Poullet, Prins, *Concise European IT Law* (2nd edn, 2010), Article 6 of Directive 2002/58/EC, p. 201.

Rowe, B. et al. *The Role of Internet Service Providers in Cyber Security, Institute for Homeland Security Solutions*, available at: http://citeseerx.ist.psu.edu/viewdoc/download?doi=10.1.1.473.2323&rep=rep1&type=pdf (June 2011).

Ruan, K. et al., *Cloud Forensics: An Overview*, in Advances in Digital Forensics 7, 40 (2011).

Ryan, P.S. *War, Peace, or Stalemate: Wargames, Wardialing, Wardriving, and the Emerging Market for Hacker Ethics*, 9 Va. J.L. & Tech. 1 (2004).

Samani, R. *Digital Laundry, An Analysis of Online Currencies, and their Use in Cybercrime*, available at: http://www.mcafee.com/us/resources/white-papers/wp-digital-laundry.pdf.

Schjolberg, S. *The History of Global Harmonization on Cybercrime Legislation – The Road to Geneva.* (Cybercrime Law, December 2008), available at: cybercrimelaw-.net.

Schmitt, M. *Computer Network Attack and the Use of Force in International Law: Thoughts on a normative framework*, Columbia Journal of Transnational Law, vol. 37, available at http://papers.ssrn.com/sol3/papers.cfm?abstract_id=1603800 (1999).

Schwartz, P.M. & Janger, E.J. *Notification of Data Security Breaches.* Michigan Law Rev., 105 at 936 (2007).

Shackelford, S.J. *Managing Cyber Attacks.* In *International Law, Business, and Relations: In Search of Cyber Peace*, 15 (Cambridge University Press 2014).

Sicke, D., Ohm, P. & Grunwald, D. *Legal Issues Surrounding Monitoring during Network Research*, Proceedings of the 7th ACM SIGCOMM conference on Internet measurement, ACM, 141 (2007).

Sieber, U. *Straftaten und Strafverfolgung im Internet.* Gutachten C zum 69. Deutschen Juristentag. Munich: C.H. Beck. 147–148 (2012), and Gercke, M. *Understanding Cybercrime: Phenomena, Challenges and Legal Response*, 278 et seq. (ITU, 2012).

Sieber, A.J. *Presentation on CEN BT/WG 161 – Standards for Security and Protection of the Citizens.* in Security Research Conference (Ankara, 2008).

Sieber, U. *General Report.* In *Computer Crimes, Cyber-Terrorism, Child Pornography and Financial Crimes* (Dionysios Spinellis (ed.) Athens-Komotini: Sakkoulas, 2004).

Sieber, U. *Straftaten und Strafverfolgung im Internet.* Gutachten C zum 69. Deutschen Juristentag. München 144–145 (2012).

Sieber, U. *The International Handbook on Computer Crime* (1986).

Simou, S. et al. *Cloud Forensics: Identifying the Major Issues and Challenges.* In *Advanced Information Systems Engineering*, 271 (Springer International Publishing 2014).

Skibell, R. *The Myth of the Computer Hacker.* 5(3) Info., Comm. & Society (2002).

Slatalla, M. *A Brief History of Hacking*, Online, Discovery Communications (October 28, 2003), available at: http://tlc.discovery.com/convergence/hackers/articles/history.html.

Sloot, B. van der, *Privacy in the Post-NSA Era: Time for a Fundamental Revision?* JIPITEC, 2014-1 (May 2, 2014).

Smith, G.J.H. *Internet Law and Regulation* (4th edn Sweet & Maxwell 2007).

Sommer, P. *Criminalising Hacking Tools*, 3(2) Digital Investigation, 68–72 (June 2006).

Sommer, P. *Evidence in Internet Paedophilia Cases*, Computer and Telecommunications Law Review, 183 (2002).

Sommer, P. *Digital Footprints: Assessing Computer Evidence*, Criminal Law Review – Special Edition (1998).

Strozer J.R., Collins, Matthew L. & Cassidy Tracy. *Unintentional Insider Threats: A Review of Phishing and Malware Incidents by Economic Sector* (CERT, July 2014).

Summers, S. et al. *The Emergence of EU Criminal Law, Cyber Crime and the Regulation of the Information Society*, 269 (Hart Publishing 2014).

Synodinou, T. *Intermediaries' Liability for Online Copyright Infringement in the EU: Evolutions and Confusions*, 31(1) Computer Law & Security Report, 57–67 (02/2015).

Tcherni, M. et al. *The Dark Figure of Online Property Crime: Is Cyberspace Hiding a Crime Wave?*, Justice Quarterly 1–22 (2015).

Tikk, E. *IP Addresses Subject to Data Protection Regulation*. In *International Cyber Security Legal and Policy Proceedings* (E. Tikk & A.M. Taliharm (eds) Talinn: NATO Cooperative Cyber Defense Center of Excellence) (2010).

Timelex. *Study of Case Law on the Circumstances in which IP Addresses are Considered Personal Data*. Final Report (2 May 2011).

Tokson, M.J. *The Content/Envelope Distinction in Internet Law*, 50 William & Mary Law Rev. 2105, (2009), available at: http://scholarship.law.wm.edu/wmlr/vol50/iss6/5.

Tsoutsanis, A. *Privacy and Piracy in Cyberspace: Justice for all*, J. Intellectual Property Law & Practice Advance Access published (October 24, 2013).

Tully, S. *A Human Right to Access the Internet? Problems and Prospects*, 14(2) Human Rights Law Rev., available at: http://hrlr.oxfordjournals.org/content/14/2/175.full#fn-93.

US Department of Justice, Office of Justice Programs, National Institute of Justice, *Forensic Examination of Digital Evidence: A Guide for Law Enforcement*, 46 (2004). https://www.ncjrs.gov/pdffiles1/nij/199408.pdf.

United Nations Office on Drugs and Crime (hereafter UNODC). *Comprehensive Study on Cybercrime*, Draft 2013, available at: https://www.unodc.org/documents/organized-crime/UNODC_CCPCJ_EG.4_2013/CYBERCRIME_STUDY_210213.pdf, 51 (2013).

Upton, D.M. & Sadie, C. *The Danger from Within*. Harvard Business Rev. (September 2014), available at: https://hbr.org/2014/09/the-danger-from-within.

Van Quathem, K. *Security Breach Notification in the European Union: First Step Taken, More to Come*, 01/10 World Data Protection Report, 19 (2010).

Venancio, P.D. *Similarity and Competition between Cybercrimes Related to Computer Data in the Council of Europe's Convention on Cybercrime*. 7 Masaryk UJL & Tech. 97 (2013).

Von Solms, R. & van Niekerk J. *From Information Security to Cyber Security*, Computers and Security 3, 897 e102 (2013).

Walden, I. *Computer Crime*. In *Computer Law*, 295 (C. Reed & J. Angel (eds), London 2003).

Warkentin M. & Willison, R. *Behavioral and Policy Issues in Information Systems Security: The Insider Threat*, 18 Eur. J. Info. Systems 101–105 (2009).

Wei, W. *Online Child Sexual Abuse Content: The Development of a Comprehensive, Transferable International Internet Notice and Takedown System*, in Independent report for Internet Watch Foundation, at 76 (May 2011), available at: https://www.iwf.org.uk/assets/media/resources/IWF%20Research%20Report_%20Development%20of%20an%20international%20Internet%20notice%20and%20takedown%20system.pdf.

Weir, A., *Overwhelming Majority of UK Broadband Users Opting Out of Porn Filters*, Neowin (Jul. 23, 2014), available at: http://www.neowin.net/news/overwhelming-majority-of-uk-broadband-users-opting-out-of-porn-filters.

Wiebe, A. *The New Fundamental Right to IT Security – First Evaluation and Comparative View at the U.S.*, Datenschutz und Datensicherheit, 713 et seq. (2008).

Wiebke, A. *Agents, Trojans and Tags: The Next Generation of Investigators*, 23(1-2) International Review of Law, Computers & Technology, 99 (2009).

Winn, J. *Are Better Security Breach Notification Laws Possible*, 24 Berkeley Tech. L.J. 1133 (2009).

Wong, R. *Data Security Breaches and Privacy in Europe*, 44 (Springer 2013).

Wright, J. & Breindl Y. *Internet Filtering Trends in Liberal Democracies: French and German Regulatory Debates*, 2(2) Internet Policy Rev., available at: http://policyreview.info/articles/analysis/Internet-filtering-trends-liberal-democracies-french-and-german-regulatory-debates.

Zahed, J. *Cybercrime Model Laws, Discussion Paper Prepared for the Cybercrime Convention Committee*, available at: www.coet.int/cybercrime (December 23, 2014).

Zetter, K. *NSA Whistleblower: The Ultimate Insider Attack*. Wired.com, (September 06, 2013), available : http://www.wired.com/2010/06/leak/.

Index

www.ingramcontent.com/pod-product-compliance
Ingram Content Group UK Ltd.
Pitfield, Milton Keynes, MK11 3LW, UK
UKHW020241290926
15470UKWH00002B/666

9 789403 509334

[152] Timmann, C., Thye, T., Vens, M., Evans, J., May, J., Ehmen, C., Sievertsen, J., Muntau, B., Ruge, G., Loag, W., Ansong, D., Antwi, S., Asafo-Adjei, E., Nguah, S. B., Kwakye, K. O., Akoto, A. O., Sylverken, J., Brendel, M., Schuldt, K., Loley, C., Franke, A., Meyer, C. G., Agbenyega, T., Ziegler, A. and Horstmann, R. D. (2012) Genome-wide association study indicates two novel resistance loci for severe malaria. *Nature,* 489, 443-446.

[153] Tsuneshige, A., Imai, K. and Tyuma, I. (1987) The binding of hemoglobin to red cell membrane lowers its oxygen affinity. *Journal of biochemistry,* 101, 695-704.

[154] Vandorpe, D. H., Xu, C., Shmukler, B. E., Otterbein, L. E., Trudel, M., Sachs, F., Gottlieb, P. A., Brugnara, C. and Alper, S. L. (2010) Hypoxia activates a Ca2+-permeable cation conductance sensitive to carbon monoxide and to GsMTx-4 in human and mouse sickle erythrocytes. *PloS one,* 5, e8732.

[155] Wagner, G. M., Chiu, D. T., Yee, M. C. and Lubin, B. H. (1986) Red cell vesiculation--a common membrane physiologic event. *The Journal of laboratory and clinical medicine,* 108, 315-324.

[156] Walder, J. A., Chatterjee, R., Steck, T. L., Low, P. S., Musso, G. F., Kaiser, E. T., Rogers, P. H. and Arnone, A. (1984) The interaction of hemoglobin with the cytoplasmic domain of band 3 of the human erythrocyte membrane. *The Journal of biological chemistry,* 259, 10238-10246.

[157] Wang, J., van Bentum, K., Sester, U. and Kaestner, L. (2014) Calcium homeostasis in red blood cells of dialysis patients in dependence of erythropoietin treatment. *Frontiers in physiology,* 5, 16.

[158] Wasserman, M. (1990) The role of calcium ions in the invasion of Plasmodium falciparum. *Blood cells,* 16, 450-451.

[159] Wasserman, M., Alarcon, C. and Mendoza, P. M. (1982) Effects of Ca++ depletion on the asexual cell cycle of Plasmodium falciparum. *The American journal of tropical medicine and hygiene,* 31, 711-717.

[160] Wasserman, M. and Chaparro, J. (1996) Intraerythrocytic calcium chelators inhibit the invasion of Plasmodium falciparum. *Parasitology research,* 82, 102-107.

[161] Waugh, S. M., Willardson, B. M., Kannan, R., Labotka, R. J. and Low, P. S. (1986) Heinz bodies induce clustering of band 3, glycophorin, and ankyrin in sickle cell erythrocytes. *The Journal of clinical investigation,* 78, 1155-1160.

international journal of experimental cellular physiology, biochemistry, and pharmacology, 28, 847-856.

[119] Olivieri, O., De Franceschi, L., Capellini, M. D., Girelli, D., Corrocher, R. and Brugnara, C. (1994) Oxidative damage and erythrocyte membrane transport abnormalities in thalassemias. *Blood,* 84, 315-320.

[120] Olorunsogo, O. O., Agbolade, F. O., Owojuyigbe, S. O., Adebisi, J. A., Adebayo, A. O. and Okunade, W. G. (1990) Comparative action of calpain on erythrocyte Ca2(+)-pumping ATPase in sickle cell anaemia, essential hypertension and kwashiorkor. *Bioscience reports,* 10, 281-291.

[121] Oonishi, T., Sakashita, K., Ishioka, N., Suematsu, N., Shio, H. and Uyesaka, N. (1998) Production of prostaglandins E1 and E2 by adult human red blood cells. *Prostaglandins and other lipid mediators,* 56, 89-101.

[122] Ortiz, O. E., Lew, V. L. and Bookchin, R. M. (1986) Calcium accumulated by sickle cell anemia red cells does not affect their potassium (86Rb+) flux components. *Blood,* 67, 710-715.

[123] Ortiz, O. E., Lew, V. L. and Bookchin, R. M. (1990) Deoxygenation permeabilizes sickle cell anaemia red cells to magnesium and reverses its gradient in the dense cells. *The Journal of physiology,* 427, 211-226.

[124] Pace, B. S., Shartava, A., Pack-Mabien, A., Mulekar, M., Ardia, A. and Goodman, S. R. (2003) Effects of N-acetylcysteine on dense cell formation in sickle cell disease. *American journal of hematology,* 73, 26-32.

[125] Pauling, L., Itano, H. A. and et al. (1949) Sickle cell anemia a molecular disease. *Science,* 110, 543-548.

[126] Perutz, R. R., Liquori, A. M. and Eirich, F. (1951) X-ray and solubility studies of the haemoglobin of sickle-cell anaemia patients. *Nature,* 167, 929-931.

[127] Peters, L. L., Jindel, H. K., Gwynn, B., Korsgren, C., John, K. M., Lux, S. E., Mohandas, N., Cohen, C. M., Cho, M. R., Golan, D. E. and Brugnara, C. (1999) Mild spherocytosis and altered red cell ion transport in protein 4. 2-null mice. *The Journal of clinical investigation,* 103, 1527-1537.

[128] Platt, O. S., Falcone, J. F. and Lux, S. E. (1985) Molecular defect in the sickle erythrocyte skeleton. Abnormal spectrin binding to sickle inside-our vesicles. *The Journal of clinical investigation,* 75, 266-271.

[129] Puchulu-Campanella, E., Chu, H., Anstee, D. J., Galan, J. A., Tao, W. A. and Low, P. S. (2013) Identification of the components of a glycolytic

[141] Scott, M. D., van den Berg, J. J., Repka, T., Rouyer-Fessard, P., H(R. P., Beuzard, Y. and Lubin, B. H. (1993) Effect of excess ε hemoglobin chains on cellular and membrane oxidation in model thalassemic erythrocytes. *The Journal of clinical investigation,* 91, 1712.

[142] Soupene, E., Kemaladewi, D. U. and Kuypers, F. A. (2008) AT activity and phosphatidylserine transbilayer movement. *Journ receptor, ligand and channel research,* 1, 1-10.

[143] Soupene, E. and Kuypers, F. A. (2006) Identification of an ery ATP-dependent aminophospholipid transporter. *British journ haematology,* 133, 436-438.

[144] Steffen, P., Jung, A., Nguyen, D. B., Muller, T., Bernhardt, I., Ka L. and Wagner, C. (2011) Stimulation of human red blood cells le Ca2+-mediated intercellular adhesion. *Cell calcium,* 50, 54-61.

[145] Steinberg, M. H., Eaton, J. W., Berger, E., Coleman, M. E Oelshlegel, F. J. (1978) Erythrocyte calcium abnormalities ar clinical severity of sickling disorders. *British journal of haema* 40, 533-539.

[146] Sugihara, T. and Hebbel, R. P. (1992) Exaggerated cation leal oxygenated sickle red blood cells during deformation: evidence unique leak pathway. *Blood,* 80, 2374-2378.

[147] Sukati, S., Svasti, S., Stifanese, R., Averna, M., Panutdapor Penglong, T., Melloni, E., Fucharoen, S. and Katzenmeier, G. Clinical severity of beta-thalassaemia/Hb E disease is associate differential activities of the calpain-calpastatin proteolytic systen *one,* 7, e37133.

[148] Tanabe, K., Mikkelsen, R. B. and Wallach, D. F. (1982) C transport of Plasmodium chabaudi-infected erythrocytes. *The Jou cell biology,* 93, 680-684.

[149] Terra, H. T., Saad, M. J., Carvalho, C. R., Vicentin, D. L., Costa and Saad, S. T. (1998) Increased tyrosine phosphorylation of bai hemoglobinopathies. *American journal of hematology,* 58, 224-23

[150] Tiffert, T., Etzion, Z., Bookchin, R. M. and Lew, V. L. (1993) Eff deoxygenation on active and passive Ca2+ transport and cytop Ca2+ buffering in normal human red cells. *The Journal of phys* 464, 529-544.

[151] Tiffert, T. and Lew, V. L. (1997) Cytoplasmic calcium buffers ir human red cells. *The Journal of physiology,* 500 (Pt 1), 139-154.

enzyme metabolon on the human red blood cell membrane. *The Journal of biological chemistry,* 288, 848-858.

[130] Rank, B. H., Hebbel, R. P. and Carlsson, J. (1984) Oxidation of membrane thiols in sickle erythrocytes. *Progress in clinical and biological research,* 165, 473-477.

[131] Rees, D. C., Williams, T. N. and Gladwin, M. T. (2010) Sickle-cell disease. *Lancet,* 376, 2018-2031.

[132] Rhoda, M. D., Giraud, F., Craescu, C. T. and Beuzard, Y. (1985) Compartmentalization of Ca2+ in sickle cells. *Cell calcium,* 6, 397-411.

[133] Rifkind, J. M., Mohanty, J. G. and Nagababu, E. (2014) The pathophysiology of extracellular hemoglobin associated with enhanced oxidative reactions. *Frontiers in physiology,* 5, 500.

[134] Rodighiero, S., De Simoni, A. and Formenti, A. (2004) The voltage-dependent nonselective cation current in human red blood cells studied by means of whole-cell and nystatin-perforated patch-clamp techniques. *Biochimica et biophysica acta,* 1660, 164-170.

[135] Ronquist, G., Rudolphi, O., Engstrom, I. and Waldenstrom, A. (2001) Familial phosphofructokinase deficiency is associated with a disturbed calcium homeostasis in erythrocytes. *Journal of internal medicine,* 249, 85-95.

[136] Roth, E. F., Jr., Friedman, M., Ueda, Y., Tellez, I., Trager, W. and Nagel, R. L. (1978) Sickling rates of human AS red cells infected in vitro with Plasmodium falciparum malaria. *Science,* 202, 650-652.

[137] Rotter, M. A., Chu, H., Low, P. S. and Ferrone, F. A. (2010) Band 3 catalyzes sickle hemoglobin polymerization. *Biophysical chemistry,* 146, 55-59.

[138] Rubin, E., Schlegel, R. A. and Williamson, P. (1986) Endocytosis in sickle erythrocytes: a mechanism for elevated intracellular Ca2+ levels. *Journal of cellular physiology,* 126, 53-59.

[139] Sabina, R. L., Wandersee, N. J. and Hillery, C. A. (2009) Ca2+-CaM activation of AMP deaminase contributes to adenine nucleotide dysregulation and phosphatidylserine externalization in human sickle erythrocytes. *British journal of haematology,* 144, 434-445.

[140] Schwartz, R. S., Tanaka, Y., Fidler, I. J., Chiu, D. T., Lubin, B. and Schroit, A. J. (1985) Increased adherence of sickled and phosphatidylserine-enriched human erythrocytes to cultured human peripheral blood monocytes. *The Journal of clinical investigation,* 75, 1965-1972.

[162] Weinstein, R. S., Warth, J. A., Near, K. and Marikovsky, Y. (1989) Sequestrocytes: a manifestation of transcellular cross-bonding of the red cell membrane in sickle cell anemia. *Journal of cell science,* 94 (Pt 3), 593-600.

[163] Weiss, E., Cytlak, U. M., Rees, D. C., Osei, A. and Gibson, J. S. (2012) Deoxygenation-induced and Ca(2+) dependent phosphatidylserine externalisation in red blood cells from normal individuals and sickle cell patients. *Cell calcium,* 51, 51-56.

[164] Williams, T. N. (2006) Red blood cell defects and malaria. *Mol. Biochem. Parasitol.,* 149, 121-127.

[165] Williamson, P., Puchulu, E., Westerman, M. and Schlegel, R. A. (1990) Erythrocyte membrane abnormalities in sickle cell disease. *Biotechnology and applied biochemistry,* 12, 523-528.

[166] Yuditskaya, S., Suffredini, A. F. and Kato, G. J. (2010) The proteome of sickle cell disease: insights from exploratory proteomic profiling. *Expert review of proteomics,* 7, 833-848.

[167] Zarychanski, R., Schulz, V. P., Houston, B. L., Maksimova, Y., Houston, D. S., Smith, B., Rinehart, J. and Gallagher, P. G. (2012) Mutations in the mechanotransduction protein PIEZO1 are associated with hereditary xerocytosis. *Blood,* 120, 1908-1915.

[168] Zipser, Y., Piade, A., Barbul, A., Korenstein, R. and Kosower, N. S. (2002) Ca2+ promotes erythrocyte band 3 tyrosine phosphorylation via dissociation of phosphotyrosine phosphatase from band 3. *The Biochemical journal,* 368, 137-144.

In: Sickle Cell Disease
Editor: Marilyn E. Lewis
ISBN: 978-1-63482-828-4

Chapter III

Antisickling and Radical Scavenging Activities of Anthocyanin Extracts from the Leaves of *Gardenia Ternifolia Subsp. Jovis-Tonantis* (Welw.) Verdc. (Rubiaceae)

P. T. Mpiana[1,*], *K. N. Ngbolua*[2], *D. S. T. Tshibangu*[1], *D. T. Mwanangombo*[1] *and P. V. Tsalu*[1]
[1]Department of Chemistry, Faculty of Science, D. R. Congo
[2]Department of Biology, Faculty of Science, D. R. Congo

Abstract

Background: Sickle cell disease (SCD) is a genetic disorder caused by an abnormality of hemoglobin. The disease is characterized by a chronic hemolytic anemia. The search for affordable and accessible

* Corresponding Author: Prof. Dr. Pius T. Mpiana, E-mail: ptmpiana@yahoo.fr; Tel.: +243 81 81 160 19

medicines mainly from plants and having various modes of actions for managing SCD is a priority in Africa where the disease is endemic.

Materials and Methods: The antioxidant activity of crude extracts of *Gardenia jovis tonantis* leaves was carried out using DPPH free radical scavenging assay while *in vitro* antisickling activity was assessed on sickle erythrocytes by the Emmel's test as previously reported.

Results and Discussion: Methanol soluble fraction, ethyl acetate soluble fraction and anthocyanin crude extracts displayed interesting *in vitro* radical scavenging and antisickling activities. These results confirm those already given by our research team with anthocyanins from other Congolese medicinal plants traditionally used in folk medicine for the management of SCD. As reducing agent/drug, anthocyanins based medicine could prevent *in vivo* oxidative reactions, often by scavenging free radicals before they can damage cells.

Conclusion: This study has validated the pharmacological relevance of *Gardenia ternifolia* and sustains the use of this herbal medicine in the management of SCD in traditional medical system.

Keywords: Sickle cell disease, herbal medicine, *Gardenia ternifolia,* anthocyanins, antioxidant activity

Introduction

Sickle cell disease (SCD) is a genetic disorder caused by an abnormality of hemoglobin. The disease is characterized by a chronic hemolytic anemia. It is a genetically inherited disease in which a single base substitution in the gene encoding the human β-globin subunit results in replacement of β6 glutamic acid by valine, leading to the devastating clinical manifestations of SCD [1, 2]. This substitution causes drastic reduction in the solubility of sickle cell hemoglobin (Hb S) when deoxygenated. Under these conditions, the Hb S molecules polymerize to form long crystalline intracellular mass of fibers which cause the deformation of the biconcave disc shaped erythrocyte into a sickle shape. The consequences of this defect are hemolytic anemia and tissue damage [3]. Each year about 300,000 children are born with pathological hemoglobin of which 70% are affected by SCD. Most of them die before the age of five years when they do not receive regular medical care. In Democratic Republic of the Congo, almost 2% of the population is sicklers [3-5].

The first-line clinical management of SCD includes medullar transplantation, repeated blood transfusion to stabilize the patient's hemoglobin level, and the use of drugs which interfere with the kinetics of the erythrocyte sickling process. Unfortunately, the available therapies are expensive for poor African population and have attendant risk factors in terms of clinical use [6-8]. Therefore, there is a need for cheap and effective treatments for the disease. Herbal medicines have been used in African folk medicine for decade to cure diseases [9-12].

The Democratic Republic of the Congo (DRC) is reputed for the extraordinary richness of its biodiversity and boast a wide variety of plant species of ethno-medicinal relevance. These plant species represent an enormous reservoir of secondary metabolites with biopharmaceutical potential for modern industries [13, 14]. Recently, we validated scientifically the sickling inhibitory effect of some medicinal plants traditionally used in Congolese indigenous medicine for managing SCD and showed that this activity is mainly due to anthocyanins [15-20]. As several other flavonoids, anthocyanins are plant naturally occurring secondary metabolites with a large spectrum of biological activities including free radical scavenging effects [21-22]. *Gardenia ternifolia subsp. jovis-tonantis* (Welw.) Verdc. (Syn: *Decameria jovis-tonantis* Welw.; *Gardenia jovis-tonantis* (Welw.) Hiern; *Gardenia lutea* Fresen.; *Gardenia ternifolia var. jovis-tonantis* (Welw.) Aubrév.; *Genipa jovis-tonantis* (Welw.) Baill.) is an infraspecific taxon of the species *Gardenia ternifolia* Schumach. & Thonn. in the genus *Gardenia* (Family Rubiaceae) *Gardenia ternifolia subsp. jovis-tonantis* (known under the vernacular name of "Lembanzau", Kikongo name) is traditionally used by indigenous peoples to treat malaria (bark decoction), worms (decoction of leaves and roots), coughs and respiratory ailments (bark decoction) [23].

The present research was assessed with the aim of evaluating the antisickling and free radical scavenging activities of some extracts from the leaves *Gardenia ternifolia subsp. jovis-tonantis*.

Materials and Methods

- Plant material collection

The plant *Gardenia ternifolia subsp. jovis-tonantis* was collected during a field work in the Bas Congo province in April 2012 and were authenticated by Mr. B.L. Nlandu of the INERA (Institut National d'Etudes et Recherches Agronomiques). Voucher specimen is on deposit at the INERA Herbarium of the Faculty of Science (Université de Kinshasa).

❖ Extraction and chemical screening

The dried and powdered plant material (stem bark, 10 g) was repeatedly extracted by cold percolation with 95% ethanol (EtOH) and water (100 mL x 2) for 48 hours. Chemical screening was done in aqueous and organic extract according to a well-known protocol as previously reported [24]. Fractions were filtered and concentrated to dryness under reduced pressure using a rotary evaporator. Extraction of anthocyanins was then done using 100 g of dried powdered plant material with acidified methanol (1% HCl) following an established protocol [13-20]. Anthocyanins extract was then defatted by n-hexane.

❖ Preparation of methanol extract and increasing polarity extracts

Plant powder (100 g) was macerated in methanol 80% (1L x 2) for 48 hours. After filtering the mixture, the aqueous-methanolic filtrate was concentrated under reduced pressure using a rotary evaporator. The methanolic extract was suspended in distilled water and sequentially partitioned with n-hexane, dichoromethane, ethyl acetate, ethanol, and methanol (1:1, v/v) three times at room temperature. The resulting fractions were evaporated to dryness on an evaporator apparatus. All extracts were stored at +4 °C.

❖ Biological material and in vitro assays

Blood samples used to evaluate the antisickling activity of the plant extracts in this study were taken from known drepanocitary adolescent patients attending the "Centre de Médecine Mixte et d'Anémie *SS*" and "Centre Hospitalier Monkole", both located in Kinshasa area, DRC. None of the patients had been transfused recently with Hb AA blood. All antisickling experiments were carried out with freshly collected blood. In order to confirm their *SS* nature, the above-mentioned blood samples were first characterized by Hemoglobin electrophoresis on cellulose acetate gel, as previously reported [5]. They were found to be *SS* blood and were then stored at ± 4 °C in a refrigerator. An informed consent was obtained from all the patients participating in the study. All the research procedures have received the approval of Department of Biology Ethics Committee.

- Antisickling assay

Sickle cell blood was diluted with 150 mM phosphate buffered saline (NaH_2PO_4 30 mM, Na_2HPO_4 120 mM, NaCl 150 mM) and mixed with an equivalent volume of 2% sodium metabisulfite. A drop from the mixture was spotted on a microscope slide in the presence or absence of ethyl acetate, methanolic or anthocyanins extracts and covered with a cover slip. Paraffin was applied to seal the edges of the cover completely to exclude air (Hypoxia). Duplicate analyses were run for each extract. The RBCs were analyzed by measuring various parameters including the area, perimeter and the radius of each RBC using a computer assisted image analysis system (Motic Images 2000, version 1.3; Motic Chine Group Co LTD) and statistical data analysis were processed using Microcal Origin 7.5 package software.

- Free radical scavenging assay

The DPPH free radical (1,1-diphenyl-2- picrylhydrazyl) scavenging assay was carried out as previously reported [25]. The radical scavenging activity of extracts for DPPH free radical was measured on the principle that antioxidants reduce the DPPH radical to a yellow-coloured compound (diphenylpicrylhydrazin) and the extent of the reaction will depend on the hydrogen donating ability of the antioxidant. Briefly, a 100 μM solution of DPPH radical in methanol was prepared. 3.5 mL of this solution were added to 0.5 mL solution of each extract in methanol at concentrations ranging from 0.1 to 1.0 mg/mL, thus obtaining the desired final concentrations in the reaction mixture. The mixture was shaken vigorously and incubated in the dark at room temperature for 30 min. The absorbance was measured at 515 nm using a UV-Vis spectrophotometer SP- 1105 Brand model. Methanol was used as a blank. The control solution consist of 0.5 mL of methanol and 3.5 mL of DPPH radical solution. The antiradical activity of a sample (calculated by the following formula) is given as percentage of reduced DPPH free radical: $\%I = [(OD\ control - OD\ sample)/OD\ control] \times 100$. The EC_{50} value (μg/mL) is the effective concentration at which DPPH radicals were scavenged by 50%. L-ascorbic acid was used as positive control. Duplicate analyses were run for each extract.

- Kinetics study

Kinetics study was assessed in order to determine the rate of the DPPH free radical reduction at a given concentration of extract. The values of absorbance A_{515nm} (t = 0) - A_{515nm} (t = x) as a function of time could be expressed as power function by the following mathematic model: A_{515nm} (t= 0) - A_{515nm} (t= x) = a* t^b [equation 3] where a and b are parameters that could be determined by nonlinear regression analysis and t the time. The value A_{515nm} (t= 0) - A_{515nm} (t= x) refers to the content of DPPH free radical scavenged at t=x.

To quantify the kinetic behavior of the investigated extracts, the reaction speed rate of DPPH free radical scavenging effect was estimated as the first derivative of equation 3: $R_S = a*b*t^{b-1}$ [equation 4] as previously reported [26-28]. By comparing the reaction speed rate at t= 0.25 min (the initial rate), 10 min (after the end of the initial rapid reaction step), 15 min, 20 min, 25 min and 30 min (at the end of the observation period when the reactions are presumably completed), it is possible to compare the curve slopes in order to identify extract with high effectiveness activity.

Each test was performed in triplicate and the results were expressed as mean±standard deviation.

Results and Discussion

- Antisickling activity of Gardenia ternifolia subsp. jovis-tonantis (Welw.) Verdc.

Figures 1 and 2(a-C) show respectively the micrographies of SS blood alone in a NaCl 0.9% solution (control, Figure 1) and the SS blood incubated with the aqueous extract (Figure 2a), alcoholic extract (Figure 2b) and anthocyanins extract (Figure 2c) from *Gardenia ternifolia subsp. jovis-tonantis* leaves.

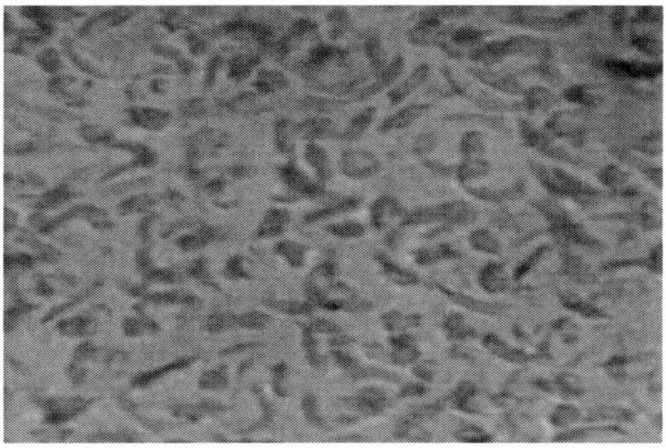

Figure 1. Morphology of drepanocytes of untreated SS blood (control) (x500) [NaCl 0.9%; $Na_2S_2O_5$ 2%,].

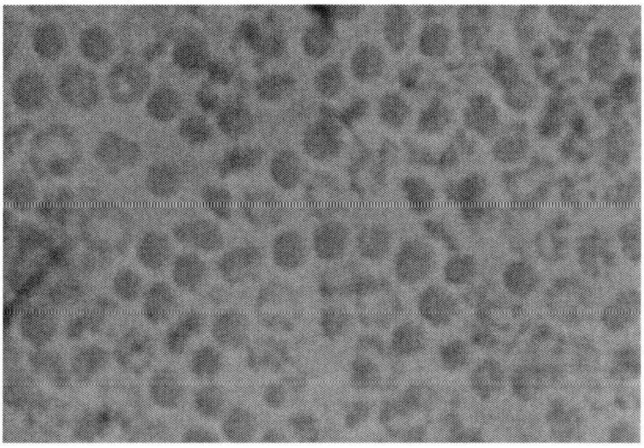

Figure 2a. Morphology of drepanocytes treated with 30 µg/ml of methanol extract of *Gardenia ternifolia subsp. jovis-tonantis* leaves (X500), [NaCl 0.9%; $Na_2S_2O_5$ 2%,].

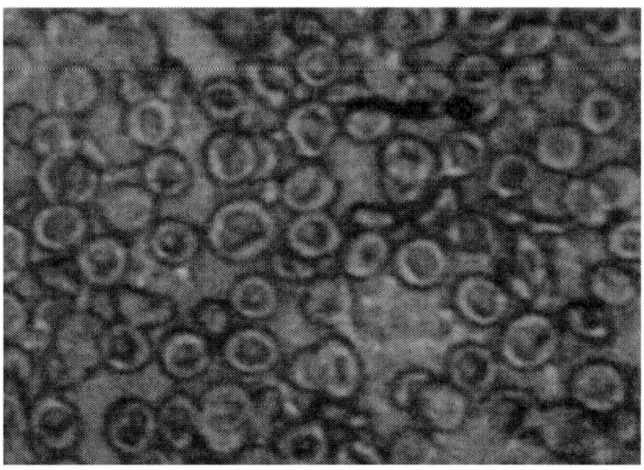

Figure 2b. Morphology of drepanocytes treated with 50 µg/ml of ethyl acetate extract of *Gardenia ternifolia subsp. jovis-tonantis* leaves (X500), [NaCl 0.9%; $Na_2S_2O_5$ 2%,].

Figure 1 shows that the control contains in majority sickle-shaped erythrocytes, confirming the SS nature of the blood. Mixed together with both aqueous extract, ethanol and anthocyanins extract (Figure 2, a-c), the majority of erythrocytes are reversed normal-shape. This indicates that *Gardenia ternifolia subsp. jovis-tonantis* leaves have antisickling effects, thus justifying the use of this plant in Congolese traditional medicine.

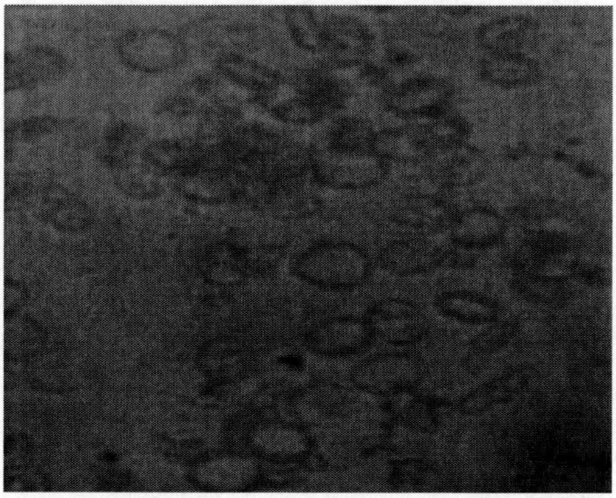

Figure 2c. Morphology of drepanocytes treated with 50 μg/ml of anthocyanins extract of *Gardenia ternifolia subsp. jovis-tonantis* leaves (X500), [NaCl 0.9%; $Na_2S_2O_5$ 2%,].

Perimeter, surface and radius were calculated for untreated and treated sickle red blood cells plant extracts in order to confirm the modification showed by micrographies (Table 1).

Table 1. Average values of the perimeters, surfaces and the radius of untreated and treated sickle Red blood cells

extracts	Cellular Perimeters (μm)	Cellular surfaces (μm^2)	Cellular radius (μm)
Control	32.66±2.32	21.14 ±1.78	-
methanol extract	21.03±2.07	34.02±3.02	3.30±0.59
ethyl acetate extract	20.12±2.14	34.18±3.23	3.28±0.54
anthocyanins extract	20.43±2.21	33.86±3.17	3.11±0.55

As it can be seen in table 1 the average radius for the RBCs of the sickle blood could not be calculated because sickled red blood cells of untreated blood are not circular. The average radius appeared after treatment of sickle red blood cells with different extracts indicating the re-appearance of the normal form of red blood cells. Statistical treatment indicated a significant difference (threshold of 0.05) between the average values of both the perimeter and the surface of blood cells on the micrographies. This confirms the red blood cells morphology modification in the presence of plant extracts.

A similar result was already obtained for some medicinal plant species used for the management of SCD by Congolese traditional healers. This activity is due to anthocyanins [13-20, 15, 23]. In fact, it is possible that anthocyanins have the ability to interact with hemoglobin S [19, 29]. Interaction of these pigments with hemoglobin S could compete with the polymerization of this abnormal hemoglobin and prevent the sickling of sickle cells. In addition, anthocyanins (for which intestinal catabolism gives phenolic acids), also known for their antioxidant properties, could affect the Fe^{3+}/Fe^{2+} higher ratio in sickle cells and the stability of erythrocytes membranes by preventing the oxidation of membranes phospholipids [30]. As SCD is a chronic disease, using anthocyanins as medicinal foods or nutraceuticals would be a good approach instead of giving pharmaceutical products to sicklers during all their life.

- ❖ Free radical scavenging activity and kinetics study

Figure 3 shows the DPPH radical reduction kinetics by the methanol, ethyl acetate and anthocyanin extracts of *Gardena jovis tonantis* compared to ascorbic acid as positive control.

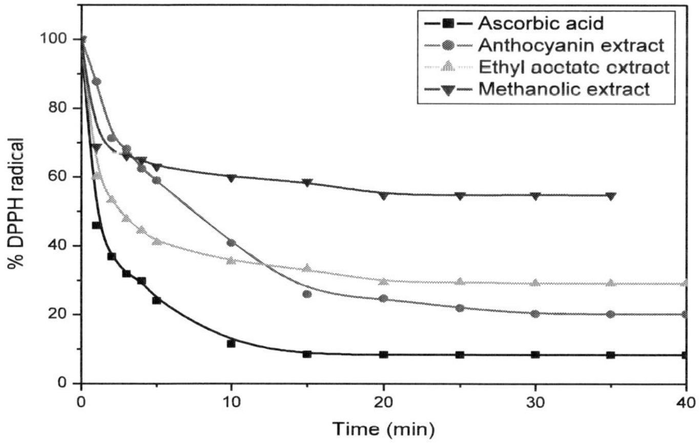

Figure 3. The dependence of DPPH radical reduction (80 μM) on time of incubation in a reaction mixture of ascorbic acid, anthocyanin, ethyl acetate and methanol extracts (10 μg/ml) respectively.

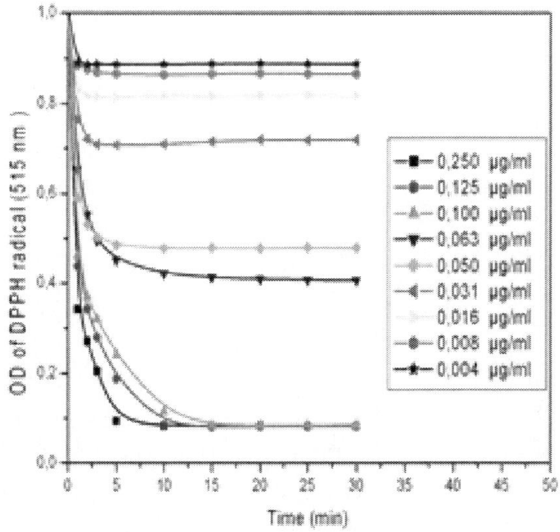

(a)

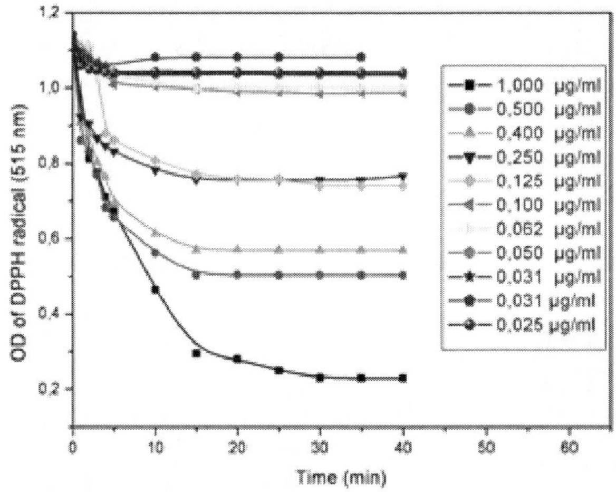

(b)

Figure 4. The dependence of DPPH radical reduction on antioxidant dose and time of incubation in a reaction mixture: (a) Ascorbic acid and (b) anthocyanin extract at various concentrations.

These curves display an exponential decrease characteristic of the kinetic curves of disappearance depending to the time. All these curves present two phases: a fast decrease phase and a stage indicating the end of radical scavenging reaction (equilibrium). The curve of the ascorbic acid (positive control) shows a faster decrease than those of all plant extracts. It is followed respectively by anthocyanin, ethyl acetate and methanol extracts.

Figure 4 shows the dependence of DPPH radical reduction on antioxidant dose and time of incubation in a reaction mixture for ascorbic acid and anthocyanin extract at various concentrations.

These curves indicate that the radical scavenging activity of a given drug/extract increases with it dose as shown by the falling speed and the appearance of the slope.

The calculated values of EC_{50} (after 30 minutes of the reaction) of different extracts are given in Table 2.

Table 2. Radical scavenging activity of extracts from *Gardenia ternifolia* subsp. *jovis-tonantis*

Tested drug	EC_{50} (µg/ml)	Radical scavenging activity
Ascorbic acid (positive control)	0.548	1.82
Anthocyanin extract	1.136	0.88
Ethyl acetate extract	0.867	1.15
Methanolic extract	1.254	0.80

As it can be seen in Table 2, Ethyl acetate extract has high radical scavenging activity followed by anthocyanin extract and methanol soluble fraction respectively.

It could be inferred from these results that the higher activity of the ethyl acetate soluble fraction could be attributed to the higher content of this extract in flavonoids as previously reported. Indeed, ethyl acetate is very selective solvent for extracting the flavonoids [31].

The reduction of radical DPPH reaction speed (figure 6) is a significant additional parameter to take into account in evaluating the radical scavenging property of the extracts. Indeed, it comes out from this figure that the reaction speed of the ascorbic acid (positive control) remains higher than that of the tested extracts for the first 10 minutes. This activity is followed respectively by anthocyanin extract (EC_{50} = 1.136 µg/ml), ethyl acetate (EC_{50} = 0.867 µg/ml) and methanol (EC_{50} = 1.254 µg/ml) soluble fractions as revealed by the slopes of different curves. Thus, the best extract is that which has a high speed of reduction of the free radicals.

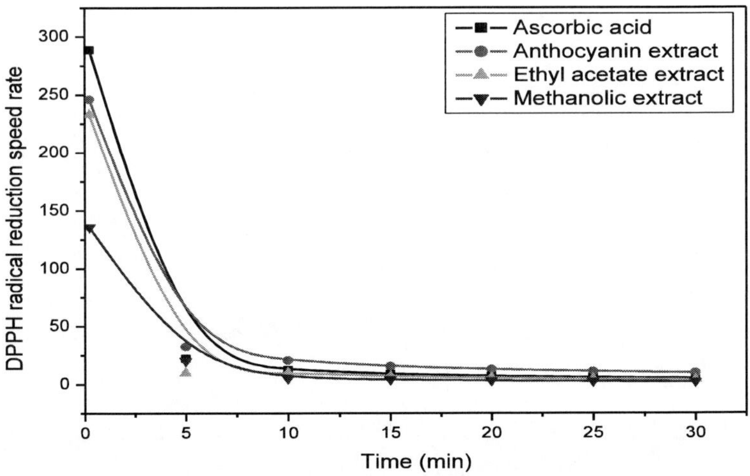

Figure 5. The dependence of DPPH radical reduction speed rate on time.

Recent findings indicate that reactive oxygen species (ROS) play a key role in the pathophysiology of chronic diseases including SCD. The oxidative stress in SCD is likely the result of intravascular sickling and transient vaso-occlusive event leading to the decrease of nitric oxide (NO) probably due to consumption of NO by free oxygen radicals, and/or by cell-free plasma heme as a result of hemolysis [32]. The results outlined in this paper, indicate the antisickling and scavenging effects of *Gardenia ternifolia subsp. jovis-tonantis* , as attractive potential candidate for SCD therapy for improving the quality life of sicklers. As valuable source of reducing leads/hits, *Gardenia ternifolia subsp. jovis-tonantis* could prevent *in vivo* oxidative reactions, often by diminishing oxidative stress-induced tissue damage resulted from chronic diseases such as SCD.

Conclusion

The present study evaluated the *in vitro* radical scavenging and antisickling activities of *Gardenia ternifolia subsp. jovis-tonantis* leaves. This plant species displayed promising antisickling and radical scavenging effects *in vitro*. The study has validated the pharmacological relevance of *Gardenia ternifolia* and sustains the use of this herbal medicine in the management of SCD in traditional medical system. Further studies involving the chemical profiling of the active fractions are in progress.

Acknowledgments

This research was founded by the International Foundation for Science (IFS, Stockholm, Sweden) and the Organization for the Prohibition of Chemical Weapons (OPCW) (IFS Research Grants N0 F/4921-1 and F/4921-2), research grant offered to Dr. Koto -te- Nyiwa NGBOLUA. Special thanks are addressed toward the "Centre de Medécine Mixte et Anémie SS" for proving us the sickle cell blood.

References

[1] Mpiana PT, Ngbolua KN, Mudogo V, Tshibangu DST, Atibu EK. The potential effectiveness of medicinal plants used for the treatment of Sickle cell Disease in the Democratic Republic of Congo folk medicine: A review. In: Progress *in Traditional and Folk herbal medicine* Vol. I, pp 1-11, 2012.

[2] World Health Organization, "Drépanocytose et Autres Hémoglobinopathies". [Online] Available from: http://www.who.int/ mediacentre/ factsheets/ fs308/ fr/ index.html (accessed on 15 January 2012).

[3] Mpiana PT, Tshibangu DST, Shetonde OM, Ngbolua KN. *In vitro* antidrepanocytary activity (anti-sickle cell anaemia) of some Congolese plants. *Phytomedicine* 14: 192-195, 2007.

[4] Mpiana PT, Mudogo V, Tshibangu V, Kitwa EK, Kanangila AB, Lumbu JBS, Ngbolua KN, Atibu EK, Kakule MK. Antisickling Activity of Anthocyanins from *Bombax pentadrum, Ficus capensis, Zizyphus mucronata*: Photo-degradation effect. *Journal of Ethnopharmacology* 120: 413-418, 2008.

[5] Mpiana PT, Mudogo V, Tshibangu DST, Ngbolua KN, Shetonde OM, Mangwala PK, Mavakala BK. *In vitro* Antisickling Activity of

Anthocyanins Extracts of a Congolese Plant: *Alchornea cordifolia M. Arg. Journal of Medical Sciences* 7 (7): 1182-1186, 2007.

[6] Mpiana PT, Mudogo V, Ngbolua KN, Tshibangu DST, Shetonde OM, Mbala BM. *In vitro* Antisickling Activity of Anthocyanins from *Ocimum basilicum L.* (Lamiaceae). *International Journal of Pharmacology* 3 (4): 371-374, 2007.

[7] Mpiana PT, Mudogo V, Kabangu YF, Tshibangu DST, Ngbolua KN, Atibu EK, Mangwala KP, Mbala MB, Makelele LK, Bokota MT. Antisickling Activity and Thermostability of Anthocyanins Extract from a Congolese plant, *Hymenocardia acida Tul.* (Hymenocardiaceae). *International Journal of Pharmacology* 5 (1): 65-70, 2009.

[8] Kambale JK, Ngbolua KN, Mpiana PT, Mudogo V, Tshibangu DST, Wumba R, Mvumbi LG, Kalala LR, Mesia KG, Ekutsu E. Evaluation *in vitro* de l'activié antifalcémiante et effet antioxydatif des extraits d'*Uapaca heudelotii* Baill. (Euphorbiaceae). *International Journal of Biological & Chemical Sciences* 7(2): 523-534, 2013.

[9] Ngbolua KN, Fatiany PR, Robijaona B, Randrianirina AYO, Rajaonarivelo PJ, Rasondratovo B, Raharisololalao A, Moulis C, Mudogo V, Mpiana PT. Ethno-botanical survey, Chemical composition and *in vitro* Antimicrobial activity of essential oils from the root bark of *Hazomalania voyroni* (Jum.) Capuron (Hernandiaceae). Journal of *Advancement in Medical and Life Sciences* 01(01): 01-06, 2014.

[10] Ngbolua KN, Mpiana PT, Mudogo V, Ngombe NK, Tshibangu DST, Ekutsu E, Kabena ON, Gbolo BZ, Muanyishay L. Ethno-pharmacological survey and Floristical study of some Medicinal Plants traditionally used to treat infectious and parasitic pathologies in the Democratic Republic of Congo. *International Journal of Medicinal Plants* 106: 454-467, 2014.

[11] Kasali FM, Mahano AO, Nyakabwa DS, Kadima NJ, FM Misakabu, Tshibangu DST, Ngbolua KN, Mpiana PT. Ethnopharmacological survey of medicinal plants used against malaria in Bukavu city (D.R. Congo). *European Journal of Medicinal Plants* 4(1): 25-31, 2014.

[12] Tshilanda DD, Onyamboko NV, Mpiana PT, Ngbolua KN, Tshibangu DST, Mbala MB, Bokolo MK, Taba KM, Kasonga KT. Antisickling activity of butyl stearate isolated from *Ocimum basilicum* (Lamiaceae). *Asian Pacific Journal of Tropical Biomedicine* 4 (5): 393-398, 2014.

[13] Ngbolua KN, Rafatro Herintsoa, Rakotoarimanana Hajatiana, Ratsimamanga Urverg Suzanne, Mudogo V, Mpiana PT, Tshibangu DST. Pharmacological screening of some traditionally-used antimalarial

plants from the Democratic Republic of Congo compared to its ecological taxonomic equivalence in Madagascar. *Int. J. Biol. Chem. Sci.* 5 (5): 1797-1804, 2011.

[14] Ngbolua KN, Hajatiana Rakotoarimanana, Herintsoa Rafatro, Urverg Suzanne Ratsimamanga, V Mudogo, PT Mpiana, Tshibangu DST. Comparative antimalarial and cytotoxic activities of two Vernonia species: V. *amygdalina* from the Democratic Republic of Congo and V. *cinerea subsp vialis* endemic to Madagascar. *Int. J. Biol. Chem.* Sci. 5(1): 345-353, 2011.

[15] Ngbolua KN, Mudogo V, Mpiana PT, Malekani MJ, Rafatro Herintsoa, Urverg Ratsimamanga U, Takoy L, Rakotoarimana H, Tshibangu DST. Evaluation de l'activité anti-drépanocytaire et antipaludique de quelques taxons végétaux de la République démocratique du Congo et de Madagascar. *Ethnopharmacologia* 50: 19-24, 2013.

[16] Mpiana PT, Kimbadi BL, Ombeni AM, Ngbolua KN, Tshibangu DST, Tshilanda DD, Misengabu NM, Muanyishay CL, Muyisa SK. *In vitro* inhibitory effects and anti-sickle erythrocytes haemolysis of *Dicliptera colorata* C.B. Clarke, *Euphorbia hirta* L. and *Sorghum bicolor* (L.) Moench. *Open Journal of Blood Diseases* 3: 43-48, 2013.

[17] Mpiana PT, Dianzenza EN, Ngbolua KN, Tshibangu DST, Mbala BM, Shetonde OM, Atibu EK, Kakule MK, Bokota MT. Antisickling properties, thermal and photochemical degradations of anthocyanins extract from *Annona senegalensis* (Annonaceae). *International Journal of Biological & Chemical Sciences* 6 (5): 2241-2251, 2012.

[18] Mpiana PT, Ngbolua KN, Mudogo V, Tshibangu DST, Atibu EK, Tshilanda DD, Misengabu NM. Antisickle erythrocytes haemolysis properties and inhibitory effect of anthocyanins extracts of *Trema orientalis* (ULMACEAE) on the aggregation of human deoxyhemoglobin S *in vitro. Journal of Medical Sciences* 11 (3): 129-137, 2011.

[19] Mpiana PT, Ngbolua KN, Bokota MT, Kasonga TK, Atibu EK, Mudogo V. In *vitro* Effects of Anthocyanins Extracts From *Justicia secunda* VAHL on the Solubility of Hemoglobin *S* and Membrane Stability of Sickle Erythrocytes, *Blood Transfusion* 8: 248-254, 2010.

[20] Mpiana PT, Bokota MT, Mbula JP, Ngbolua KN, Tshibangu DST, Atibu EK, Kwembe JTK, Kakule MK. Effet of Anthocyanins Extracts from *Justicia matammensis* and *Justicia laxa* on Sickle cells. In: Anthocyanins, Structure, Biosynthesis and Health benefits (Series:

Biochemistry Research Trends, Nutritional and Diet Research Progress); Noboru Motohashi (ed.), pp. 111-124, 2013.

[21] Kahkoonen MP, Heinamaki J, Heinonen M. Antioxidant activity of anthocyanins and their aglycons. *Journal of Agricultural & Food Chemistry* 52: 628–633, 2003.

[22] Satué Gracia MT, Heinonen M, Frankel EN. Anthocyanins as antioxidants on human low–density lipoprotein and lecithin-liposome systems. *Journal of Agricultural & Food Chemistry* 45: 3362-3367, 1997.

[23] Neuwinger HD. African Traditional Medicine: A dictionary of plant use and applications, Mepharm Scientific Publisher, Stuttgart: Germany, 2000.

[24] Bruneton J. Pharmacognosie, Phytochimie des Plantes Médicinales. 3rd Edition, Revue et Augmentée, Tec & Doc, Paris, 1999.

[25] Ngbolua KN, Bishola TT, Mpiana PT, Mudogo V, Tshibangu DST, Ngombe KN, Ekutsu EG, Tshilanda DD, Gbolo ZB, Mwanangombo DT, Fatiany PR, Baholy R. Ethno-botanical survey, *in vitro* antisickling and free radical scavenging activities of *Garcinia punctata* Oliv. (Clusiaceae). *Journal of Advanced Botany & Zoology* V1I2. DOI: 10.15297/JABZ.V1I2.04, 2014.

[26] Terpinc P, Bezjak M, Abrahimovic H. A kinetic model for evaluation of the antioxidant activity of several rosemary extracts. *Food Chemistry,* 2009, DOI 10, 1016/J. FoodChem. 2008.12.033.

[27] Terpinc P, Abramovic H. A kinetic approach for evaluation of the antioxidant activity of selected phenolic acids, *Food Chemistry* 2010, 121: 366-371, 2010.

[28] Gulpa S, Cox S, Abu-Ghannam N. Effect of different drying temperatures on the moisture and phytochemical constituents of edible irish brown Seaweed. *LWT Food Science and Technology* 44 (5): 1266-1272, 2011.

[29] Mpiana PT, Ngbolua KN, Mudogo V, Tshibangu DST, Atibu EK, Tshilanda DD, Misengabu NM. Antisickle erythrocytes haemolysis properties and inhibitory effect of anthocyanins extracts of *Trema orientalis* (ULMACEAE) on the aggregation of human deoxyhemoglobin S *in vitro. Journal of Medical Sciences* 11 (3): 129-137, 2011.

[30] Mpiana PT, Makelele LK, Oleko RW, Bokota MT, Tshibangu DST, Ngbolua KN, Mbala MB, Atibu EK, Nshimba SM. Antisickling activity of medicinal plants used in the management of Sickle cell Disease in

Tshopo district, D.R.Congo, *Australian Journal of Medical Herbalism* 22 (4): 132-137, 2010.

[31] Nan Wu, Kuang Fu, Yu-Jie Fu, Yuan-Gang Zu, Chang FR, Chen Y-H, Liu X-L, Kong Y, Liu W, Gu Cheng-Bo. Antioxidant Activities of extracts and main components of pigeonpea [Cajanus cajan (L.) Milsp.] leaves. *Molecules* 14: 1032-1043, 2009.

[32] Dasgupta T, Hebbel RP, Kaul DK. Protective effect of arginine on oxidative stress in transgenic sickle mouse models. Free *Radical Biology & Medicine* 41: 1771-1780, 2006.

In: Sickle Cell Disease
Editor: Marilyn E. Lewis
ISBN: 978-1-63482-828-4

Chapter IV

Bioactivity of Medicinal Plants Traditionally Used for the Management of Sickle Cell Disease in Democratic Republic of the Congo: State of the Art and Future Directions

K. N. Ngbolua[1,], P. T. Mpiana[2], D. S. T. Tshibangu[2] and B. Z. Gbolo[1]*

[1]Department of Biology, Faculty of Science, University of Kinshasa, Democratic Republic of the Congo

[2]Department of Chemistry, Faculty of Science, University of Kinshasa, Democratic Republic of the Congo

Abstract

Background: The search and the development of antisickling herbal drugs are a priority in Africa, where the Sickle cell disease (SCD) is

[*]Corresponding Author: Dr. Koto-te-Nyiwa Ngbolua, Associate Professor, E-mail: jpngbolua@unikin.ac.cd; Tel.: +243 81 68 79 527

endemic. Our research program had as initial objectives - to identify plants traditionally used in folk medicine for the management of SCD in Democratic Republic of the Congo (DRC), - to identify other/new sources of antisickling bioactive secondary metabolites mainly from non human primate (great apes) pharmacopeia/diet or zoopharmacognosy - to validate their bioactivity scientifically, - to identify the chemical groups responsible for this bioactivity, to elucidate the structures the bioactive molecules and finally - to formulate the bioactive plants based medicines for managing SCD in DRC.

Study design and Methodology: The plant extracts were screened for antisickling activity using Emmel test, polymerization of haemoglobin S assay; osmotic fragility assay; anti-hemolytic test; radical scavenging assay and Met-hemoglobin profiling assay. The molecular structures of the active compounds were characterized by combining the chromatographic and spectroscopic methods. The acute toxicity bioassay of herbal medicine was carried out using the Wistar rats as animal model.

Results: To date, 100 antisickling plants were scientifically validated; - the anthocyanins, betulinic, maslinic, oleanolic and lunularic acid as well as the butyl stearate are responsible for this bioactivity. The results of the pre-clinical evaluations allowed us to select by bio-guidance three most active plants for the formulation of a polyherbal medicine Drepanoalpha®. This herbal drug displayed *in vitro* sickling inhibitory of effect on drepanocytes in hypoxia as well anti-hemolytic and anti-oxidative properties. The acute toxicity test in Wistar rat model showed that the DL_{50} of Drepanoalpha® is higher than 4000 mg/kg. The analysis of the biochemical and hematologic markers showed the safety of Drepanoalpha®. Thus, Drepanoalpha® is not toxic and has moreover the property of boosting the rate of hemoglobin in the treated rats. A preliminary clinical trial of Drepanoalpha® in a pilot scale on a sample of 20 sicklers indicates that this drug alleviate significantly clinical manifestations in patients after some period probably by epigenetic modulation of the gene expression of fetal hemoglobin or by inhibiting *in vivo* hemolysis of sickle erythrocytes. Non-recourse to blood transfusion is done for a long period after cessation of medication.

Conclusion and future directions: The results of fundamental research obtained led us to develop Drepanoalpha® from Congolese Traditional Medicine knowledge. The biochemical and hematological data showed that this polyherbal formula does not interfere with the physiological functions of the liver and the kidneys. A double blind and randomized clinical trial (Phase II), is thus necessary for confirming the in vivo biosafety of the medicine before it industrial valorization.

Keywords: Sickle cell disease,Polyherbal medicine, Drepanoalpha®, Clinical trials, DR Congo

Sickle Cell Disease: Pathophysiology and Treatment

Sickle Cell Disease (SCD) or sickle cell anaemia (SCA) is due to the polymerization of abnormal haemoglobin S when oxygen tension decreases. This lead to the erythrocytes shape modification and anaemia [1, 2].

Clinical symptoms of SCD are associated to the polymerization of unstable haemoglobin S under hypoxic conditions. These symptoms include erythrocytes shape modification as well as anaemia [3]. The intracellular polymerization of deoxy-haemoglobin S occurs as a result of the activation of both KCl-cotransport system and Gardos channel, leading into sickle erythrocyte dehydration [4-6] while anaemia occurs as a result of radical oxygen species (ROS) induced erythrocyte (RBC) membrane damage. At biochemical level, SCD is characterized by the low activity of the glutathione reductase system [7] and the hexose metabolism in sickle erythrocytes is very reduced [8], so methaemoglobin and other ferriprotoporphyrin (containing Fe^{3+}) breakdown products builds up in the SCD patients' blood system as result of oxidative stress. It is known also that sickle cell patients contain more than the normal concentration of the calcium ions. These ions are bound to membrane proteins resulting in dehydration and loss of red blood cells deformability and RBC/leukocyte adherence to the endothelium making SCD patient in a chronic inflammatory state [9]. Nuclear factor-kappa B (NF-kB) is a transcription factor that activates expression of endothelial adhesion molecules in SCD. The NF-kB activity could increase leucocyte adhesion leading into the decrease of microvascular blood flow [10-12].

Several others complications are also associated with the pathophysioloy of SCD. These include the abnormalities in blood coagulation related to increased generation of thrombin and the defective fibrinolytic activity (activation of the coagulation system) and pro-inflammatory events (elevation in the inflammatory mediator secretory phospholiapse A_2) [2, 13, 14]. Except the bone marrow transplant, SCD has currently no widely available cure. However, the treatment is based on the inhibition of the naturally occurring pathophysiological events of the disease: anemia, vaso-occlusives crises, infections, pain, pulmonary hypertension, etc. [15, 16].

In regions where SCD is endemic, herbal medicines are widely used to relieve the symptoms of the disease. Clinical improvement has been observed in SCD patients undergoing treatment with medicinal plants [17]. In our efforts to search for novel and bioactive antisickling hits from indigenous plants, we recently investigated 100 plants species native to Democratic Republic of the Congo (DRC) which are prescribed by traditional practitioners or sold in markets for the management SCD. The aim of this research program is - to validate their bioactivity scientifically, - to identify the chemical groups responsible for this bioactivity, - to elucidate the structures of the bioactive molecules. The additional goal of the program is - to identify other/new sources of antisickling bioactive secondary metabolites mainly from non human primate (great apes) pharmacopeia/diet or zoopharmacognosy, - to formulate the bioactive plants based medicines for managing SCD in DRC.

Great Apes Plant Foods As Sources of New Antisickling Secondary Metabolites: A Validated Hypothesis

Humans and great apes (bonobos, chimpanzees, gorillas, and orangutans) share a common gut anatomy. Although, some diseases that cause countless deaths in humans are ineffective or have minor non disturbing effects in apes. Because of their phylogenetic closeness and common neural pathways of chemosensory perception, humans and great apes, when displaying symptoms of illness could alter their foraging to ingest non-nutritive chemical as diet (pharmacophagy) [18-21]. In the case of malaria infections, the animal self-medicative behavior aid in the control of malaria by inhibiting erythrocytes hemolysis. So malaria does not seem cause any harm or illness to the great apes like bonobos (*Pan paniscus*, figure 1b) [22].

It is well-known that, the high frequency of SCD gene occurred in tropical regions (figure 1d) where malaria is endemic (figure 1c) [23].Thus, in such regions, the great apes especially bonobos, endemic to Democratic Republic of the Congo, control the malaria infections through their diet. The control of a hemolytic disease such as malaria by the non human primates (NHP) through medicinal plants based diet indicates that the plants consumed by these animals would be displayed anti-hemolytic and anti-inflammatory effects and could be beneficial for people suffering from SCD [18-21]. Since great apes (bonobos) are infected by malaria parasite but they cannot develop malaria disease, it was therefore, hypothesized that great apes plant foods could protect sickle erythrocyte against hemolysis by inhibiting the polymerization of sickle hemoglobin and radical oxygen species formation within sickle erythrocyte as it does for *Plasmodium falciparum* infected erythrocytes in bonobos [21].

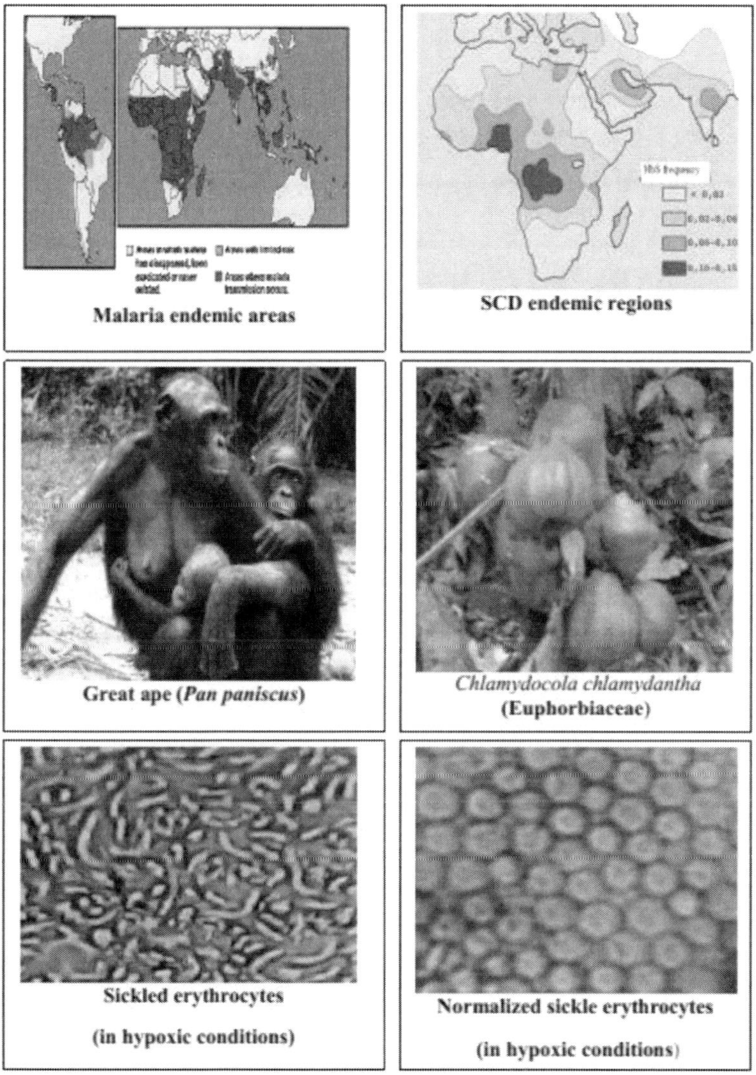

Figure 1.

This approach also knows as zoo-pharmacognosy constitutes an alternative and valuable therapy strategy for identifying effective medicinal plants as revealed by our research bio-prospection program [18-21, 24].

Antisickling Bioassays: State of the Art

When searching for active antisickling plants/extracts/compounds, it is necessary to have relatively simple biological tests available in order to validate the bioactivity the chosen plant species. Recent findings in biochemistry and cell biology of SCD have indicated that three main targets are of chemotherapeutic relevance. These include erythrocyte membrane, unstable haemoglobin S and free radicals which are spontaneously produced within red blood cells (RBCs) [25]. It is possible therefore to act directly on each target involved in the pathophysiology of SCD. For example, plant extract which inhibit the sickling of RBCs or the polymerization of deoxy form of haemoglobin S in hypoxic conditions and free radicals scavengers will alleviate all the clinical symptoms of SCD by preventing cell dehydration, cell haemolysis and haemoglobin oxidative damage.

In our bio-prospecting program, a RBCs sickling inhibitory test (Emmel test) has been adapted and used successfully to test systematically a library of Congolese plants for their reported antisickling properties. The testing procedure consists of exposing sickled erythrocytes to plant extracts and the number of the normalized RBCs is evaluated microscopically. A 6x zoom CANNON-type digital camera is used to convert the photonic micrograph image into a digital image, which is then digitalized with the help of MOTIC Images 2000 ver. 1.3 software [26-46]. An extract/compound is considered to possess: very high activity (+++) if normalization >70%; high activity (++) if 50 < normalization <70%; weak activity (+) if 10<normalization <50%; no activity (–) if normalization <10% (Mpiana*et al.,* 2008). The modes of action are investigated by evaluating the effects of extracts/compounds on inhibition of Hb S polymerization and erythrocyte membrane stability using Itano and osmotic fragility tests respectively (Mpiana*et al.,* in press). The solubility of the deoxygenated sickle cell hemoglobin (Itano test) is expressed as the increase of the optical density at 540 nm after its treatment with active extracts/compounds. Fragility of RBCs is evaluated by placing cells in graded series of hypotonic saline solutions (from 0.2% to 0.8% NaCl) buffered with phosphate at pH 7.4. The number of RBCs not lysed by saline concentration is determined microscopically. Extract/compound is considered as active if the mean corpuscular fragility (which is the concentration of saline causing 50% haemolysis of the RBCs) value of treated cells is greater than that of the untreated sickle erythrocytes and means that RBCs are rehydrated.

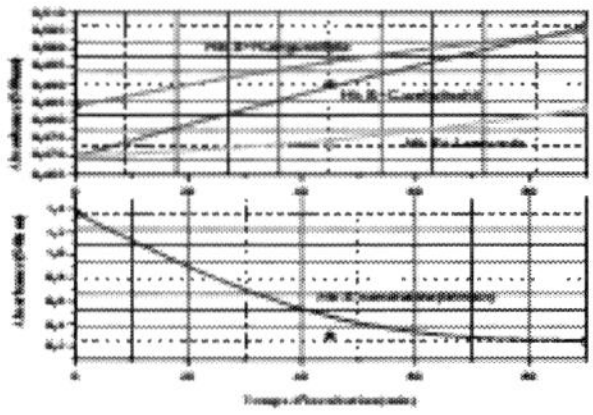

The increase of optical density at 540 nm wavelength (Hb S): Hb S polymerization inhibitory effect

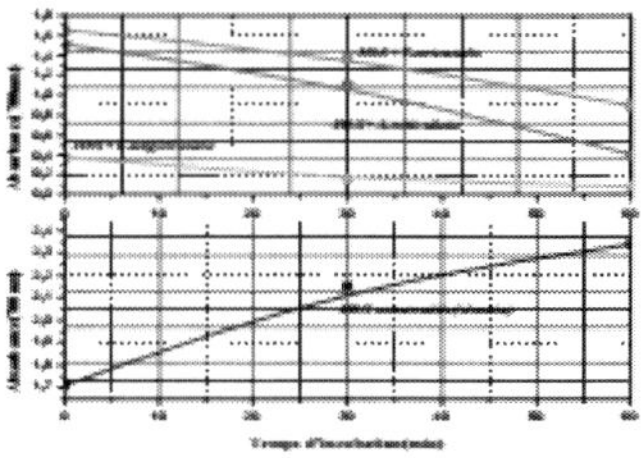

The decrease of optical density at 700 nm wavelength (tactoïd): tactoid formation inhibitory effect

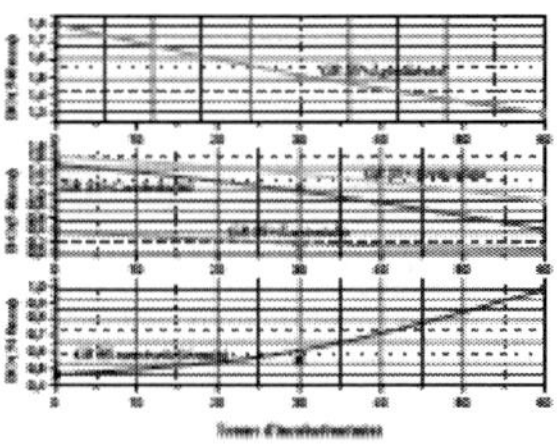

Optical density at 540 nm (Hb S): Inhibition of Sickle erythrocyte hemolysis (Isotonic conditions)

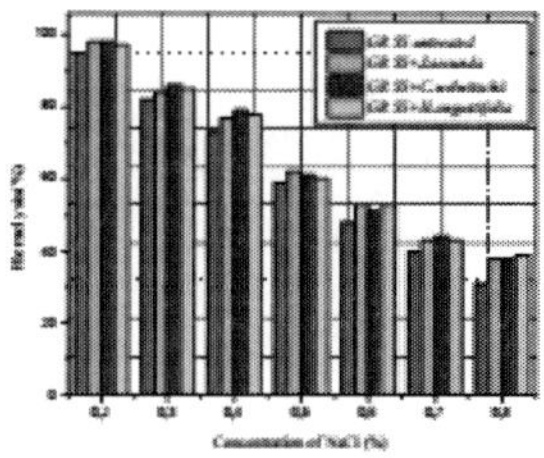

Hemolysis (%) of Sickle erythrocyte: stabilization of erythrocyte membrane

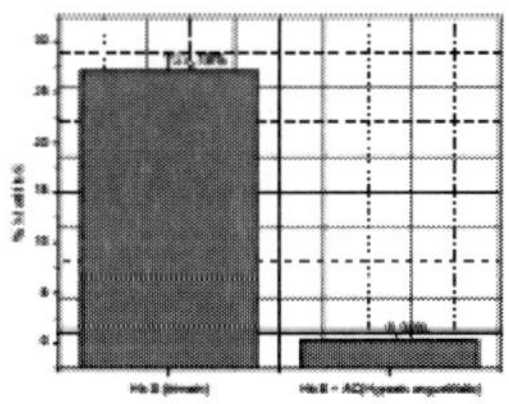

Decease of %MetHb S:

Iinhibition of MetHb S formation in solution

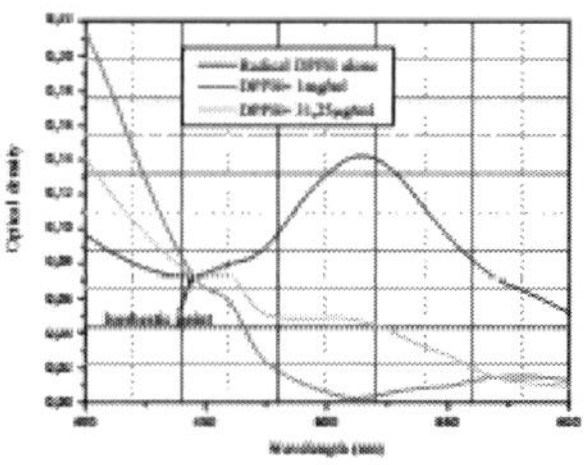

Titration of DPPH radical by anthocyanin extract : Isosbestic point revealed radical scavenging activity of anthocyanins

Results of Our Research Program

- ❖ Congolese antisickling plants

The knowledge of traditional herbal practice has played a positive role in the use of medicinal plants in the management of sickle cell disease with a great degree of success over time. This traditional knowledge has been scientifically validated through preclinical study process. Hence much information on the active constituents and possible mode of action of the plant derived secondary metabolites has been reported in the literature. 100 plant species were screened for their antisickling activity and the major/active metabolites responsible for the observed activity identified by the combination of chromatographic and spectroscopic techniques for some plant taxons [18-21, 24-48]. Plants reportedly used in Congolese SCD ethno-medicine as medicinal foods are *Anonidiummannii (Oliv.) Engl. & Diel* (Annonacea), *Cajanuscajan* (L.) Millsp. (Leguminosae), *Glycine max* (L.) Merr.(Leguminosae), *Ipomoea batatas*(L.) Lam. (Convolvulaceae), *Ocimumbasilicum*L. (Lamiaceae), *Psophocarpusscandens* (Endl.) Verdc. (Leguminosae), *Sorghum bicolor* (L.) Moench (Poaceae), *Treculiaafricana Decne. exTrécul* (Moraceae), *Vignaunguiculata*(L.) Walp. (Leguminosae).The field of nutrigenomics which involves the study of how genes and dietary components interact to influence human phenotype (epigenetic modulation) is a valuable strategy to be developed in SCD management.

- Chemicals constituents isolates from Congolese plants and their role in SCD

The major phytochemicals in Congolese medicinal plants traditionally used for the management of SCD include phenolics (lunularic acid) [46], polyphenolics (anthocyanins) [25-31, 35-47], pentacyclictriterpenoids (oleanoic acid, maslinic acid and betulinic acid) [49] and esters (butyl stearate) [50]. It is observed that some plant species which have not been displayed any antisickling properties are still very useful as they could help to relief pains and reduce inflammation and other complications associated with SCD. However, most of the active principles have antioxidant activity. Thus, the roles of antioxidants in SCD management were investigated *invitro* using DPPH radical scavenging assay and met-hemoglobin profiling assay. Plant phenolics and polyphenolics displayed interesting antioxidant activities, and may play key role in SCD management. Indeed, as reducing agent, such bioactive secondary metabolites could prevent *in vivo* oxidative reactions, often by scavenging free radicals before they can damage cells.

❖ Drepanoalpha®: The polyherbal formulafrom Congolese flora

Drepanoalpha® is a polyherbal medicine produced through a bio-guided based plant selection after eight years of intensive advanced laboratory research by the research team of Professor Pius T. Mpiana at the University of Kinshasa, Democratic Republic of the Congo. Drepanoalpha® possess a significant antisickling (normalization rate >80%) and antioxidant activities *in vitro* (ED_{50}= 0.604 ± 0.028 μg/mL) and have the medium lethal dose (LD_{50}) higher than 4000 mg/kg (in Wistar rat model). The product has non-toxic effect on immune cells and blood clotting factors. This poly-herbal formulation increases the hemoglobin rate in the rats (500-4000 mg/kg bodyweight) and preserves the histological architecture of the liver cells compared with the control. The aqueous and alcoholic extracts of Drepanoalpha® contain phenolic compounds especially anthocyanins as the biologically active constituents [51]. In human clinical use, this nutraceutical is taken three times daily for the treatment of SCD. Drepanoalpha® reduces the frequency of crises in SCD and improves the general state treated patients. The oral administration of Drepanoalpha® does not induce any signs of toxicity (no side effects). All the treated patients have normal phenotype if compared them to normal individuals and have not made any more crises for more than six months last. Non-recourse to blood transfusion is done for a long period after cessation of medication. The preliminary clinical trial of Drepanoalpha® in a pilot scale on a sample of 20 sicklers indicates that this poly-herbal formulation increases also the hemoglobin rate in human (from 7.6 to13.2 g/dL). However, the heterogeneity of drug response in was observed among treated SCD patients [17]. We postulated that Drepanoalpha® couldalleviate the clinical manifestations in SCD patients probably by epigenetic modulation of the gene expression of fetal hemoglobin or by inhibiting *in vivo* the hemolysis of sickle erythrocytes [17].

Conclusion and Future Directions

The use of herbal remedies in Africa especially in DRC has made treatment more affordable and accessible for poor population. The results of fundamental research (pre-clinical evaluations) obtained led us to develop Drepanoalpha® from Congolese Traditional Medicine knowledge. The biochemical and hematological data showed that this polyherbal formula does not interfere with the physiological functions of the liver and the kidneys. A double blind and randomized clinical trial (Phase II), is thus necessary for confirming the *invivo* bio-safety of the medicine before it industrial valorization. Studies targeting inflammatory events (anti-inflammatory effect), cyto-adherence (anti-adhesive effect) and blood clotting (anti-thrombotic, fibrinolytic and fibrinogenolytic effects) are necessary for completing the available data on Drepanoalpha®.

Acknowledgments

This research program was founded by the International Foundation for Science (IFS, Stockholm, Sweden) and the Organization for the Prohibition of Chemical Weapons (OPCW) (IFS Research Grants N0 F/4921-1 and F/4921-2), research grant offered to Dr. Koto -te- NyiwaNgbolua. The authors are also indebted to the Faculty of Science, University of Kinshasa (DRC) for the facilities provided.

References

[1] Kunle OF, Egharevba HO. Chemical constituents and biological activity of medicinal plants used for the management of sickle cell disease - A review. *Journal of Medicinal Plants Research* 7(48): 3452-3476, 2013.

[2] Hankins J, Banu A. Pharmacotherapy in sickle cell disease – state of the art and future prospects. *Br. J.Haematol.* 145(3): 296–308, 2009.

[3] Okpuzor J, Adebesin O, Ogbunugafor H, Qmadi I. The potential of medicinal plants in sickle cell disease control: a review. *International Journal of Biomedical and Health Sciences* 4(2):47-55, 2008.

[4] Stocker JW, De Franchesi L, Naughton-Smith GA, Corrocher R, Beuzard Y, Brugnara C. ICA-17043, a novel Gardos channel blocker, prevents sickled red blood cell dehydration in vitro and in vivo in SAD mice. *Blood* 101:2412-2418, 2003.

[5] De Franceschi L, Saadane N, Trudel M, Alper SL, Brugnara C, Beuzard Y. Treatment with oral clotrimazole blocks Ca(2+)-activated K+ transport and reverses erythrocyte dehydration in transgenic SAD mice. A model for therapy of sickle cell disease. *J.Clin. Invest.* 93:1670-1676, 1994.

[6] Brugnara C, Gee B, Armsby CC, Kurth S, Sakamoto M, Rifai N, Alper SL, Platt OS. Therapy with oral clotrimazole induces inhibition of the Gardos channel and reduction of erythrocyte dehydration in patients with sickle cell disease. *J Clin.Invest.* 97:1227-1234, 1996.

[7] Hebbel RP, Eaton JW, Balasingam M, Steinberg MH. Spontaneous oxygen radical generation by Sickle cell erythrocytes. *J. Clin. Invest.*70: 1253-1259, 1982.

[8] Osuagwu CG, Mbeyi CU. Altered plasma hexose sugar metabolism in Sickle cell anaemia. *African Journal of Biochemistry*, 1(3): 37-40, 2007.

[9] Mpiana PT, Ngbolua KN, Bokota MT, Kasonga TK, Atibu EK, Mudogo V. *In vitro* Effects of Anthocyanins Extracts From *Justiciasecunda*VAHL on the Solubility of Hemoglobin *S* and Membrane Stability of Sickle Erythrocytes, *Blood Transfusion* 8: 248-254, 2010.

[10] Hebbel RP, Osarogiagbon R, Kaul D. The endothelial biology of sickle cell disease: inflammation and a chronic vasculopathy. *Microcirculation* 11:129-151, 2004.

[11] Kaul DK, Liu XD, Choong S, Belcher JD, Vercellotti GM, Hebbel RP. Anti-inflammatory therapy ameliorates leukocyte adhesion and microvascular flow abnormalities in transgenic sickle mice. *Am.J.Physiol Heart Circ.Physiol.* 287:H293-H301, 2004.

[12] Gupta K, Gupta P, Solovey A, Hebbel RP. Mechanism of interaction of thrombospondin with human endothelium and inhibition of sickle erythrocyte adhesion to human endothelial cells by heparin. *Biochim. Biophys. Acta.* 1453:63–73, 1999.

[13] Nsimba MM, Lami JN, Hayakawa Y, Yamamoto C, Kaji T. Decreased thrombin activity by a Congolese herbal medicine used in Sickle cell anemia. *J. Ethnopharmacol.* 148: 895-900, 2013.

[14] Nsimba MM, Yamamoto C, Lami JN, Hayakawa Y, Kaji T. Effet of a Congolese herbal medicine used in Sickle cell anemia on the expression of plasminogen activators in human coronary aortic endothelial cells culture. *J. Ethnopharmacol.* 146(2): 594-599, 2013.

[15] Mpiana PT, Tshibangu DST, Shetonde OM, Ngbolua KN. *In vitro*antidrepanocytary activity (anti-sickle cell anaemia) of some Congolese plants. *Phytomedicine*14: 192-195, 2007.

[16] Villagra J, Shiva S, Hunter LA, Machado RF, Gladwin MT, Kato GJ. Platelet activation in patients with sickle disease, hemolysis-associated pulmonary hypertension, and nitric oxide scavenging by cell-free hemoglobin. *Blood* 110:2166-2172, 2007.

[17] Ngbolua KN, Mpiana PT. The Possible Role of a Congolese polyherbal formula (Drepanoalpha®) as source of Epigenetic Modulators in Sickle Cell Disease: A Hypothesis. J. *of Advancement in Medical and Life Sciences*. V2I1. DOI: 10.15297/JALS.V2I1.02, 2014.

[18] Ngbolua KN, Bishola TT, Mpiana PT, Mudogo V, Tshibangu DST, Ngombe KN, Ekutsu EG, Gbolo ZB, Kabena NO. Ethno-pharmacological survey, *invitro*antisickling and free radical scavenging activities of *Carapaprocera*DC. stem bark(Meliaceae). *Nova Journalof Medical and Biological Sciences* 2(2): 01-14, 2014.

[19] Ngbolua KN, Bishola TT, Mpiana PT, Mudogo V, Tshibangu DST, Ngombe KN, Ekutsu EG, Tshilanda DD, Gbolo ZB, Mwanangombo DT, Fatiany PR, Baholy R. Ethno-botanical survey, *invitro*antisickling and free radical scavenging activities of *Garciniapunctata*Oliv. (Clusiaceae). *Journal of Advanced Botany & Zoology* V1I2. DOI: 10.15297/JABZ.V1I2.04, 2014.

[20] Ngbolua KN, KambaleSaa-Sita DD, Malekani MJ, KyunguKasolene JC, Kasereka KO, Maloueki U, Musuyu MD, Mpiana PT, Mudogo V. Phytochemical investigation and TLC screening for antioxidant activity of 24 plant species consumed by the Eastern Lowland Gorillas *(Gorilla beringei ssp. graueri:*Hominidae, Primates) endemic to Democratic Republic of the Congo.*Journal of Advancement in Medical and Life Sciences* V1I3. DOI: 10.15297/JALS.V1I3.02, 2014.

[21] Ngbolua KN, Bishola TT, Mpiana PT, Mudogo V, Tshibangu DST, Ngombe KN, Tshilanda DD, Baholy R. *In vitro*antisickling and free radical scavenging activities of *Pentaclethramacrophylla*Benth. (Fabaceae).*Journal of Advancement in Medical and Life Sciences* V1I2. DOI: 10.15297/JALS.V1I2.03, 2014.

[22] Krief S, Escalante AA, Pacheca MA, Mugisha L, André C. On the diversity of malaria parasites in African apes and the origin of P. *falciparum* from bonobos. *PLosPathog.*, 6(2): e 1000765, 2010.

[23] Pagnier J, Wajcman H, Baudin V, Labie D. Genetic polymorphism of drepanocytosis. *Annals of Genetics* 28: 5-12, 1985.

[24] Kambale JK, Ngbolua KN, Mpiana PT, Mudogo V, Tshibangu DST, Wumba R, Mvumbi LG, Kalala LR, Mesia KG, Ekutsu E. Evaluation *in vitro* de l'activié antifalcémiante et effet antioxydatif des extraits d'*Uapaca heudelotii* Baill. (Euphorbiaceae). *Int. J. Biol. Chem. Sci.* 7(2): 523-534, 2013.

[25] Mpiana PT, Ngbolua KN, Mudogo V, Tshibangu DST, Atibu EK, Tshilanda DD, Misengabu NM. Antisickle erythrocytes haemolysis

properties and inhibitory effect of anthocyanins extracts of *Tremaorientalis* (ULMACEAE) on the aggregation of human deoxyhemoglobin S *in vitro.Journal of Medical Sciences*11 (3): 129-137, 2011.

[26] Mpiana PT, Misakabu FM, Kitadi JM, Ngbolua KN, Tshibangu DST, Lombe BK, Tsalu PV, Atibu EK, Gbolo BZ, Muanishay CL.Antisickling activity and physico-chemical stability of anthocyanin extracts from *Hypoxisangustifolia* Lam. (Hypoxidaceae) bulbs. M. Noboru (Ed.), in: Anthocyanins: Occurrence, Structure, Biosynthesis and Health benefits Based on their Evidences of Phytochemicals in Vegetables and Fruits, NOVA Science Publishers, Inc., New York, USA, Vol. 2, pp: 97-113, 2014.

[27] Mpiana PT, Misakabu FM, Yuma PM, Tshibangu DST, Ngbolua KN, Muanyishay CL, Gbolo BZ, Misengabu NM, Kayembe JS. Antisickling activity and physico-chemical stability of anthocyanin extracts from *Ipomoea batatas* leaves. *Journal of Life Medicine* 2(1): 25-31, 2014.

[28] Mpiana PT, Misakabu FM, Tshibangu DST, Ngbolua KN, Mwanangombo DT. Antisickling activity and membrane stabilization effect of anthocyanins extracts from *Adansoniadigitata* L. bark on sickle blood cells. *International Blood Research and Reviews* 2(5): 198-212, 2014.

[29] Mpiana PT, Bokota MT, Mbula JP, Ngbolua KN, Tshibangu DST, Atibu EK, Kwembe JTK, Kakule MK. Effet of Anthocyanins Extracts from *Justiciamatammensis*and*Justicialaxa*on Sickle cells. In: *Anthocyanins, Structure, Biosynthesis and Health benefits* (Series: Biochemistry Research Trends, Nutritional and Diet Research Progress); Noboru Motohashi (ed.), NOVA PUBLISHERS, New York, USA, pp. 111-124, 2013.

[30] Mpiana PT, Kimbadi BL, Ombeni AM, Ngbolua KN, Tshibangu DST, Tshilanda DD, Misengabu NM, Muanyishay CL, Muyisa SK. *In vitro* inhibitory effects and anti-sickle erythrocytes haemolysis of *Diclipteracolorata* C.B. Clarke, *Euphorbia hirta* L. and *Sorghum bicolor* (L.) Moench. *Open Journal of Blood Diseases* 3: 43-48, 2013.

[31] Mpiana PT, Dianzenza EN, Ngbolua KN, Tshibangu DST, Mbala BM, Shetonde OM, Atibu EK, Kakule MK, Bokota MT. Antisickling properties, thermal and photochemical degradations of anthocyaninsextract from *Annonasenegalensis*(Annonaceae), *Int. J. Biol. Chem. Sci.*6(5): 2241-2251, 2012.

[32] Mpiana PT, Ngbolua KN, Mudogo V, Tshibangu DST, Atibu EK. The potential effectiveness of medicinal plants used for the treatment of Sickle cell Disease in the Democratic Republic of Congo folk medicine: A review. In: Progress *in* Traditional and Folk herbal medicine, DAYA PUBLISHING HOUSE, NEW DELHI, Vol. I, pp 1-11, 2012.

[33] Mpiana PT, Makelele LK, Oleko RW, Bokota MT, Tshibangu DST, Ngbolua KN, Mbala MB, Atibu EK, Nshimba SM. Antisickling activity of medicinal plants used in the management of Sickle cell Disease in Tshopo district, D.R.Congo, *Australian Journal of Medical Herbalism*22 (4): 132-137, 2010.

[34] Mpiana PT, Bokota MT, Ndjele MBL, Mudogo V, Tshibangu DST, Ngbolua KN, Atibu EK, Kwembe JTK, Makelele LK. Antisickling activity of three species of Justicia from Kisangani (DR Congo):*Justiciatenella, J. gendarusa and J.insularis, International Journal of Biological and Chemical Sciences* 4(6): 1953-1961, 2010.

[35] Mpiana PT, Mudogo V, Ngbolua KN, Tshibangu DST, Atibu EK. *In vitro*antisickling activity of anthocyanins extracts from *Morindalucida*Benth (RUBIACEAE) *in* Medicinal Plants: Phytochemistry, Pharmacology and Therapeutics, VK Gupta, GD Singh, Surjeet Singh and A Kaul (Eds): DAYA PUBLISHING HOUSE, NEW DELHI, Vol. 1, pp. 330-337, 2010.

[36] Mpiana PT, Mudogo V, Tshibangu DST, Ngbolua KN, Mangwala PK, Atibu EK, Kakule MK, Makelele LK, Bokota MT. Antisickling Activity and Thermodegradation of an Anthocyanin fraction from *Ocimumbasilicum L.* (LAMIACEAE). *Comp. Bio. Nat. Pro*. Vol. 3. Effects, Safety & Clinical (Pt II), pp. 278-287, 2010.

[37] Mpiana PT, Mudogo V, Kabangu YF, Tshibangu DST, Ngbolua KN, Atibu EK, Mangwala KP, Mbala MB, Makelele LK, Bokota MT. Antisickling Activity and Thermostability of Anthocyanins Extract from a Congolese plant, *HymenocardiaacidaTul.* (Hymenocardiaceae), *Int. J. Pharmacol.* 5 (1): 65-70, 2009.

[38] Mpiana PT, Balangayi EK, Kanangila AB, Kalonda EM, Ngbolua KN, Tshibangu DST, Atibu EK, Lumbu JBS.Activité anti-drépanocytaire et thermo-dégradation des anthocyanes extraits de *Sterculiaquinqueloba*et *Ficus capensis,Int. J. Biol. &Chem. Sci.*3 (3): 551-560, 2009.

[39] Mpiana PT, Mudogo V, Ngbolua KN, Tshibangu DST, Atibu EK, Kitwa EK, Kanangila AB. *In vitro*antisickling activity of anthocyanins extracts of *Vignaunguiculata* (L.) walp., *In* Recent progress in Medicinal Plants:

Chemistry and Medicinal Value, JN Govil, VK Singh (Eds): DAYA PUBLISHING HOUSE, NEW DELHI, Vol.25, pp. 91-98, 2009.

[40] Mpiana PT, Mudogo V, Nyamangombe L, Kakule MK, Ngbolua KN, Atibu EK, Mbala MB,Mbongo AK, Ntumba JN. Antisickling Activity and Photodegradation Effect of Anthocyanins Extracts from *Alchorneacordifolia (*SCHUMACH&Thonn.*)* and *Crotalaria retusa L. Ann. Afr.Med.* 2 (4): 240-245, 2009.

[41] Mpiana PT, Mudogo V, Tshibangu DST, Ngbolua KN, Atibu EK, Kitwa EK, Kanangila AB, Makelele LK. Activité antifalcémiante et thermodégradation d'une fraction d'anthocyanes extraits de *Zizyphus mucronata*, *Ann. Afr. Med.*2 (2) : 91-97, 2009.

[42] Mpiana PT, Mudogo V, Tshibangu DST, Ngbolua KN, Tshilanda DD, Atibu EK. Antisickling activity of anthocyanins extract of *Jatrophacurcas* L. *In* Recent progress in Medicinal Plants: Chemistry and Medicinal Value, JN Govil, VK Singh (Eds): DAYA PUBLISHING HOUSE, NEW DELHI, Vol.25, pp. 104-108, 2009.

[43] Mpiana PT, Mudogo V, Tshibangu DST, Kitwa EK, Kanangila AB, Lumbu JBS, Ngbolua KN, Atibu EK, Kakule MK. Antisickling Activity of Anthocyanins from *Bombaxpentadrum, Ficuscapensis, Zizyphusmucronata*: Photo degradation effect. *J. Ethnopharmacol.*120: 413-418, 2008.

[44] Mpiana PT, Mudogo V, Ngbolua KN, Tshibangu DST, Shetonde OM, Mbala BM. *In vitro*Antisickling Activity of Anthocyanins from *Ocimumbasilicum L.* (Lamiaceae). *Int. J. Pharmacol.* 3 (4): 371-374, 2007.

[45] Mpiana PT, Mudogo V, Tshibangu DST, Ngbolua KN, Shetonde OM, Mangwala PK, Mavakala BK. *In vitro*Antisickling Activity of Anthocyanins Extracts of a Congolese Plant: *AlchorneacordifoliaM.Arg. J. Med. Sci.*7 (7): 1182-1186, 2007.

[46] Ngbolua KN, Mudogo V, Mpiana PT, Malekani MJ, Rafatro H, Urverg RS, Takoy L, Rakotoarimana H, Tshibangu DST.Evaluation de l'activité anti-drépanocytaire et antipaludique de quelques taxons végétaux de la République démocratique du Congo et de Madagascar. *Ethnopharmacologia* 50: 19-24, 2013.

[47] Yuma PM, Mpiana PT, Bokota MT, Wakenge IB, Muanishay LC, Gbolo ZB, Mathina Di Mathina G, Tshibangu DST, Ngbolua KN. Etude de l'activité anti-falcémiante et de la thermo et photo-dégradation des anthocyanes de*Centella asiatica, Thomandersia hensii* et *Maesopsis eminii.Int. J. Biol. Chem. Sci.* 7(5): 1892-1901, 2013.

[48] Ngbolua KN, Tshibangu DST, Mpiana PT, Mihigo SO, Mavakala BK, Ashande MC, Muanyishay LC, 2015. Anti-sickling and antibacterial activities of Some Extracts from *Gardenia ternifolia* subsp. *jovis-tonantis* (Welw.) Verdc. (Rubiaceae) and *Uapacaheudelotii*Baill. (Phyllanthaceae).*Journal of Advances in Medical and Pharmaceutical Sciences*2(1): 10-19, 2015.

[49] Tshibangu DST, Shode FO, Koorbanally N, Mudogo V, Mpiana PT, Ngbolua KN. Antisicklingtriterpenoids from *Callistemon viminalis, Meulaleucabracteata*var. Revolution Gold *Syzygiumguineense*and *Syzygiumcordatum*. The 14th NAPRECA Symposium and AAMPS Ethnoverterinary Medicine Symposium 8th-12th August. Internatiuonal Centre For Insect Physiology and Ecology (ICIPE) :Kasarani, Nairobi, Kenya., pp.296-300, 2011.

[50] Tshilanda DD, Onyamboko DNV, Mpiana PT, Ngbolua KN, TshibanguDST,Mbala MB, Bokolo KM, Taba KM, Kasonga KT. Antisickling activity of butyl stearate isolated from *Ocimumbasilicum* (Lamiaceae). *Asian Pacific Journal of Tropical Biomedicine* 4 (5): 393-398, 2014.

[51] Ngbolua KN, Mpiana PT, Tshibangu DST, Mazasa PP, Gbolo BZ, Atibu EK, Kadima JN, Kasali FM. *In vitro* anti-sickling and radical scavenging activities of a poly-herbal formula (Drepanoalpha®) in Sickle cell erythrocyte and acute toxicity study in Wistar albino rats. *European Journal of Medicinal Plants*4(10): 1251-1267, 2014.

In: Sickle Cell Disease
Editor: Marilyn E. Lewis
ISBN: 978-1-63482-828-4

Chapter V

Pain, Sexual Activity and Partner Support in Jamaicans with Sickle Cell Disease

Kai A. D. Morgan[1, *]***, Naila Smith***[4]***, Roger C. Gibson***[1]***, Wendel D. Abel***[1]***, Monika Parshad-Asnani***[2]***, Marvin Reid***[2]***, Keisha N. O'Garo***[3] ***and Christopher L. Edwards***[3]

[1]Department of Community Health & Psychiatry, University of the West Indies, Mona Campus, Kingston, Jamaica W. I.
[2]Sickle Cell Unit, University of the West Indies, Mona Campus, Kingston, Jamaica W. I.
[3]Duke Medical Centre, Duke University, North Carolina, US
[4]Fordham University, New York, US

Abstract

Sickle Cell Disease (SCD) and other chronic diseases can certainly have a significant impact on sexual functioning as well as relationship dynamics, especially with the importance of support systems within the

* Corresponding author: Dr. Kai A. D. Morgan, kaiandito@gmail.com.

framework of a chronic illness. The sample consisted of 140 Jamaican adults between the ages of 19 and 79 years (mean age = 35.97 ± 12.11 years). Diagnosis of SCD was based on results of hemoglobin electrophoresis. Correlations were conducted with types of SCD pain, intensity of pain, sexual activity and social support from spouse with special attention paid to the emotional, instrumental, informational and comparison aspects of social support from the patient's spouse/significant other. Various questions regarding sexual functioning were utilized to explore this area. Results indicated that there were a number of significant correlations between sexual activity and support, pain and support, pain and quality of intimate relationship, spouse's reaction to pain and patient's pain ($p < .05$). Conclusions support the importance of social support and its far-reaching impact into the coping mechanisms of patients with chronic illness as well as quality of life.

Background

Sickle Cell Disease is the most common genetic disorder of the blood. The term Sickle Cell Disease (SCD) refers to several diseases, all of them associated with the presence of abnormal hemoglobin (S). SCD is characterized by a predominance of abnormal hemoglobin (Hgb) molecules in red blood cells (RBC). Sickle cell trait (AS), the heterozygote carrier state, is not a disease and is seen in approximately 1 in 10 African Americans, while similarly 10% of Jamaicans are carriers of the trait, with 1 in every 300 having the SS (anemia) genotype and 1 in every 500, the SC (disease) genotype. Because tissue damage can occur all over the body as a result of the disease, patients with SCD are at risk for other medical complications including, but not limited to: delayed growth and sexual maturation, acute and chronic pulmonary dysfunction, stroke, aseptic necrosis of the hip and/or shoulders, sickle cell retinopathy, dermal ulcers, severe and chronic pain, and psychosocial dysfunction (Abrams, Phillips, Whitworth, 1994; Schaeffer, Gil, Burchinal, Kramer, Nash, Orringer, Strayhorn, 1999).

The clinical course of SCD includes periods of acute and chronic hematological crisis that often result in marked psychosocial and physical disability, and at other times even early death. Although most sickle cell disease variants can be diagnosed prenatally, symptoms of the disease usually do not appear for months after birth due to increased levels of fetal hemoglobin that tend to suppress symptom expression (Huntsman, 1987). The characteristics of SCD symptoms tend to vary with age and appear to be progressive (Embury, Hebbel, Mohandas, Steinberg, 1996).

Of the sickled cell disease syndromes, sickle cell anemia (SS hemoglobinopathy) is the most common. Other Hgb S related hemoglobinopathies include the double heterozygous states (Sickle b-thalassemia; SC disease; SD disease), Hgb C, Hgb SO_{-arab} and SHPFH. The mean life expectancy of patients with sickle cell anemia is 42 years for men and 48 for women, almost 28 and 27 years below the normal population, respectively (Platt, Brambilla, Rosse, 1994).

Pain and Psychosocial Factors

Chronic pain and other complications of SCD requiring frequent hospitalization and medical management significantly impact the general lifestyle of patients with the disease, specifically, reducing quality of life, affecting intra- and interpersonal relationships and impairing overall psychosocial functioning (Edwards et al., 2005). Edwards et al. (2005) asserts, therefore, that "understanding the pathophysiology of SCD in the absence of a thorough understanding of the psychological, psychiatric, cultural and social influences is really misunderstanding SCD." (p. 177) They posit that the definition of adequate care for persons with SCD must encompass both pharmacological and non-pharmacological preventive and intervention strategies to improve quality of life for persons with the disease. In addition to advocating for cognitive behaviorally and psychosocially oriented therapies, they propose that these opportunities be made proactively available to the caregivers of persons SCD in order to combat potential psychosocial complications (Edwards et al., 2005).

Using a phenomenological approach, Thomas and Taylor (2002) identified six themes encapsulating the psychosocial experience of individuals with SCD and its resulting impact on their quality of life. These six themes are: (1) Hospitalization (2) Impact of the unremitting nature of the disease, (3) Employment, (4) Education, (5) Effects on relationships and (6) Growing up with SCD. These domains they argue are equivalent to those on the World Health Organization Quality of Life (WHOQOL) and therefore undermine quality of life (Thomas & Taylor, 2002).

SCD patients reported disliking hospitalization due to the "immense disruption" it causes in their lives and the hurt inflicted by unempathic hospital staff. Patients reported that the unremitting nature of the disease was also problematic as painful crises were unpredictable, felt as if they were taking over their lives, lead to pessimistic and negative thoughts and resulted in restrictions, e.g., in activity level, and impacted on living a "normal life". Fear about disclosing their SCD status to potential employers, high level of absenteeism due to illness, being turned down for or having to leave jobs because of SCD are employment issues that individuals with SCD grapple with (Thomas & Taylor, 2002). Similarly, with respect to education, school-aged children with SCD miss many days of school due to painful crises, fall behind at school and experience difficulty catching up, sometimes due to unsupportive teachers and staff, and disruption of peer relationships. Relationships were also found to be impacted by SCD. Results showed that significant others would display a myriad of reactions including distancing, frustration, helplessness and anger. This typified the difficulty they experienced coping with the recurrent painful crises experienced by their partners (Thomas & Taylor, 2002). Finally, growing up with SCD posed difficulties specifically, their parent's inability to accept their child's condition, denial of said condition usually (arising from guilt), lack of understanding of the disease, over-protective and restrictive behavior. Additionally, some children experience difficulty making friends due to thoughts and beliefs about their shortened lifespan, and different appearance (jaundiced eyes and smaller stature for boys) (Thomas & Taylor, 2002).

According to Thomas and Taylor (2002), results showed that persons with SCD have experiences that have impacted the psychological domain of their quality of life. The study identified thoughts and feelings generally associated with depression, helplessness and loss of control. Patients also experienced distress and pressure to "prove" their pain as hospital staff disbelieves them. Individuals also report negative feelings about their present, past and future situation and impacted self-esteem due to disruptions in the development of self-esteem (Thomas & Taylor, 2002)

Quality of life for patients with SCD was found to be lower than that of the general population. SCD patients had a mean score of 83.6 on the Burckhardt and Anderson Quality of Life Scale. This scale measures satisfaction on a seven item Likert scale that ranges from delighted – 7 to terrible -1.This was lower than the average scores for healthy populations which is 90. Scores ranged between 52 and 112 (the maximum score). The item related to less active entertainment, specifically, "reading, listening to music or observing entertainment" received the highest (M=6.05) average scores. This suggests that these activities are perhaps used to distract patients from SCD related symptoms and issues. The lowest (M=4.18) score received was for “work – job or in home”. This underscores the psychosocial difficulties experienced by patients with SCD.

Sexual Maturation

Both boys and girls with SCD experience the impact of the disease on their sexual maturation and development. Typically, children with the disease will experience a delay in maturation and the development of secondary sexual characteristics of about two years. The median age for menarche in women without SCD is 13 years old but for girls with SCD the median age is 15.4 years old (Sergeant, Singhal, & Hambleton, 2001).

Due to these developmental delays adolescents experience adjustment difficulties that may or may not be resolved as they progress into adulthood. Specifically, they grapple with distorted body perceptions and low self-esteem and have difficulty asserting their independence due to the unpredictability of their disease (Pinckney & Stuart, 2004); this may have an impact on the task of gaining autonomy, which is an important developmental task for adolescents. According to Newland (2008) African-American adolescents with more severe SCD, less knowledge about the disease and poorer family relationships were more independent and such an unusual and almost inexplicable finding ultimately suggests that the issues for adolescents with SCD are more complex and still need further investigation.

Sexual Functioning

Chronic illness not only has an impact on general quality of life, but more specifically in areas such as sexual functioning and the dyadic relationship. Human sexuality / sexual health and intimate interpersonal relationships are critical areas of human existence and can be severely affected in persons with SCD yet the area is severely under-studied (Burnett, 2012). Relationship and sexual satisfaction are important factors of quality of life, a significant, but of times unvoiced concern for patients who live with chronic illness. When one’s life is physically restricted by one’s illness, sex can be an indubitable source of comfort, and intimacy, and an affirmation of gender when other gender roles are virtually impossible to carry out. Sex can become a way to feel like one is “normal”. In one study looking at persons with chronic respiratory failure, 383 patients were sampled who began non-invasive mechanical ventilation,

46% did not change their level of sexual activity, 36% were less active sexually, and 13% were more active. The average frequency of intercourse was about five times per month. Conclusions stated that the need for and the experience of sexual activity will still persist even in the face of significant levels of disability. (Schonhofer, Von Sydow, & Bucher, 2001). In yet another study of 20 Brazilians with Sickle Cell Disease, eleven (55%) respondents considered that they had an active sex life with the frequency of sexual activity ranging from one to three times per week. Moreover, 82.3% of the patients rated their sexual activity as satisfactory; it was classified as excellent by 47.0% and as good by 29.4%. The majority of subjects (60%) had a partner in the previous year. Out of the 20 patients, 70% said they had had the desire to engage in sexual intercourse; 76.4% of those who had had intimate relationships said that they had enjoyed the experience. Thirteen (65.0%) of the 20 interviewees reported having impaired sexual functioning due to SCD or the associated clinical complications. In particular 12 (92.3%) of these 13 patients reported that the impairment was due to painful crises; the other patient reported fear of priapism (Cobo et. al., 2013).

The most common sexual issues surrounding Sickle Cell Disease often affect men, seemingly more than women, and include delayed sexual maturation, sex hormone disturbances, priapism (persistent painful erection usually requiring medical attention), erection problems (Burnett et. al., 1995) sexual mobility problems, and reduced fertility. Sexual mobility problems not only include difficulty with particular sexual positions but it also includes restricted levels of activity. It is important to note that these sexual mobility issues are typically due to the chronic pain that persons with Sickle Cell Disease endure which can affect sexual activity.

These issues would be particularly critical issues facing our Jamaican men who define themselves as masculine based on their virility, ability to procreate and general sexual acumen (Chevannes, 1995). Some studies, however, have found conflicting results. For example, Chavis & Norman (1993) found no difference in sexual functioning as measured by the Derogatis Sexual Functioning Inventory (DSIF) for a group of 44 persons with sickle cell anemia when compared to a control group of 42 persons with no chronic illness. Nonetheless, the same study found a significant difference in the area of sexual information which meant that persons with SCD had much less accurate knowledge pertaining to facts about sex. In another qualitative study however, Afro-Caribbean participants reported the following sexual issues: delayed sexual development, prolonged detumescence times (erection subsides very slowly), priapism, erectile problems, reduced fertility and sexual mobility problems (Duffy, 2009).

Partner Support

As previously mentioned, spousal relationships are often strained and burdened and characterized by distress especially depending on the severity of the pain and SCD (Thomas & Taylor, 2002). However, very few studies have really examined the impact of the spouse's reactions to their partners with SCD, despite the reality that social support has been lauded as the single most critical factor in determining the quality of life of persons with chronic illnesses. In a study done in Alameda County (Berkman & Syme, 1979), where 4725 participants with Cardiovascular Disease were surveyed, individuals with the fewest social ties suffered the highest mortality rates. Unfortunately, the details and nuances pertaining to Sickle Cell are woefully absent.

This chapter explores the important psychological, social and interpersonal issues, specifically those of a sexual and intimate relationship nature, that patients with SCD struggle with. The knowledge gained from such an investigation will assist persons with the disease and their medical care team to be better informed about the total management of the disease and more informed ways to approaching their general health care and psychosocial management. This chapter uses findings from the study to examine two primary areas in the experiences of individuals with SCD: 1) how pain is related to reports of sexual activity and 2) how partner support is related to experiences of pain.

Overview of Psychosocial Impact on Sickle Cell Project

This project was a study designed to examine the complete psychosocial experiences of individuals with SCD disease and these results form part of that larger project. Patients were recruited from the complete patient list as well as by referrals of medical staff at the Sickle Cell Unit, University of the West Indies (UWI). We recruited 143 Jamaican adult patients between the ages of 19 and 79 (average age = 35.97) to be members of our sample. Persons participating in the study had aconfirmed diagnosis of SCD as determined by clinical characteristics and haemoglobin (Hgb) electrophoresis conducted by the University of the West Indies, Sickle Cell Unit's hematologist based on hemoglobin (Hgb) electrophoresis demonstrating Hgb SS, Hgb S/O+-thalassemia, Hgb S/00- thalassemia or Hgb SC . Study participants genotypes included: Sickle Cell Anemia (Hgb SS), Hgb SBO- thalassemia, Hgb SB+ (all variants except SBO) or Hemoglobin Sickle Cell Disease (Hgb SC). Of these types 69.6% were noted as having the more severe Hgb SS genotype, while 23.9% had the milder Hgb SC. The remaining sample reported being either of the SBO (1.4%) or SB+ (5.1%) genotypes.

Most persons included in the study indicated that they were Black (98.6%), female (52.1%), and single (68.6%). Fewer participants were married (15.7%), living with a significant other (12.9%), separated (2.1%) or widowed (0.7%). The majority of the sample had attained schooling up to the Secondary/High School level (55.6%), the Tertiary level (21.1%), or Vocational/Skills Training/Post Secondary level (11.3%). Only a small portion of the sample reported that they had received no formal education (3.8%), or had been educated up to the Pre Primary (0.8%) and Primary (7.5%) levels. Only 58 respondents indicated that they were employed (42.3%) at the time of the study; the majority of whom were employed in the Private Sector (60.7%). To ensure confidentiality, all participants were assigned an identification number that will be used to track their activities throughout the study.

All participants completed a questionnaire which comprised eight measures with items on religion, social support, depression, social desirability, pain, coping and psychological disturbances. Questionnaires were administered by members of the data collection team, specifically, the study co-ordinator, investigators or other trained personnel during the patients' regular clinic visits. Questionnaire administration took place in a small private room that was kept at a constant temperature. The paper and pencil survey administration took approximately two hours and participants who requested a break were allowed to take one and frequent breaks were encouraged. The order of the questionnaire administration was counterbalanced to eliminate order effects. The measures specifically utilized for this aspect of the study included:

The Alford-Edwards Social Support Inventory (AESSI). The AESSI was developed using empirical literature, focus groups, and consultations with mental health professionals with expertise in social support. It assessed satisfaction with four theory-driven components of social support (Emotional,

Instrumental, Informational, Comparison) from five primary sources (Spouse/ Significant Other, Friends, Family, Co-workers, Other Social Contacts).

Emotional Support refers to the degree to which one feels listened to, understood, and cared for by significant persons. Instrumental Support refers to the practical assistance that others provide when needed such as helping with household chores, picking up groceries, babysitting one's child/children, giving a ride to the store. Informational Support refers to the knowledge, information, wisdom, and/or advice that others provide and Comparison Support refers to the information and advice that is received from someone who is experiencing a situation that is the same or similar.

The Multidimensional Pain Inventory (MPI-2). The Multidimensional Pain Inventory is a short form of the West Haven-Yale Multidimensional Pain Inventory (WHYMPI;Kerns, Turk, & Rudy, 1985). The MPI-2 contains three sections. Only Section II was utilized for these analyses. Section II measured perceptions of the individual as to how a spouse or significant other responds to the person when he or she is in pain.

Short-Form McGill Pain Questionnaire (MPQ). The MPQ is an assessment of the subjective feeling of pain. The visual analog scale (VAS) (Melzack, 1987) and the McGill Pain Questionnaire (Melzack, 1987) are probably the most widely used self-rating instruments for the assessment of pain in clinical and research settings. The Short Form McGill Pain Questionnaire (SF-MPQ) was developed for use in specific research settings and consists of 15 descriptors (11 sensory, 4 affective) which are rated on an intensity scale as 0 = none, 1 = mild, 2 = moderate, or 3 = severe. Three pain scores are derived from the sum of the intensity values of the words chosen for sensory, affective and total descriptors. The SF-MPQ also includes the Present Pain Intensity (PPI) index from the standard version of the MPQ and a VAS that conjointly provide indices of overall pain intensity. The MPQ and SF-MPQ were designed to assess the multidimensional nature of pain and have been demonstrated to be reliable, valid, and consistent measurement tools (Melzack & Katz, 1992).

Sexual activity was measured by indicating whether one was active, inactive or active, but no current partner, in addition to 2 other questions from other surveys asking about rectal bleeding or pain during sex and the frequency with which one engages in sexual behaviour.

Participants were referred to mental health care when their responses to the questionnaires or observed behaviour during survey administration were concerning and when they directly requested referral. All data was carefully secured in a locked file cabinet in a locked room. Researchers when writing or talking about this study to doctors or others ensured that none of the patients or subjects could be identified.

Results and Discussion

The average, as well as percentages of participants responses on each dimension measured was calculated. T-tests were also conducted to examine differences in frequency of sexual activity by reported level of pain. Pearson's correlations were conducted with types of SCD pain, intensity of pain, sexual activity and social support from spouse with special attention paid to the emotional, instrumental, informational and comparison aspects of social support from the patient's spouse / significant other.

Pain and Sexual Activity

The average rating of pain during a one-week period and in a month were both approximately 3 out of 10, with a score of 10 representing excruciating pain. Both ratings were relatively low and suggest that the pain levels in this sample were well under control.

Fifty-four percent (54%) of the sample indicated that they were sexually active while 39% reported that they were not. The remaining 7% did not indicate their status. Nineteen percent (19%) of the men in the sample admitted to having difficulties achieving or maintaining an erection while 22% reported priapism (painful erections), 7.7% indicated ejaculatory difficulties and 3% of the total sample confirmed that they had experienced rectal bleeding, injury or infection related to their sexual behaviour.

Individuals who were sexually active consistently reported lower levels of pain based on a 6 point scale, whether average rating of pain for the week, month, or current pain was reported. However, this was only significant for average rating of pain for the week ($t(117) = -2.6$; $p = 0.01$). There were no significant differences between the sexually active and inactive group by reports of priapism, ejaculatory difficulties, rectal bleeding or erectile dysfunction.

There were significant results obtained for types of pains noted in SCD as well with those that stated they were sexually inactive reporting more gnawing pain ($t(83) = -2.46$; $p = 0.016$), throbbing pain ($t(93) = -2.4$; $p = 0.018$) and tenderness ($t(78) = -2.5$; p=0.013). Other types of pain did not yield significant differences between sexually active and inactive persons, such as cramping, stabbing, sharp, aching, shooting, sickening and hot-burning pains.

These results suggest that sexual activity might play an important role in the experience of pain for persons with SCD. Not only did those that were active report less pain but they reported less gnawing, throbbing and tenderness. More research needs to be done to flesh out why these pains were reported more often in those that were sexually inactive.

Many authors have advocated a cautious approach to dealing with sexual functioning in chronically ill patients with other chronic diseases such as cancer, musculo-skeletal issues, and cardiovascular diseases (Nusbaum, Hamilton, & Lenehan, 2003). There is a serious lack of information about sexual functioning in the Sickle Cell population which has made it difficult to provide solid, evidence-based advice about how persons with this disease should manage challenges in their sexual functioning. In this cohort of patients, with generally low levels of painful crises and general pain, sexual activity appeared to play a role in subjective experience of pain. This finding underscores the importance of addressing sexual functioning as a part of general health care management.

Sexual functioning and relationships in general, are greatly impacted by chronic illnesses. From a biological perspective, sexual arousal or desire, and mobility may be altered by the disease process through interference with the hormonal, vascular and neural integrity of the genitalia, as well as the effects and side effects of medications. From a psychological perspective, depression anxiety, and loneliness, which have been shown to be highly comorbid with Sickle Cell Disease, are of pertinent concern and also can heavily impact sexual functioning (Asnani, Fraser, Lewis, & Reid, 2010). Finally, socially, there is a general discomfort with the idea of persons who are ill thinking about sex or even wanting to still have sex, especially if these persons are youth or aging. Hence, there's a reticence by society and healthcare professionals to discuss these critical issues related to sex. Therefore, healthcare professionals must be keenly aware that Sickle Cell can impair / affect sexual functioning in pre-pubertal individuals and this sets up a longstanding challenge with dealing with sex and relationships. Additionally, longstanding challenges dealing with sex and relationships might lead to vulnerability to sexual abuse. In one study which sampled more than 36,000 adolescents with chronic illness, results indicated that adolescents with non-visible disabilities were more likely to be sexually abused (Suris, Resnick, Cassuto, Blum, 1996).

Persons with sickle cell are not always easily / readily identifiable by outward appearance and so this study highlights the importance of the risk that can be associated with being chronically ill. Other applicable concerns include single, separated or divorced persons, and their very relevant need for sex, issues around sexual orientation which all require sensitivity and analysis of one's sexual stereotypes (McInnes, 2003). This again becomes particularly relevant in our Jamaican population where masculinity is defined by heterosexual behaviour and many stereotypes exist of the homosexual male in particular. So, not only is the person with Sickle Cell dealing with their chronic illness but they are also trying to manage their sexual orientation and perhaps transgender issues and possible challenges with same and the situation becomes layered.

There are many barriers to this type of an open discussion despite the strong biopsychosocial implications. Some of these barriers include the lack of training of health care workers in dealing with matters of sex, and the general unwillingness of patients to discuss sexual matters (McInnes, 2003). The training of health care workers is usually very focused on physical and mental health and the discussion of relationship and sexual health tends to be minimal (McInnes, 2003). In addition to this, there is usually quite a bit of discomfort with discussing these aspects of patients' lives as socially, in the Jamaican context, sex is conceptualized as personal information and most are not willing or comfortable with neither divulging nor asking pertinent questions.

Pain and Spousal / Partner Support

Most participants reported that their partner provided support and / or was helpful during their pain crises with an average rating of 4.7 on a 6 point scale for the level of partner's support. Average responses asking if the pain had changed the marriage / family relationships yielded less than 1 on a 6 point scale. Lastly, most persons on average felt that their partners were attentive to their pain problem (4.48/6).

A more detailed analysis revealed that there was a significant negative correlation (r = -.233, $p < .05$) between the support/helpfulness of a spouse/partner towards the partner in pain and the average amount of pain for the past week, on a 0-10 scale. This suggests that the more helpful the partner was, the less pain was reported for the past week. However, there were significant positive correlations between partner support and gnawing experience with SCD pain (r = .356, $p < .01$), and a fearful experience of SCD pain ($r = .277$, $p < .05$) which indicates that the more gnawing and fearful the experiences, the more support the person received from his / her partner. Similarly, there were positive correlations between a spouse/partner ignoring the partner in pain and the overall level of pain ($r = .300$, $p < .01$) and between spouse/partner expressing frustration at the partner feeling pain and the overall pain experience ($r =. 270$, $p>.05$). So here we note that the more the partner ignored or expressed frustration at the person in pain, the higher the overall levels of pain.

There was also a significant positive correlation between how worried a spouse/ significant other was in relation to their partners' SCD pain problem and the current level of pain($r = .301$, $p < .01$) as well as between a partner/ spouse expressing frustration at the partner experiencing SCD pain and the highest level of pain experienced on a 0-10 scale while remaining normal ($r = .349$, $p < .01$). Additionally, there was a significant positive correlation between a partner or spouse expressing anger at the partner affected by the SCD pain and the highest level of pain experienced on a 0-10 scale while remaining normal($r =.235$, $p < .05$). This indicates that a partner's anxieties / worries and expressions of frustration and anger may be important factors in increasing the person's level of pain.

There was a significant negative correlation between a heavy SCD pain and satisfaction with the amount of comparison support received from spouse/partner, ($r = -.357$, $p < .05$) between a splitting SCD pain and satisfaction with the amount of emotional support received from spouse/partner($r = -.317$, $p < .05$), and between a spouse talking to his/her partner to relieve the pain and punishing-cruel SCD pain ($r = -.259$, $p < .05$). Although these results suggest that as the various types of pains, that is heavy and splitting, increased, the satisfaction with the comparison support and emotional support decreased, this can possibly be explained by both the type of support being represented and the intensity of the pain and the partner's ensuing response. In other words, comparison support speaks to feeling like the other person is going through a similar experience and we can understand how this may not be possible given that the partner does not also experience a chronic illness. Secondly, partners may feel sometimes inequipped to deal with the intensity of the pain being felt and may feel that emotional support at that point of splitting pain, may neither be acceptable or helpful.

With correlational data it is difficult to determine the direction of influence between variables. Nevertheless, the results clearly indicate that there is a significant relationship between spouse/significant other support on intensity and types of pain experienced. These results showed that there are clear relationships amongst pain, sexual functioning, social support and intimate relationships. The results suggest that in many cases, social support and nurturance is likely to mitigate both pain levels and types of pain while a spouse/significant other's anger, frustration or ignoring the person with SCD was likely to impact their pain status negatively. These findings are supported by the literature that discusses a more general relationship between chronic illnesses and social support. Once social support is positive, uplifted and engendered emotionally, that support has a great positive impact on the individual's ability to manage one's pain (Berkman & Syme, 1979; Teeman et al., 1987).

Recommendations

Whilst the results pertaining to partner support are not particularly surprising, the findings relating to sexual activity are novel in the area of Sickle Cell Disease, particularly in this Jamaican cohort. The following recommendations are being put forward based on the conclusions that both sexual activity and partner support are critical in the improvement of quality of life. From a health care professional's perspective, the overall objective should be to improve the openness of discussion regarding sex with ones' patients so that both patient and health care worker can be more comfortable doing same. In order for this to happen, healthcare workers must evaluate entrenched negative attitudes, myths and stereotypes and embrace the following ideals: (1) sex and relationships are critical aspects of health; (2)it is the health care worker's role to address quality of life issues including sexual health; (3) people of all ages may still be sexually interested and active despite their chronic illnesses; (4) and sex encompasses more than just penetration (McInnes, 2003). McInnes (2003) further recommends a model for sexual counseling which includes 4 graded levels of intervention and is called PLISSIT which is explained below. Some health care workers may be more comfortable at various levels than others but this model allows for flexibility in referrals at the higher levels and most health care workers will be involved at Level 1.

Level 1: Permission (P)

This involves broaching the subject of sex and actively screening for any possible sexual concerns in any patient regardless of age. Culture must be considered and if a patient declines to discuss such matters, this should be respected however, patients are more likely to be open if they understand the rationale and framework within which such questions are being asked. Including the partner in this discussion is sometimes very helpful. Open-ended questions are also very useful in the form of routine questioning such as: "Your sexual health is a very important part of your overall health. How has your relationship been going?" Or generalizing, "People with sickle cell often experience challenges with their sexual functioning. How have you been affected?" Or normalizing, "It's normal to be concerned about your sex life once you have a chronic illness. What worries have you had?" Or using statistics, "Approximately, 80% of persons with SCD have issues with pain and sex such as priapism. What changes have you noticed? Of course other open-ended questions can be utilized.

Level II: Limited Information (LI)

At this level, information can be provided about the impact of illness on sexuality and the effects of treatments on sexual function.

Level III: Specific Suggestions (SI)

Suggestions might include reading printed material about sexuality and illness, taking pain relief before sexual activity, or advice about alternative sexual techniques or coital positions. Treatment may involve counselling, medication, or both. Some couples may require relationship counseling, in addition to sexual counselling.

Level IV: Intensive Therapy (IT)

This level requires further training and is usually given by an expert counsellor, psychologist, social worker or psychiatrist.

Conclusion

The age of sex as taboo is fast closing. Whether we are dealing with our adolescents or the elderly, chronically physically ill or mentally ill, dealing with sex and relationships should not be avoided, as these are crucial elements of quality of life and impact daily functioning. In one particular study, Cobo et. al., (2013) showed that 80% of Sickle Cell participants were not aware of what priapism was and they were not knowledgeable about the risks of pregnancy in persons with Sickle Cell. This study highlights that persons with SCD might need more sexual health information than they are currently exposed to. More research needs to be conducted in the area of sexual health of persons with Sickle Cell Disease, which can inform more programs and training opportunities for individuals who work with this population.

References

Abrams, M., Phillip, G. & Whitworth, E. (1994). Adaptation and coping: A look at sickle cell patient population over 30-An integral phase of the lifelong developmental process. *Journal of Health & Social Policy*, *5* (3/4) 141-160.

Asnani, M. R., Fraser, R., Lewis, N. A. & Reid, M. E. (2010). Depression and Loneliness in Jamaicans with Sickle Cell Disease. *BMC Psychiatry*, *10*(40), 1-7

Berkman, L. F. & Syme, S. L. (1979). Social networks, host resistance and mortality: a nine-year old follow-up study of Alameda County residents. *American Journal of Epidemiology*, *109*, 186-204.

Burnett A. L.(2012). Sexual health outcomes improvement in sickle cell disease: A matter of health policy? *Journal of Sexual Medicine*, *9*, 104–113.

Burnett, A. L., Allen, R. P. Tempany, C. M., Dover, G. J. & Brendler, C. B. (1995). Evaluation of erectile function in men with Sickle Cell Disease. *Urology*, *45*(4), 657-63.

Chavis, W. M. & Norman, G. S. (1993). Sexuality and Sickle Cell Disease. *Journal of the National Medical Association*, *85* (2), 113-116.

Chevannes, B. (1995). *Jamaican men: Final report to the National Family Planning Board on the in-depth study of Jamaican male sexual belief and behaviour*. University of the West Indies, Kingston: Institute of Social and Economic Research.

Cobo, V. A., Chapadeiro, C. A., Ribeiro, J. B., Moraes-Souza, H. & Martins, P. R. J. (2013). Sexuality and sickle cell anemia. *Revista Brasileira de Hematologia E Hemoterapia, 35* (2), 89-93. doi: 10.5581/1516-8484.20130027

Duffy, T. (2009). Sexual experiences in men with Sickle Cell Disease – A phenomenological inquiry. Retrieved on February 19, 2014 from http://www.sicklecellsociety.org/information/resrep/res7.html

Edwards, C. L., Scales, M. T., Loughlin, C., Bennett, G. C., Harris-Peterson, S., De Castro, L. M., Whitworth, E., Abrams, M., Feliu, M., Johnson, S., Wood, M., Harrison, O. & Killough, A. (2005). A brief review of the pathophysiology, associated pain and psychosocial issues in sickle cell disease. *International Journal of Behavioral Medicine, 12*(3), 171-179.

Embury, S. H., Hebbel, R. P., Mohandas, N. & Steinberg, M. H. (1996) (eds). *Sickle Cell Disease: Basic Principles and Clinical Practice.* New York: Lippincott-Raven

Huntsman, R. G. (1987). *Sickle cell anemia and thalassemia.* Toronto, Canada: Canadian Sickle Cell Society

Kerns, R. D., Turks, D. C. & Rudy, T. E. (1985). The West Haven-Yale Multidimensional Pain Inventory (WHYMPI). *Pain, 23*(4), 345-356.

Mann-Jiles, V. & Morris, D.L. (2009). Quality of life of adult patients with sickle cell disease. *Journal of the American Academy of Nurse Practitioners, 21*, 340-349.

McInnes, R. A. (2003). Chronic illness and sexuality. *Medical Journal of Australia, 179* (5), 263- 266

Melzack, R. (1987). The short form McGill pain questionnaire. *Pain, 30*(2), 191-197.

Melzack, R. & Katz, J. (1992). The McGill pain questionnaire: appraisal and current status. In *The Handbook of Pain Assessment*. Edited by: Turk DC, Melzack R. New York: The Guildford Press, 152-168

Newland, J. A. (2008). Factors influencing independence in adolescents with sickle cell disease. *Journal of Child and Adolescent Psychiatric Nursing, 21* (3), 177-185.

Nusbaum, M. R., Hamilton, C. & Lenehan, P. (2003). Chronic illness and sexual functioning. *American Family Physician, 67* (2), 347-354.

Pinckney, R. B. & Stuart, G.W. (2004). Adjustment difficulties of adolescents with sickle cell disease. *Journal of Child and Adolescent Psychiatric Nursing, 17*, 5-12.

Platt, O. S., Brambilla, D. J., Rosse, W. F., Milner, P. F., Castro O., et. al. (1994). Mortality in sickle cell disease: Life expectancy and risk factors for early death. *New England Journal of Medicine*, *330*, 1639-1644.

Schaeffer, J. J., Gil, K. M., Burchinal, M., Kramer, K. D., Nash, K. B., Orringer, E. & Strayhorn D. (1999). Depression, Disease severity and Sickle Cell. *Journal of Behavioural Medicine*, *22* (2), 115-26

Schonhofer, B., Von Sydow, K. & Bucher, T. Sexuality in patients with noninvasive mechanical ventilation due to chronic respiratory failure. *American Journal of Respiratory Critical Care in Medicine*, *164*, 1612 – 1617.

Seeman, T. E., Kaplan, G. A., Knusden, L, Cohen, R. & Guralnik, J. (1987). Social network ties and mortality among the elderly in the Alameda County study. *American Journal of Epidemiology*, *126* (4), 714-723.

Sergeant, G., Singhal, A. & Hambleton, I. (2001). Sickle cell disease and age at menarche in Jamaican girls: Observations from a cohort study. *Archives of Disease in Childhood* , *85* (5), 375-378. doi: 10.1136/adc.85.5.375

Suris, J. C., Resnick, M. D., Cassuto, N. & Blum, R. W. (1996). Sexual behaviour of adolescents with chronic disease and disability. *Journal of Adolescent Health, 19,* 124- 131.

Thomas, V. J. & Taylor, L. M. (2002). The psychosocial experience of people with sickle cell disease and its impact on quality of life: Qualitative findings from focus groups. *British Journal of Health Psychology*, *7*, 345-363.

Index

A

B

C

D

E

F

G

H

O

P

Q

R

S

T

U

V

W

Y

Z